SURVEY OF WORLD CULTURES

Editor, THOMAS FITZSIMMONS

POLAND

its people its society its culture

Clifford R. Barnett

IN COLLABORATION WITH

Robert J. Feldman

John C. Fiske

Peter Malof

Florence K. Nierman

Otto R. Reischer

Egon R. Tausch

GROVE PRESS, INC.   NEW YORK

Grove Press Books and Evergreen Books
are published by Barney Rosset at Grove Press Inc.
795 Broadway   New York 3, N.Y.

Distributors in Great Britain:
John Calder Ltd., 17 Sackville St., London, W. 1

PERHAPS at no other time in history has so much been written about the behavior of peoples in the different countries of the world. While there remain critical areas of ignorance about motivation and behavior, the dynamics of society, culture and its power, there do exist quantities of recorded observations and information, and of highly detailed analyses of this or that aspect of life as it is lived by given groups of people. Observations, information, analysis—all usually are scattered, available but separate. The books of this series represent an endeavor to gather and interpret the separate pieces. The series itself proceeds from an earlier group of studies—the Country Series—issued experimentally in limited quantity to discover what needs they might fill and how they might be improved. The need has been defined, it is enormous. The series will present works on representative societies in each major culture area of the world.

This, then, is a different kind of book in that it is concerned with the relationship of aspects usually studied separately. The focus of the book is a society as it functions, the interrelationship of its parts and of the parts to the whole. Emphasis is on the dynamics of that interplay, on constants of attitude and behavior, abiding values, the presence and impact of forces for change. Containing a great deal of information, and thus useful as a reference, it is not merely a collection of data. Covering the political, economic, and sociological aspects of a society, it presents no minute analysis of any element within these catagories. Asserting as valid only what has stood up to the simultaneous and systematic challenge of the various social science disciplines represented by the persons who wrote it, the book has no recourse to the citation of authorities.

Much that has remained implicit in previous separate studies is here made explicit, and should generate controversy. In the course of challenging the available materials, and consequent selection, gen-

11115

eralization, and implication, many gaps in existing knowledge have been exposed. In some cases it has been possible to indicate the general outline and probable significance of such gaps, and this should be useful as a guide to further exploration. These are, in short, books out of which should come many questions. That there may also come some increased understanding of the seemingly endless and confusing diversity of ways by which men approach the experience of living with one another is the wish of all who have participated in the making of the series.

Thomas Fitzsimmons

Washington, D. C.

ACKNOWLEDGMENTS

PUBLICATION of this study, and of the series, is possible because many individuals gave unstintingly of time, talent, critical and creative energy. Review procedures designed to tap all the resources of the HRAF research staff as well as those of outside specialists were supervised by Dr. Herbert H. Vreeland, who read and commented upon each chapter as it was drafted. Mr. Percy Winner of the senior staff rendered especially valuable assistance to Dr. Vreeland and to the Editor.

The authors were fortunate in having the use of working papers prepared under contract at the University of Chicago under the general supervision of Professor Bert F. Hoselitz and the editorship of Miss Alicja Iwańska. Professor George L. Trager, University of Buffalo, provided basic linguistic materials and analysis. Dr. Margaret Mead, Director of the Institute for Intercultural Studies, graciously made available valuable research materials developed by Dr. Sula Benet and others.

Other individuals who provided critical comment on several chapters include: Mr. Alfons Sergot and Dr. Kazimierz Grzybowski of the Mid-European Law Project, Library of Congress, Dr. Myron Gordon, Mrs. Lucia Glicksman, and Mr. Leon Lewins.

While these and many others contributed to the Poland study, whatever shortcomings it may have are the sole responsibility of its authors and the Editor.

CONTENTS

Contents (*continued*)

THE CULTURE AND THE SOCIETY

CAPTIVE, ECONOMICALLY IN CHAOS, POLITICALLY IN FERMENT, unable, militarily, to defend or assert itself, Poland nonetheless has embarked on a dramatic and bold attempt to preserve itself as a nation on its own terms—terms meaningful in the context of Polish culture. Yet the dominant values and cultural ideals of the Polish people— in part conditioned by nearly a century and a half of foreign domination—have frequently shown themselves to be antithetical to the requirements of a modern industrialized Polish state.

The dismembering of their state at the end of the eighteenth century forced the Polish people to live under the simultaneous rule of three foreign nations for over a century, thus preventing them from evolving attitudes and social institutions related to the changing terms of life in Europe. The people, however, clung tenaciously and successfully to their language, their religion, and to values and modes of living which they identified as Polish. Dominant among those values is an intense, almost fierce individualism. That trait has been a serious obstacle to Polish efforts to establish the institutions which, when they function, assure the state a firm base of political and economic concord that permits it to exercise its sovereignty to the limits of strength and opportunity. The same individualism, however, has proven an effective shield against attempts to reshape the Pole to models preferred by foreign masters or by the champions of some abstractly defined utopia—socialist, communist, or whatever.

Poland's dismemberment and absorption by Germany and the Soviet Union during World War II rekindled a long tradition of intense resistance to foreign oppression. Communist rule since World War II not only has kept that tradition alive but has strengthened it by deeply violating many basic Polish values. Communist programs and methods of control are associated with Russian domination and eastern despotism by the Poles, who are culturally part of the West and have been Roman Catholic since the tenth century.

Resentment of authoritarian methods of government which deprive the individual of respect and dignity, coupled with the feeling of national indignation at Russian hegemony, produced widespread unrest in Poland. After Stalin's death in 1953 that unrest progressively challenged Communist goals, programs, and power. Since October 1956 the Polish Government, under Gomułka, has to a degree responded to the popular appeal for national and individual freedom. It has secured a limited degree of independence from rigid Soviet control, and it is attempting to create a system of rule more compatible with the traditional relationship of the individual to the state. While this has strengthened the government's popularity, it has also weakened its ability to direct the people's efforts toward greater economic and political stability.

Individual, Society, and State

The Pole dreads anonymity and resists every effort to draw him into communal activities that threaten it. His society reflects the high value placed upon the individual assertion of differences. In so doing, it comes into conflict with the needs of the state, since the state in any form—and most especially in the Communist form—requires the organizational submergence of differences. The interplay between these two elements provides a great measure of the drama in Poland today.

There are in Polish culture no dominant values requiring the individual to subordinate himself to the state. Centralized authority— indeed, any form of depersonalized power—is viewed more as a goad to objection and resistance than as the instrument of group consensus. The Pole tends to respect authority only to the degree that he can associate it with some one person who fits the traditional image of the dedicated, selfless hero. He will rally to a leader who seems to personify highly valued traits: integrity, strength, vision, boldness. Since a man capable of marshaling the devotion of great masses of Poles appears but rarely on the national scene, the institutions of Polish society are characterized by internal fragmentation and discord; political organizations, trade unions, public associations, and similar groups are subjected to continual internal tension as numerous small cliques militate for their own special interests.

That an institution or an organized group is subject to enormous tensions in Poland does not mean that inevitably it is torn apart. Much can depend upon the versatility of a leader and upon the kind of appeal made to the group. The more ideal, in Polish terms, the goal to be striven for—the degree to which it can tap the great reservoir of emotion associated with the central values of the culture—

the greater the organization's potential for survival. The army, for example, the actual or potential guardian of Poland, has never lacked for men or suffered from serious internal dissension. On the contrary, it has been able to maintain its tradition and its high prestige despite the catastrophes that have befallen the nation it serves.

Intensely patriotic, the Poles will submerge individual differences to come to the support of the nation—but only when the nation is threatened, and only when that threat is so immediate that every action required of the individual has an obvious meaningful relation to the crisis at hand. If the government defines the nation's needs in more subtle or diffuse terms and requires of the people a series of seemingly unrelated small actions and sacrifices, those needs are apt to be subordinated to individual desire. A Pole on horseback will charge a tank with pistol and saber. Require him, however, in the interest of the "common good," to pile economic brick upon brick in an aura of sweat and his attention will wander. Today, appeals for support of the ideal of national independence and for preserving the integrity of the Polish Church are the most effective rallying points for the Polish people as a whole.

The leaders of both the Polish United Workers' (Communist) Party and the Roman Catholic Church have come together in urging the people to abjure individual heroics (without, however, forgetting that they are heroes), to join together in doing the innumerable dull and repetitive tasks which must be done if the nation is to prosper. But the people continue to assert their independence, acquiescing only in part to the appeals of the leaders—continuing, in short, to behave in the ways by which, in their culture, an individual can define himself.

The Church

The Roman Catholic faith in Poland is closely identified with the people's sense of national identity, and the Church has served since the nineteenth century as a symbol of national freedom. Roman Catholicism has been a central influence on all aspects of Polish culture, differentiating it from the culture of Orthodox Russia to the east, and that of the Protestant countries to the west. The Polish Church provided a spiritual mainstay during the decades of partition; it emerged from World War II as a chief source of national unity and spiritual strength; it has survived the assault of communism to function now as one of the strongest voices insisting that there shall be a distinct and autonomous Poland.

To achieve that end, the Polish Church hierarchy has chosen, despite the Church's abhorrence of the Communist system, to side at least temporarily with those Polish Communists who seek to minimize Russian domination without provoking Russian intervention. At the same time, the Church has insisted that its internal autonomy be respected. The actions of Gomułka since October 1956 indicate his belief that Catholicism is perhaps the single most important cohesive force in the nation today; the support given him, as the lesser evil, by the Polish Episcopate is without doubt the single most important source of his own strength.

Acceptance of the Roman Catholic faith, with little of the challenging and questioning that mark the intellectual history of many western European nations, has and does cut across all classes in Poland. Participation in ceremony and conformity to dogma varies, being more a part of the peasants' life than of the intelligentsia's. But such variation is far less significant than what is shared.

The link between a Pole's religious faith and his patriotism may be hard to measure, hard to describe; it is nonetheless real and viable. It is one of the keys to political power in the nation, for such power finally is dependent upon cohesion in the society, and cohesion in Polish society in large part depends upon Polish Catholicism.

In theory, communism—fundamentally an attempt to harness every human energy, dictate every motive, and control every social act—cannot tolerate the existence of religious faith, much less of an organized Church. But to a far greater degree than in Russia, communism in Poland not only has had to permit the existence of the Church, it has had to treat with it as a political power. The Polish Communists, seizing control of the state on the heels of vast devastation and chaos, could little afford an attempt in the name of theory to destroy or supplant those institutions which in fact are the base of order and predictability of behavior in a society. A successful attempt to destroy the Church would have been in fact to dissolve an essential cementing ingredient in the society and an essential reference point for the actions of individuals. In Poland the price of avoiding anarchy was to come to terms with Polish Catholicism and the mystique of Polish patriotism. Today, to the degree that Poland's political leaders seek to maintain their power, they depend upon the existence and strength of religious faith.

Politics and Economics

Poland's political and economic affairs are directed by a small group of Communists placed in power by the Soviet Union toward the end of World War II. Their political instrument, the Polish United Workers' Party, has the "directing role" in Polish political life, but it has been found necessary to work with a number of non-Communist parties as well as with the Church. The economy presents a similarly "impure" aspect, being a mixture of socialism, state capitalism, and private enterprise, and it has not yet come close to resembling the productive machine envisioned by Party planners.

The effort to "build socialism" in Poland has been marked by three distinct stages: (1) 1945–48, the consolidation of Communist control and the linking of Stalinist socialism with nationalism; (2) 1948–55, the abandonment of nationalism, the open subordination of Poland's needs to those of the Soviet Union, and the adoption of Soviet methods and patterns in the drive to transform Poland from an agricultural into an industrial nation; (3) 1956–present, the return, following a mounting degree of popular protest, to nationalism in policy and to the realities of Polish culture, without, however, renouncing the goal of communism.

During the interwar period and World War II there was a great increase in popular awareness of politics in Poland; and the experience of the German occupation inured much of the population to many forms of intimidation. Moving to centralize the government's powers and functions and to extend them to control not only the actions but also the thoughts of the individual, the Communists met a populace which eventually resisted at every level. Intellectuals protested. Workers rejected, totally or in part, the discipline of the state-run factory. Peasants rejected and wrecked the collectivization program and withheld their produce from the government. Producing for the Soviet Union rather than for Poland, the economy could offer few material incentives to entice the population into activities alien to them.

The crisis reached its climax in June 1956 when the workers in Poznan demanded "Bread and Freedom." The result of that crisis was to reinstate Władysław Gomułka—the previously discredited exponent of a Polish as distinct from a Russian "road to socialism"—as head of a badly divided party and chief of a badly disrupted state. Moving boldly he was able to redefine the relationship of Poland to the Soviet Union and of the Polish United Workers' Party to the USSR's Communist Party: henceforth that relationship was to be, at least theoretically, based on "sovereign equality." Gomułka gained the support of the Church in the large matters affecting Poland's survival. Some of the most detested social, political, and economic controls were eased. The immediate crisis was weathered, the people in part satisfied by the assertion of Polish autonomy and the easing of internal controls. In terms of permanent solution, however, everything still is left to do.

In the immediate future the Polish Government must weigh its every decision against the possibility of Russian intervention. On the one hand are the demands of a people aroused, on the other the watchful might of a power which has demonstrated its willingness to move, swiftly and brutally, should it consider itself endangered. In the middle are the Polish Communists, determined that they, and they alone, know what is best for the people, but seriously split among themselves both as to the methods and the tempo of transition and as to the specific intermediate goals on the road to communism. Basic to all these factors is a culture which contains little that will motivate Poles to accept the discipline and the grueling drudgery which their political and spiritual leaders alike assure them are the only means by which they can achieve a better life and preserve the limited strength and independence their nation now enjoys.

HISTORICAL SETTING

EMERGING FROM POLITICAL OBSCURITY IN THE TENTH CEN-
tury, Poland by the fourteenth century had become one of the great
powers of Europe. The Poles, differing from the Eastern Slavs in
their use of the Latin alphabet and their adherence to Roman Catholicism, played a major part in building from the fourteenth century to the sixteenth a federation which linked Poles, Lithuanians,
Ukrainians, and Belorussians into a Polish-Lithuanian Commonwealth.

The Commonwealth, in which the Polish state was dominant, attempted to maintain an expansionist policy. By the seventeenth century, however, political instability, economic weakness, and foreign
wars had sapped its strength and left it helpless before the rising
power of the Germans to the west and the Russians to the east. In
1795, after a series of partitions, Poland was completely dismembered
by the military empires of Prussia, Austria, and Russia; it was to
remain under alien domination for over a century.

Poland disappeared from the political map of Europe but survived
as a cultural entity. Although the mass of Polish peasants, like other
peasants of eastern Europe, had no highly developed sense of nationality, they clung to their native speech, their Catholic faith, and
their land. Many educated Poles, more conscious of their nationality,
refused to be reconciled to the dismemberment of their country.
From the latter group came the leaders of several bitter but hopeless insurrections, after which, to escape repression, thousands of the
intellectuals took refuge in exile.

Abroad, these men continued the struggle as exiled revolutionaries
and apostles of Polish nationalism. Poets, writers, and scholars endowed the suffering nation with their vision of a bright future, proclaiming their faith in the eventual triumph of "spiritual" forces over
the brute reign of material power. Many, easily fired by idealistic

proposals, lost contact with political reality. Among themselves they were divided by numerous quarrels. The patriotic fervor and dedication that pervaded their works, however, contributed much to the survival of the concept of Polish nationality and independence when Poland possessed no political existence.

Poland re-emerged only after all three partitioning empires collapsed during World War I. The experience of partition had, however, left a deep mark. Poles within each of the partitioned territories had gone through different social and economic processes at a crucial period of modern history—the nineteenth century, a period that saw developing nationalism, the emancipation of the peasants, the industrial revolution, the rise of capitalism. The difficult task of creating a united political, economic, and social system confronted a nation discordant, divided by hatreds, and lacking practical experience in politics beyond that of opposition, intrigue, and conspiracy.

A relatively short and unstable period of experimentation with parliamentary democracy, accompanied by mounting economic and social problems, was followed in 1926 by a military coup and authoritarian rule, paralleling developments elsewhere in eastern Europe. The revival of German and Russian power during the 1930's once more threatened an independence that had been won in a moment of German and Russian weakness. The Polish Government's attempt to pursue an "independent" policy and to act as counterweight to both Germany and Soviet Russia failed to prevent another partition in 1939.

Germany invaded Poland on September 1, 1939, unleashing World War II. Soviet forces moved across the Polish eastern frontier on September 17. Twelve days after the Soviet attack both powers signed a treaty dividing Poland between them according to a previous agreement.

After the Nazi invasion of Russia in 1941 all of Poland fell under German rule. The bestiality of the German occupation assumed unparalleled proportions. Planning to transform Poland into an essentially German land, the Nazis undertook the political, cultural, economic, and biological annihilation of Poles, beginning with the systematic killing of those of the upper classes. The resulting hatred of Germans gave the Soviet regime its major, and perhaps sole, political asset in dealing with Poland after the war.

Poland's subsequent political fate was decided largely by the distribution of power in Europe at the end of World War II. Occupied by Russian forces at the close of the war, Poland was slowly transformed into a Soviet satellite. The horror and suffering experienced by the Poles at the hands of Germans did much to facilitate the gradual process of Sovietization. The devastation and chaos of war, moreover, had uprooted many old values and ideals and destroyed, at least for a time, the will of many to resist. Faced with the issue of survival, most Poles sought to reconstruct a semblance of normal life within the framework of the inevitable. Communist Poland increasingly began to resemble its "liberator" in administrative structure as the Soviet regime implemented its police and other controls with the help of an indigenous, though weak, Polish Communist movement.

Of all the satellites, however, Poland was perhaps the most difficult for the Soviet Union to absorb. Poles remained proud of their ties with western civilization. They retained their centuries-old tradition of Polish-Russian animosity—reinforced by a growing record of Communist atrocities. They continued to cherish their history as a symbol of the indestructibility of their national consciousness and of the vitality of their culture.

The Piast Kings

Of the scattered Slavic tribes who, in the middle of the tenth century, lived between the Oder and Vistula rivers, the Polanie, or "dwellers of the plain," proved to be the strongest and politically best organized. Uniting with neighboring tribes to resist German invaders, they produced the able Piast dynasty, which ruled the land until 1370.

One of the earliest accounts of Poland deals with a frontier struggle between Polish Prince Mieszko and German forces in the year 963. To secure his position, Mieszko entered into a tribute-paying relationship with the newly revived Holy Roman Empire. Wedding a Bohemian princess, he accepted the Roman Catholic faith for himself and his people, hoping thereby to deprive the Germans of an evangelizing pretext for aggression. Poland was thus drawn into the orbit of Rome and western civilization. The Eastern Slavs of Russia, in the meantime, embraced the Greek rite and fell under Byzantine influence. In later centuries this division led to a deep estrangement between the two leading Slavic nations.

The date for the founding of Mieszko's kingdom is traditionally given as 966. The Polish state soon broke out of its original territorial limits to push eastward, abandoning its western territories early in its history and returning to them only after World War II. Under Mieszko's successor, Boleslav the Brave (r. 992–1025), the Polish state grew in strength and standing, extending its authority as far east as the Dnieper River. The conquest of eastern lands opened up commercial routes to the Black Sea, securing Poland's prosperity through the Middle Ages.

The first manifestation of Polish power and independence was followed in the thirteenth century by a period of disintegration and chaos. The appanage system of inheritance, whereby the ruler divided his land among his sons, disrupted the unity of the state. Brothers and cousins competing for the throne sought the support of wealthy landowners and the higher clergy by offering them privilege and power. Quarrels among Polish dukes invited foreign intervention. Poland lost more and more of its land. Foreign invasions soon overwhelmed a great part of the country. Tatar forces swept through southern Poland as far as Silesia. The Tatars left no lasting imprint upon Poland's history, as they did on Russia's, but Poles have since regarded this period as an example of the burden they bore in the past, when, as they see it, they guarded Europe and Christendom from devastation by Mongol hordes.

The requirements of military defense greatly strengthened the internal position of Polish knights and warriors, who formed the core of Poland's landed nobility. Organized on a clan basis, members of the nobility carefully guarded their individual rights from encroachment by royal power, considering themselves, at least theoretically, all equal. This tradition of "liberty" paved the way for later constitutional government in Poland, but in the interim it contributed to the State's eventual destruction.

Early in the fourteenth century the Polish state regained its unity and enjoyed a revival under Casimir the Great (r. 1333–70), whom many Poles consider one of their greatest rulers. The administration was reformed to strengthen the central government. Marshes were drained and forests cleared to foster agriculture; roads, bridges, and trading posts were built and improved. The first Polish university, and the first in Central Europe, was founded at Cracow in 1364 with the active cooperation of the leading Polish clergy. Modeled on the Paris Sorbonne, the university developed into a great center of theological learning. The Polish Church acquired highly gifted leaders, many of European renown, who were eminent as scholars and active in political affairs. The Church gained in strength and contributed much to the restoration of stability and order.

In foreign relations, Poland under Casimir sacrificed Pomerania to the Teutonic Knights, Silesia to Germanized Bohemia, and once more directed its attention toward the east. Its territorial and political aims would in time bring it into conflict with a resurgent Muscovy, but it was first to enjoy a period of true greatness.

The Jagiellos

The eastward expansion under Casimir the Great brought about an important internal transformation. Increasingly absorbing non-Polish elements, Poland became a multinational state. Casimir died in 1370. In 1386 one of his descendants, Queen Jadwiga, married the Grand Duke of Lithuania, Vladyslav Jagiello, founding the Jagiellon dynasty. This union between Poland and Lithuania laid the foundations for what became one of the greatest powers in eastern Europe: a commonwealth which embraced vast territories, including most of Belorussia and the Ukraine.

The growing menace of German pressure served as the main motive for the union. In 1410 the forces of Poland and Lithuania succeeded in defeating the Teutonic Order at Stebark (also known as Tannenberg) in one of the greatest battles of medieval times. In 1569 the two nations bound themselves together by a more organic and permanent political union which gave them a common king and extended the privileges and rights of Polish nobles to the Lithuanian nobility.

Sixteenth-century Poland experienced an impressive development of national culture. The period is spoken of by Poles as their "golden age." The University of Cracow became an international center of humanism. New universities were built. Poles created a brilliant literature, first in Latin, then in Polish.

The Church by now had considerable influence in state affairs. The clergy was assured a voice in the management of the country and enjoyed self-government. Although the Roman Catholic faith remained the state religion, the idea of religious tolerance was accepted as a constitutional principle. The religious trends of the Reformation swept through the Polish upper classes and for a short while became fashionable, contributing to the development of a Polish national literature. Among the masses, however, Protestantism took no deep roots and lost ground rapidly. Reaction against Protestantism was spearheaded by the Jesuits, and the Counter Reformation gained strength after the middle of the sixteenth century.

Beneath the brilliance of the "golden age" social and political decay had begun. Members of the Polish landed nobility (*szlachta*) had by this time acquired impressive privileges and rights, greatly reducing the authority and strength of the Crown; Polish kings became increasingly dependent on their good will and support for political and military undertakings. The rise of the gentry was accompanied by a deterioration of the status of other social groups. Showing little taste or skill in commerce and handicrafts, the gentry had in earlier centuries welcomed foreign merchants and Jewish tradesmen. A great number of Jews, persecuted in the rest of Europe during the Middle Ages, had flocked to Poland for refuge and had prospered. The position of this emergent middle class was, however, undermined when the gentry enacted legislation harmful to merchants and tradesmen. By the second half of the sixteenth century Polish merchants were restricted more stringently than foreign traders. The peasants, comprising the chief source of labor on the land, were compelled to work on gentry estates and prohibited from leaving the land without the permission of their landlords. Deprived of freedom of movement and forced to do service to the nobility in ever-increasing amounts, the peasant was gradually reduced to serfdom.

The gentry now possessed immense political power. Their assemblies had been transformed into a parliament (*Sejm*), which secured control over the legislative functions of the state. They had won the right to elect members of the dynastic family to the throne. They had evolved an extraordinary practice, called the *liberum veto,* whereby any single deputy to the *Sejm* could block any measure indefinitely merely by voicing dissent. While these privileges and rights produced a proud upper-class tradition of political equality and liberty for the few, they eventually degenerated into irresponsible license to perpetuate internal political weakness and confusion. Citizenship was the right only of the gentry, who constituted a relatively numerous group by the end of the sixteenth century—roughly ten percent of the total population. Among the various strata of gentry, however, differences in economic position largely nullified nominal equality. At the bottom of at least six grades of nobility were a great number of families who had lost much of the land once given them in return for military service and who lived not much better than the peasants. These generally offered their political allegiance to the relatively few leading families who constituted the real source of power.

Unlike the Prussian Junkers, the Polish nobility never developed the concept of service to the Crown, and the struggle for position and wealth among competing gentry families gradually robbed the state of its cohesion. After the death of the last of the Jagiellos (Sigismund August) in 1572, Poland continued to enjoy moments of imperial expansion, but it could not long hide its growing weakness from foreign powers.

The Elective Monarchy

Sigismund August left no heir, and succession to the Polish throne was opened to the quarrels and intrigues of rival European courts. Further, a new monarch was required to sign a pact which bound him to respect the rights and privileges of the nobility, and to solemnly contract to transfer most of his prerogatives to the *Sejm*.

Wars with Russians, Turks, and Swedes began to drain Poland's strength despite occasional military triumphs. Several victories against

Russia were won by Stefan Batory (r. 1575–86), who died in the midst of plans for a vast expedition against Turkey. The reign of Sigismund III (r. 1587–1632) coincided with a period of great internal disorder in Russia and offered Poles a unique opportunity to interfere in Russian affairs. Polish forces invaded a Russia convulsed by dynastic troubles and economic chaos. King Sigismund laid claim to the throne of Muscovy. The Poles were soon repulsed, however, by a Russian people roused to defend their Orthodox faith and their land. Subsequent clashes were to reveal the growing strength of Russian rulers.

To Poles the seventeenth century is still known as "The Deluge." Enemies poured over the land from almost every direction. Incessant wars exhausted the country. Brilliant military exploits against Turkey by Poland's last great ruler, Jan Sobieski (r. 1674–96), were but an afterglow of waning Polish power. Russia's drive toward the Baltic and Black Seas and the rise of the Kingdom of Prussia began to menace Poland's very existence.

Internal political anarchy frustrated all efforts to resist the growing pressure from outside. Eighteen foreign candidates competed for the Polish throne in 1697; the combined powers of Russia, Prussia, and Austria succeeded in imposing upon the Poles Augustus II of Saxony. Russian troops soon enjoyed free passage through Polish territory and Poland was deprived of an independent foreign policy.

Poland's powerful neighbors profited greatly by the weakness of the Polish governmental structure. The gentry, jealous of their privileges, refused to cooperate with the monarchy in providing funds for the modernization of the armed forces, which were steadily reduced in strength. Time after time the *Sejm* was paralyzed by the exercise of the *liberum veto.* By the middle of the eighteenth century Poland maintained neither a regular army nor a diplomatic service.

Meanwhile, the country had experienced increasing economic and social disintegration. Landed estates were exploited so harshly that Poland became known in Europe as the "peasants' hell." By persecuting Jewish shopkeepers and foreign merchants and by arbitrarily forbidding all imports and exports over long periods of time, the gentry destroyed once flourishing cities and towns—depriving Poland of a prosperous middle class which might have bridged the cleavage between the upper nobility and the masses. The Polish Church represented the only important element of unity and cohesion in the country. Foreign invaders had all been of different religions—Protestant Swedes and Prussians, Orthodox Russians, Moslem Turks and Tatars. The Poles increasingly identified themselves with their Catholic faith, and they began to persecute religious dissenters.

Early in the eighteenth century Russian pressure exacted from the Polish state a promise to respect the Orthodox religion in Polish territories. This became a pretext for increasing Russian intervention in Polish affairs. After becoming Empress of Russia, Catherine the Great secured the election of Stanisław August Poniatowski to the Polish throne (r. 1764–95), a pro-Russian Polish noble who had been her lover. Frederick the Great of Prussia then joined with Catherine in a campaign to win certain "rights" for Orthodox and Lutheran minorities in Poland. In 1768 this campaign sparked an outbreak of armed resistance to Russian interference by a group of Polish noblemen led by Józef Pułaski and his son, Kazimierz (who later fought in the American Revolution). The rebellion, though maintained for almost four years, was crushed. It precipitated the first partition of Polish lands.

Fearing that Russia would take the lion's share of Poland if he did not act quickly, Frederick the Great arranged an agreement in 1772 whereby none of the interested powers—Austria, Prussia, and Russia—would acquire Polish territory to the exclusion of the others. Austria then annexed most of Galicia, and Prussia occupied the provinces of Ermeland and Pomerania, as well as the region at the mouth of the Vistula River. Russia seized the outlying eastern border regions. Poland had lost almost one third of its territory and one half of its population.

This disaster shocked the Polish nobility into a belated effort to restore cohesion to the state. Lulled into a false sense of security by a temporary estrangement between Prussia and Russia, the *Sejm* on May 3, 1791 adopted a new Constitution which abolished the *liberum veto*, established a hereditary monarchy, strengthened executive authority, and gave political rights to the urban middle class.

In 1792 Russian troops invaded Poland to defend the "golden liberties" of Polish nobles who had opposed the new Constitution. A second partition of Poland was agreed upon with Prussia in 1793. This led in 1794 to an insurrection under the leadership of Tadeusz Kościuszko, who unsuccessfully sought to enlist the support of Polish peasants. Though scoring initial military successes, the uprising was crushed after the invasion of Poland by Prussian forces. The inhabitants of Warsaw staged a heroic struggle but capitulated to Russian troops after a massacre organized by General Suvorov in the suburb of Praga.

A third partition, in which Austria again claimed a share, wiped the Polish state off the map in 1795. The heart of former Polish lands, including Warsaw, went to Prussia. Austria's Galician acquisitions were enlarged. Russia took the remaining territory east of a line drawn from Grodno to Brest-Litovsk and to the new Austrian border. For over a century Poles were to live divided—under three separate alien governments.

The Dismembered Nation

After 1795 leading Polish gentry either lost their privileges or transferred their allegiance to the courts of the conquerors. Peasants barely noticed the change. Many Polish intellectuals, political leaders, and officers emigrated, giving birth to "Poland in exile."

Emigrés in Paris, seeking the support of revolutionary France, organized, under the command of General Jan Henryk Dąbrowski, a Polish Legion that fought valiantly on the side of France in the Napoleonic Wars. Fighting under the French flag in numerous countries throughout Europe, divisions of the Legion gave their nation a heroic military tradition. The Napoleonic epic brought Poles fame as incomparable soldiers, but all efforts to revive the "Polish Question" among the governments of Europe failed.

In 1807 Napoleon carved out of Prussia's Polish provinces the Grand Duchy of Warsaw, a puppet state which served as a French military outpost in the east. The Duchy was ruled by Napoleon's ally, the King of Saxony, under a Constitution which provided for a *Sejm,* a system of independent courts operating under the Napoleonic Code, and a strongly centralized French administration. A decree abolishing serfdom and introducing civil equality was opposed by Polish nobles and never put into practice.

After Napoleon's defeat at Waterloo the Grand Duchy of Warsaw was swept away by the Congress of Vienna (1815), which rearranged the map of Europe. Poland remained partitioned. Out of the remnants of the Duchy the Russian Tsar, Alexander I, created a small Kingdom of Poland—generally known as the Congress Kingdom—which was given a Constitution modeled on that of Napoleon's Grand Duchy. Many Polish landowners under Russian rule began to hope that ultimately all Poles would be united in a new state with the tsar as king.

At the Congress of Vienna the partitioning powers had agreed to respect the rights of their Polish subjects. Prussia and Austria nevertheless embarked almost immediately on a policy of national oppression, but initially Alexander I was ready to play the part of a benign constitutional monarch. The Congress Kingdom enjoyed a decade of liberties. Many of the enlightened measures introduced by the French were preserved. Industry was developed and education fostered; the kingdom was given a separate Polish administration and army.

This interlude of peaceful development was soon over. Stimulated by romantic ideals of nationalism, Polish extremists demanded the transfer from Russia of the lands that had belonged to the Polish state before partition. Russian policies became increasingly repressive. Poles organized numerous secret societies and prepared themselves for a revolution. An insurrection was finally launched by a group of army cadets in 1830.

The uprising was doomed from the start. The Poles were split into two major hostile camps, one representing the upper nobility, the other the lesser gentry. Neither group gained the support of the peasants, whom both had long suppressed. The uprising was followed by ruthless Russification. The Congress Kingdom was made an integral part of the Russian Empire and ruled directly by a governmental department in the Russian capital. Nicholas I imposed upon Poles a regime of martial law. The use of the Polish language in schools was prohibited, and Polish universities, the chief centers of nationalist propaganda, were closed.

Thousands of Polish intellectuals fled the country in what is now called the "Great Emigration." Abroad, they played an important part in keeping alive the Polish national spirit. Some sought escape in reveries and contemplation of the heroic past, forgetting the subsequent periods of anarchy and dissension; Poland, they declared, was too noble to exist in a world of wickedness. Others exalted the national suffering, endowing it with a religious and messianic character; the poet Adam Mickiewicz, for instance, spoke of Poland as "the Christ of the nations," which by its suffering would redeem the guilt of a corrupt humanity. Some saw in their own past the source of all calamities and called for a regeneration of the Polish spirit. Still others, realizing that Poland could not be restored so long as the political order that had permitted the partitions endured, proclaimed that a new universal moral order would have to be established before Poland could rise from the tomb. Although the Poles abroad were split into various cliques and factions, they gave each successive generation at home a sacred cause, to be sponsored regardless of the propitiousness of the times. A Pole was measured by the manner in which he fought for his ideals, not by the outcome of the struggle.

Unrest inside the former Polish territories continued to express itself intermittently throughout the middle years of the nineteenth century. An ill-fated uprising broke out in Cracow in 1846, spread to Galicia, and was put down by the Austrian Government—in some areas with the help of peasants who were rewarded for every severed head of a nobleman. In 1863 the conscription of Poles into the Russian Army led to one of the most bitter and bloody insurrections in Polish history. Poles clashed with Russian troops in hundreds of encounters. Again, however, the Poles were divided—some favoring gradual reform within the framework of Russian political supremacy, others wanting an all-out revolution—and again the hoped-for mass revolt of Polish peasants failed to materialize. The rebellion, crushed by numerically superior Russian forces, was the last Polish attempt at armed opposition until 1914.

A new attitude emerged after the failure of the 1863 insurrection. An atmosphere of realism replaced the former spirit of romanticism. Many branded the romantic temper as folly and sought an outlet for their creative energies in what they called "organic labor"—the support of internal economic and social progress. Young Poles who had never known a free Poland could no longer look toward a restoration of old foundations. They found that the old Poland had been a land of class privilege and serfdom, and sought to adapt themselves to the present by engaging in practical and constructive labor.

Meanwhile, important social and economic changes were taking place. Prussia had emancipated Polish peasants in 1823, Austria in 1849, and Russia in 1864—something Polish landlords persistently sought to prevent. As the Polish landed aristocracy decreased in numbers and wealth, sons of the gentry turned to the towns for careers in business and the professions, forming the nucleus of a new middle class. As a result, Polish Jews lost a number of their traditional economic functions and suffered many hardships. An upsurge in industrial development brought with it the problems of a growing urban proletariat. Changing times and the Polish response to them assumed a different character in each of the three territories.

To Russian Poland, despite continued repression and persecution, the practice of "organic labor" brought about a transformation in industry and agriculture. Poles cooperated in administrative reforms and the development of municipal and civic institutions. Huge Russian markets were opened to Polish industries. The pressure of Russification continued, however, and gradually drove many Poles underground. Some began to intrigue with disaffected factions in Russia for the eventual overthrow of the tsarist regime. Others felt they could still win a measure of freedom without complete separation from Russia; these looked upon Germany as the real enemy of Polish independence. In both cases political objectives once more came to the forefront of Polish aspirations.

Austrian Poland, or Galicia, was economically the most backward of all the Polish lands. Much of its soil was poor and many areas suffered from overpopulation. Many of its peasants emigrated to North America, and hundreds of thousands became seasonal migrants to Prussian areas and elsewhere. Despite limited economic opportunities, however, the Austrian Poles managed to win important political privileges. After a defeat by Prussia in 1866, the Austrian Government felt it necessary to secure greater political support from its Slavic subjects. The Poles in Galicia were given a large measure of autonomy and self-government; in return for various concessions, they almost invariably supported the existing government in the Austrian *Reichsrat* when other elements for a majority were lacking. Making skillful use of their advantages, they became masters at bargaining and compromise. Considerable numbers entered the Austrian governmental service and acquired training and experience which later proved of great value. Universities were revived and an Academy of Sciences was opened. Galicia became in time an important Polish artistic and intellectual center. The concessions won, however, were primarily for the benefit of the Polish upper classes, at the expense of the peasantry.

Prussian Poland was perhaps the most severely ruled of all the territories. In 1873 education, which had been largely in the hands of the Polish Roman Catholic clergy, was placed under the control of the state. Prevented from engaging in any political activity, the Poles turned to economic fields. Attempting to free themselves from dependence on German capital and management, they built a strong system of cooperative organizations which contributed greatly to economic progress. Cooperative credit associations provided Polish artisans and tradesmen with much-needed capital. Polish funds were withdrawn from German banks and deposited in Polish cooperative banks. Agricultural "circles" trained peasants in new agricultural techniques. Large estates were bought up and the land was parceled out among Polish peasants. By the end of the nineteenth century the Poles in Prussia possessed a strong and financially independent economic organization which helped to integrate the economy of the entire province. The Poznan area became the richest and economically the most highly developed of all the Polish lands.

At the turn of the century Poles once more became restive. A new generation reacting against the "call to reason" of its elders revived some of the romantic fervor of the past. A revolt against the "quietism" of Polish life produced an impressive number of gifted writers and artists.

Various political groupings at home and abroad also began to show renewed signs of life. A socialist movement developed among workers in Russian and Austrian Poland but made little headway in the industrial areas of Prussian Silesia. Peasants in Galicia, prodded by intellectuals representing various political factions, began to organize parties of their own. A large part of both the Polish gentry and the conservative intelligentsia found its political temper embodied in a group calling itself the National Democrats.

Notions of active struggle for Polish independence were revived. Except for professed devotion to their nation, however, Poles were still divided in allegiance and social outlook. Socialists were split into "nationalists" and "internationalists." Some Poles were pro-Russian, others pro-German or pro-Austrian. Many Poles, in 1914, could not foresee a solution to their problems without the support of one or another of their oppressors.

The outbreak of World War I caught most Poles unprepared. Both Russia and the Central Powers, in a struggle for the loyalty of their Polish subjects, promised them an independent state. Many Poles were elated, then disillusioned, as it became clear that neither side intended to keep its promises. When President Wilson declared in January 1917 that "men everywhere were agreed that there should be a united, independent, and autonomous Poland," Poles turned their hopes toward the Allies.

In the summer of 1917 Polish political leaders from Russia and Galicia formed a Polish National Committee in Paris, which was accepted by the Allies as spokesman for the Polish cause. In January 1918, President Wilson proclaimed his Fourteen Points. The thirteenth stated:

> An independent Polish state should be erected, which should include the territories inhabited by indisputably Polish populations, which should be assured a free and secure access to the sea, and whose political and economic independence and territorial integrity should be guaranteed by international covenant.

A Polish army organized in France by the Polish National Committee took part in the final battle on the Western Front in 1918.

Inside Poland a separate independence movement took shape under the leadership of Józef Piłsudski, a Polish officer who had succeeded in forming a small Polish fighting force of his own. With the collapse of the Central Powers, Piłsudski quickly organized a Polish government in Warsaw. Strongly anti-Russian and viewed by his rivals as a Socialist, he assumed the title of temporary Chief of State and formed a Cabinet of Ministers. The National Committee in Paris, represented by conservative and pro-Russian Polish leaders, refused to accept his government as legitimate. The breach between the two groups was healed by the arrival in Poland of Ignace Jan Paderewski, who belonged to no political party and had the backing of the United States. He became Premier and Foreign Minister of a coalition government, and Poland was formally recognized by the United States on January 30, 1919.

Complete independence, a result of the outcome of the war, brought the leaders of the Polish nation many new and difficult problems. No lasting solution was found that could determine with finality the territories inhabited by "indisputably Polish populations." The settlement of frontiers proved a torturous process which planted the seeds of constant tensions and future dangers. Lack of capital and developed resources was to undermine economic stability. Poland's "territorial integrity," finally, was once again to be violated by powers which would choose not to respect the order created at Versailles.

The Years of Independence

Frontier struggles, carried on at the conference table and on battlefields, determined the climate in which the Polish state functioned for the next twenty years. By the Versailles Treaty (1919) Poland recovered the main part of the lands formerly under Prussian rule, but access to the Baltic Sea was limited to a narrow strip of land which terminated at the almost wholly German city and port of Danzig. The distribution of power between Germans and Poles in Danzig was left in suspense. Danzig was made a Free City under the protection of the League of Nations. East Prussia remained a German enclave; separated from the rest of Germany by the Polish Corridor, which Germans had to cross in sealed trains, it became a permanent threat to Polish security.

By plebiscite Upper Silesia was partitioned between Germany and Poland, the latter receiving very important industrial regions. A conflict between Polish and Czech interests in the region of Cieszyn (Teschen) in Silesia was resolved in favor of Czechoslovakia in 1920; in 1938, however, when the Czechs were forced to surrender part of their territories to Germany, Poland seized the opportunity to demand the cession of the disputed area. The city and region of Vilna (Vil'nyus), to which both Poles and Lithuanians laid claim became part of Lithuania in 1920 but was occupied by Poland in 1922 over the protests of Britain and France.

Conflict with Russia's new Soviet regime prevented any quick settlement of Poland's eastern frontiers. The Supreme Council of Allied and Associated Powers had made an attempt to define a provisional Polish-Russian frontier in 1919 corresponding roughly to the eastern frontier of the Congress Kingdom and known later as the Curzon Line. The Poles refused to accept this line, however, insisting they were entitled to the "historical" frontier of 1772.

An offensive to "liberate" the Ukraine was undertaken by

Piłsudski in the spring of 1920. Polish forces captured Kiev but were soon compelled to retreat in the face of a Soviet counteroffensive. The Red Army now hoped to carry the Revolution over a crumbling Poland to a Germany thought to be ripe for revolution, but was stopped at the gates of Warsaw. Both sides were now exhausted and ready for an armistice. A peace treaty between Poland and Russia was signed at Riga in March 1921, and the Ukrainian and Belorussian territories were divided between the two countries, restoring to Poland a little more than the area acquired by Russia in the third partition.

Poland now sought to buttress its security through various treaties and by participation in the League of Nations. France and Poland, both distrusting the good faith of Germany, signed on February 19, 1921 an alliance which remained one of the cornerstones of Polish foreign policy until 1939.

In domestic affairs the Polish Government worked to provide the state with a legal foundation. A constitution was prepared and came into force on June 1, 1921. Poland was declared a republic in which sovereignty belonged to the nation. Inspired by western democratic ideals, the Constitution provided for a relatively weak executive—an attempt to escape "the possible man on horseback"—by creating a presidency dependent upon an all-powerful parliament. The first elections under the new Constitution took place in 1922. Piłsudski, who had been an opponent of the Constitution, declined to stand as a candidate for the office of president and soon withdrew to his estate.

Free elections brought into the legislature a multitude of political groups and factions unable to produce a stable majority except in extreme situations. The next four years witnessed numerous changes in cabinets, frequent parliamentary crises, continuous bickerings, personal quarrels, and clashes of ambitions.

Those who became the leaders of the country—in the professions, government, and army—possessed a high sense of patriotism but lacked practical political experience and often failed to display a sense of responsibility. Intellectuals, businessmen, landowners, bureaucrats, and politicians from the three formerly partitioned territories confronted each other in an atmosphere of mutual suspicion and dislike. As a group they formed a slowly rising upper and middle class which acquired many of the habits and traditions of the old gentry. They were ready to concern themselves with the abstract welfare of the nation but frequently disregarded the concrete needs of living people, whom they tended to look upon as a "mob." Those with property and influence repeatedly blocked sorely needed agricultural reforms.

By 1926 the existing Polish Government had failed to give the country political stability and to solve many of the problems left by the years of war and occupation. In the eyes of men like Piłsudski the experiment in parliamentary democracy had only revived the anarchy of the seventeenth and eighteenth centuries. Entering Warsaw at the head of a regiment in May 1926, Piłsudski carried out a coup. He then sought the support of influential landowners and industrialists, with whose help he built an authoritarian regime.

Piłsudski exercised virtually dictatorial powers until his death in 1935. He attempted to rally support for his regime around a program of action which closely paralleled that of Mussolini, for whom he professed a profound admiration, but failed to win broad popular backing. After his death a single group of close political and military associates held on to the levers of power by sheer force.

A new Constitution was prepared in 1935; it imbedded authoritarian principles into the Polish political system. A new electoral law abolished extensive electoral rights and excluded opposition parties from parliamentary elections. Scores of opposition leaders were arrested and incarcerated in a concentration camp at Bereza on the edge of the Pinsk Marshes.

The unrest in Europe tempered Polish internal political life during the late 1930's. Opposition parties refused to accept the domination of the self-constituted ruling group and boycotted elections held under the Constitution, although they declined to resort to violence. Under the mounting threat of danger in the international field, the pressure for a return to a democratic system of government was eased.

Poland had followed a conciliatory policy in regard to Germany during the early 1930's. As the threat of German expansion increased, Foreign Minister Józef Beck attempted to pursue an "independent" policy which would maintain a balance between Poland's two most dangerous neighbors—Germany and Soviet Russia. In Beck's opinion the League of Nations had outlived its usefulness, and in August 1938 Poland gave up its seat on the Council of the League. Poland's efforts to improve relations with Russia while at the same time maneuvering for diplomatic position with Germany ended in disaster.

The German absorption of Czech lands foreshadowed Poland's destruction. In a last-minute reversal of policy Poland accepted in March 1939 a British guarantee of Polish independence. A military alliance with Great Britain (April 5, 1939), which included a specific territorial guarantee, was an attempt to preserve at least the *status quo* on the eastern German frontier. The critical issues were now whether or not Britain would live up to its guarantee and fight and what the attitude of the Soviet Union would be. Hitler apparently believed that British and French appeasement would continue. On August 23, 1939, he signed a nonaggression pact with Stalin and reached an agreement on the partition of Poland.

On the morning of September 1, 1929, Germany attacked Poland, and Polish troops retreated in confusion to the east. Britain and France declared war on Germany on September 2. Soviet forces, invading Poland on September 17, met hardly more than token resistance. Germany and Russia partitioned Polish territory along a frontier which corresponded roughly to the Curzon Line proposed by the Allies in 1919.

World War II and After

On September 30, 1939, the President of the Polish Republic, Ignacy Mościcki, transferred his presidential powers to Władysław Raczkiewicz (under a provision of the 1935 Constitution) and fled to Rumania. The new President took his oath of office in Paris and formed a government-in-exile with General Władysław Sikorski, a long-time opponent of the Piłsudski regime, as Prime Minister. A new Polish army was created on French soil. After the fall of France the Polish Government moved to London, evacuating a substantial part of the Polish army to Britain.

The new government, representing four major Polish political parties which had kept out of parliamentary activities in the last prewar years, decreed that all forms of government by a single individual or by an oligarchic group would in the future be prohibited. This government was to struggle abroad for the Polish cause as well as its own legal existence, only to find itself excluded from the most important decisions affecting Poland's future.

In German-occupied Poland an underground resistance movement was soon organized; it functioned under the direction of the government-in-exile. Nazi atrocities against the Polish and Jewish population assumed monstrous proportions. Millions died before firing squads and in concentration camps. Those left alive were deliberately condemned to undernourishment and starvation. The Nazis openly embarked upon the methodical extermination of Poles as a national group. A leading Nazi propagandist (W. Best) declared:

> Historical experience has shown that the destruction and elimination of a foreign nationality is not in the least against the laws of life, provided that destruction and elimination are complete.

In Soviet-occupied Poland large numbers of Poles and Ukrainians were deported to the interior of Russia. Following the German invasion of the USSR in 1941, however, the Polish government-in-exile reached an agreement with the Soviet regime providing for the restoration of diplomatic relations, the release of interned Polish civilians and military prisoners of war, and the creation of a Polish army on Russian soil. This army was subsequently moved to the Near East and supplied with American and British arms.

The Soviet regime had begun entertaining long-range political objectives in regard to Poland early in the war, and Soviet diplomacy worked ceaselessly to discredit the Polish government-in-exile. At the same time an indigenous Polish Communist movement was given new life and entrusted with the tasks of exploiting the fear and hatred of Germany in Poland and making the most of the chaos and disruption created by war.

The Polish Communist Party had played an insignificant role in prewar Poland. It had been unable to compete with other parties for influence, and was declared illegal, but it had suffered more from its own internal purges than from persecution by the Polish Government. Its top leaders perished in Moscow during the Russian purges of 1937–38, and the Party itself was dissolved by the Comintern.

Polish communism resumed its organized existence in 1941 under the name of the Polish Workers' Party (Polska Partia Robotnicza—PPR). The Communists embarked upon a struggle both against the Germans in Poland and against the "official" Polish underground —the Home Army—connected with the Polish London government. Simultaneously, a small group of Polish Communists who resided in the USSR set up a separate organization in Moscow known as the Union of Polish Patriots.

On the diplomatic front, friction between the Soviet Union and the Polish government-in-exile increased as it became clear that the USSR had no intention of abandoning its 1939–40 territorial claims. A request by the Polish London government in April 1943 for a Red Cross investigation of German charges that in 1940 the Russians had killed about 10,000 Polish officers in the Katyn forest, near Smolensk, was seized upon by the Soviet regime as a pretext for severing all relations.

Soviet diplomacy now sought to gain British and American concurrence in its territorial demands. The USSR wished to restore the Curzon Line as the postwar frontier between Russia and Poland and to reward Poland with German areas in Silesia, Pomerania, and East Prussia. In the interests of Allied unity, Great Britain agreed to the Curzon Line at the Teheran Conference in November 1943. The matter of Poland's western frontiers, however, remained an unsettled and highly controversial issue.

That same month Gomułka assumed the leadership of the Polish Workers' Party (PPR). The PPR now organized an underground Communist government—the Home National Council—which could take over in Poland as soon as the Red Army had pushed the Germans out of the country. Conscious of its numerical weakness, the Home National Council made no pretense to a wide national reputation and placed its hopes for the future on the reoccupation of Poland by Soviet forces.

By the summer of 1944 the Soviet offensive had liberated a large part of Poland. Gathering in Lublin, Polish Communists issued a manifesto, on July 22, which proclaimed the Home National Council and the Polish Committee of National Liberation the sole sources of authority in Poland. The Lublin Committee, as this body became known, declared that it would function on the basis of the 1921 Constitution, rejecting the 1935 Constitution and hence the legality of the Polish government-in-exile. It was clear that the Lublin Committee was a Russian-sponsored agency, but a considerable amount of potential opposition to the Communists apparently was neutralized and disarmed by the Russian claim that the Soviet Union had rescued Poland from total annihilation by the Nazis. For many Poles inside Poland the threat of Communist or Soviet domination appeared, at this time, less important than the memory of Nazi occupation.

As Soviet forces approached Warsaw, Radio Moscow's Polish-language broadcasts called upon the people of the city to rise in revolt against the Germans. The Soviet offensive, however, broke down at the outskirts of Warsaw in the last days of July 1944. Simultaneously, the underground in Warsaw, under the direction of the Polish government in London, staged an uprising, apparently in the hope of liberating the city before its capture by the Russians. Savage fighting in the city lasted for over two months, during which time the Russians refused to allow Allied planes supplying the insurgents to land in their territory for refueling. The revolt was crushed.

On January 5, 1945, the Soviet Government officially recognized the Lublin Committee as the "Provisional Government of Liberated Democratic Poland." The Red Army resumed its offensive on January 17, entered the ruins of Warsaw, and then advanced rapidly through Poland in its march to Berlin.

In London the British Government urged the Polish *émigré* government to reach an agreement with the Soviet Union and the Lublin Committee. Division among the Polish *émigré* leaders had by this time seriously weakened the government-in-exile. General Sikorski, killed in an airplane crash in 1943, had been succeeded in the premiership by Stanisław Mikołajczyk, the leader of the Polish

Peasant Party. Mikołajczyk went to Moscow in October 1944 to confer with Soviet leaders and representatives of the Lublin Committee. On his return to London he urged his colleagues to accept the Curzon Line as the basis for a territorial settlement with Russia. Unable to obtain their consent to a policy which would result in an agreement with the Soviet Union, he resigned the premiership on November 24, 1944.

Although the United States and Great Britain continued to give official support to the Polish government-in-exile, they agreed at the Yalta Conference in February 1945 to the creation of a new "Provisional Polish Government of National Unity." The Lublin Committee was to be reorganized on a broader basis to include non-Communist Polish leaders in the government.

In March 1945, sixteen leading Polish underground leaders were invited to Moscow to help organize the Government of National Unity. They were then arrested, tried in June for "sabotage," and imprisoned.

The Poles in exile, meanwhile, split into further rival factions. Many of them denounced the Yalta agreement, insisting that the rights of the Polish people to create their own government had been usurped. Mikołajczyk and his supporters, on the other hand, decided to join the Lublin Committee in Poland. A coalition government was formed on July 5, 1945. America and Britain assented to the settlement and withdrew their recognition of the Polish government-in-exile.

Four weeks later, at the Potsdam Conference, the Big Three agreed to place the eastern part of Germany to the Oder-Neisse line under "the administration of the Polish state." As a result of this and previous agreements Poland was transplanted bodily westward, losing 75,000 square miles in the east and gaining half of that area in the west and north. The lost land was chiefly agricultural; the areas gained had a substantial industrial potential.

The western powers regarded the new Polish-German frontier as provisional, to be determined finally at the peace settlement. The USSR, on the other hand, subsequently insisted that the frontier had been definitively determined by the Potsdam agreement. A final territorial arrangement could not be agreed upon. The existing arrangement became a source of permanent tension between Poles and Germans and helped also to reinforce the dominance of Russian power in eastern Europe.

With the period of armed struggle over, Poland began to undergo a new process of transformation. In 1945 Polish Communists had neither the ability nor the personnel to run the state by themselves. They had come to power on the bayonets of the Red Army, but bayonets alone could not collect grain, rebuild cities, or dig coal. The Party itself, moreover, could not count on a large degree of genuine popular support. A united front and coalition government accordingly became necessary steps in the transformation of Poland into a Soviet satellite.

By the inclusion of non-Communists in the government the Party avoided the threat of civil war. It acquired and was able to harness for its own purposes the skills and energies of sorely needed technicians, administrators, and economists. At the same time it shifted the arena of struggle to the political level, confident of eventual victory. The subsequent successes of Polish communism owed much to the skill with which its leaders took full advantage of war exhaustion, the failure of *émigré* Poles to hold the broad respect of the population, the burning hatred of Germany in Poland, and the emerging pattern of power in the world.

The first stage in the Sovietization of Poland was a period of moderation. The non-Communist parties enjoyed considerable latitude and freedom, as long as the consolidation of Communist power was not openly opposed. The degree of freedom allowed in the intellectual sphere compared favorably with conditions in other satellites. No determined attack was made upon the position of the Catholic Church and its economic privileges were not yet curtailed. Peasants were frequently reassured that their status would not be disturbed. The official Party line maintained that Poland would not have to pattern all its policies on the experiences of the USSR. The Party's leader, Gomułka, had often stated that Poland could achieve socialism without repeating the violence and disruption of the Soviet experiment. Socialism, he declared in 1947, could be achieved in Poland through evolutionary means; Poland was to follow its own road to socialism.

The government, representing a coalition of several political parties, proceeded to guide the country along the road of economic reconstruction and expansion. Its program included fairly radical social reforms—such as the breakup of large landed estates—and a foreign policy friendly to both the western Allies and the USSR. Within the coalition, however, the Communists gradually secured the decisive positions of power. Once entrenched in key posts in the government, the police, and the army, they removed their strongest enemies from positions of influence and built up an administrative staff of their own.

Aided by the threat of the Red Army, the Party then slowly broke the power of opposition parties and their leaders through legal chicanery, intimidation, and terror. Opposition leaders were purged or forced to flee the country. Other parties were still represented in the government, but by persons chosen by the Communists. Mikołajczyk escaped to the West in October 1947, and by the end of 1947 the Polish Peasant Party, which had attempted to compete with the Communists, had been completely destroyed. The only important "independent" party left was the Polish Socialist Party. Its leadership was purged of anti-Soviet elements and, in response to a "demand" for "workers' unity," it was merged with the Communist Party in December 1948 to form a Polish United Workers' Party (Polska Zjednoczona Partia Robotnicza—PZPR). The merger brought into the Communist fold a wealth of needed talent in the shape of experienced administrators, trade unionists, and organizers and helped to strengthen the Communists' grip upon the country.

The Party thus built up its power to a point where it could itself afford a purge. Up to 1948 the regime had been able to apply a veneer of nationalism and economic success to its policies. Increasing Soviet pressure was to rub off some of this coating.

The creation of the Cominform in September 1947 foreshadowed that hardening of Soviet control in the satellites which was to become increasingly evident in 1948. Gomułka, however, continued to appeal to national sentiment in his speeches. In particular he praised the traditions of the Polish Socialist Party and its attachment to Polish independence. He appeared to be starting to look upon the problems of his country from the inside and from the viewpoint of the man who had to handle those particular problems, rather than from the standpoint of a disciplined servant of international communism.

As the Soviet-Yugoslav dispute was reaching its climax in June 1948, Gomułka supported a conciliatory attitude toward Tito. Soon, however, he found himself in opposition to the majority of the Polish Politburo. He was severely criticized for various deviations and errors, but refused to retract his views. In July 1948 he was removed from all Party posts and forced into retirement. For a year and a half after his public disgrace, however, he was treated with considerable caution, for he had acquired tremendous prestige and the crisis had almost split the Party. While other Communists were at this time easily broken and treated with contempt, Gomułka preserved a certain personal dignity. For a brief period he was re-elected to the Party's Central Committee, then expelled in November 1949. Nineteen months later he was arrested and disappeared from public life.

In September 1948 the leadership of the Party was assumed by Bolesław Bierut, a man with considerable Moscow training. Under his leadership Poland was increasingly required to subordinate its national aims to those of the "socialist camp," as defined by the Soviet leadership. The pattern of Soviet political, economic, and cultural organization and practice was now forcibly imposed upon Polish society.

The Church had continued to be the last center of independent influence in Poland. During the nineteenth century it had frequently acted as a powerful national symbol; in the interwar period it had been fairly active in Polish politics, generally supporting the existing government as long as the position of the Church was respected. The majority of Poles had always been deeply religious; after the postwar border changes there was more religious homogeneity than ever before.

The Bierut regime began to undermine and indirectly curb Church activities through legislation. Aware of the strength of its adversary, the regime firmly indicated that it would not tolerate the crystallization of any opposition around the Church. It attempted, but unsuccessfully, to force Church leaders to sever their ties with the West. Spectacular trials were staged to prove that some priests and Catholic laymen had contacts with subversive organizations. The increasing pressure of the state was opposed by the Church with skill and determination. It refused to become a subservient instrument of the Communist regime; at the same time it also exhibited caution and did not openly seek martyrdom.

The actions taken against the Church—part of an over-all Sovietization plan—indicated Moscow's determination to enforce its will with absolute vigor. But these actions violated deep feelings of nationalism and thereby weakened the Polish Communist administration. The Soviet regime, under Stalin, was forced into an increasing degree of direct responsibility for the implementation of policies in Poland and into an ever-growing reliance on its troops stationed there.

When Stalin died in 1953 his successors embarked upon a cautious reform of Stalinist policies. In regard to the satellites they apparently hoped to find a more efficient and flexible substitute for the stringently centralized controls.

Polish intellectuals and Party theoreticians began groping for the limit to which they could depart from the rigidly held pattern of behavior of the past. Discussions in the Polish press increasingly criticized past theories and practices. Early in 1955 the Party announced it would "democratize" the Polish security police and restrict its powers. A discussion and criticism of managerial and trade union practices accompanied trade union elections in the summer of 1955. Later that year Party ideologists held a raging discussion on intellectual creativity and communistic dogma. Communist writers began expressing bitter disillusionment with the existing Communist order. This movement toward qualified independence of action gathered momentum as the Soviet leaders unleashed their anti-Stalin campaign early in 1956. The Poles became increasingly restive. The oppressive features of the past no longer seemed to be part of the unalterable order of things, and the demand for greater independence from Soviet dictation became sharper.

During the spring and early summer of 1956 almost all of Poland's leading intellectuals were involved in the ferment, demanding freedom in art, greater cultural contact with the West, and governmental reforms. In April the *Sejm,* for the first time since 1947, publicly discussed important economic and social problems and promised reforms. An amnesty released 200,000 persons from confinement.

Party leader Bolesław Bierut died in Moscow on March 12, 1956, and a factional struggle for power and mass influence soon developed within the Party and the government. Some of the unrest among the general population could no longer be contained. Riots broke out in Poznan on June 28, 1956; the disorders were put down by armed detachments of police the following day, but the regime now had to choose between a policy of outright repression and one of further concessions. Apparently fearing the outbreak of revolutionary incidents, it chose the latter course.

Under great internal strain, the Party leadership sought to re-enlist the support of Władysław Gomułka, who had recently been released from house arrest and had been reinstated in the Party (August 4, 1956). Gomułka dictated his terms—economic reforms and national independence in internal affairs—and resumed leadership of the Party as First Secretary in October. Simultaneously, a showdown took place between the Polish leaders and a Soviet "delegation" headed by Nikita Khrushchev. The threat of naked Soviet force hung ominously in the air, but the Russian leaders apparently did not want to risk an open rebellion. They accepted Gomułka's internal political victory as an accomplished fact, but only after obtaining assurances that Poland would remain Communist and stand loyally by the Soviet alliance. Some Polish Communists soon referred to the events of October as their "second revolution."

A *rapprochement* with the Church came as one of the most important features of Gomułka's program immediately after his return to power. The Roman Catholic Primate of Poland, Cardinal Stefan Wyszyński, was quickly released from confinement. The support of the Church gave Gomułka the best safeguard he could find against a repetition in Poland of Hungary's bloody rebellion and Russian intervention.

Gomułka's resurrection as the leader of Polish political life stirred many Poles both within and outside the Party. His outspoken and frank appraisal of the current political crisis contrasted vividly with previous official speeches and pronouncements. He hailed the intellectual ferment in Poland thus:

> The silent, enslaved minds began to shake off the poison of mendacity, falsehood, and hypocrisy. The stiff clichés previously predominant on Party platforms and at public meetings as well as in the press began to give place to creative, living words.

He insisted that those who ruled had to win the confidence of the masses or lose their "moral basis" for exercising power. He demanded that the people be told the truth, about the past and the present:

> There is no escaping from truth. If you cover it up, it will rise as an awful specter, frightening, alarming, and madly raging.

The first official Polish reaction to the Poznan riots had been that the disorders were provoked by enemy agents. Gomułka described the riots as a protest against "the evil which was widespread in our social system" and outlined his program for reform: decentralization of economic planning, greater "workers' control" over industry, abolition of enforced collectivization, "democratization" of Party and governmental life, greater internal freedom from Soviet direction and control, and "mutual confidence and equality of rights" in Polish-Soviet relations.

As a result of its stand, at least verbal, for national independence, the Polish regime can no longer count on the sanction of Soviet power and has been forced into greater reliance on popular backing. It has sought internal support by promising greater freedom for popular political initiative. Gomułka has called for greater creative and progressive thinking—"which is the monopoly of no party and of no single man"—in solving Poland's economic problems, stating, "It is a poor idea to maintain that only Communists can build socialism, only people holding materialist views."

Possible Soviet intervention is, perhaps, the gravest threat the regime must face. Gomułka seems acutely aware that the formula for "independence" must be worked out within circumscribed limits, and that the people must be made to realize these limits. An official pronouncement defined the goal of Gomułka's policies as "a harmonious fusion of demands arising from our geographical and political position with demands arising from the right of nations to full sovereignty." But this fusion, declared Gomułka, could be achieved only if the people remained calm, disciplined, and avoided demonstrations and meetings.

Gomułka's regime must prevent the growth of popular unrest, which might undermine its stability or provoke the Soviet Union; it must also safeguard its position from rival factions within the Party (see chap. 6) and maintain the Party's dominance in Polish political life. A great effort has been made to persuade the people that the only alternative to Communist rule is Poland's extinction. The Party, Gomułka has insisted, must remain the "guide" of the country. He warned that no one will be permitted to use the process of "democratization" to undermine socialism. A Party resolution declared: "For the enemies of socialism and of the working people there can be no freedom."

GEOGRAPHY AND POPULATION

WITH NO NATURAL BOUNDARIES ON EITHER THE EAST OR THE west, the existence and location of Polish borders during the past two hundred years have depended on the political decisions of non-Polish governments. The Baltic Sea and the Carpathian Mountains mark the northern and southern limits of the Polish portion of the European plain, which extends from the Atlantic Ocean and the North Sea to the Urals—an area which is easily crossed by both military forces and migrating peoples. All Poles feel that the territory now within Polish borders, including the western provinces acquired in 1945, are rightfully and traditionally Polish lands. Many also feel that some of the territory to the east, now part of the Ukraine, Belorussia, and Lithuania, should also be within the Polish frontiers (see Map, Interwar and Postwar Frontiers of Poland).

The present boundaries of Poland were drawn by diplomatic agreements among the Big Three at Yalta (February 1945) and Potsdam (July–August 1945), and modified by bilateral agreements (1945, 1950, and 1951) between Poland and the USSR. The general effect of the agreements was to shift Polish territory some 150 miles to the west of its interwar location. The eastern boundary was placed at the Curzon Line, with slight modifications in the south, giving to the USSR considerable territory that had been Polish between 1921 and 1939. The southern boundary with Czechoslovakia remained as it had been before World War II. The western boundary was placed along the Oder River and the Neisse pending final settlement by a peace treaty between the Allies and Germany. The former German territories thus falling within Polish jurisdiction (German Silesia and Pomerania, southern East Prussia, and the Free City of Danzig) are still, in theory, only temporarily under Polish administration.

The treaty fixing western borders has not yet been concluded. Three official positions have developed which make a potentially ex-

Interwar and Postwar Frontiers of Poland

PRESENT BOUNDARY OF POLAND
BOUNDARY 1920-1939

0   50   100
Miles

plosive international situation and create domestic problems. The United States and other western powers hold that the boundary has not been settled and refer to the former German areas as "territory under Polish Administration" or "administered territories." The Soviet Union has given official recognition to the borders as agreed upon at Potsdam and in subsequent bilateral treaties. The Polish Government, in its political and economic policies, acts as if they were permanent. The unsettled boundary situation strengthens the hand of the Soviet Union as the "protector" of Poland against Germany.

The territorial integrity of Poland, then, is still dependent upon international power politics.

In comparison to interwar boundaries, the present boundaries are considerably shorter, follow geographical features more closely, and include five times as much seacoast. Instead of seven bordering countries there are only three—East Germany, Czechoslovakia, and the USSR. Access to the sea, long desired by Poland, is provided through three major ports on the Baltic—Szczecin (Stettin), Gdynia, and Gdansk (Danzig)—which are connected by rail and water to the interior. The newly acquired agricultural lands are generally more productive than those ceded to Russia, but of perhaps greatest importance is the acquisition of the rich mineral deposits and industrial enterprises of upper Silesia. These more than balance economically the loss of agricultural lands, oil resources, and industries in the Lvov area. Resources are now available for development of a well-balanced economy. In addition, the new areas have provided needed living space and economic opportunity for the surplus population of central Poland.

Emigration of Poles and forcible transfer of ethnic groups had been common during the years of independence. During and following World War II, however, there were far greater changes in both the size and ethnic composition of the population. Between 1939 and 1949 Poland lost nearly a third of its population through death, expulsion, and repatriation. The Nazi policy of extermination wiped out all but some 30,000 to 70,000 of the 3,500,000 Jews of interwar Poland as well as a very large number of non-Jewish Poles. Large German, Ukrainian, Belorussian, and Lithuanian groups were reduced by expulsion or voluntary return to their homelands. On the other hand many Poles were repatriated from territories ceded to the USSR and from other countries, and repatriation from the USSR is continuing. Today the population of Poland is slightly over 28 million, still below the prewar figure, but increasing rapidly. In contrast to the prewar period, it is ethnically almost homogeneous—approximately 98 percent Polish.

Geography

Poland has an area of 121,130 square miles. About the size of the State of New Mexico, it is the largest and most important of the Soviet satellites and fourth in size among European countries. It is in the same latitude as England, and extends some 400 miles south from the Baltic Sea and approximately 428 miles east of the Oder and Neisse. Its southern borders lie approximately along the same parallel as the United States–Canadian boundary.

The territory of Poland is a plain which slopes gently to the northwest from the Carpathian Mountains to the shores of the Baltic. Though there are peaks reaching 6,000 to 8,000 feet, about 90 percent of the total area is less than 1,000 feet above sea level.

The plain may be divided into three fairly distinct areas—the Baltic highland and the coastland, the central lowlands, and the southern uplands. Though there is considerable variation within each area, in general the most productive lands lie toward the west, decreasing in quality toward the east.

Except for the moraines left by the last glaciation, the Baltic heights would be perfectly flat. From Szczecin Province to Bialystok Province the land is poor and drainage difficult and there are frequent swamps and lakes, particularly in Olsztyn Province. Thick coniferous forest covers most of the area although some of it has been cleared, drained, and put under cultivation. Potatoes, rye, and hay are the chief crops; large herds are maintained and the forests are exploited. Until World War II absentee German owners generally held large tracts which were cultivated by both German and Polish peasants. Along the Baltic shores are found the urban concentrations and fishing villages.

Extending southeasterly from the Baltic heights, through the provinces of Bydgoszcz and Warsaw to the border, the central lowlands have better drainage and soils upon which are grown wheat, sugar beets, potatoes, and rye. This region has a number of large villages and commercial cities, such as Bydgoszcz and Torun, as well as industrial centers such as Warsaw and Lodz.

The richest Polish lands both in soil and mineral resources are located in the southern uplands, which extend from Poznan through Cracow and Rzeszow, taking in most of lower and upper Silesia. Here much of the land is rich loam, well-drained and watered. Sugar beets, wheat, rye, and potatoes are the chief crops, as they are in the areas to the north; the extensive mineral deposits, chiefly coal, provide the base for a well-balanced economy. Mining and metallurgical development, considerable before World War II, have been stepped up in recent years, the greatest concentration being in the area between Wroclaw (Breslau) and Cracow, which includes the urban industrial complex of Katowice—a belt which has been called the Polish Ruhr.

Below the national level, Poland is divided into 19 provinces (*województwo,* "voivodship"). Two of these provinces are the cities of Warsaw and Lodz which also serve as capitals of the provinces of Warsaw and Lodz. All provinces are named after their capital cities (see Map, Provinces of Poland). The provinces are subdivided into 371 rural and urban counties (*powiat*), below which are smaller local units—some 40,000 rural districts (*gromada*)—as well as towns and precincts.

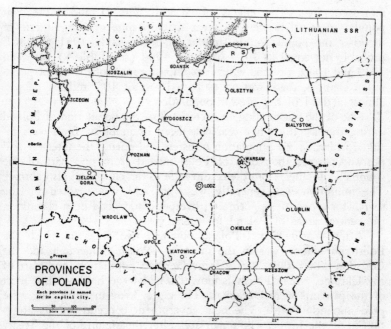

PROVINCES
OF POLAND

Each province is named
for its capital city.

Population

Though there is no shortage of Polish population statistics, they have
certain limitations, particularly when adapted to conform to today's
boundaries. While there were censuses of interwar Poland (1931)
and of the German Reich (1933), both countries tended to overestimate the number of their nationals in those territories which are
now under Polish administration. Projections and estimates based upon
these data are only approximate. The February 1946 census contains
many inaccuracies due to unsettled conditions. The December 1950
census is, however, considered moderately reliable. While the statistical information included in the following pages is not precise, it can
be relied upon for the direction and approximate magnitude of population changes.

SIZE AND DISTRIBUTION

The population of Poland was estimated at 27,544,000 in 1955, and
28,070,000 as of December 1956. Among European countries only
the United Kingdom, West Germany, Italy, France, and Spain are

more populous. The effects of World War II and subsequent population transfers were so great that, in spite of a rapid rate of increase, the population is smaller than it was in 1931 and will probably not equal its 1939 size until 1960 (see Table 1). Between 1939 and 1949, a period which encompasses most of the major population changes, there was an estimated loss of 10.7 million people, almost a third of the prewar population.

One of the outstanding characteristics of the population of Poland during the last thirty-five years has been its mobility. Both wars resulted in large-scale population transfers and during the interwar and postwar periods thousands of Poles moved from one part of the country to another, from the countryside to the cities, and also abroad. The migration was generally westward and was sparked by the search for economic opportunity; overpopulation had been chronic in the central areas of Poland for many years.

After World War I Poland obtained two areas in which the Polish population was in the minority—Polish Pomerania and the Corridor, where there was a large German population, and part of the Ukraine, where Polish landowners had large holdings but most of the peasants were Ukrainian. The cities, Lvov in particular, were predominantly Polish. The new government concentrated its attention upon the former Ukrainian area after the signing of the Treaty of Riga (1921). The large landholdings were broken up and offered without cost to demobilized Polish soldiers, who constituted a pressing social and economic problem. This gratuitous distribution was halted, however, within a few years. Many of the Poles who had moved into the region sold out to the Ukrainian peasants. At the root of the failure to settle Poles in the area was the fact that the land was heavily populated and individual holdings were too small to support the people already there. The net result was a decline rather than an increase in the Polish population.

Polish settlement of the former German areas was far more successful, though it was given less official emphasis. There, lands were available because of the largely voluntary return of Germans to their homeland. In addition, industrial development in the areas of Silesia and Poznan provided employment for large numbers of Poles from the crowded, war-devastated central areas.

In addition to these two population shifts, an estimated 1.5 million refugees and repatriates—some Poles, but many Lithuanians, Belorussians, and Ukrainians—fled the Bolshevik territories in the guise of repatriates. Most of these settled in the eastern Polish territories and in the urban centers of Warsaw, Vilna, Lodz, and Lvov.

The net result of these movements was an increase in the proportion of non-Polish minorities in eastern territories and successful settlement of Poles in western Poland. The congestion and unemployment in the central provinces, created by the influx of repatriates and refugees from Soviet territories, was greatly relieved by the migration of Poles to the former German territories. Simultaneously, central Poland and Galicia profited by commerce with the western area, where industry had not been destroyed by the war.

In the face of the rapid advance of the German Army in September 1939 there was a mass flight of people to the east, particularly to Warsaw, the area which resisted longest. Most of the refugees, however, remained in German-occupied territory. After the formal German-Russian partition (September 28, 1941) the "incorporated provinces" along the German borders were subjected to an intense process of expulsion, extermination, and property confiscation, to make way for German settlers. Expulsion was halted in 1942, however, largely because of the need for labor in both the occupied territories and in Germany proper. At first Poles who remained in the area were recruited; later they were forcibly transferred to man the productive machine of the Reich. Southern regions of Poland along the Carpathians remained to a large degree outside the combat area, and many refugees settled there.

After World War II the westward movement of the Polish population began again, owing to the migration policy of the new government, as well as to economic pressure. By 1947 some 3 million Poles from the congested central regions and 1 million from the areas ceded to the USSR had moved to the former German territories from which the German residents had fled or been expelled. In general the repatriates moved as families to the agricultural lands, but the migrants from the central areas, predominantly young adults, gravitated to the developing industry of the cities.

Large-scale internal migration to the western territories had all but stopped by 1948. Today the government is encouraging movement to these areas. During the last two years the bulk of the migrants have been Poles repatriated from the USSR and West Germany. According to official figures released in July 1957, some 79,000 Poles had returned from the USSR alone and 22,000 more are expected during the second half of 1957. The number of repatriates from West Germany is not known.

Concurrent with the movement of population within Poland, large numbers of Poles left the country. Overpopulation and unemployment in peacetime and the two world wars led many to take refuge in foreign countries. During the period of Polish independence the exodus was largely to western countries. Large numbers of seasonal as well as permanent immigrants moved to Germany; others settled in France, where they were actively recruited for work in the mines. Still others settled in the United States (until establishment of the quota system), Canada, and South America. Some Jews went to Palestine. World War II forced Polish refugees into the USSR, the Near East, and most of the countries of Europe. Many have returned to Poland, but the majority have remained in foreign countries. Probably the largest group to settle in a single country were those members of the Polish army and their families, some 160,000 in all, who went to Great Britain. Emigration largely stopped under the Communist government after 1948; now is again being allowed, though the policy fluctuates. It is reported that the Jewish exodus to Israel has been large and includes Communists and non-Communists, professional people and manual workers (see chap. 4).

Poland is today a moderately urbanized country; approximately 43 percent of its people live in areas classified as urban. This proportion is higher than that in any of the other Soviet satellites except Czechoslovakia (58 percent), slightly less than that of Austria (49 percent) and Sweden (49 percent), but far less than that of such highly industrialized countries as Great Britain (81 percent) and the United States (64 percent).

The movement of the people from the countryside to the cities has been going on for many years. Since 1946 the movement has accelerated in conjunction with industrial expansion. It has been based largely upon four types of industrial development—the coal and associated industries of upper Silesia; textile manufacture in the central region; scattered lumbering, sawmills, and associated chemical and paper manufacture; and water transport, both on the rivers and the Baltic.

In general, the cities and more highly urbanized provinces suffered greater population losses during World War II than did the rural areas. The cities, especially those in the center of the country, were the scenes of the heaviest fighting as well as centers for the German policy of systematic extermination. The greatest population loss was suffered by the province and city of Warsaw. The population of the cities to the south, such as Cracow and Katowice, was swelled, however, by the large number of refugees who fled in that direction from the areas of intense fighting, and they thus showed a relatively smaller net population loss.

The depopulation of the cities in the former German territories did not take place until after the war, when the German population fled or was moved. Since the Germans tended to live in the urban areas, the highly urbanized provinces of Wroclaw and Szczecin sustained the greatest population losses. The rural provinces of Olsztyn, Koszalin, and Zielona Gora and the cities of Gdansk and Gdynia, which had a high proportion of Poles, showed less of a decrease.

While the population of the predominantly rural provinces has not increased appreciably since the end of the war, the cities have recovered rapidly. By 1956, of all the major cities within the prewar Polish boundaries, only Warsaw had a significantly smaller population than in 1939, although it remained the largest city in the country. Most of the others have grown above their 1939 figure, particularly those in the southern industrial region. Those in the former German territories have repopulated more slowly. Wroclaw is just over half the size it was before the war; Szczecin, with the most rapid rate of growth of any city, is about 85 percent of its prewar size; Gdansk has remained about the same as in 1939 (see Table 2).

Despite the population shifts that have occurred in Poland in the past thirty-five years, the general pattern of population concentration has remained fairly constant except for the radical but relatively temporary reductions in the territories acquired as a result of World War II. The area of greatest concentration lies along the southern borders, where there is extensive development in both agriculture and industry. The latter development consists of a series of industrial cities and towns stretching from Wroclaw through Cracow, with Katowice as the hub.

There are three other regions of moderate density. In the southern uplands there are few towns—Lublin is the only town of commercial importance—but a rather heavy rural population. On the central plain are two of the largest cities, Warsaw and Lodz, a number of smaller cities such as Poznan, Bydgoszcz, and a number of towns. The rural population density is low. Along the Baltic Coast there are the ports of Gdansk and Gdynia at the mouth of the Vistula and Szczecin on the Oder.

GROWTH OF THE POPULATION

Though the size of the Polish population was drastically reduced by World War II, its net rate of increase in the postwar period has been higher than that of most western nations. Considerably short of the 1939 population of approximately 34.8 million, the 1956 population nevertheless represented an increase of approximately 19 percent (almost 4 million people) in the short period of eleven years. The rate of increase between 1945 and 1950 was comparatively slow, owing to the unsettled conditions and the losses from the expulsion of ethnic minorities—far larger than the gains from repatriation. Between 1950 and 1955, however, the population has been increasing by slightly over 2 percent per year. (The annual rate of increase in the United States between 1940 and 1950 was 1.4 percent.)

There have been wide variations in the rate of growth in the various provinces. In the former German areas of Gdansk, Koszalin, and Zielona Gora the population increase between 1950 and 1955 was somewhat more than 20 percent, while in Szczecin it was 28 percent. Even with these high rates the population has not yet completely replaced the German population. Warsaw, particularly the city, has continued to draw population; its increase is considerably higher than that of most other central and eastern provinces. Katowice and Cracow, areas where industrial development had been rapid before the war and from which relatively few non-Polish peoples were removed, are the only provinces in which there has been any significant increase over the 1931 population. Wroclaw lost nearly a third of its population as the result of postwar population transfers but is sharing in the rapid industrial development of the other upper Silesian areas. Olsztyn, though located to the east, is made up to a considerable extent of territory recovered from Germany and, like the western territories, had a population vacuum created by the removal of ethnic Germans. Though its land is generally poor, the fact of its availability and the development of some light industry based upon excellent forest resources have been sufficient to draw population from the central areas.

For many years the rate of natural increase of the population of Poland has been considerably higher than that of most other European countries. An increase of 1 percent per year is not unusual, but during the entire period between 1895 and 1913 rates of 1.5 per year were characteristic of Poland and in some years the rate was as high as 1.8 percent. There was a marked fall in the rate of increase during World War I, but it rose immediately thereafter and remained above 1.5 percent per year until the 1930's, when it began to fail. By 1938 it was only slightly above 1 percent.

In all the years since 1948 the rate of natural population increase in Poland has exceeded that of the United States (which has been experiencing a "baby boom"). In 1948 the rate was 1.79 percent per year; by 1953 it was 1.95, in 1954 only slightly lower—1.88 percent.

Differences between the rates of increase in the various provinces are marked (see Table 3). During the interwar period the most rapid rate of increase occurred in the central and eastern areas, where the population was predominantly Polish, Ukrainian, and Belorussian; the slowest rate was in the western and northern provinces, where there was a large German population. Since 1943 the position of these areas has been reversed. In the six provinces that are made up entirely or in part of former German territory (Oslsztyn, Gdansk, Koszalin, Zielona Gora, and Wroclaw), the natural rate of increase ranged in 1955 between 26 and 32 per thousand population. The next highest rate was in Bydgoszcz (20.5 per thousand) and the lowest in Lodz (15.3). Since ethnic differences between provinces no longer exist, this large differential is undoubtedly a reflection of the high proportion of young adults who have settled in the recently acquired territories.

AGE AND SEX

In spite of the tremendous impact of World War II, the age and sex structure of the population has remained much the same as it was in 1939. Poland is a country of young people: the median age in 1954 was 25.2 years—23.66 years for men and 26.6 for women (see Table 4). Almost all the countries of western Europe and the United States have median ages over 30 years. The Polish population is, however, older than that of some countries of eastern Europe and most of Asia and Africa; it is approximately the same as the population of the USSR. The difference between the median ages of the men and women is not as great as in some other countries, notably the USSR where the war losses among young males were far more pronounced.

The official 1950 statistics indicated that females outnumbered males in almost all age groups. (It is not clear whether men in military service were included in the calculations; if they were not the imbalance would be reduced but not eliminated.) For the whole of Poland the ratio was 91 males to 100 females with the greatest deficit of males occurring in urban areas.

Considerable differences are found in the ratios of the various provinces, with the ratios of men generally lowest in the more highly industrialized areas and highest in the western provinces. Only in Szczecin do the men outnumber the women in both urban and rural regions.

The new lands have attracted large numbers of young adults, making the population of those areas markedly younger than that of central areas, where many of the repatriates settled. Women have tended to be drawn to the older cities.

PROBLEMS AND PROSPECTS

The characteristics of the population of Poland have created certain problems and certain advantages. During the interwar period the rapid increase and relatively high density of the population of the central areas, the predominantly rural population throughout the country, and the lack of industrial development combined to produce "overpopulation"—a term indicating the inability of the economy to provide a reasonably adequate standard of living. It is estimated that with the methods of cultivation then in use from 30 to 50 percent of the agricultural population was "surplus," that is, the same level of production could have been maintained without their labor. Industrial urban development was not sufficient to absorb this surplus. The new and unpopulated farmlands and the newly acquired and rapidly expanding industrial capacity of postwar Poland has reduced surplus employment in agriculture to the point where it no longer is a major problem. But the planned industrial expansion of the government has not been able to provide employment for the increasing urban population.

In the years of reconstruction and reorganization since 1945, Poland has been in a favorable position so far as its population is concerned. Over half of the people have been concentrated in the age groups with the greatest potential productivity. The burden of dependency (proportion of population under 14 and over 65 years of age) has been low. In spite of the great population changes of the war years, there are no marked gaps in the younger age groups to indicate future shortages in the labor force.

These favorable characteristics may, however, become liabilities as the vacant lands of western Poland are settled. As the death rate continues to decline, the number of dependents will increase. Though the birth rate seems to be dropping somewhat, the population will continue to grow at a rapid rate. Mounting population pressure thus is one of the cardinal problems to be solved by any government in Poland; at present it figures importantly in the Gomułka plan for rapid industrialization and increased agricultural production.

ETHNIC GROUPS AND LANGUAGES

MORE THAN 98 PERCENT OF THE POPULATION WITHIN THE present boundaries of Poland may properly be considered a single ethnic group. Ethnic minorities, which in interwar Poland included about ten million people, or almost 30 percent of the population, now comprise only slightly over half a million people, or less than 2 percent of the population. Numerically, then, the minorities present no major problem in Poland today, but attitudes toward them have carried over from the interwar period and are reflected in both the national and international scene.

Between the two world wars the problem of ethnic minorities loomed very large in the affairs of the Polish nation. The Poles themselves prior to 1918 had been minority groups in the Russian, German, and Austro-Hungarian Empires; in 1918 they were transformed into the ruling group of a nation with German, Jewish, Ukrainian, Belorussian, Lithuanian, and other minorities within its borders. The Polish-Lithuanian Commonwealth, before the partitions of the late eighteenth century, had been a multinational state; and the concept of Polish patriotism which shaped the interwar period involved more than citizenship in a Polish national state. The Polish language, the Roman Catholic faith, and a certain view of life that many Polish writers spent a lifetime defining (see chap. 22) all were and are essential characteristics of a Pole.

Examples of popular and official ethnic discrimination are abundant through the interwar period, and Polish statistics of 1937–38 show that only a fraction of the ethnic minorities were allowed their own schools (which had been guaranteed them in a treaty signed by the Polish Government, on June 28, 1919, with the Allied and Associated Powers). Boundary disputes and minority nationalism heightened minority tensions during this period.

The great reduction in numbers of the minority peoples in Poland after World War II has not brought an end to the minority problem. While Poles from all walks of life have expressed great satisfaction over the increased "homogeneity" of their state, popular feeling against the relatively few remaining minority group members—especially Germans, Jews, and Ukrainians—has run high, threatening at times the control of the government over public order. Antiminority activity seems to be, as it is in other countries as well, an expression of frustration over difficult social and economic conditions; in Poland it is also a vehicle for masked criticism and defiance of the government and Party.

Since March 1957 the Gomułka government has attempted to counter some of this feeling by stressing and facilitating the contribution which the various ethnic remnants have made and can make to Polish life. Various minority committees and associations have been established throughout the country, and a special Minorities Committee, part of the Central Committee of the Party, was appointed in May 1957 to combat "nationalist attitudes opposed to the basic principles of our Party." This program also makes excellent propaganda abroad, supporting "democratization" claims of the government; and the Polish treatment of Germans within the country has a bearing on Polish-German relations (see chap. 10).

Poles

The Poles of today are descendants of various Slavic tribes who settled in and around the area of present-day Poland well before the eighth century A.D. Regional distinctions among Polish peasants today —in dialect, dress, manners and customs—follow very roughly the old tribal divisions. Many of the old tribal names persist in modified form. The Polanie ("plainsmen"), who lived in the neighborhood of modern Poznan, gave their name to the whole nation; the Mazowszanie were presumably the ancestors of the Mazurs, who now live in the area around Warsaw and northward through Olsztyn to the Soviet border. In the region between these two tribes were the Kujawanie, presumably in the area now known as Kujawy, around Wloclawek and Inowroclaw. To the north, along the Baltic shore, the area called Pomorze ("seaboard") and known in English as Pomerania was inhabited both by the Pomorzanie and by a closely related tribe, the Kaszubie (Kashubs). The Slazanie, in the hilly southwestern part of the country, gave their name to Slask, now Katowice, in Silesia, and to the peasants dwelling there today.

Under German rule some of the Kashubs were converted to Protestantism, as were a group of "Mazurians" in East Prussia. But German attempts to identify these groups as "non-Polish" appear to have been ineffectual, although the Kashubian dialect is of all Polish dialects the furthest removed from the standard language. Dialectal distinctions are disappearing today, and old local customs and costumes are dying out. Mazurians and Silesians, Cracovians and Kashubs, all today consider themselves Poles, and are so considered by each other.

Minority Groups

GERMANS

For the last thousand years large numbers of Germans have lived in what is now Poland; they have been there as missionaries, tradesmen, artisans, technicians, farmers, landowners, even as kings. Many living in the major Polish cities became thoroughly assimilated, with only their family names to indicate their origin.

The number of Germans in Poland between the two world wars is difficult to estimate, since there was an almost infinite variation in degrees of assimilation. The Polish census of 1931 set the figure at 741,000, officially on the basis of mother tongue, but the Germans themselves claimed 1.7 million. American analysts have suggested that a more reasonable figure would be about 970,000. Boundary changes and population shifts since World War II have made it even more difficult to arrive at an estimate. It seems probable that there are now 200,000 to 300,000 people in Poland who consider themselves German. Most of these are in the newly acquired territories of the north and west in and around Gdynia in the old Polish Corridor, in the mining areas around Katowice, and in a few cities such as Lodz.

Before the rise of Prussia as a dangerous neighbor in the late seventeenth and eighteenth centuries, Poles had seen the Germans as able and industrious people, rather stolid and unimaginative, lacking in social graces, but highly successful as farmers, artisans, and administrators. The growth of German power created a continuing threat to the very existence of Poland, but the Polish *szlachta* (landed nobility), concerned with internal rivalries, failed to heed the threat until too late. For the peasant, the possibility of German rule was a matter of little moment—provided he was permitted to continue his familiar way of life—since German landowners had already shown themselves more enlightened and efficient as masters than most of the Polish gentry.

Though the Germans made considerable efforts to Germanize the Poles within their territory after the partitions, their rule was somewhat more enlightened than that of the Russians. Anti-German feeling was not strong among the Polish peasants; through the nineteenth and early twentieth centuries it was strongest among exiled patriots. Until World War I there was much intermarriage between Germans and Poles, in urban as well as rural society. In communities with a Polish majority, the German partner in such a marriage seems to have often accepted the language and—if he had been Protestant—the religious creed of his spouse. Under the exigencies of war such families could and did call themselves Polish or German according to the need of the moment.

In interwar Poland the treaty of 1919 was supplemented by the convention on Silesia signed by Germany and Poland on May 15, 1922, which defined the rights of Polish and German minority groups on each side of the new frontier. The agreements did not, however, prevent the government of Poland from trying to forcibly assimilate the Germans; Polish measures became especially harsh as the Germans, encouraged by the rise of Hitler, began to demand virtual autonomy.

Those Germans who did not leave Poland after World War II have been the object of hostile discrimination and are deeply dissatisfied with their lot. The Poles, on the other hand, vividly remember the brutalities of the German occupation, and there seems little hope of reconciliation between the two peoples.

BELORUSSIANS

After the eastern provinces were ceded to Russia in 1945, Poland retained less than 300,000 of the nearly 2 million Belorussians it contained during the interwar period. The majority of those remaining live in Bialystok Province on poor land in conditions that compare unfavorably with those of most minorities in Poland. Never as nationalistic as the Ukrainians, they show little evidence of dissatisfaction.

UKRAINIANS

The largest minority group in interwar Poland (more than 4 million), the Ukrainians were chiefly found in the southeastern provinces, where they constituted a majority in the rural areas although such major cities as Lvov were predominantly Polish. The majority of Ukrainians lived in the Ukrainian SSR, within the Soviet Union, and a smaller group inhabited the "Sub-Carpathian Ukraine," which until 1938 was part of Czechoslovakia. All areas where Ukrainians formed a high percentage of the population have now been incorporated into the USSR, and the number of Ukrainians remaining in Poland is probably less than 100,000.

Before the partitions Poland included a large part of the Ukraine. The Ukrainian people had not yet begun to think of themselves as a nation, but their language and their Uniate religion set them off as distinct from the Poles and their association with Cossacks and occasionally with Russians made them sometimes a troublesome minority. Ukrainian nationalism grew in the nineteenth century, and when, after World War I, hopes for an independent Ukraine did not materialize, Ukrainians in Poland became dissatisfied and restless. In the early years of the Republic, Ukrainian uprisings and disorders were frequent; "pacification" by Polish troops only increased the tension. In the 1930's recognition in the form of Ukrainian-language schools and other institutions lessened this tension, but in 1938, when Poland approved the Hungarian take-over of Czechoslovakia's Ukrainian lands, Ukrainian nationalist leaders in Poland were again indignant. Since the cession of Poland's eastern provinces to the USSR, the Ukrainian nationalist underground in former Polish territory has created a considerable problem for Soviet authorities.

Ukrainian nationalistic activities in the interwar period gave the Ukrainians a reputation as troublemakers. Apparently such activities continued after World War II and as a result the government forcibly moved most of the Ukrainian population from the southeastern area to the western territories. In March 1957 the government announced that those whose farms are still unoccupied may return to them; others will receive compensation for property left behind. Undoubtedly the majority will remain in the western territories, and the government has promised the removal of "obstacles and discriminations applied to Ukrainian schools and culture."

Historically, the majority of Ukrainians in Poland have been peasants. The Poles were inclined to look down on them as a people of lesser culture and to belittle their claims to national identity.

JEWS

Before World War II there were almost 3.5 million Jews—one tenth of the total population—in Poland; today there are between 30,000 and 70,000, living chiefly in Silesia. Some of these are repatriates who fled to the Soviet Union during the war; the Nazis destroyed all but a small fraction of the Jews that did not leave Poland.

Jews have been an important element in the population of Poland since medieval times. For centuries they found the country a refuge from the persecutions inflicted on them in western Europe. Under the Polish kings they received the right to semiautonomy in their own communities, and with the rise of commerce and cities they made a place for themselves as traders and shopkeepers. The pattern of Polish society from the later Middle Ages through the eighteenth century worked in their favor in the latter regard: the nobility and landed gentry, as elsewhere in Europe, scorned to enter commerce, considering it a debasing occupation, and the peasants were practically bound as serfs to the fields; thus the Jews filled a gap in the economic life of the country. Along with the Germans, they formed the bulk of an emerging urban middle class.

To the Polish peasant, however, the Jew was an outsider—different in appearance, customs, and religion—profiting from what the peasant felt was his more honest and productive labor. The landed nobleman also considered the Jew an outsider—who often became his creditor since many landowners had little taste for efficient management of their estates. The economic decline of Poland from the late seventeenth century to the middle of the nineteenth was especially disadvantageous to the Jews. Under the anti-urban policies of the nobility, trade in the once flourishing cities stagnated.

With the end of serfdom in the nineteenth century, the Polish upper and lower classes began to converge on the field where the Jews had been pre-eminent, and trade acquired new respectability. Semiofficial discrimination increasingly limited Jewish activities. Anti-Semitic feeling was widespread, and Poland, like Russia, became a place of persecution. Large numbers of Jews emigrated to Germany, the United States, and other western lands. The persecution, however, was not highly systematized or universal, the worst pogroms taking place in the eastern provinces, and many Jews in Warsaw, Cracow, and elsewhere were partially assimilated to the Polish community—emerging from the ghetto, speaking Polish rather than Yiddish, entering professions other than trade, and even becoming landowners.

The liberation of Poland in 1918 raised new problems for Jews. Included within the boundaries of the country were large numbers of Jews from the Russian "pale of settlement," highly concentrated in such cities as Grodno, Baranowicz, and Pinsk. These Jews were, in general, not assimilated to either Polish or Russian culture and were to some extent looked down on by the upper level of Polish Jews. Many of them, and many of the Polish Jews as well, had as oppressed minorities shown sympathy with various leftist groups, including the Communists. For the more chauvinistic Poles in the new Republic, this furnished an excuse for characterizing all Jews as a politically dangerous minority.

After World War I the rights of Jews were asserted in the Minorities Treaty of 1919 and in the Constitution of 1921. A more detailed statute in 1927 restored semiautonomous, limited self-government to the Jewish communities—making them almost entirely responsible for their own religious, educational, and social needs.

Despite these provisions, discrimination and active anti-Semitism existed in Poland through the entire interwar period. As early as 1919 mobs attacked the Jews in various towns, and until 1926 the acquisition of citizenship was made difficult for Jews. Institutions of higher learning introduced quotas restricting enrollment of Jewish students. The establishment of government monopolies in certain trades worked against Jews, and hardly any were admitted to government service. Under the Piłsudski regime there was not much increase in official tolerance of anti-Semitism, but after Piłsudski's death in 1935 measures against Jews were frequently introduced in the *Sejm* (parliament) and some were enacted. In 1936, Polish representatives in the League of Nations emphasized Poland's interest in arranging for emigration of Jews from Poland. Pogroms took place in 1937 in several cities. Some of this activity was undoubtedly the result of propaganda from Germany.

In the face of these abuses, Jews in Poland managed to survive, increase, and in some cases even to flourish. Many played a considerable part in the social, economic, and intellectual life of the country, though they had little part in political affairs. At the same time, Polish Jews were among the leaders of the Zionist movement, and there was some emigration to Palestine.

Following World War II a few of the Jews who returned to Poland from their refuge in the Soviet Union were among the leaders of the Moscow-sponsored Polish Government. Again there was occasion for many Poles to associate Jews in general with a political creed to which they were violently hostile. The government's efforts to show itself strictly nondiscriminatory were widely interpreted as specially favoring the Jews, and it is probable that expressions of anti-Semitism were and are often a cloak for anticommunism. Under the Gomułka regime many Jews in the government—including such prominent figures as Jakub Berman and Hillary Minc—have lost their posts. Antigovernment feeling has been materially reduced, but incidents of anti-Semitic activity are repeatedly reported in the Polish press and on the radio. According to official sources, as of June 1957, 6,000 Jews had been repatriated from the Soviet Union and, of these, 2,000 had already emigrated to Israel. There have been demands in the press and in the *Sejm* that the government limit repatriation to "those who intend to settle in Poland." The government, however, has claimed that it issues an average of 1,500 passports per month to Jews who wish to emigrate.

Officially approved reports from Poland tell of a Jewish state theater in Warsaw, of the continued publication of books in Yiddish, and of the existence of Jewish cultural associations. There are Jewish state schools in Wroclaw, Lodz, Walbrzych, Szczecin, Dzierzoniow, Liegnitz, and Bielawa. Two daily newspapers, as well as a quarterly magazine, are published in Yiddish. Jewish affairs are now handled by a central Jewish committee in Warsaw, and Yiddish-language broadcasts may be heard over Warsaw Radio. In general, it appears that the government is officially combating anti-Semitism and seeking to protect the remnant of the Jewish population. But Jews in Poland still appear eager to emigrate.

KARAITES. The Karaites, or Karaim, are a small Jewish sect which has held itself separate from the Jewish community in general. The largest concentration was formerly in the neighborhood of Vilna (now Vil'nyus, in the Lithuanian SSR). Though no figures are available regarding the number remaining in Poland, according to official sources the largest centers of Karaites are in Warsaw, Gdansk, Gdynia, Wroclaw, and Opole. More assimilated than the orthodox Jews, the Karaites have been in the rather difficult position of being regarded as Jews by Gentiles and as "outsiders" by Jews. The Polish Government now considers them a separate "nationality," and their religion is one of the seven denominations legally recognized in Poland.

RUSSIANS

During the interwar period Russian settlements in Poland—with a population estimated in 1931 as 139,000—were chiefly in the eastern provinces, now ceded to the USSR. Many of the inhabitants are reported to have been members of the Old Believer sect, presumably descendants of those who had fled central Russia from the seventeenth century on to escape religious persecution. Except for Soviet troops and officials stationed within the country, little is known about Russians in Poland today.

CZECHS AND SLOVAKS

In 1931 Czechs in Poland were estimated at 38,000. A few Czech primary schools existed in Poland in 1937–38, but there is no evidence of such schools today. Slovaks were not recognized as a Polish minority in the interwar period, though several thousand are reported to have lived near the border south of Cracow.

LITHUANIANS

Lithuanians in Poland in 1931 were numbered in the census at 84,000. (Lithuanians themselves claimed a total of 300,000.) The present-day number is undoubtedly less, since most of them had lived in the neighborhood of Vilna.

In the long history of the Polish-Lithuanian state the association of the two peoples—both Roman Catholic and with a common government—was very close. Numerically and culturally the Poles were the dominant group; upper-class Lithuanians often adopted Polish as their own tongue, and even many peasants became bilingual. Many people in Poland with Lithuanian names are by now completely assimilated. Polish seizure of Vilna in 1920 caused much hard feeling between the two states, for Lithuanian nationalism had developed rapidly. The city contained a very mixed population of Poles, Jews, Belorussians, Germans, and Russians, as well as Lithuanians, but the surrounding rural area was predominantly Lithuanian and the seizure undoubtedly caused resentment among these peasants. A few Lithuanian schools were established by the Poles but they could accommodate only a fraction of the Lithuanian child population.

GYPSIES

The Polish radio reports that there are about 30,000 Gypsies in Poland today, but since the counting of Gypsies is obviously difficult the figure must be accepted with reservations. Since World War II there have been attempts to settle them on the land, but here, as elsewhere, such efforts have met with only partial success. The wandering Gypsy has traditionally been, and probably still is, a familiar figure in the Polish countryside, and Gypsy tinkers and horse traders always appear at local fairs. In general the Gypsy is surrounded by the same disreputable but rather romantic aura as in other countries. Some distinctions can be made between Polish Gypsies, who are more or less permanent residents of the country and generally speak Polish as well as their mother tongue, and those who have traditionally wandered back and forth across the borders of Rumania, Hungary, and Czechoslovakia. Gypsies are less numerous in Poland than in its neighbors to the south and east, and Gypsy music and dances appear to be less a part of the national scene than in Hungary or Rumania.

OTHER MINORITY GROUPS

There are various other groups of wholly or partly foreign origin, who are almost completely assimilated. During the last three centuries Armenians had fled to Poland from the Turkish Empire. Present-day Armenians in Poland have retained their own religion in most cases, but they are likely to speak Polish as their mother tongue and have been virtually absorbed in Polish urban communities. There are also Moslems, of Turkish or Tatar origin, most of whom have completely lost their original language but retain their religious faith; mosques are found in several major cities in Poland. A colony of Greek Communist refugees also is reported.

The Polish Language

The Polish language belongs to the western branch of the Slavic language group. After Russian and Ukrainian it is the most widely spoken of the Slavic languages. More than 98 percent of the population of Poland today considers it their mother tongue, and it has been carried by extensive immigration to various European and American countries, where, however, it is gradually disappearing.

Although there are many similarities in vocabulary and structure among the Slavic languages, Polish cannot be easily understood by other Slavic peoples—even by the Czechs and Slovaks, whose languages are also West Slavic. Polish is the only major Slavic language that preserves the old Slavic nasal vowels. It is also characterized by two sets of "shushing" sounds and by a modification of the common Slavic hard *l* into a sound which in most areas of the country is much like the English *w*.

The Poles, like the other western Slavs as well as the Croats and Slovenes, use the Latin alphabet—a mark of their conversion to the Roman Catholic Church rather than the Eastern Orthodox. To provide for Polish sounds not found in Latin, accents and other diacritical marks have been added and special values have been given to certain consonant combinations, most of which involve the letter *z* (see Chart, The Polish Alphabet and Diphthongs, with Approximate Pronunciation). The result in the written language is a proliferation of *z*'s and a massing of consonants which make almost any page of Polish easily recognizable as such. Such town names as Bydgoszcz, Białobrzegi, and Szczebrzeszyn are cases in point. Words incorporated into Polish from Latin and other western languages are often respelled in Polish orthography. Thus "scout" becomes *skaut,* and "feuilleton," *felieton.*

THE STANDARD LANGUAGE

Standard literary Polish had its origins in the speech of the Polish upper classes of about the sixteenth century. Until that time there was very little writing in Polish, most literary and official documents being written in Latin. During the Reformation period both Protestants and Catholics sought to reach the people by producing religious works in the native language, and at the same time there was a

The Polish Alphabet and Diphthongs with Approximate Pronunciation

Words are regularly stressed on the next to last syllable.

a	*a* in father	l	like French *l* in *bel*
ą	nasalized, like the *an* in want	ł	*w* in wall (in some areas like *l* in bell)
b	as in English	m	as in English
c	*ts* in hats		
ć	*ch* plus slight *y* sound, as in tea*ch y*ou	n	as in English
		ń	*ny* in canyon
ch	between English *h* and German *ch* as in *ach*	ni*	like *ń*
		o	*o* in coffee
ci*	like *ć*	ó	*u* in rule
cz	*ch* in chore	p	as in English
d	like English *d*	r	*r* strongly trilled
dż	*j* in judge	rz	*z* in azure
dź	*jy* in jud*g*e *y*ou (cf. *ć*)	s	as in English
dzi*	like *dz*	ś	*sh* in pu*sh y*ou (cf. *ć*)
e	*e* in set	si*	like *ś*
ę	nasalized like French *in* in *fin*	sz	*sh* in shore
f	as in English	t	like English *t,* but dental
g	as in English get (never as in gem)	u	*u* in rule
		w	*v* in very
h	equals Polish *ch*	y	*y* in rhythm
i	*i* in machine	z	as in English
j	*y* in yard or boy	ż	*z* in azure (tongue back)
k	as in English	ź	like *ż* but with *y* effect (cf. *ć*)
		zi	like *ź*

* If these combinations are not followed by a vowel, the *i* also retains its original vowel sound.

flowering of secular literature in Polish. The sixteenth-century poet J. Kochanowski is credited with crystallizing the literary language; since he lived in Cracow, it has been said that the language is actually a literary form of the Cracow dialect. The various circumstances of the last four centuries have been such, however, that literary Polish is really the urban educated speech in any Polish city.

The vocabulary of standard Polish reflects the various historical influences in the country. The Catholic religion had been brought in by Czech and German priests, who introduced terms from their native languages as well as Czech and German modifications of Latin words. During the time that literary and official documents were written in

Latin, educated people—a small minority—considered it fashionable to interlard their speech with Latinisms, producing a macaronic Polish; some of these usages have persisted in the standard language. From the fifteenth century on, German and Italian craftsmen and technicians contributed to the technical vocabulary of the language, and during the eighteenth century many French words came in.

During the years of Poland's partition (1772–1918) the German and Russian governments made strenuous efforts to assimilate the Poles under their rule. Many Poles learned German or Russian, but the Polish language was little affected since few Polish families stopped speaking Polish in their home and social activities. In the nineteenth century an upsurge of nationalism led to a movement aimed at "cleansing" the language of foreign elements. The poet Adam Mickiewicz (see chap. 21) is often credited with preserving the unity of literary Polish, reflecting the desire of educated Poles to adhere to certain nationalistic standards of elegance and choice of words.

Technological changes in the nineteenth century brought in new vocabulary items; Greco-Latin terms, often in German or Russian adaptations, were adopted for scientific and technical use. As happens in all languages, these terms were adapted to Polish usage; they were also respelled to give in Polish orthography the pronunciation of the form as taken from German, Russian, or direct from Latin. There has been little effort to devise Polish-based words instead of the international forms of these terms except during a period in the 1920's and 1930's when the effort met with little success.

DIALECTS

Polish, like many languages, is spoken in several dialects, some of which differ rather widely from one another. The most divergent is Kashubian, so much so that it is considered by some to be a separate West Slavic language. Kashubian has an orthography of its own, and a literature. Its 200,000 or so speakers inhabited the Baltic Coast area in Pomerania and before World War I were all bilingual, speaking German as their language of contact with officialdom. During the interwar period the Kashubians were in the Polish-governed Corridor between East and West Prussia, and attempts were made to assimilate them to Polish culture. During World War II they were scattered; their number is now reduced and their location not precisely determinable.

The remaining dialects may be grouped as follows: Great Polish, in the northwest with Poznan as the center; Kuyavian, in the area east of "Great Poland," with Inowroclaw and Wloclawek as the principal cities; Little Polish, centered around Cracow; Silesian, in the largely industrial area which includes Katowice and Wroclaw; and Mazovian, in the area around Warsaw and extending north and east. Within these major divisions various subdivisions are also found. Population shifts since 1939, as well as increased urbanization, education, and communication, have blurred the regional speech distinctions, but Poles can still generally recognize a man's place of origin by his speech.

In the cities educated upper-class people speak a standard form of speech with little specifically local flavor; however, the legend has it that the Cracow variety of this educated speech is "best," that of Lvov (before its incorporation in the USSR) almost as "good," and Warsaw's "least desirable." Middle-class Warsaw speech reflects more localisms and is reputed to have a "Jewish" flavor. Lower-class people, largely of recent peasant origin, retain the characteristics of their local dialects. Of these, the Mazovian (Mazurian) speakers are the special butt of jokes in Warsaw. There are also, of course, various special jargons (thieves' argot, student slang, technical jargons, and so forth).

NAMES AND FORMS OF ADDRESS

Like most western Europeans, Poles have one or more given names and a family name. Unlike the Russians, they do not use a patronymic. Polish given names are generally taken from the saints (Jan, Józef, Maria) or from traditional Slavic names (Stanisław, Zbigniew, Kazimierz), some of which have also become saints' names. French given names are not uncommon. Such distinctions as once existed between peasant and noble names have by now disappeared, but some nicknames (Maciek, Wojtek, Jagna) are still used for scornful reference to peasants. Polish Jews have traditionally used names taken from Hebrew, largely from the Old Testament. Moszek (a diminutive of Moses) was used as an opprobrious name for Jews, not only by Gentiles but also by Jews themselves.

Among family names, the most numerous are made of a given name or place name plus an adjective ending, generally *-ski, -cki;* the ending *-icz* is also common. Many of these names belonged originally to the nobility, were later adopted by the lower classes. Names ending in *-ik,* or *-ak,* generally connected with a trade, are of humbler origin, and some family names, such as Gomułka (cheese loaf) and Krupa (groats) were arbitrarily given to peasants when the use of family names became mandatory in the eighteenth century. German family names are frequent in Poland, not only among Germans and Jews but also in families whose German origin is almost forgotten. A few aristocratic names, among them Radziwiłł, were originally Lithuanian.

Women use the feminine form of the family names. When an adjective ending is used, this is formed by changing the final *i* of the family name to *a*; thus the wife or daughter of Adamowski will be Adamowska. If the adjective ending is not used, the common feminine termination is *-owa* for a married woman or *-ówna* for a single one, but under certain circumstances *-ina* and *-ianka* (or *-anka*) are used instead.

Polish, like most European languages, uses the second person singular pronoun—*ty* "thou"—in address to friends, relatives, and inferiors (especially children and animals). In all ordinary and polite address and to strangers the word used is *pan* for males and *pani* for females, with the verb in the third person singular; for the plural, *panowie* (m.) and *panie* (f.) are used, with a plural verb. *Pan* and *pani* used alone are equivalent to "sir" and "ma'am"; with names they are equivalent to "Mr.," and "Mrs., Miss" (given names in friendly situations, family names in formal ones). Upper-class Poles use *pan* or *pani* even in addressing their servants. The form *panna* for unmarried girls has almost disappeared as a form of address, as have *panicz* and *panienka,* formerly applied to "the young master" or "the young mistress." The form *towarzysz* (comrade) is today used in formal address among Party officials, and *obywatel* (citizen) also has some currency in official circles. The form *pan,* however, despite its noble origins, shows no sign of dropping from the language.

Polish peasants in formal address have continued the older usage of *wy* (you) for the second person plural. Within the last century this has been in the process of being replaced by the urban *pan,* but the older form has been somewhat revived by the present regime as a semiformal mode of address, and it has also for some time been current between professional colleagues.

A complete cataloging of all the nuances of address in Polish is not possible here. The complexity of the subject reflects the "elegance" and "politeness" of Polish speech in general, a vestige of the social attitudes of Poland's "golden age."

Minority Languages

In the period between the two world wars the Polish state included within its boundaries areas where the native inhabitants were and always had been speakers of languages other than Polish: in the east, Ukrainians, Belorussians, Lithuanians; in the west and south-west as well as in the Corridor to the Baltic, a certain number of German speakers; and throughout the country, especially in the cities and villages, a large number of speakers of Yiddish. These minorities constituted about 30 percent of the population. By the treaties establishing Poland after World War I, the minorities had various special rights, including the right to schools in which their respective languages could be the primary languages of instruction or could be taught as second languages after Polish. Pre-World War II figures show about 600,000 students in schools using or teaching German, Ukrainian, Belorussian, Lithuanian, Czech, Russian, Yiddish, and Hebrew.

During World War II all but a fraction of the Jews (a large number of whom spoke Yiddish) were exterminated; the remainder were deported or managed to escape. After the war boundary changes and exchanges of population removed most of the other non-Polish speakers. At present less than 2 percent of the population is listed as having a native language other than Polish.

The question of native language in Poland has for many decades been connected with political and social problems. Before World War I when the ruling German and Russian governments were seeking to eradicate Polish language and culture, many non-Polish (principally Jewish) inhabitants of the areas claimed German or Russian as their language even if they also—or principally—spoke Yiddish, Ukrainian, Belorussian, or Lithuanian. In the Austrian-ruled part of Poland linguistic autonomy of a kind was permitted, but even there many Jews preferred to list themselves as speakers of German rather than Yiddish. Between the two wars many Jews were actually Polish speakers but listed themselves as speakers of Yiddish (or sometimes Hebrew) in order to receive the tenuous protection of the treaty-instituted minority rights. Speakers of German in the west and of Ukrainian, Belorussian, and Lithuanian in the east usually also insisted on being listed by their native language, again in order to receive minority rights, but Polish officials often distorted the figures to strengthen the Polish claims to these areas.

Newspapers and books were being published in Russian, Belorussian, Ukrainian, Lithuanian, Slovak, Czech, and Yiddish in early 1956.

GERMAN

The relatively few speakers of German left in Poland still are chiefly in the Silesian provinces. Official sources report some 120 schools in which German is the language of instruction.

BELORUSSIAN AND UKRAINIAN

Belorussian and Ukrainian belong, like Russian, to the eastern branch of the Slavic languages. Of the two, Ukrainian claims more speakers and greater development as an independent language. The dialects of the eastern Poles have affected and been affected by those of the western Belorussians and Ukrainians across the border. There is a very close similarity between western Belorussian and Polish.

On March 1, 1957, a "nationalities committee" was established by the Bialystok Provincial Committee of the Polish United Workers' Party to deal with textbook publication and other special problems of the Belorussian, Ukrainian, and other minority groups in the area. According to official reports there are in Poland 2 schools and a new teachers' college in which Ukrainian is the language of instruction. It is also taught in 140 Polish schools and 2 teacher-training colleges.

YIDDISH

Many of the Jews of Poland in the interwar period spoke Yiddish as their mother tongue, but all but a few knew at least one other language. Yiddish, developed on a base of Middle High German dialects, became widely spoken in Poland when large numbers of Jews were invited into the country in the fifteenth century. Words from Hebrew, Polish, and other languages were incorporated, and regional variations developed. The Yiddish of Cracow, for example, remained in some ways closer to German than did that of Warsaw. Yiddish was written in the Hebrew alphabet, and a considerable body of Yiddish literature was created. With the emigration of Polish Jews, the language spread into other parts of Europe—especially the Russian Empire—and to the Americas. The segregation of Jews in the major cities of Poland strengthened the development of Yiddish as part of a culture distinct from that of the Poles, but by the twentieth century many Jews had emerged from this isolation and had come to speak Polish rather than Yiddish. Most Jews in Poland retained a distinctive accent in speaking Polish; it is also true that Yiddish in Poland acquired a Polish accent.

As noted, Jews in Poland have since 1939 been reduced to a small fraction of their former numbers. The number migrating from Russia since the end of the war has been almost balanced by the number going to Israel. Although a broadcast in Yiddish is still (early 1957) offered on Warsaw Radio, the number of Yiddish speakers in Poland cannot be much more than 30,000 today.

Yiddish-language theaters are still operating in Lodz, Wroclaw, and Warsaw, and the Yiddish newspaper *Folksztyme* appears three times weekly. A Yiddish historical quarterly magazine and a Jewish library in Katowice are reportedly still in existence.

OTHER MINORITY LANGUAGES

Russian was a recognized minority language in interwar Poland, spoken chiefly by members of the "Old Believer" sect. There is no available record as to the fate of this group. Five Russian schools, four of them private, were reported in 1937–38. Soviet troops and other officials stationed in Poland today constitute a rather fluid Russian-speaking minority. Slovak and some Czech are still spoken in a few spots along the southern border. Lithuanian is still used in Lithuanian schools in Bialystok but the number of speakers is unknown. Recent information indicates that there are 4 elementary schools and only 1 secondary school in which all instruction is given in Lithuanian. The language is also taught in 26 Polish-language schools. An indeterminate number of Gypsies within the country probably retain their Romany language, though it receives no official recognition. Latin, which until the eighteenth century was an artificially spoken language among upper-class Poles, remains as the ecclesiastical language of the Roman Catholic Church. Hebrew was taught in Jewish schools in the interwar period.

Foreign Languages

Poland's history and geographical position in Europe made the learning of a foreign language a necessity for many Poles. The importance of Latin as a second language until the eighteenth century has been mentioned above. French was spoken by many educated people in the eighteenth and nineteenth centuries and is still a language that is liked or looked up to even by those who do not know it. Occupation for more than a century by Russia, Prussia, and Austria caused many Poles to learn German and Russian; they were less likely to learn from their less powerful neighbors—during the long association with Lithuania, for example, few Poles learned Lithuanian, while many upper-class Lithuanians adopted Polish as their own language.

During the interwar period French and German were the foreign languages most widely studied. Polish animosity toward the Russians made the study of that language unpopular, but many Poles had perforce learned Russian before 1918, and there was considerable knowledge of the language in Poland between the wars, despite its unpopularity. After World War II, Russian became a required language in the schools and was very strongly stressed, but on January 1,

1957, it was made optional, on a par with French, German, and English. Russian words such as *kolkhoz* (collective farm) and others directly connected with the Soviet system have acquired a pejorative sense in Polish popular usage today, and the introduction of a Russian word in a Warsaw music hall skit has long been a way to evoke laughter.

Literacy

Until 1918 educational opportunities for Poles were severely limited, and Polish peasants, except those in the German part of the country, received little schooling. After Poland achieved its independence much attention was given to raising the literacy rate among adults as well as children (see chap. 18), and by 1931 the government claimed a literacy rate of 77 percent among citizens over 10 years of age. A large number of illiterates were in the eastern regions later ceded to Russia; this may partially explain the figure of only 2 million illiterates (about 10 to 11 percent of the population over 10 years of age) claimed by Polish authorities in 1945. The drive against illiteracy was stepped up by the postwar regime. In 1949, 1.2 million persons (6.1 percent of the population over 10 years of age) unable to read or write were registered in response to a government order. Illiteracy has undoubtedly been further reduced since that time.

RELIGIONS

POLES HAVE BEEN PREDOMINANTLY ROMAN CATHOLIC SINCE THE tenth century, and the Polish Catholic Church has played a dominant role in the political and intellectual life of the nation, molding the customs, morals, and attitudes of the people since the Middle Ages. For the vast majority of the people, the Catholic faith and ritual is a deeply ingrained part of everyday life, closely associated with the sense of being a Pole. Catholicism also brought to Poland the Latin alphabet and Latin aspects of culture—permanently setting Poland apart from Orthodox Russia and making the country a member of the western community of Christian nations.

Throughout Poland's history the ecclesiastical hierarchy has served as an element of unity in times of internal division and strife. During the period of partition the Church was the spiritual mainstay of the nation. The hardships suffered by the people and by the Catholic Church under Orthodox Russian and Protestant Prussian rule resulted in a lasting identity of Polish nationality with the Catholic faith. Religious and patriotic ideals have been interwoven in the minds of Poles ever since.

The Polish Church emerged from the horrors of World War II as the chief source of spiritual unity and national strength in the country. Common suffering, persecution, and resistance during the war and German occupation reinforced the ties between the clergy and the people. For the Polish Communist leadership, however, Catholicism represented a potential source of organized political opposition as well as a serious ideological challenge. From 1949 the government followed a program that increasingly restricted the activity of the Church and culminated in the arrest of the Polish Primate, Cardinal Wyszyński, in September 1953. Other leading clergymen, priests, and seminarists were also arrested and imprisoned. Church estates were confiscated, most of the Church's source of income thus coming under state control. Catholic publications were controlled, and religious instruction was effectively eliminated from the schools.

For the Polish people, however, the Church once more became the symbol of their resistance to foreign repression. Worshipers crowded the churches; Communion became a political as well as a religious act.

In the crisis of October 1956—which brought Gomułka back to power as head of the Party—the Polish Government found itself in desperate need of national unity. Promising to resolve the differences between the Church and the state, Gomułka released Cardinal Wyszyński and secured the support of the Church hierarchy for his policy of "liberalization" and national independence. This support proved of crucial importance to the survival of Gomułka's government and helped, by marshaling popular support, to forestall the threat of Soviet armed intervention in Polish affairs. Since the October crisis Gomułka has acted in the full awareness that Polish Catholicism, permeated with national feeling, is perhaps the most important source of cohesion and solidarity in Polish society today.

Polish Catholicism

RELIGION AND THE PEOPLE

The Church in Poland is a powerful political and moral force by virtue of the fact that it enjoys the support of the overwhelming majority of the people; approximately 95 percent of the total population in Poland today is Roman Catholic. For Poles of all classes, moreover, Catholicism is an essential part of Polish identity and is closely linked with feelings of national patriotism.

For the Polish people action and ritual seem to have greater appeal and significance than meditation. In contrast to Russian Orthodox believers, for example, educated Poles are not greatly concerned with questions regarding mystical truths or ultimate reality. Beliefs and practices divergent from those of the Church have never assumed sufficient importance to become popular heresies, and throughout its history the Polish Church has suffered little from schisms.

While Poles of all classes are united in their acceptance of the Catholic faith, different social groups exhibit somewhat different attitudes toward religion and the institution of the Church. A member of the intelligentsia is likely to be less conformist in his religious practices than a peasant. He may be skeptical about the authority of priests. His participation in parish life is limited; frequently he may not know to which parish he belongs. He feels free to interpret religious dogma in his own way and does not worry about whether or not his way conforms exactly to the teachings of the Church. He considers himself, however, a good Catholic. The ceremony and tradition of Catholicism is for him a source of patriotic pride and deep emotional and aesthetic satisfaction.

To Polish peasants and urban workers, who together make up the bulk of the population, religion is an integral part of daily existence. There is little direct information regarding the religious attitudes and behavior of workers in Poland, but the majority of this group come from rural backgrounds and current descriptions of religious celebrations, processions, and other such activities in the urban centers show little variation from the peasant pattern. For a growing number of industrial workers, religion may no longer offer all the answers, but churches in the cities are crowded, and many working-class people apparently still rely upon religious ritual and prayer to help them surmount the difficulties of daily life.

The peasant's religion is interwoven with his practical interests and is to some extent fused with long-harbored folk superstitions. One of the first things a peasant does upon rising is to kneel, inside his hut or outdoors, to pray. Later in the morning, at the sound of the church bell, he may stop his work and say another prayer. Throughout the day he will exchange with the neighbors and strangers he may meet the customary greeting "Praised be Jesus Christ!" —to be answered, "World without end!" Occasionally, he may cross himself and say a Hail Mary to ward off fiends and spirits or to protect himself from possible evil spells. When passing a roadside shrine or cross—a characteristic of the Polish landscape—the peasant may doff his hat and cross himself, or he may stop to kiss the feet of the figure of Jesus.

The passing of time for the peasant is closely connected with religious observances and ritual. His daily speech is studded with such expressions as "after the space of a few Our Fathers" and "before you could say a Hail Mary." When giving his age he may refer to a saint's day or declare, "Last Assumption Day I rounded my 35th year." Throughout the year he will refer to the calendar of saints' days in rhymes which remind him of his annual round of duties:

> *Before the Virgin is born,*
> *Sow rye ahead of corn [i.e. wheat].*
> *But once Our Lady is born,*
> *Then get busy with corn!*

> *Now has come St. Luke's day,*
> *Put your plough and harrow away!*

The major events and crises of a peasant's life cycle—birth, mar riage, death—are connected with religious ceremonies.

Sunday is a day of rest and prayer, as well as a time to drink and gossip with one's neighbors. Similarly, other holidays and religious festivals are social events and times when absent relatives may visit as well as days of devotion. The yearly pilgrimage to a famous shrine such as that of Our Lady of the Black Madonna at Czestochowa, is anticipated by a peasant community as another welcome break in the monotony of life, frequently involving a week-long absence from home and a gypsylike existence on the way.

Common worship is an important means of binding communities and villages together. All inhabitants of one parish or area usually express devotion to the same patron saint. Each region has a shrine which houses its own particular holy figure or painting, an image that may be known for its special powers. On feast days and holidays all people of one locality gather and demonstrate their common ties to a particular place. During a pilgrimage each community or region travels as a group, often led by the local priest. In times of drought or great need all the peasants of a given area may share the cost of a votive Mass.

An entire village participates in the numerous religious processions that are held in the course of the year. Upon the death of a prominent member of the community, the house of the deceased may be the scene where a long line of people chant, weep, beat their breasts, and pray. The coffin, sprinkled with holy water, is carried to the churchyard in a long procession, amid great lamentation.

On other occasions, processions are festive and gay. In the spring the priest may lead his parishioners around the boundaries of the village. Trees, earth, and worshipers are sprinkled with holy water, prayers against plague and misfortune are recited. The entire procession moves forward to the sound of chanting, women's shrill voices, children's cries, and jingling bells. Holy banners and pictures and statues of saints, veiled in gauze and decorated with flowers, are held aloft in front of the surging crowd.

The worship of innumerable saints, represented in holy figures or paintings, is characteristic of the peasant's religious life. Special qualities are attributed to the holy paintings which adorn every peasant home; during particularly stormy weather, for instance, they may be taken outside as a safeguard against the powers of evil abroad. The paintings are approached with both solemn respect and a sense of familiarity. In the mind of the peasant, the saints possess distinct personalities and are subject to ordinary human emotions and drives. He may argue and bargain with them, and if he feels that they have failed him he can always appeal to the boundless sympathy of the Holy Mother. The Virgin Mary is for all Poles the supreme symbol of benevolence, understanding, compassion, and tolerance toward human weakness.

Regular attendance at church, partaking of the Holy Sacrament, going to confession, observing fasts, and other forms of ritualized behavior are part of the peasant's routine of life and help to sustain and renew his faith. The beautiful and rich décor of the church, the use of Latin in the service, the solemnity of the songs and ritual make a deep impression upon his emotional life.

His village church represents God, Christ, and the saint to whom it is dedicated. The priest is regarded as a holy man and has great influence over the members of the parish. The peasant looks to him for words of comfort, advice, help in time of need, and will offer in return his unbounded gratitude and love. The priest is often listened to as though he spoke with the words of Jesus; his censure or blame, especially when expressed in church, can evoke deep remorse and fear.

The peasant also recognizes that the priest may be subject to ordinary human weaknesses. This became an important factor in his attitude toward the clergy in the latter part of the nineteenth century, when peasants first began to question the permanence of the existing social order. For centuries the clergy had been identified with the upper classes and, recruited almost entirely from the *szlachta,* had always shared their style of life and outlook. The hierarchy of the clergy paralleled the stratification of the nobility: bishops lived in the style of the higher nobility; priests were associated with the landed gentry, and many of them subjected their flocks to harsh economic exploitation. The peasant viewed the existing social and economic order as permanent and natural. That a priest would seek profit as well as honor was accepted as necessary, just as a church building necessarily had to be of a certain size and aesthetic perfection.

This attitude began to change in the nineteenth century. The peasant began to want to overcome his poverty and inferior position. Although an increasing number of peasants were themselves becoming priests many of the clergy continued to support the old social order. After World War I the clergy were recruited from all social strata, but whatever their social origin, were often very willing to be identified with the intelligentsia, who had become the dominant political and social class in the country. The higher clergy continued to live in the grand style, often on a much better economic level than the sometimes impoverished aristocracy.

During the interwar period priests of peasant origin often pursued their careers solely for the benefit of their families. Although there were some who never gave up their loyalty to their original social class, most village priests had at best a patronizing attitude toward the peasants. The peasant, in turn, viewed the privileges and abuses of the Church hierarchy with increasing bitterness. Some of this feeling was expressed in common sayings such as, "A priest's kith and kin will never grow thin," and "This shepherd only cares for the sheep he can shear: we have no wool for him!" Another peasant saying likens the bright stars in the heavens to the souls of bishops, the smaller ones to the souls of priests, while the souls of peasants, missing from the heavens, are to be found in the fires of hell.

Thus, prior to World War II many peasants came to view the Church as an institution representing the rich and powerful. The ecclesiastical hierarchy not only kept its ties with upper-class traditions but often exploited the poorer segments of the population; the frequent collection of money by the priest or various Catholic organizations—often for goals as distant from the life of parishioners as the support of missions to "pagan" countries—was felt as a real plague in the villages.

The peasant's dissatisfaction during the interwar period with the Church as an institution was matched by a growth of anticlerical sentiment among the intelligentsia and the urban working class. The general European trends of positivism and religious skepticism influenced an increasing number of Polish intellectuals. The utilization of religious fervor—chiefly by exponents of extreme nationalism—to promote anti-Semitism gave some Poles an opportunity to challenge the Church as being reactionary or "fascist."

Much of the near-hostility that had grown up between at least a part of the clergy and large numbers of the population was burned away in the crucible of World War II. The intimacy of common suffering forged new bonds between the people and their Church. The Polish Catholic hierarchy played a courageous role in the anti-German resistance movement and won the unbounded admiration of the entire nation. In the eyes of many Poles the Church was transformed from a prosperous institution that strongly defended the *status quo* to a champion of the poor and persecuted. The shift from a conservative to a "fighting" Church appealed to those intellectuals who considered themselves "progressive" as well as those who still identified themselves with the *szlachta* and cherished the traditions of rebellion against authority and to the peasants, who saw that many priests had become poorer than themselves. When Poland's Communist regime assumed political power after the war, the Church enjoyed an influence over the people far exceeding that of any secular authority.

THE CHURCH IN NATIONAL LIFE

Throughout Polish history the hierarchy of the Catholic Church has played a prominent part in the educational, cultural, and political life of the nation. In the course of time the Church acquired great political power as well as moral authority.

THE MIDDLE AGES TO THE RENAISSANCE. Poles still identify the adoption of Christianity in 966—referred to as the "Baptism of Poland"—with the creation of their state. It was by entering into the fold of the Roman Catholic Church that Poland's first rulers attained the status of European sovereigns. Poland's self-defence against pagan or schismatic neighbors was supported by the Popes, and throughout the Middle Ages direct relations with the Holy See served to buttress the country's independence.

With the appointment of a Polish archbishop at Gniezno in the beginning of the eleventh century, the Polish Church grew in influence, attracting monks and bishops from countries as far away as Italy and France. By the thirteenth century the new faith had become a controlling force in the life of the Polish people.

The Catholic hierarchy served as Poland's most important and sometimes only link with western Christendom. The impress of Latin Christianity on Poland's cultural life was deep and lasting. Latin monks were the first to develop the grammar of the Polish language. At the same time, Latin, the language of the Church, became a vehicle for the introduction of western religious, artistic, and scientific trends in Polish life.

In addition to making Poland culturally part of the West, the Church became an important source of political cohesion. During the internal chaos of the thirteenth century, when Poland split into numerous rival duchies, the ecclesiastical organization served as a rallying point in an otherwise divided country. The clergy and church chronicles developed and preserved an awareness of this unity and helped to give the country a sense of destiny. The canonization in 1253 of Stanisław, Poland's patron saint, brought together bishops and laymen from all parts of Poland—symbolizing the revival of national solidarity. Poland's political, social, and economic reconstruction at the end of the thirteenth century took place under the leadership of prominent members of the Catholic hierarchy.

From the fourteenth to the sixteenth century the Church played a role of supreme importance in the national life of the country. The rest of Europe looked upon Poland as an outpost of western Christianity. The Holy See confirmed the coronation of Polish kings. The Polish Catholic hierarchy possessed distinguished statesmen and men of learning who enjoyed considerable influence in state affairs. The Renaissance in Poland had as its leading representatives outstanding members of the Church.

THE REFORMATION. In the middle of the sixteenth century the Church in Poland found itself challenged by the spread of Protestant doctrines. The Reformation movement reached Poland soon after its outbreak in Germany and won a considerable number of followers among Poland's upper class. Its success, however, proved temporary and superficial, for the Polish nobility had seized upon the ideas of the Reformation, not out of deep religious convictions, but as a weapon in the struggle with the ecclesiastical hierarchy for political, social, and economic power.

Except for the lasting contribution it made toward the development of a national literature, the Reformation by the end of the sixteenth century had lost most of its force in Poland. Having largely attained their political objectives, most members of the nobility were ready to discard this weapon in order to hold and protect their gains. The effectiveness of Roman Catholic counteraction, the zealous reforms of the Jesuits (particularly in the field of education), the inability of the Reformation movement to produce an able native-born leadership (which could come only from the mother Church), the lack of internal unity in the movement, and the continued devotion of the mass of peasants to the Roman Catholic Church—all contributed to the Polish Reformation's decline and decay.

The Church became a symbol of resistance against Orthodox Russian and Lutheran German pressure. The tie between the Catholic faith and Polish national feeling was intensified. Poles worshiped an increasing number of national rather than foreign saints. In 1656 the leaders of the state dedicated the Polish-Lithuanian Commonwealth to the Black Madonna of Czestochowa. The Madonna was crowned "Queen of Poland," and since then Poles have annually renewed their vows to her.

PARTITIONED POLAND. After Poland's partition at the end of the eighteenth century, the Church, as the only unifying factor in the nation's internal life, became the backbone of national resistance to foreign rule. Although the failure of the Holy See to protest the destruction of the Polish state created much bitterness, the Catholic faith, together with the continued use of the Polish language, helped the people to resist efforts of their neighbors to separate and destroy them as a nation.

In the absence of political freedom and indigenous state institutions, the responsibility of political leadership inside Poland was thrust upon the Catholic hierarchy. The struggle for elementary human rights, especially the right to use the native Polish tongue, involved the clergy of all ranks. Abroad, the deeply religious and patriotic works of Poland's poets and writers provided another link between Catholic tradition and Polish nationalism.

INTERWAR POLAND. When Poland regained its independence after World War I, the Church was ready to support the existing government so long as its own position of dominance in the religious, social, and cultural life of the nation was fully respected. Throughout the interwar period, accordingly, the Church was supported by the government in every way, and enjoyed considerable influence in politics and legislation.

The Constitution of 1921 officially recognized the "leading position" of the Catholic Church "among all the denominations enjoying equal rights." While 95 percent of the Poles were Roman Catholics, Roman Catholicism was the religion of only 65 percent of the total population. With the exception of a small number of Lithuanians, the ethnic minorities were almost all religious minorities as well (see chap. 4).

The Catholic Church enjoyed numerous privileges. It was one of the largest owners of property—land and buildings—in the country. The teaching of the Catholic faith was made compulsory in all elementary and secondary schools. The Catholic university founded in Lublin in 1918 exercised a strong influence upon the academic life of the country. All of the state universities, with the exception of Poznan, possessed faculties of theology. The Church established a large number of monastic institutions, and it directed as well the activities of at least 80 Catholic seminaries. Catholic welfare agencies functioned in more than 4,000 parishes. Over 200 Catholic periodicals were published under the auspices of the Church. Numerous lay associations formed by workers, students, and alumni of the universities supported the work of the Church and played a prominent part in the life of the country; they gathered to discuss contemporary problems and organized various social and cultural activities and pilgrimages to famous shrines.

The privileged position of the Church was reinforced by the establishment of close contacts with the Holy See. Monsignor Achille

Ratti, sent to Poland in 1918 and appointed Papal Nuncio at Warsaw in 1919, showed a deep interest in the reconstruction of independent Poland. His sympathy for Poland continued to manifest itself after he was elected Pope, as Pius XI, in 1922. A concordat between the Holy See and the Polish Government, signed on February 10, 1925, formally recognized the Catholic Church as an autonomous body and confirmed its extensive privileges, although the government reserved the right to intervene in certain matters, including ecclesiastical appointments.

The higher clergy were appointed by Rome, subject to confirmation by the President of the Republic. Each bishop chose his parish priests in consultation with the Minister of Education. Members of the clergy were exempt from military service. In breaches of the law they were subject to the secular courts.

The Polish Church produced a number of highly distinguished leaders who sought to adapt religion to the needs and demands of modern times. With the growth of industry, the needs of the urban population, quite different from those of the countryside, presented a new challenge to the Church. Cardinal August Hlond, who became the Primate of Poland in 1926, instituted reforms to narrow the gap between religion and everyday life. His pastoral letters thoroughly discussed all major contemporary problems. He actively supported the Catholic Action movement in which Pius XI, his personal friend, was particularly interested. The Primate's interest in social progress and welfare was shared by some of the most eminent Polish clergymen.

POSTWAR POLAND. The relations between the Polish hierarchy and the Vatican during and after World War II were colored by the fact that Cardinal Eugenio Pacelli who had been Papal Nuncio to Bavaria and had lived for many years in Germany and negotiated concordats with Bavaria, Prussia, and Germany, was consecrated Pope in March 1939 as the successor of Pius XI. There was a feeling in Poland that the new Pope harbored strong sympathies for Germany—a suspicion that was reinforced when the Vatican suggested in the latter part of August 1939 that Poland cede territory to Germany in order to save the peace.

Whatever tensions this may have created, the attitude of Polish clergymen toward German ambitions was very clear from the beginning. Cardinal Hlond firmly rejected a German offer to head a regency in Nazi-occupied Poland. Great numbers of Polish religious leaders participated in the underground resistance, and many of them were executed or died in concentration camps. The performance of their routine religious duties during the pressures of the German occupation was in itself often an act of heroism.

Thus, in postwar Poland the Catholic Church represented an extremely difficult and sensitive problem for the new Communist regime. Subscribing to an ideology which itself is an exclusive and intolerant form of religion, Poland's Communist leaders could not ignore the tremendous prestige enjoyed by the Church nor the fact that Poland was now almost entirely Roman Catholic as a result of territorial and population changes.

1945–1949. Fearful of provoking a possible civil war, the regime initially followed a cautious and conciliatory policy toward the Church, and from 1945 until the end of 1948 the policy in regard to the Polish Catholic hierarchy was one of relative liberalism. In 1945 jurisdiction over marriage, divorce, and vital statistics was removed from the Church, and the regime denounced the Concordat of 1925, since the Vatican continued to recognize the Polish government-in-exile; otherwise, the Communists moved cautiously. The official Communist line maintained that the coexistence of Catholicism and communism in Poland was both feasible and desirable, and it urged Catholics to support the government's endeavors to build a new Poland.

Cardinal Hlond, interned by the Germans during the last phase of the war, returned to head the ecclesiastical administration in July 1945. Catholic publications, educational establishments, and charitable institutions were quickly reorganized. Numerous churches were reconstructed with state assistance. Religion was included in the curriculum of primary and secondary schools, much as before the war. The estates owned by the Church were exempted from the agricultural reform of 1945. The rapid reorganization of Church activities was accompanied by a revival of religious practice throughout Poland. More than two million persons went on pilgrimages to the shrine at Czestochowa during 1946.

The Communist leaders went out of their way to show not only tolerance but friendliness toward the Catholic Church. Government dignitaries attended religious ceremonies. When Bierut was elected President, he took a religious oath; following his lead, other prominent Communists proclaimed their religiosity, and some of them continued to give their children religious education. The Church, in turn, though critical of the Party's atheistic doctrine, did not explicitly repudiate the existing regime, nor did it condemn all changes instituted by the Communists. Accepting the new regime as the legitimate government of Poland, the hierarchy awaited further developments.

Cardinal Hlond died on October 22, 1948, and was succeeded to the Primacy by Archbishop Stefan Wyszyński (elevated to Cardinal in January 1953). The new Primate's personal influence and prestige in Poland was considerable. The son of a church organist and village schoolteacher, Wyszyński during the interwar period, when the clergy were often accused of identifying with the upper classes, always allied himself with the working man. He earned a doctorate in Canon Law and Social Sciences at the University of Lublin. Writing books on such subjects as unemployment and the rights of labor (he had begun to act as a counsel in labor disputes just prior to World War II), Wyszyński became known as a "labor priest." He was active in the underground resistance movement during the war and was appointed Bishop of Lublin in 1946. As Primate of Poland he became the greatest moral authority in the country.

While preserving the façade of toleration, the regime concentrated its propaganda attacks on the Holy See, effectively playing upon fears in Poland that the Vatican harbored pro-German sympathies: the Vatican's readiness during the war to confirm the appointment of German clergy as administrators of dioceses in Polish territory seized by the Nazis had created resentment among many Poles. The Communists vigorously denounced the Vatican's refusal to recognize the postwar regime and to approve the reorganization of the Catholic hierarchy in German territories allotted to Poland by the Potsdam Conference. The regime exerted continuous pressure on the Vatican to reorganize the apostolic administrations in the "recovered territories," an act which would indirectly indicate an acceptance of the Oder-Neisse line as Poland's western frontier. It was supported in this objective by a large proportion of the Polish people and the Polish hierarchy.

By 1949 the Communists were ready to test the strength of the Polish Church. They began to sponsor various groups of so-called "patriotic" or "progressive" priests—chiefly those military chaplains and priests who had been inmates of Nazi concentration camps—who were willing to back the regime against the Vatican on political and social issues. The regime also gave extensive support to a lay group of "Social Catholics" who sought to reconcile Marxism with Catholicism.

The group became the backbone of the regime's attempt to mobilize opinion against the higher clergy and to marshal Catholic laymen, particularly intellectuals, behind the programs of the government. They operated a government-controlled publishing house, known as PAX, which became the keystone of a group of so-called Clerical Lay Catholic National Front Activists.

The PAX association possessed a cadre of about 350 members and was headed by Bolesław Piasecki, who had been leader of the "Falanga," a prewar Polish fascist movement. It published numerous books and periodicals justifying Marxism in terms of Catholic dogma. A considerable amount of its propaganda was geared for Catholic consumption abroad and stressed that only in "socialist" countries could Catholicism find the proper conditions for its universal mission —asserting that in the West this mission was warped and bound up with reaction, imperialism, and war. But, while PAX denounced the Holy See for being allied with the "camp of reaction," it did not advocate a break with the Vatican and often asserted its members' filial obedience to the Pope.

1949 TO OCTOBER 1956. From 1949 Church and government engaged in a tug of war interrupted sporadically by attempts to reach some kind of agreement. On July 13, 1949 the Vatican issued a world-wide decree debarring from the sacraments all Catholics who either belonged to the Communist Party or were its willing adherents, and excommunicating Communist activists. The Polish Government denounced this move as an act of aggression against the Polish state and on August 5, 1949, it published a law providing prison sentences of up to five years for any clergyman refusing the sacraments to citizens because of their political opinions or activities. Religious associations and orders were now required to register with the government, and possession of all religious property was made dependent on government permit.

The pressure on the Church was intensified in the autumn of 1949, when the Party organized a series of strikes among laborers on Church estates. On January 23, 1950 the largest welfare institution of the Church, Caritas, was placed under state control. Simultaneously, numerous priests and bishops were accused of graft, embezzlement, hostility to "People's Poland," and, finally, espionage and sabotage. By the end of January 1950 over 500 priests, nuns, and monks had been placed under arrest. In March 1950 the government passed a bill which called for the seizure of all Church estates in excess of 250 acres; about 375,000 acres of Church property were affected.

On April 14, 1950, an agreement stipulating that the Episcopate would seek the Vatican's recognition of the Oder-Neisse line as Poland's permanent boundary was negotiated between the government and the Polish Episcopate. The Church also agreed to punish members of the clergy guilty of misuse of religious feeling for "antistate" activity, and it was to help teach respect for the authority and laws of the state. In matters of faith and ecclesiastical jurisdiction, the

Pope was to remain the supreme authority of the Polish Church; in other matters the Episcopate would be guided "by the Polish *raison d'état.*" The government, in turn, agreed to refrain from interference with public worship. The rights of Catholic associations were to be recognized. Catholic publications were to have the same privileges enjoyed by other publications. The agreement represented a supreme effort on the part of the Episcopate to avoid an open clash with the regime. In essence it was not an ideological compromise but a *modus vivendi* through which the Church hoped to enjoy a bearable existence at least for the time being.

The experiment in coexistence lasted not quite three years. The regime launched a new offensive against the Catholic hierarchy at the end of 1952. Large numbers of clergymen, including some bishops, were accused of subversion and arrested. Pressure was exerted to confine religious instruction to the churches. Instructors of religion were refused admittance to professional teaching organizations and sometimes dismissed from their positions in the schools. A Society of Children's Friends was formed to establish schools based on atheistic principles. Officially, religious instruction was still included as a subject in the curricula of public and secular schools, but the provision was circumvented in practice.

On February 9, 1953 the regime issued a decree giving the government control of all appointments to Church posts. The authority of the Pope in matters of Church jurisdiction was now drastically limited. The Party press declared on February 13:

> The decree insured that only patriots will be appointed, that only persons who support the Polish state's interests will hold ecclesiastical posts.

The regime simultaneously suspended a large number of Catholic publications, some of which reappeared later under new editorial boards composed of proregime Catholics.

On May 8, 1953 the Polish Episcopate sent a memorandum to the government accusing it of violating the agreement of 1950. The Episcopate listed its grievances: growing persecution of the Church; abrogation of religious instruction in educational institutions; intervention of the government in the internal affairs of the Church; efforts to instigate dissension among the clergy; destruction of the Catholic press and publications; use of political pressure against the clergy and the faithful.

In its memorandum the Episcopate declared that the government's decree of February 9, 1953 definitely closed the period of experimental coexistence opened on April 14, 1950. In assessing the reasons for the failure of the experiment, the Polish bishops commented:

The hostility toward the Church was not so much a matter of the people involved, but of the system; with the people we negotiated, as a rule, in a friendly atmosphere.

This statement strongly suggests that in its relations with the Church the Party had acted as an instrument of Moscow, not as an independent agent. It is known that there was a special section of the Soviet Embassy in Warsaw which supervised the execution of the Party's policy toward ecclesiastical affairs in Poland.

In June 1953 Cardinal Wyszyński denounced the Party for the "intolerable attempt" to suppress religion in individual and social life. The Polish hierarchy, he declared, would defend religion "even to the point of shedding blood." In September the regime accused Bishop Czesław Kaczmarek of Kielce (a prominent Church leader) of espionage, put him on trial, and sentenced him to twelve years in prison. A few days after the trial Cardinal Wyszyński was suspended from his functions and forced to retire into a monastery. In October two of the Primate's auxiliaries were imprisoned. Nine bishops and several hundred priests were held in prisons or were under arrest at the beginning of 1954.

From 1954 to October 1956 the struggle continued unabated. The majority of seminaries in the country were closed, and Catholic institutions of higher learning were placed under strict political supervision. The regime continued to use the "progressive patriotic" priesthood and the PAX association as its main weapons to split Polish Catholicism from within. A number of PAX publications were put on the Roman Index.

The PAX movement, however, exercised little influence on Catholic life in Poland; the vast majority of the people opposed its activities. Similarly, the small group of priests collaborating with the regime failed to win the respect of the population. The nation almost overwhelmingly continued to manifest its wholehearted devotion to the mother Church and its persecuted leaders.

The Church once again became a rallying point for national feeling and unity. Poles filled their churches for political as well as religious motives. Attendance at Mass or Confession became a means of exhibiting open hostility toward Communist rule. When Władysław Gomułka returned to power in October 1956, the new government found that it could not contain the growing restiveness of the population or win popular backing for Gomułka's policies without reaching a new understanding with the Church.

SINCE OCTOBER 1956. Gomułka assumed leadership at the Eighth Plenary Session of the Party's Central Committee, held October 19–21, 1956. On October 22 a mass student demonstration in Warsaw adopted a resolution demanding the release of Cardinal Wyszyński and the "clearing up of the reason for his imprisonment." The Polish Episcopate at the same time indicated to the regime that the Primate of Poland would help to rally the people behind the government if three wishes were granted: freedom of expression for non-Marxist Catholics; restoration of an independent Catholic press outside the control of PAX; and independence of social and intellectual activity for "authentic" Catholic groups.

In need of popular support, the Gomułka government recognized the necessity of settling its differences with the Church. On October 29 the government announced that Cardinal Wyszyński had been restored to office. The Cardinal resumed his duties as Primate of Poland and Archbishop of Warsaw and Gniezno. Speaking that same day to a crowd assembled before the Primate's Palace, Wyszyński asked the people to preserve their calm and dignity.

A new spirit of cooperation marked the relations between the state and the Church after the Cardinal's release, although the undercurrent tension occasionally rose to the surface. Wyszyński issued appeals for national unity and support of the new programs of the government, and groups of prominent Catholic laymen expressed their readiness to mobilize Catholic society to implement the new and difficult tasks facing the nation.

The PAX association was bitterly attacked by Catholic writers and intellectuals, who now expressed their opinions more freely and openly. The head of PAX, Bolesław Piasecki, was accused of building up a personal political apparatus and denounced for attempting to represent the PAX movement as the voice of Polish Catholicism. Appeals were made to PAX activists not to "live in isolation from the whole nation." During November 1956 numerous PAX leaders publicly broke with Piasecki and resigned from their posts.

Before the year was over the government had given in on several issues that it had previously fought most bitterly. A new policy of "unhampered freedom" for religious teaching effectively reintroduced religious education into the schools. The most influential Catholic newspaper of those suspended in March 1953, *Tygodnik Powszechny* (a Cracow weekly), was permitted to resume independent publication. The government agreed to "substantive" modifications in the decree of February 9, 1953, by which it had acquired veto power over all church appointments in Poland: it retained its rights to withhold consent to any church appointment, but in case of disagreement would enter into negotiation with representatives of the Catholic hierarchy.

The government indicated, however, that it would require of every clergyman an oath of allegiance to the Polish People's Republic, and it insisted that any clergyman who lost his civic rights through court action should be removed from his Church post. These demands created considerable dissatisfaction in Catholic circles.

Despite such dissatisfaction, Catholic leaders did their best to unite the people behind the new government and its policies. A meeting between Premier Cyrankiewicz and Cardinal Wyszyński took place on January 15, 1957. The following day the Secretary of the Episcopate, Bishop Zygmunt Choromański, issued a statement urging Catholics to "fulfill the duty of conscience" by voting in the national elections for a new *Sejm* on January 20.

Various Catholic organizations and numerous priests took part in the election campaign in an attempt to persuade the people to vote for the National Unity Front candidates. Where necessary, the time of Mass was adjusted to permit the faithful to go to the polls; entire congregations were led to the voting booths by their priests.

Twelve of the 458 deputies of the new *Sejm* were elected as open adherents of the Catholic Church. Nine of them formed a separate group under the name of Znak (The Banner), led by Professor S. Stomma, a noted sociologist and author. They declared that Gomułka symbolized for them the "true Polish political road." They made clear, however, that they would continue to show confidence in Gomułka only so long as the ideals of "October"—a democratization of political life, a greater respect for the rule of law, economic reforms, sovereignty in the conduct of foreign relations—were not abandoned. At the same time they recognized that a Polish-Soviet alliance must be the cornerstone of Polish policy and criticized "those of our countrymen at home and abroad who want to preserve the past, who have learned nothing and forgotten nothing." Self-preservation, in their view, demanded that Poles remain within the Soviet bloc and that Poland be ruled, at least for the time being, by Communists, who alone enjoyed Russia's confidence.

Leading Catholic intellectuals, writers, journalists, students, and educators had by this time organized various clubs and associations. Catholic debating societies and groups were formed in Warsaw, Lublin, Cracow, Poznan, Katowice, Lodz, and Torun. Catholic intellectuals from the major Polish cities joined forces in the All-Polish Club of Progressive Catholic Intelligentsia. This group was led by the prominent writer and dramatist J. Zawieyski, and its members included a number of noted Catholic laymen: A. Golubiew, vice-chairman of the Union of Polish Writers; J. Turowicz, editor of *Tygodnik Powszechny;* S. Stomma, S. Pigon, and J. Kleiber, professors of Cracow University; A. Makarczyk, professor of the Catholic University in Lublin; and K. Górski, professor of Torun University. Leading members declared in January that they had no intention of concealing the differences between Catholics and Communists but that they would cooperate with the government "in everything which is good and moral for the individual and the country." The Party, they stated, would have to be supported if the nation was to avoid catastrophe:

> This is dictated to us by a sense of the *raison d'état,* of political realism, as well as by our faith in the good will of others.

The leaders of the club did not wish to organize into anything resembling a political party, since this, in their view, would be "unrealistic and inexpedient" in the Poland of 1957; however, they would not avoid political activity "in so far as it might contribute to social, cultural, and educational work."

A degree of tension accompanied the reintroduction of religious education in the schools. The president of the Polish Academy of Sciences, Tadeusz Kotarbinski, expressed fear in January 1957 that the government's new policy toward religion might result in practices "contrary to the freedom of conscience." He noted that tremendous social pressure was being exerted against parents who did not want their children to attend religious classes. He did not criticize the new policy, which he described as a concession on the part of rational people in favor of a majority "who unfortunately do not think rationally," but he defended the right of persons who opposed religious instruction to organize themselves and to support lay schools which would not teach religion. He observed that many Poles felt that only a religious education could give a child a "high moral standard," and he urged that the lay schools "prove in practice that they too can provide ethical education."

A Lay Schools Society, with branches in twelve provinces, began functioning early in February 1957. It was composed of Communist intellectuals, professors, and teachers, who in some cases had lost their jobs because they were "nonbelievers." The society asserted that its purpose was, not to combat religion, but to disseminate a belief in secular education and to demonstrate "the superior quality of lay school education." It also expressed a desire to introduce lessons on "lay ethics" into the regular school curricula.

Early in March the Party leadership spoke out against the Church for the first time since October 1956. The official Party paper, *Trybuna Ludu,* accused the Church of teaching intolerance and complained that children who did not attend religious classes were treated "as Jews or even anarchists" by the majority of their classmates. At the same time the paper tried to calm Communists and "non-Communist atheists" who charged that their children were being "terrorized" into attending religious classes. The paper noted that the Party's lack of tolerance in the past had only increased the strength of religious feeling in Poland, and it insisted that Communists must prove the superiority of "materialism" in a free contest of ideas with believers. Education and propaganda, *Trybuna Ludu* predicted, would eventually win over "the religious illusion."

Subsequent statements in the Party press later in March indicated that manifestations of "intolerance" were receding, thanks to the tactful behavior of state authorities and teachers and to the intervention of Church authorities. A number of articles attempted to explain the government's new policy toward the Church. It was stated that Gomułka's aim was to prevent the division of the nation on matters of faith and to rally all patriotic forces round the difficult "October" tasks. The government would endeavor to give satisfaction to the religious needs of the faithful, observe the principles of tolerance, and prevent religious strife.

Despite occasional friction, relations between the government and the Church continued to be marked by a spirit of cooperation. A number of priests, nuns, and bishops, among them Bishop Kaczmarek, were rehabilitated and permitted to resume their normal duties. The government approved plans for the construction of a new church at Lodz, which would resemble St. Peter's Basilica in Rome and hold 5,000 people. It also authorized the erection of the first Roman Catholic church at Nowa Huta, Poland's largest steel city. Nowa Huta had been built according to Russian specifications to serve not only as a steel center but also as a Communist stronghold to counter the influence of neighboring Cracow, traditionally a leading center of Polish Catholicism. When originally planned, the city was never to have a church.

Relations with the Vatican represented an important unsettled problem facing the Gomułka government. When still under confinement, Cardinal Wyszyński had broken Vatican rules to confirm the government's appointments of vicars for dioceses in the western territories, a move that enhanced his prestige at home. It had been the Vatican's policy, however, not to make such appointments until a peace treaty was signed. A desire to move toward a settlement may have been indicated in December 1956 when the Vatican appointed five Polish bishops for the formerly German territories, at Wroclaw, Opole, Olsztyn, Gorzow, and Gdansk. The appointments suggested at least *de facto* recognition of Polish control in this area, but not necessarily formal acceptance of the postwar frontiers.

On May 8, 1957, Cardinal Wyszyński arrived in Rome to pay a long-deferred visit to Pope Pius XII. The Polish Primate received from the Pope the red hat of a Cardinal of the Roman Catholic Church on May 18—a belated sequel to the Pope's second consistory in January 1953 when Wyszyński was elevated to Cardinal. Wyszyński had not attended the consistory for fear that Polish authorities might prevent his return to Poland.

The outcome of the Cardinal's visit to Rome has been a matter of considerable and conflicting speculation among western observers. Some writers have noted that the Pope received Wyszyński with signs of special esteem and affection, and expressed paternal confidence in the fate of Poland, and that the Pontiff and his top aides greatly admire his piety, courage, and skill. Others have stressed the fact that, in contrast to the solemn public consistories of January 1953, the Pontiff conferred the hat on Cardinal Wyszyński in an austere and private ceremony, and have insisted that the Vatican was firmly opposed to a general collaboration between the Church and the Communist government in Poland which might set precedents for other states in the Soviet orbit. Some analysts have suggested that Polish religious leaders are disappointed in the degree of understanding and sympathy found in the Vatican for the unusual position of the Church in Poland. Whatever the facts behind these commentaries, the Polish hierarchy, the goverment in Poland, and the Vatican are likely to face each other in uneasy relationship for a considerable time to come.

Religious Minorities

Less than 5 percent of the population within the present boundaries of Poland adheres to faiths other than Roman Catholicism. In an attempt to counterbalance the influence of the Roman Catholic Church, the postwar regime sometimes sought the cooperation of non-Catholics against the Catholics, but this propaganda tactic proved ineffective and was never tried on a large scale.

Poland's eastern territories had embraced a large number of members of the Russian Orthodox Church, most of them Belorussians or Ukrainians. After Poland's loss of this area, the Orthodox in Poland numbered no more than 100,000. Uniates who follow the Greek Catholic rite (mostly Ukrainians) also number about 100,000.

Protestant denominations of all kinds included approximately 330,000 members in 1956; the largest part of these were Lutherans. Protestant sects are found mainly in Warsaw, the region of Mazury, and in Silesia. They were accorded favorable treatment after World War II, but state supervision was stricter after 1951.

The 30,000 to 70,000 Jews in Poland today are located chiefly in the cities of Lodz, Warsaw, Wroclaw, and Walbrzych. All Jewish denominational schools were closed after World War II, and only in the larger Jewish centers were Jewish pupils permitted to attend extracurricular instruction in Yiddish. Over the centuries Jews in Poland have suffered varying degrees of persecution because of their faith, but the roots of anti-Semitism, particularly today, go beyond mere religious differences (see chap. 4).

The Karaites, a small Jewish sect, are recognized by the regime as a separate religious denomination. Their number is not known (see chap. 4).

An unknown number of Moslems, the majority of them farmers, live in Bialystok Province and around Gdansk and Warsaw. A Warsaw Moslem Religious Union has supervisory powers over the Moslem communities, which have received financial support from the state for the repair and conservation of mosques.

There are in Poland, finally, a very small number of "National Catholics," who do not acknowledge the authority of the Vatican.

DYNAMICS OF POLITICAL BEHAVIOR

MEMBERS OF A SMALL GROUP OF POLISH COMMUNISTS PLACED in power in Lublin by the Soviet Union during the final period of World War II have since then been the directing force in Polish political life. At first depending for power on the presence of the Red Army, they offered a program appealing to Polish nationalism, but from 1944 to 1948 they sought to control all aspects of life in Poland and to secure a complete monopoly of political and intellectual expression. By 1948 they felt sufficiently sure of their power to try to impose, with little regard for Polish conditions or traditions, the Soviet model for "building socialism," but the attempt met a serious obstacle in the increased popular awareness of politics that had developed slowly during the interwar period and had been given impetus during World War II.

The Sovietization program conflicted with the traditional nationalism, Roman Catholicism, and deep-seated anti-Russian attitude of the Polish people. Eventually the effort to lead Poland down the "Soviet road to socialism" produced an economic and political crisis; the workers went out into the streets in June 1956 demanding "Bread and Freedom," in full support of the intellectuals who were struggling for a reassertion of Polish identity and for a national program allowing free political expression.

At the October 1956 Plenum of the Central Committee of the Polish United Workers' Party (Polska Zjednoczona Partia Robotnicza—PZPR) some of the demands of the people were met by the return to power of the Party group led by Władysław Gomułka, who from 1944 to 1948 had been the exponent of a specifically "Polish road to socialism." Since his return Gomułka has maintained a degree of independence of Soviet leadership, has refrained from using extreme coercive measures, and has based his control largely on the popular support he won during the October days.

At that time he made clear that the "new era" had definite limitations. Although a "good Pole," he remained a Communist, and the demands of political realism, as represented by the necessary link with the Soviet Union, had been underscored by the fate of the Hungarian workers and intellectuals. He explained the framework within which his government would attempt to hold the Polish nation: the "directing role" of the PZPR was to be unchallenged; the dedication of all elements of the nation to the "building of socialism" was to be maintained; and the basic international orientation of Poland as a member of the "international camp of socialism" and a participant in the Soviet Union's east European defense organization was to be continued. So long as the Poles remained within the established framework they would be allowed to criticize and the Party, in making policy, would be responsive to their needs.

Gomułka faced the problem of maintaining discipline in a country where lack of discipline, especially political discipline, has been the rule. A program of "building socialism" adapted to Polish needs and experiences has replaced the attempted imposition of the Soviet experience and patterns. A *rapprochement* with the Roman Catholic Church has been achieved; in return for guarantees of freedom from government and Party interference in its internal affairs, the Church has supported Gomułka's attempt to maintain popular discipline as an alternative to the probable imposition of order by the Soviet army. A new basis for Polish-Soviet relations has been worked out; the Soviet Union is to deal with Poland more as a sovereign, independent state than as a subordinate political unit. The Soviet commander of the Polish Army has been removed, and limitations have been placed on the Soviet troops stationed within Polish boundaries. Poland has begun to pursue a more independent role in foreign relations. Cultural, economic, and political contacts with the West have been re-established on a scale unprecedented for a member of the Communist bloc.

Gomułka's domestic program, as outlined in October 1956, included greater popular participation in government, workers' participation in management, and greater freedom of expression for all segments of the population. Nevertheless, the Polish people have remained restive, and the problem of maintaining discipline and public order has become increasingly acute. Furthermore, Gomułka's major weapon of political control, the Party apparatus, suffered severely from the shift to the "Polish road," and a major bloc of opposition to the government appears to be centered within the Party itself.

These difficulties have been compounded by the problem of preventing Poland from becoming a second Hungary. In an effort to achieve greater internal discipline and to strengthen its authority, the government has limited the concessions, both economic and political, which most Poles felt would be achieved through Gomułka's return. The feeling that the government has "retreated from October" has weakened the popular support on which it calls. Given the failure of the repressive methods of the past, a return to Soviet discipline would at best serve as a temporary solution and risk a second and more violent Poznan—and with it, the entry of the Soviet army. Thus the government finds only a severely limited area of political maneuver open to it.

Popular Political Attitudes

The touchstones for popular political issues from the time of the partitions down to the contemporary period have been nationalism, Roman Catholicism, and the general anti-Russian and anti-German attitude of the Polish people. Fed for more than a century by the writings of Poles in exile, Polish nationalism was a source of unity but could not serve as a guide to practical political life. It ceased to serve as a widely unifying force when independence was achieved in 1918; in the interwar period all political parties except the Communists firmly embraced the national cause, but wide areas of agreement on any other question were nonexistent. Not until the struggle for survival against the German's planned extermination campaign did nationalism again serve as a force counteracting the divisive tendencies in Polish political life. After World War II nationalism became fused with the anti-Russian and anti-Soviet sentiment of the bulk of the populace and contributed to the pressures from within the Party and among the population that made possible the return to a "Polish road to socialism" in October 1956.

Roman Catholicism has political significance because of the close identification of the Church with Polish nationalism during the period of partition and during the struggle against the Germans in World War II. The Church was the strongest unifying force in the three areas of partitioned Poland—Russian, Prussian, and Austrian. The general denationalization campaigns waged by the Protestant Prussians and the Orthodox Russians firmly planted in the popular mind the association of Catholicism with Polish nationality. In the pre-World War I struggle for independence the clergy provided leadership at the local level. During the interwar period the Church's influence declined among workers and peasants, who began to identify it with the middle and upper classes. But during World War II the Church shared in the whole people's suffering under German persecution, and again provided leadership and assistance in the struggle for national survival and liberation. At present the Church accepts "coexistence" with the government, but only so long as the government continues to respect its autonomy and to fight for Poland's national and international freedom.

Out of Poland's long history of direct contact with both Imperial Russia and the Soviet Union has developed a general anti-Russian and anti-Soviet feeling. The Poles have always tended to feel themselves culturally superior to the Russians and to consider their country the outpost of western culture against eastern forays. Soon after Poland regained independence, following World War I, a Soviet army reached the gates of Warsaw. Later, the knowledge of what went on in Russia during its period of forced collectivization was not calculated to win sympathy for the Soviet regime. And for the Poles, the Molotov-Ribbentrop pact of 1939 (see chap. 10), under which Russia occupied the eastern areas of Poland, was the preface to the German attack from the west. The experience of Poles of all classes in the Soviet-occupied areas, and especially of those who were deported to the interior of the USSR and were thus under direct Soviet jurisdiction, increased anti-Soviet feeling.

The anti-Russian feeling was tempered for a time because of the extreme brutality of the German occupation, during which the upper classes especially were the subject of the Germans' deliberate policy of mass extermination. Thousands died in concentration and forced labor camps. The bulk of the population was subjected to a policy of slow starvation. In the immediate postwar period the Communists skillfully exploited the fear and horror of Germany, but as the postwar government consolidated its political power hatred of Russia revived.

The capstone to the anti-Russian and anti-Soviet feeling, characterized as a "complex" by the present leadership of Poland, was the period from 1948 to 1956 when the attempt was made to force Poland onto the Soviet path of "building socialism." Today, the persistence of anti-Russian and anti-Soviet "complexes" constitutes a major threat to the preservation of the Polish-Soviet alliance, and is kept in check largely by the fear of German resurgence.

Closely related to the traditional issues of Polish politics are the political characteristics of the various Polish social strata. During the interwar period the politically conscious elements of the Polish working class aligned themselves with the Polish Socialist Party (Polska Partia Socjalistyczna—PPS), which had rejected internationalism in favor of a program based upon the primacy of Polish national interest. In October 1956 the support given to the exponents of the "Polish road" by the workers indicated clearly that this primacy of national feeling had not been eradicated even under the pressures of more than eight years of Soviet repression and "re-education."

The present political consciousness of the peasants is largely a result of World War II. Peasant insularity—the distrust of the urban populace and its behavior, values, and aims—was dealt a crushing blow by the German extermination campaign, transfers of population, the mingling of refugees from the towns with the peasantry, and the participation of peasant detachments in the underground struggle. The widespread peasant resistance to forced collectivization and Communist indoctrination reflects the continuing political awareness of the peasantry.

Leadership for the peasant and working-class political movements had come from the intelligentsia group in both partitioned and interwar Poland (see chap. 20). Most members of the intelligentsia, however, tended to identify themselves with the political Right. Their traditions and standards had been taken from the old landed nobility, whose unique position in Polish society had made them an almost independent political force. As the bearers of Poland's cultural heritage, the intelligentsia constituted a group which felt itself to be the guardian of the Polish way of life, a feeling reinforced by their unchallenged dominance in the government administrative apparatus, the officer corps of the army, the educational system, the organs of mass communications, and in almost all political parties, including the Communist.

The ferment which preceded the reversal in October 1956 of the attempted Sovietization of Poland was created by the intellectuals, both within and without the Party. The present "Polish" leadership of the PZPR has continued to make concessions to the intellectuals, concessions limited only by the framework imposed by the Gomułka faction.

The Interwar Period

Polish interwar political life was characterized by a profusion of political groupings. The achievement of independence had removed nationalism as a basis for joint action. All groups, with the exception of those involved in the then insignificant Communist movement, put. forward platforms that stressed nationalism, but in all other areas and on all other issues it was never possible to achieve agreement among a sufficiently large number among the many factions to support a government.

Most of the political parties fell into fairly well-defined class groupings, but personal considerations rather than principles determined alignments on specific issues. The extreme Right was composed of the industrialists and the few remaining large landowners organized in the Conservative Party. Numerically small, the membership of the party helped to provide the support needed by the post-1926 government. The major political force of the Right was the National Democratic Party—more a coalition of a number of cliques than a party. It dominated the first modern Polish legislature (1919–21) and was responsible for selecting the French Constitution of 1875, with its weak executive, as the model for the Polish Constitution of 1921 (see chap. 7). Organized before independence by exiles, it tended, as a by-product of its extreme anti-Prussianism, to be pro-Russian. Especially strong in the former Prussian areas, it received the support of almost the entire middle strata as well as the bulk of the intelligentsia. Its appeal was socially conservative (opposing even moderate land reform), clerical, and extremely nationalistic, including a "Poland for the Poles" type of appeal with strong anti-Semitic and anti-Ukrainian sentiments. After the 1926 coup many of its supporters, as well as some of its ablest leaders, went over to the "nonparty bloc" supporting Józef Piłsudski and his successors.

The Peasant Party (*Piast*) of Wincenty Witos is generally accorded the place of political Center in interwar Poland, largely as a result of its movement from an alliance with the National Democrats to one with the Socialists and the Left (Thugutt) Peasant group. Organized in the Austrian portion of partitioned Poland, it not only had sent delegates to the Austrian parliament but had developed a strong organization which formed the bulk of the peasant movement in interwar Poland. Except for its land reform program, it was strongly conservative and nationalistic, and on many issues it worked with the National Democrats despite their opposition to land reform.

In 1931 the Piast Party merged with the peasant movement which had been led by Stanisław Thugutt in the former Russian area. With a social program far more radical than that of the Piast and taking an anticlerical stand, Thugutt's party had tended to ally itself with the Socialists. In general, however, the programs of the Polish peasant parties tended to be vague as soon as they moved away from the basic issues of land reform and questions of direct interest to the peasant. The Piast, especially, remained suspicious of the Left.

The Polish Socialist Party, organized in 1893 in Paris, was the major Left element on the interwar Polish scene. Strongly nationalistic, its main strength came from the trade union movement and a small segment of the intelligentsia. The basic economic demands of the Socialists were largely met in the labor legislation of the early years of independence (see chap. 12). The major weakness of the Polish Socialist Party and of worker influence in politics was the relative numerical weakness of the workers (trade union membership in 1939 was only 1.6 million) in the face of the mass of peasants under largely conservative leadership and an intelligentisa which tended to identify itself with the parties of the Right. Further, the Socialist Party was unable to mobilize the workers on purely political issues during periods of economic well-being and was thus prevented from taking effective action in the struggle to restore the constitutional system after 1926.

A small and relatively insignificant Communist Party existed in interwar Poland—underground after 1919—until officially dissolved in 1938 by the Comintern. Founded in 1895 as the Social Democracy of the Kingdom of Lithuania and Poland (Social-Demokracja Królestwa Polskiego i Litwy—SDKPiL), it merged in 1918 with the Left faction of the Polish Socialist Party and took the name Communist Workers' Party (Komunistyczna Partia Robotnicza Polski —KPRP). In 1925 it changed its name to Communist Party of Poland (Komunistyczna Partia Polski—KPP).

Pursuing a policy which opposed Polish independence, it at no time gained the support of any appreciable segment of either the working class or the poorer peasantry of interwar Poland. Before being forced underground in 1919 it did elect two delegates to the first legislature, and under the increasing economic distress of the mid-1930's the workers and the peasant proletarians began moving left faster than their own leadership. But the party was greatly weakened by penetration by agents of the Polish police and by the decimation of its leadership during the Soviet purges of the 1930's under charges of "Trotskiism" and "Luxemburgism." The Comintern delivered the death blow with its 1938 dissolution order.

The first *Sejm* of the interwar period (1919–21) was marked by deep divisions among the political groups represented, and the Constitution of 1921 represented a compromise (see chap. 7). The demands of the Right were reflected primarily in the bicameral legislature and the provisions relating to private property. The forces of the Left were able to secure provisions protecting labor, but little else. The Constitution was ratified, over the opposition of the Socialists and the Thugutt peasant group, by an alliance of the parties of the Right with the conservative peasant party, the Piast of Wincenty Witos. The regime established by the Constitution placed the preponderance of power in the lower house of the legislature, which was designated the *Sejm,* the name formerly applied to the whole of Polish assemblies, and made the Cabinet responsible, collectively and individually, to it.

The 1921 elections, the first under the new Constitution, resulted in a multiplicity of parties represented in the *Sejm*. The expansion of the borders of Poland beyond the Curzon Line in the east had brought a large number of Ukrainians and Belorussians within the borders of the state, and the successful military campaign against the Lithuanians in 1920 led to the inclusion of still more non-Poles. Within the Polish state, the Belorussians, Ukrainians, and Lithuanians of the borderlands and the Germans and Jews scattered throughout the country constituted approximately one third of the population. Never integrated into the life of the nation, the minorities served as a divisive factor among the Polish political groups. In the first constitutional *Sejm* the minority parties held the balance of power.

The inability of any one political group to control a majority, as well as the inability of many of the leaders to rise above personal antagonism, prevented the establishment of a stable Cabinet. Governments rose and fell; none was able to meet the demands of the economic and international crises which afflicted the nation. The squabbling of politicians in a *Sejm* which could not be dissolved without its own consent produced a general disillusionment with the parliamentary process. The general political apathy of the peasantry concerning anything but the question of land reform allowed the leadership of the major peasant party, the Piast, to pursue personal ends and struggles. The Right, the largest group in the *Sejm,* had adopted a general policy of "Poland for the Poles" which antagonized the minority representatives. The Socialists abjured the national issue in regard to the minorities but were too weak numerically to form a government. The minority parties, ranging from extreme conservative to extreme radical, especially reflected the fractionalism of the Poles. Fiscal policies which the Right supported were opposed by the Left, and inflation and instability continued unchecked. The opposition of the Right successfully prevented any major land reform, and the peasant parties fluctuated between support of the Right coalition and joint opposition to it with the Socialists, at the discretion of their leaders and irrespective of issues.

Throughout this period changes in the views of the electorate remained difficult to assess. The members of the *Sejm,* despite their inability to produce a stable government, refused to resort to the polls. It was only after the coup of Józef Piłsudski in 1926, the political "death blow" to the constitutional era, that elections were held.

Marching into Warsaw as the hero of the nation, Piłsudski received the endorsement of both the Socialist Party and the Communist Party; the Right, which had feared and hated Piłsudski since 1918, could not offer effective resistance to the workers and the army.

Almost immediately Piłsudski set about developing a base for his regime among the elements of the upper and middle classes. Borrowing a sprinkling of social ideas from Mussolini, he attempted to create a national movement which would replace the "sterile, jabbering howling" of parliamentarism, but he was unable to win a broad basis of support. His efforts to win over the most conservative elements and his introduction of restrictions on the press quickly disillusioned his supporters on the Left. The Socialists joined with the Peasant Party of Wincenty Witos in opposition and began a fruitless attempt to preserve the parliamentary system.

The regime presented its "nonparty bloc" (Bezpartyjny Blok Współpracy z Rządem—BBWR) at the polls in 1928 and captured almost a third of the seats in the *Sejm*. The gains were made at the expense of the parties of the Right, as the BBWR became the rallying point of the upper and middle classes. The coalition of Socialists and the Peasant Party also increased its representation.

Control of 135 seats out of 444 by the BBWR was insufficient to rule the *Sejm*, and not enough support could be rallied to amend the Constitution so as to strengthen the executive, a need expressed even by the peasant leader Witos. Extra-constitutional government was continued.

The improvement in Poland's economic situation following Piłsudski's assumption of power (largely the result of the strikes in England which allowed Poland to capture the European coal market) strengthened the regime's self-confidence. In 1930 the country again went to the polls, and it became evident that the time of free elections in Poland had passed: intimidation of voters, the arrest of opposition leaders, and open violence marked the day. The result was a majority for the regime's "nonparty bloc." The magnitude of the victory indicated, however, that the mass of the electorate had responded to the relatively "good times" rather than to the political appeals of various factions. But in spite of the regime's majority in the *Sejm*, the constitutional amendment was still not put through.

In 1935, by means of a questionable parliamentary maneuver, the regime was finally able to promulgate a new Constitution which strengthened the executive, making it responsible only to "God and history" (see chap. 7). Under the accompanying restrictive elective law, the regime used the polls for the third time and secured, in the face of a call by the opposition parties to boycott the election, a one-party *Sejm*. In proportion to the number of eligible voters, the vote was only 25 percent less than that cast in 1930.

The opposition political parties had been defeated by voters apathetic to issues and still disillusioned by the behavior of the politicians in the 1921–26 period. The attempts of the Socialist Party to call political strikes met with little success. Some opposition to the regime was expressed by workers and peasants, but it was based more on economic distress than political dissatisfaction.

In 1939 the response of the Poles to the German attack was a return to unity under the banner of Polish nationalism. Political, social, and regional differences were submerged in the struggle for national survival. The occupation of the eastern areas of Poland by the Soviet Union at the time of the German attack intensified the general anti-Russian feeling, but it was overshadowed by the hatred of Germans burned into all segments of the population by the Nazi policy of deliberate extermination.

The Postwar Period

The political changes produced in Poland by World War II were of major significance. The shift in boundaries eliminated the bulk of the minorities of the eastern areas, primarily Belorussians, Ukrainians, and Lithuanians, and German genocide had reduced the 3.5 million Jews of interwar Poland to less than 70,000. The German minority had either retreated with Hitler's armies or been driven out. The postwar Polish state was almost completely Polish and Roman Catholic. The acquisition of the western territories, lands which had not been Polish for over five hundred years, met with the approval of Poles of all political views and social backgrounds. The position of the Soviet Union as the only power pledged to defend the Polish western gains, in fact the only major state to recognize the Polish territorial position as definitive, made it obvious to all Poles that Soviet support of any Polish government was a necessity. The demonstration of Soviet military might and the memories of the German occupation made it equally obvious that no government antipathetic to the Soviet Union could exist in Poland. Acceptance of this new pattern of relations with the Soviet Union created a conflict with the traditional Polish attitude toward the Russians. A deepening and growing political awareness among all segments of the population was met by the Communist attempt to secure a monopoly of power.

The period since the end of World War II has been marked by three major political periods. The first, from 1945 to 1948, saw the consolidation of Communist control over all aspects of life—social, intellectual, economic, as well as political—through a program which linked "socialism" to nationalism. The second period, running from 1948 to 1956, was marked by the abandonment of the "national" policies of the period of consolidation, and the open attempt to impose Soviet methods and patterns. The mounting economic and intellectual crisis which resulted from the failure of Soviet methods during this period reached its climax in the rising of Poznan workers in July 1956. The return of Władysław Gomułka in October as First Secretary of the Party inaugurated the third, and present, period of Poland's experience as a People's Democracy.

Throughout these three periods the goal of Poland's leaders—to build socialism as a transitional stage to communism—has remained constant, the periods being differentiated only by changes in the means adopted. The relationship of Poland to the Soviet Union and of the PZPR to the USSR's Communist Party has been an important consideration in the choice of methods, but the determining factor has been success or failure, which means that the Party has had to take into account popular non-Party reactions as well as intra-Party differences.

CONSOLIDATION OF POWER

In the first period the Communist-sponsored Lublin Committee (see chap. 2) was forced to deal with a situation largely created by the decisions of the major Allied powers. The Yalta agreement of February 1945 called for the inclusion in the provisional Polish government of representatives of the Polish exile groups. This introduction of a non-Communist element into the government delayed the consolidation of Communist control over Polish political life because it forced the regime to take account of interwar political forces it had attempted to eliminate by basing itself on the Constitution of 1921 (see chap. 7).

The Yalta provision calling for free and unfettered elections made it necessary for the Communists to go through the motions of democratic processes—although they were in complete possession of the army, police, and media of mass communication—while trying to eliminate all opposition. They scheduled both a national referendum on the "basic policies" of the regime and a nationwide election of delegates to the Polish legislature, theoretically restored to its position of dominance in the Polish state structure. The referendum held on June 30, 1946, posed three questions to the electorate:

1. Are you in favor of the abolition of the Senate?
2. Are you for making permanent, through the future constitution, the economic system instituted by the land reform and nationalization of the basic industries with maintenance of the rights of private enterprise?
3. Are you for the Polish western frontiers as fixed on the Baltic and on the Oder and Neisse?

All three questions were highly loaded in the political context of postwar Poland. The issue of an upper house had been fought bitterly at the time of the adoption of the Constitution of 1921. Both the Socialists and the Left-wing peasant group had opposed it. With the elimination of the groups that had written the Senate into the Constitution, no important body of opinion favored retaining it in the postwar period. To the second question no serious opposition could be expected. State ownership of industrial establishments had been a feature of interwar Poland (see chap. 15). Neither workers nor peasants were opposed to the principle, and the magnitude of the task of reconstruction made socialization of the means of production seem necessary. The third question directly involved the key issues of Polish nationalism and the retention of the former German lands; on these, alone of present-day issues, all Poles, from Communists to monarchists, are united.

Stanisław Mikołajczyk, former premier of the London government-in-exile who had returned to Poland in 1945 and had openly opposed the Communist regime, decided to use the referendum as a test of strength. He called upon his supporters to vote "no" on the question of abolishing the Senate, despite the fact that he personally favored abolition and that his peasant party had traditionally stood in opposition to an upper house.

The regime, which had asked for a "yes" vote on all three questions, emerged victorious. Mikołajczyk charged that the returns had been falsified and that an overwhelming majority of the electorate had voted "no" on the question of abolishing the Senate, and therefore in support of him and his party. Apparently encouraged by the results of the referendum, the regime scheduled the nationwide elections for the *Sejm* to be held in January 1947.

The second condition laid down at Yalta, the holding of "free and unfettered elections," included the proviso that all democratic and anti-Nazi parties should be eligible to participate. The determination of which parties were "democratic" and truly "anti-Nazi" was left to the Communist regime.

Six political parties were recognized for the campaign. While several of them bore little relation to the interwar parties, the names remained the same. The voters in the 1947 election were presented with a government "Democratic Bloc" which included a single list of candidates representing the (Communist) Polish Workers' Party (Polska Partia Robotnicza—PPR), the Polish Socialist Party (Polska Partia Socjalistyczna—PPS), the Peasant Party (Stronnictwo Ludowe—SL), and the Democratic Party (Stronnictwo Demokratyczne—SD). In addition, a "collaborating" party, the Work Party

(Stronnictwo Pracy—SP), an interwar party with an artisan base, entered the campaign. The only opposition party permitted was Mikołajczyk's Polish Peasant Party (Polskie Stronnictwo Ludowe—PSL), organized in 1945. To increase the confusion resulting from the existence of two peasant parties—Mikołajczyk's PSL and the SL of the "Democratic Bloc"—a proregime splinter PSL list was also entered in the campaign. An attempt to enter an independent Socialist list was blocked by the government-controlled electoral boards.

The regime used all of the means at its disposal to insure the victory of the "Democratic Bloc." The campaign was later described during the first debate in the new *Sejm* in the speech of the 67-year-old Socialist leader Zygmunt Żuławski, former secretary general of the Polish Trade Union Congress and chairman of the Supreme Council of the PPS. Żuławski, after attempting to work with the regime, had left the PPS in November 1946 with a number of supporters and sought to form a joint opposition list with Mikołajczyk. He was the only independent Socialist elected to the *Sejm*.

> What I saw . . . surpassed all my . . . fears. It was not a free election, it was not an election at all, but organized violence over the the electorate and his conscience. . . .
> I shall quote only a few examples which I witnessed myself. In Kraków thousands and thousands of people were struck off the electoral lists under the pretext that they had collaborated with the Germans or with the "underground.". . .
> . . . the electoral agent covering my list and my comrades who stood as candidates with me were arrested. . . .
> . . . I was not allowed to publish even one single electoral appeal, and the printing house, in breach of an agreement, stopped printing the Polish Peasant Party weekly *Piast* which had cooperated with me. . . .

The official results of the election gave the "Democratic Bloc" 382 seats out of a total of 444. The distribution of seats among the parties of the government Bloc according to a pre-election arrangement gave the PPR (Communist) 119; the PPS 119; the SL 106; and the SD 38. Of the non-Bloc "allies," the Work Party (SP) received 17 and the splinter PSL 14, for a total of 413 government seats to 28 for the opposition—27 to Mikołajczyk's PSL and 1 to the independent Socialist, Żuławski. The remaining 3 seats went to non-Party Catholic supporters of the regime.

With the elections over and Mikołajczyk forced to flee the country, the Communists were free to consolidate their hold over the political parties. Despite the change in name in 1942 and the attempt to identify itself with the national cause, the Polish Workers' Party had not attracted the element it most desired—the workers. Although it had taken in over a million members by 1948, as compared to only 20,000 in 1944, it lacked a hard core of politically conscious workers and disciplined cadres.

The Polish Socialist Party also claimed to represent the working class; in a state based on an alliance of workers and peasants under the leadership of the working class, the continued existence of a party making such claims was not feasible to the PPR. In addition, the PPS, through its long association with the Polish workers and the trade union movement and its traditional emphasis on a national rather than international platform, represented a major source of personnel with the organizational and administrative experience that the PPR needed. Working through the leadership of the PPS, the PPR forced a purge of PPS members who were considered hostile to the regime or to a merger of the two parties. In December 1948 a "Fusion Congress" of the PPR and the PPS was held; out of it emerged the Polish United Workers' Party (Polska Zjednoczona Partia Robotnicza—PZPR) as the "directing force" in the Polish People's Republic.

Like the workers, the peasants were to have but one political party. In November 1949 the Peasant Party (SL) merged with remnants of Mikołajczyk's PSL group—which had approximately 600,000 members at the time of the merger—as the United Peasant Party (ZSL). The remaining political elements—non-Marxist intellectuals, professionals, white-collar workers, and the artisan members of the SP—were all merged with the Democratic Party (SD).

The auxiliary youth groups of the political parties had been merged in July 1948. Membership in the new youth group, the Union of Polish Youth (Związek Młodzieży Polskiej—ZMP), totaled 500,000 in February 1949, although the total 1947 membership of the four groups had been 840,000: Union of Youth for Struggle (affiliated with the PPR), 200,000; Youth Organization of the Society of Workers' Universities (PPS affiliate), 120,000; Union of Peasant Youth of the Republic of Poland (SL affiliate), 500,000; and the Union of Democratic Youth (SD affiliate), 20,000.

The organizing statute of the ZMP stated that it was to be a "mass, non-Party, independent, ideological-educational organization for young workers and students in both rural and urban areas." The statute of the PZPR stated, however, that "the Polish United Workers' Party directs the activities of the ZMP" and that "Party policy is the directive for ZMP organizations in all fields of their activity." The ZMP was to carry out indoctrination of the youth in the "spirit of socialism" and recruit Party members. The only avenue of admission to the Party for persons under the age of 20 was through the ZMP.

The ZMP was charged with ideological education of youth from the age of 15 through 25. Children within the 5 through 14 age group were organized into other Party auxiliaries. Those 9 through 14 years old were encouraged to join the Union of Polish Pioneers, officially described as the "substructure of the ZMP." The chief of the Pioneers was a member of the Central Board of the ZMP. Younger children, 5 through 8 years, could join the Braves—bearing a relationship to the Pioneers equivalent to that of the Cub Scouts to the Boy Scouts.

Political consolidation was carried out within an announced framework of Polish, rather than Soviet, patterns of "building socialism." During this period Gomułka repeatedly emphasized the differences between the Russian experiences and Polish conditions and needs. The dictatorship of the proletariat was declared unnecessary for Poland; collectivization of agriculture was a goal for the distant future which would come about as the result of a change in peasant attitudes through propaganda, rather than by force; and a relationship of mutual tolerance between the Church and the regime was fostered. The foundations for building socialism were to be laid peacefully, over a long period of time, and the means to be used were to be determined with due regard to the peculiarities of the Polish scene.

THE "SOVIET ROAD"

With the success of the Communist coup in Czechoslovakia in 1948, the inner belt of Communist-controlled states had been forged. Combined with the Soviet-Yugoslav split later in the same year, these events marked a turning point in the course of the People's Democracies. Within Poland, 1948 marked the end of the Communist use of nationalism as an element in the methods of control over Polish life.

Representatives of the "Polish road," especially those leaders associated with the wartime struggle within Poland, were purged. The Soviet model of the dictatorship of the proletariat was proclaimed and the Soviet apparatus of coercion and control introduced on a mass scale. In 1950 the new Six-Year Plan demanded enormous sacrifices to achieve accelerated industrial development. As a corollary of the Plan forced collectivization and a program of class warfare in the countryside were decreed. In 1952 an all-out attack on the Church was initiated (see chap. 5). "Socialist realism" in its Soviet form was imposed on artists, and Polish intellectuals were muzzled by the secret police and the Party's control of the media of mass communication. The Party apparatus, the "allied" parties, the Union of Polish Youth, the trade unions, the myriad of professional and social organizations were all harnessed by the Party leaders to serve as "transmission belts" from the ruling organs of the PZPR to the people of Poland. The Party apparatus grew into a shadow government with corresponding posts in the Party hierarchy for each major administrative post in the government.

The program was similar to those being carried out in the other People's Democracies of eastern Europe, but the regime, evidently fearful of a violent Polish reaction to a full-scale rapid Sovietization program, played it down in various ways. The purged Polish leaders, for example, were not brought to public trial, condemned, and executed, although the publicized charges leveled against them at the Party Plenums were no less serious than the charges placed against their fellow "national deviationists" in Hungary. The tempo of Sovietization was slow compared to that in the other satellites. Collectivization goals were extremely modest (see chap. 14) and work discipline was not strictly enforced.

Although the Sovietization program had been modified, the Poles reacted strongly against it. The workers, alienated from the Party and chafing under Soviet labor regulations, failed to meet production norms. The peasants, resentful and resisting pressure to collectivize, did not maintain grain deliveries. The intellectuals grew more and more restive under the yoke of "socialist realism." And everyone resented the lack of freedom to criticize openly, the constant feeling of being watched and spied upon, and, most importantly, the constant pressure to idolize everything Soviet at the expense of everything Polish.

Not unmindful of the breakdown of production and the tenor of popular feeling, the Polish Government took advantage of the general Soviet relaxation after the death of Stalin in 1953 and the denunciation and execution of Lavrenti Beria to dilute the Polish program even more. In November 1954 the Ministry of Public Security was broken up (see chap. 8) and its head, Stanisław Radkiewicz, removed from the Politburo. A purge of the police appears to have taken place at the same time, removing three "police" members of the Central Committee of the PZPR.

The restive Polish intellectuals, breaking through the weakened Party controls over publications, contributed to the general unrest which the economic failure had created among the workers. The effects of the denunciation of Stalin at the Twentieth Party Congress in the Soviet Union (February 1956) further weakened the position of the pro-Soviet leaders of the PZPR. For the mass of the people, and for many within the Party, the downgrading of Stalin was taken as a corroboration of their anti-Soviet, Polish position.

The crisis produced by the attempt to use Soviet means to "build socialism" with little regard for differences in Polish conditions erupted in June 1956 at Poznan during the annual international trade fair. The uprising of Poznan workers under the banner "Bread and Freedom" was immediately denounced by both Polish and Soviet leaders as the work of foreign agents and counterrevolutionary elements. The Polish leaders, however, although alienated from the masses of workers as well as from the population in general, soon recognized the true nature of the crisis and, in spite of Soviet continued insistence on the earlier interpretation, publicly admitted that the uprising had been spontaneous and of domestic origin.

In July, at the Seventh Plenum of the Central Committee of the PZPR, the Party leadership accepted responsibility for its failure. Dissolution of the shadow government of the Party was announced, and the stage was set for the re-emergence of the "national" leadership of the PZPR.

The leadership of the PZPR had never really been free from factionalism. Following World War II an alliance of undetermined stability was formed between those Polish Communists who had spent the bulk of the war years in the underground struggle in Poland and those who had spent them in the Soviet Union. The leader of the "Polish" faction, Władysław Gomułka, had risen within the underground Communist movement during the war; in the immediate postwar period he continued to serve as secretary-general of the PPR. The "Moscow" group, headed by Bolesław Bierut, shared power with the Polish faction until 1948, when a concerted drive was initiated against those leaders who had identified themselves with Polish rather than Soviet views on the "building of socialism." The purge continued through 1949 and created a split in the Party which reached down to the rank and file.

The struggle between the supporters and opponents of complete Soviet control in Polish life continued in covert form as long as Stalin was alive and became increasingly noticeable after his death. It burst out into the open after the Poznan uprising. Some of the leaders of the Polish faction were "rehabilitated" at the Seventh Plenum of the Central Committee of the PZPR in July. In October, at the Eighth Plenum, the struggle culminated in the return of the major leaders who had been denounced seven years before. Gomułka, Marian Spychalski, Zenon Kliszko, and others soon assumed positions of control within the Party and the government.

Their opponents, known as the "Natolin" faction, attempted to stage a coup, but apparently lacked sufficient support. Some leaders who previously had been identified with "Stalinist" policies—among them Edward Ochab and Prime Minister Cyrankiewicz—threw their support to Gomułka. The shifting of allegiances makes it impossible to identify the leading figures of the factions within the Party today.

Three major factions appear to have been vying for influence and power since Gomułka's return: the Stalinist Natolin group, often referred to as the "dogmatists"; the "revisionists," who favor greater liberalization and freedom than Gomułka has permitted; and the Gomułka supporters, who are trying to steer a middle course. The Natolin faction appears to possess strongly entrenched positions in the lower echelons of the Party apparatus, while the "revisionists" apparently draw much of their support from intellectuals both within and outside the Party. Infighting seems to continue at all levels of the Party, and a showdown may not be forced until the Third Congress of the PZPR.

RETURN TO THE "POLISH ROAD"

During the Eighth Plenum of the Central Committee of the PZPR, the depth of the political crisis was shown by the sudden arrival in Warsaw of the leaders of the Soviet party and state, Nikita Khrushchev and Nicolai Bulganin. The Polish Army was still commanded by the Polish-born Soviet Marshal, Konstantin Rokossovsky, and the disposition of the Soviet units stationed within Poland was unclear. As the new Polish Politburo, headed by Gomułka, met with the Soviet Leaders, the PZPR stood firm behind the new leadership. The workers of Warsaw remained under arms in their factories ready to fight any military force which might attempt to enter the city, and the police apparatus—the former guardian of the Soviet line—helped to prevent a bloody coup by the die-hard exponents of the Soviet model.

Gomułka and the Party leadership, including men like Edward Ochab who had headed the Central Committee before Gomułka's return to power, made their position clear to the Soviet Union, to the Polish people, and to the membership of PZPR. On the one hand, the goal of building socialism would not change; the Party would continue to play the leading role in directing the state and the nation; and, of primary importance to the Soviet Union, the Polish People's Republic would remain in the "international camp of socialism" and a member of the Soviet military organization in eastern Europe, the "Warsaw Pact." On the other hand, however, the means which the Party and the government had used to achieve the goal would change. The Party recognized that the old methods had failed. It proposed now to re-establish contact with the masses and to win the confidence of the workers.

The Party itself was in a far from satisfactory state. Factionalism had produced a paralysis of the upper echelons. Bureaucratization caused by the Party's "shadowing" of the state structure had also produced paralysis in the state administration and developed professional officeholders instead of cadres that could carry the Party's program to the people. Gomułka told the Eighth Plenum that "there should be a clear delineation of the roles of the Party apparatus and the state apparatus." At the Ninth Plenum, held in May 1957, he said it was equally necessary that factionalism within the Party should cease. He warned both the "dogmatists," who sought a return to the policies of the Soviet period, and the "revisionists," who wanted to go beyond the limits set by the government (even to the point of allowing western parliamentary democracy and opposition parties), that they would have to join him in supporting the Ninth Plenum program or leave the Party.

The most radical change in the Polish situation has been the redefinition of the relationship of Poland to the Soviet Union and of the PZPR to the Communist Party of the Soviet Union. The new basis, both political and economic, is the "sovereign equality" of the two states.

The effect of the return to the "Polish road" has been less satisfying to Poles in general than had been hoped in October 1956. The range within which freedom is tolerated has been greatly broadened but the limits may not be exceeded with impunity. Controls over newsprint and printing have been somewhat relaxed. Educational institutions are being freed from political direction and returned to academic control and standards. The collectivization campaign has been temporarily halted, most collective farms have been dissolved by the peasants, and any possibility of real collectivization of agriculture has again been moved far into the future. Wages have been raised and the government has promised to give greater attention to consumer needs in its economic planning.

The election of January 1957 tested the new alliance of the Church with the Gomułka government. Rejection of administrative manipulation and removal of the apparatus of direct and indirect intimidation that had been used in previous elections gave the Polish people the opportunity to cross out the names of the candidates selected by the government. The Church supported the government slate through personal appeals by the Primate, episcopal letters, and the activities of priests. The work of the Party at the local level and personal appeals by the leaders of the state also served, in the absence of the former controls over voting procedure, to keep the people in the path of moderation.

The issue in the election, however, was not the relative freedom of the electoral process; it was the question of national survival. In Gomułka's words, "to cross a Communist off the list is to cross Poland off the map." To date, the choice which the electorate was promised has shown itself to be an extremely limited one. Candidates are still chosen by inter-Party committees in which the PZPR plays the "leading role"; and the tendency in the by-elections held since the general election of January 1957 has been for the two candidates selected by the committee to be of the same political party (two PZPR members facing each other, or two ZSL members).

In addition to controlling the selection of candidates, the PZPR has forced the retention of the National Front on its "allied" parties, the ZSL and the SD, thus insuring continuance of the policy of presenting a single government list. The non-Communist parties are still prevented from entering candidates under their own colors.

The Interplay of Political Forces

Having abandoned Soviet methods of control, the government must now meet the demands of the people for means of effective expression. The auxiliary organizations, ranging from the League of Women (Liga Kobiet—LK) to the Association of Polish Lawyers (Zrzeszenie Prawników Polskich—ZPP), the "allied" parties, the United Peasant Party (Zjednoczone Stronnictwo Ludowe—ZSL) and Democratic Party (Stronnictwo Demokratyczne—SD), the Roman Catholic Church, and the youth organizations are all active participants in the contemporary political arena. The government's problem is how to keep these elements from going beyond the limits of the political framework announced by Gomułka, without alienating the population at large. The only means available to the government, barring a return to the Soviet means of coercion or dependence on the Soviet army, is the Party itself, working at all levels in these organizations.

THE POLISH UNITED WORKERS' PARTY (PZPR)

The PZPR is organized in pyramid form, with primary units of 3 to 100 persons in any work establishment or area constituting the base; the structure then ascends through local administrative units, provincial organizations, and finally to the Party Congress. Although the Party statute calls for a Congress to be held at least once every three years, only two sessions have been held: the "Fusion Congress" in December 1948, and a second in March 1954. The number of delegates to the Congresses is not fixed; at the 1954 session, there were 1,268 delegates on a representation basis of approximately 1 delegate for 100,000 members.

The primary function of the Party Congress is the adoption of Party statutes and the election of the Central Committee, which is supposed to direct the work of the Party between Congresses. The Central Committee is specifically charged with the establishment and direction of Party "institutions" and the supervision of the Party press through the appointment of editorial boards. In addition, it "guides and controls the activity of the Party members who occupy directing positions on the national level." The Central Committee (Plenum) is supposed to meet "not less than once every four months," but only nine Plenums are known to have been held between the Congress of December 1948 and that of March 1954. Most of its members hold full-time positions outside the Committee, and it appears that its functions are actually exercised by its organs, particularly the Political Bureau (Politburo) and the Secretariat.

Although technically elected by the Central Committee, the Politburo is the actual ruling body of the Party and the state. Formally charged with the direction of the Central Committee's activities between Plenums, it both makes policy and supervises its implementation. After the 1954 Party Congress the Politburo was composed of 13 full members and 2 alternates; after the October 1956 reorganization only 9 members were named. Closely related to the Politburo is the Secretariat, with 7 members, a full-time body with a salaried membership and staff, which is responsible for supervision of the day-to-day operations of the Party. The membership of the Secretariat interlocks with the membership of the Politburo; Gomułka, for example, is chairman of both.

The Secretariat has felt the effects of the October 1956 reorganization more than any other organ of the Party. The stated aim of realizing a "clear distinction between the Party apparatus and the Government apparatus," heralded at the Seventh Plenum (July 1956) and emphasized by Gomułka at the Eighth Plenum (October 1956), has resulted in a drastic reduction in the staff of the Secretariat and a curtailment of its functions. Formerly organized into 20 "sections," which included Heavy Industry, Municipal Administration, and Party History, the Secretariat appears now to have only four—Organization, Propaganda, Agriculture, and Industry. A final reorganization is to be made during the Third Congress of the PZPR.

Theoretically, intra-Party relations are conducted in accordance with the principle of "democratic centralism." Proposals are supposed to be discussed at all levels, from the primary unit up, with each group forwarding its recommendations to the next higher unit. During this process free and open discussion is encouraged. Once a final decision is handed down, whether by the Politburo in the name of the

Central Committee, the Central Committee itself, or a Party Congress, it becomes "law." All criticism must cease, and all Party members, regardless of their views, are obliged to work for the implementation of the decision without qualification.

In practice, the Gomułka regime has been faced with a nearly complete breakdown of Party discipline. The June explosion and the October reorganization wreaked havoc on its organization. According to Party leaders, the cadres were behaving like "offended virgins" and even openly criticizing policies adopted by the Central Committee. The problem of restoring discipline within the PZPR is complicated by the confusion which the abandonment of the Soviet methods, the model of half a decade, produced among Party activists. They were told that their earlier program had been wrong and dangerous, and, as abandonment of coercive measures became general, their positions of power evaporated. It was the local Party activist who felt the brunt, sometimes physically, of the first wave of extremism among the disaffected elements of the people.

As the alienation of the Party cadres developed, moreover, the need for their services increased. The Party's withdrawal from direct management of the state apparatus, the granting to the workers of a limited voice in the direction of production through the re-establishment of the workers' councils, the increasing role allotted to the provincial government apparatus created expanded problems of control for the government. Since the use of force was rejected, it became imperative for the cadres to be loyal to Gomułka or, ideally, susceptibile to the demands of "democratic centralism."

The need to restore discipline within the Party and to train new cadres is seen as matched only by the need to restore contacts with the masses. Since the October Plenum, leading government figures have been devoting a large amount of time to speaking before groups in factories and answering the workers' questions. In June 1957 the Central Committee of the PZPR took the unprecedented step of assigning members of the Politburo and Secretariat, the "full-time" employees of the Party, to primary Party units in and around Warsaw. Both Gomułka and Cyrankiewicz, for example—both Politburo members—have been assigned to units in Warsaw factories, and wide publicity has been given to their attendance and participation at meetings.

Although the formal requirements for membership in the PZPR are not rigorous—recommendation by two Party members of at least a year's standing, and a one-year period of "candidacy"—the number of members is small, about 4 percent of the population. (Party membership in Czechoslovakia is 9 percent of the population, in

Bulgaria 6 percent.) Since 1949 the working-class element in the Party has constantly been decreasing and the proportion of intelligentsia membership increasing (see Table 5) despite the repeated statements of the leadership that this trend must be reversed. The Party has also had a shortage of "activists," the dedicated zealots on whom the actual implementation of policy must, in the final analysis, rest. A committee on revision of the Party statute dealing with membership has been organized and is expected to report to the Third Congress in December 1957.

AUXILIARY ORGANIZATIONS

Many organizations have served useful functions as auxiliaries of the government in carrying out such immediate tasks as assisting with the problems of the western territories (Society for the Development of the Western Territories), as well as in long-range programs involving the shaping of attitudes (Society for Secular Schools). While it is difficult to gather detailed information concerning particular groups and their organization, membership, and leadership, some information is available about the effects of the return to the "Polish road." A recent report on the League of Women, which reported a membership of over two million in 1954, offers a good example of the effects of "October" on the auxiliary organizations. With an open statement that the League had been a "bureaucratic organization whose activities were limited to propaganda" during the Stalinist period, a new program of action was announced—a program described as allowing the League the opportunity of "fulfilling its proper functions." The heavy cuts in administrative personnel resulting from the "debureaucratization" affected women heavily; the League, in response to the problem of female unemployment, has been trying to help women find employment and has established a retraining program. In addition, it has established cooperative enterprises, opened cafés in Warsaw, and is at present planning to organize a catering service in open-air markets.

A partial listing of other auxiliary organizations indicates the scope of organized activity in Poland.

> Association of Polish Jurists
> Association of Polish Lawyers
> League of Soldiers' Friends
> Polish Atheists and Freethinkers Association
> Polish Committee of Peace Defenders
> Polish-Soviet Friendship Society
> Polish United Nations Association

THE ''ALLIED PARTIES''

The relationship of the "allied" political parties with the PZPR has undergone structural changes, but the basic nature of the relationship has changed only within the limits of the framework established by the government. Both the Democratic Party and the United Peasant Party must continue to recognize the "directing role" of the PZPR. But in place of the former method of controls exercised within the parties, affirmations of allegiance to the National Front have been exacted, none too willingly, from the executive organs of the two groups and a new control apparatus has been established— the Coordinating Committee—which gives the parties the appearance of "allies" rather than "subjects." Organized at all levels of the Party hierarchies—village, town, province—such committees have been formed of representatives of each of the three parties. Reports to date indicate that the PZPR representative assumes the chairmanship. The work of the committee is to "coordinate" the activities of the three parties in the implementation of the programs put forward by the government, thus insuring the full cooperation of the "allies" in building socialism.

Under the Soviet control pattern, the function of the allied parties was to transmit the directives of the government to their members. Decisions affecting agriculture, for example, were taken without even the gesture of consultation with the leaders of the ZSL. The allied parties will now serve to keep the PZPR leadership aware of local reactions, and, more importantly, they are to be consulted in the determination of policy relating to the interests of their membership.

With the exception of the ZSL, little is known of the political forces within the allied parties. The return to political life of amnestied political prisoners, especially former members of the Peasant Brigades (the World War II underground peasant military organization which worked with the forces controlled by the London government-in-exile), produced a crisis within the ZSL. The rehabilitated underground leaders are attempting to challenge the present ZSL leadership, and their influence appears to be growing, judging by repeated warnings of Gomułka that the worker-peasant alliance on which the government bases itself must at all costs be preserved. The goal of the returned leaders appears to be the withdrawal of the ZSL from the National Front and its transformation into a potential opposition party.

THE CHURCH

The Primate of Poland and Gomułka have recognized that they need one another in the present crisis. Both are conscious that public disorder could turn the country into another Hungary. Cardinal Wyszyński has called upon Poles to foreswear the heritage which taught them how to "die magnificently" and to learn to "work magnificently"; to rise to the need for the "greater heroism" demanded by Poland's present situation; "to live in toil, suffering, pain, and sacrifice for years." His support of Gomułka has been a crucial factor in holding the Poles to the path of moderation that Gomułka symbolizes.

A joint Church-State committee was formed in November 1956 to settle outstanding issues and outline the future course of relations. Jerzy Morawski, member of the Politburo of the PZPR, and Jerzy Sztachelski, former Minister of Health, met with the Secretary of the Episcopate (Bishop Choromański) and the Bishop of Lodz. On December 10 they announced the principles of a new agreement. The joint announcement declared that "the representatives of the Episcopate expressed full support for the work undertaken by the government aimed at the strengthening and development of People's Poland." In December, also, the Vatican announced the appointment of Polish bishops for the western territories. In return, the government agreed to permit voluntary religious instruction in the schools at state expense, with the material taught to be approved by both Church and school authorities, and to work out with the Church a new law on the matter of Church appointments (see chap. 5).

During the election of January 1957, with Gomułka's political future at stake, the Church marshaled its powerful influence behind the government. While Cardinal Wyszyński made no specific public pronouncements, the second ranking Catholic cleric, Bishop Choromański, issued a message, published shortly before the elections:

Catholic citizens . . . will have fulfilled their obligation of conscience by voting. The Catholic clergy must arrange services so that all believers can without difficulty fulfill both their religious and election obligations.

Throughout Poland the clergy took a prominent part in mobilizing the electorate. Bishops ostentatiously deposited their ballots without crossing out the names of any candidates. Parish priests led their entire congregations directly from the churches to the polling places.

The present policy of "coexistence" represents essentially a return to the agreement negotiated by Wyszyński with the government in April 1950 (see chap. 5), which the government subsequently violated. At that time the Church agreed to support the state in its claims to the western territories; to "be guided by the requirements of Polish policies of state," except that "in matters of faith, morality, and ecclesiastical jurisdiction the competent and supreme authority of the Church is the Pope"; "not to oppose the extension of the system of collective farms"; to "condemn activities against the state"; to "condemn and punish those of the clergy who might be guilty of participation in underground action against the regime and state"; and to "support all efforts for the consolidation of peace and to oppose warmongering." These obligations were assumed with the understanding that the government would "recognize the right of teaching religion in the schools"; that Catholic lay organizations would be permitted to function on a par with other organizations; that the Catholic press and Catholic publications were to enjoy the same rights as other publications; that the "public practice of religious forms . . . shall not be obstructed"; and that "monastic orders and congregations shall within the scope of their vocation and the binding laws enjoy freedom of activity."

The present relations between Church and state are not free from tension. The major outstanding issue for the Church remains that of education. Voluntary religious education continues to be obstructed by local authorities in some areas. It is known that Wyszyński would like to re-establish a system of parochial schools, but on this issue the government has remained adamant. The Church would also like to regain control over Caritas, the Catholic charitable organization which had been transformed into a state welfare agency (see chap. 5).

The journal of the PZPR Central Committee discussed the problem of Church-State relations in June 1957 from the point of view of the government. It expressed concern lest the Church become the center for a "regrouping of the forces hostile to socialism." The article welcomed the support of the Church but added, "Still, we cannot help but watch [carefully] the consolidation of our peculiar allies, who are at the same time our ideological opponents."

Both sides have the difficult task of drawing a satisfactory line between the "ideological struggle," proposed by the government and accepted by the Church, and the "political struggle," which each has abjured.

YOUTH GROUPS

The collapse of the Union of Polish Youth (ZMP) in the wake of the "October days" and the establishment of a number of youth groups with varying degrees of independence dealt the regime a heavy blow. The hope of the directors of "socialist construction" is the youth—those who must carry on the struggle and inherit the new "golden age."

The initial response of Polish youth to the October 1956 events was a return to the preconsolidation pattern of organizations. A youth group associated with the Democratic Party was re-established; the Union of Rural Youth reappeared and even a second peasant youth group, the "Wici." In response to the needs of the situation, a Union of Socialist Youth under PZPR auspices was established. The Democratic Party youth organization was quickly dissolved by its organizers after they were requested to do so by the police. The youths involved stated that there had been no threat of force associated with the request; they did complain, however, that the request for dissolution smacked of the Soviet era, but they have apparently made no attempt to reorganize or to make further public protest.

To fill the void in the "substructure" of organized Polish youth in the post-October chaos, the Polish Scout Union (Związek Harcerstwa Polskiego—ZHP) was reconstituted. The Supreme Scouting Council, the executive organ of the ZHP, adopted the organization statute at Warsaw on June 23, 1957. Declaring that the ZHP was an "independent, ideological, and educational mass organization rallying the youth for common work for People's Poland," it emphasized that "the Union works under the ideological leadership of the PZPR and educates the youth in the spirit of socialism." In line with the general return to the "Polish road," the statute states that "the Union draws its ideals from Polish cultural traditions and from the nation's struggle for freedom, independence, and progress." Although the results of the June "scouting census" have not become available, reports on Scout activities for the summer of 1957 stated that "more than 1,000 camps with over 47,000 Boy Scouts and Girl Guides will be organized." Camps for "Wolf Cubs" were also to be organized.

The Union of Rural Youth with a membership of more than 85,000 organized in approximately 4,700 local "circles," is the largest of the present youth organizations. The Fourth Provisional Plenum of the Central Board of the Union met in early June 1957. In addition to the members of the Board, the deputy chairman of the United Peasant Party (ZSL) and a member of the Central Committee of the PZPR participated. The chairman of the Board declared that it was "necessary to win over the rural youth to all forms of co-operativeness" and in a case of any "divergences" between richer and poorer peasants the Union "should always adopt a political stand toward it, helping the exploited." The representatives of the ZSL and PZPR found that "some activists" of the Rural Youth Union felt that the "right of both Parties [PZPR and ZSL] to interest themselves in the Union" was an "unavoidable evil." The PZPR participant assured the Central Board that the Union would have no difficulties in being organizationally independent, but that such independence did "not mean, of course, tendencies opposed to socialism."

While the regime appears to have achieved some success in confining the Rural Youth group within the limits it has set for popular participation in political affairs, it has not been as successful in regard to the Wici. This group apparently attracted the concerned attention of the regime and of the ZSL and Rural Youth Union, and, despite repeated demands that it merge with local Rural Youth Union units, it has, to date, refused to surrender its independent existence.

The post-October Union of Socialist Youth (Związek Młodzieży Socjalistycznej—ZMS), oriented toward the PZPR, has achieved a formal organizational status. Its Constitutional Congress in late April of 1957 adopted a statute and an "Ideological and Political Declaration." The statute declares that, while the ZMS "recognizes the ideological leadership of the Polish United Workers' Party," it is an "ideological-political, independent, vanguard organization of leading young workers, students, and working intelligentsia." Membership in the organization is open to all workers, students, and "working intelligentsia" between the ages of 17 and 30, upon written request. Admittance is to be decided by a simple majority of the local group in the presence of the candidate. The duties of a member require him to "subordinate himself to the resolutions of the authorities [the 'Assemblies' and executive organs] of the Union," but the statute declares that a member has the right, while carrying out the resolutions which have been adopted, "to retain and defend his own views." Disciplinary penalties, censure, and/or dismissal, for "infringing the statute, the ideological and basic principles, and resolutions of the authorities or [for] not realizing the program of the group" must be imposed in the presence of the member, who then has the right to appeal in writing to the "Collegiate Court of the ZMS within a period of 14 days." Any member dismissed or discharged from the Union has the right to apply for re-entry after six months.

Primary units of "group activity," composed of at least 5 members, may be created "in any work establishment, higher school, or institution." The creation of a primary unit, however, is subject to confirmation by the county, communal, or district committee. The "general assembly" of members of a unit appoints a committee of from 3 to 7 members, including a secretary. If the unit has fewer than 7 members, it appoints a secretary and a deputy-secretary, who "exercise leadership." The Council of Delegates of county, town, or district, elected by the member groups, is required to meet at least once every six months. The County Council elects a 5-man Auditing

Committee and a County Committee of from 15 to 35 members annually. The County Committee, in turn, appoints a Secretariat of from 5 to 9 persons from among its members, including a first and second secretary. The Committee is required to meet at least once every two months.

Each county, town, or district unit elects representatives to a Provincial Council of Delegates which must meet at least once a year. The Provincial Council elects a 5-man Auditing Committee, a Collegiate Court of from 5 to 7 members, and a Provincial Committee of from 35 to 51 members for a two-year term. The Provincial Committee elects from among its members a Secretariat of from 7 to 11 members, a first secretary, and 2 to 3 additional secretaries, as well as the heads of sections within the Secretariat. The Provincial Committee is required to meet at least once every three months.

At the apex of the pyramid is the National Council of ZMS Delegates, the "supreme authority of the Union." The delegates, elected in every county, town, and district, elect in turn a Central Auditing Committee of 15 members, a 7-man Central ZMS Court, and a Central Committee of from 69 to 93 members, all for three-year terms. The Central Committee, from among its membership, elects a Secretariat of from 11 to 15 persons, a first secretary, and from 3 to 5 secretaries from among the members of the Secretariat, as well as the heads of sections. The National Council is required to meet at least once every eighteen months and the Central Committee every four months.

A local Council of Delegates is responsible for adopting resolutions defining the direction of the activity of the Union in its locality, as well as making "an assessment of the activity of the organization, the Committees, Secretariat, and their members." The Committees direct the work and policy of the Union in their respective locality between sessions of the Councils. The Secretariat, serving as the executive organ, serves the same function in regard to the Committees between plenums. The decisions of superior authorities are binding on all lower echelons of the Union.

Elections to the Councils on all levels must be held by secret ballot "in the presence of at least two thirds of the elected delegates." In all Councils decisions are by simple majority of a quorum of 50 percent of the members. Every member of every authority is subject to recall, and "every political worker should be elected by an appropriate Committee."

The statute may be changed only by the National Council of Delegates through a two thirds majority of votes, "in the presence of at least two thirds of the members entitled to vote," and the Union may be dissolved only by a resolution of the National Council. The most interesting point in the statute, and a startling innovation, is the stricture that if the Councils of Delegates do not meet in the specified period of time, they lose their authority (Chapter IV, Article 14, Para. 2).

The "Ideological and Political Declaration of the Socialist Youth Union" demonstrated unequivocally the continuing reaction of the youth in Poland against the methods of the "Soviet road to socialism" and their dedication to the October spirit of popular participation. In the statute the ZMS leaders have attempted to guard against a return to arbitrary controls exercised from without at the top of the pyramid. In the Declaration they gave full expression to their feelings in regard to independence:

> Without disparaging the lasting achievements of the ZMP, we consider its model as false. We shall not consent to the role of passive executors, devoid of initiative, of the policy of the Party and of the authorities, we shall not allow our movement to dissolve into an ideological vacuum, we shall not permit our movement to suppress the creative research of the young people, we shall not desist from the principles of internal democracy. The struggle . . . to renovate the life of the country, to restore to socialist practice its humanistic essence . . . is and will remain our struggle.

The Declaration declares the ZMS to be the inheritor of the mantles not only of the interwar Communist and Left-Socialist youth organizations but also of the pre-1948 unified organizations of Socialist and Communist youth.

Continuing in the spirit that has characterized Polish popular thinking since October, the Socialist Youth demand a role in shaping their own future, a demand which assumes an importance as great as their actual role as the leaders of Polish life during the next decades.

> We want not only to interpret the policy of the Party and of the Government but also to have an influence on the shaping of this policy. Inflexible constructors of socialism and a number of future Party members among them will only then be able to grow out of the ranks of the ZMS if this organization can cooperate in working out the line of socialist construction.

LEGAL AND THEORETICAL BASE OF GOVERNMENT

THE PRESENT CONSTITUTION OF THE POLISH STATE, PROMUL-
gated in July 1952, is patterned directly upon the Constitution of
the USSR. In theory, it takes into account the specific features of the
Polish People's Republic and allows for democratic forms usually
associated with a government designed to carry out the will of the
people. In practice, these forms have been manipulated in terms of
ideological preconceptions which stress the absolute authority and
power of the Polish United Workers' Party (Polska Zjednoczona
Partia Robotnicza—PZPR).

For the Communists, the Constitution is an instrument to be used
in the struggle to accomplish the aims of the state, rather than a
"basic" document limiting governmental power in the interests of
individual liberty. It is designed, therefore, to meet three requirements: first, it describes the existing political state of affairs, the
present "relationship of the productive forces" within the state, and
the degree of progress thus far achieved in "socialist construction";
second, it indicates future lines of development; third, it explains
in detail the governmental forms through which the Communists
exercise their power, without, however, directly referring to the Party.

The Polish People's Republic is described in the Constitution as
a "People's Democracy," a state in transition from the "bourgeois
democracy" of the past to a Soviet type of "socialism." In order to
put into effect the "great ideals" of socialism, the government's task is
to work for the gradual elimination of "those classes of society which
live by exploiting the workers and peasants." State power formally is
vested in the "working people of town and country," who are to
elect, on the basis of "universal, equal, and direct suffrage by secret
ballot," representatives to a parliament traditionally called the *Sejm*.

The laws of the state supposedly express "the interests and the will of the working people."

In practice, however, the Party (PZPR) has acted as the "directing force" and policy-making center of the state, contending that it is the supreme representative of the interests of the masses. Until very recently the *Sejm* had done little more than rubber-stamp Party decisions and give ex post facto approval of government measures carrying them out. The Party has used the laws of the state as a weapon of control in the struggle to build a "new social system."

Communist constitutional practice has created resentment and bitterness among the better-educated strata of Polish society. The ideals of constitutionalism have long been a part of Poland's intellectual tradition, even though the country's experience with constitutional government has been limited and imperfect (see chap. 2), and many Poles hoped that return to a democratic system of government would be possible after World War II.

Under mounting popular pressure, the Party has since 1956 attempted to make the government function more in accord with the principles embodied in the Constitution of 1952. The *Sejm* is now allowed a somewhat greater scope for debate and activity. It is permitted to serve as a limited, popular check on policies as they are submitted by the Party through the government, and on their implementation. But no attempt has been made to give the *Sejm* power to make policy. The Party continues to interpret the interests of the people in its own way. The cleavage between political reality and constitutional ideals is still very marked and remains a source of great dissatisfaction and tension in the political life of the country.

Constitutional Development

BEFORE WORLD WAR I

Polish constitutional development has been characterized by a struggle for power between the executive and the legislative organs. After winning the first "Charter of Rights" in 1374, the Polish nobility gradually extended its legislative power at the expense of the monarchy. By the end of the sixteenth century a contract between the king and the nobility defined mutual obligations and privileges. The contract formalized the right of the nobles to freely elect anyone to the throne and gave legal recognition to the existence of a parliament which, at this time, was composed only of the nobility.

The *Sejm* consisted of two chambers, the House of Senators, and the House of Deputies. The House of Senators was composed of the magnates (the great landed nobles) and the higher clergy, with membership based on personal position rather than election. It had the power to declare war and approve treaties of peace, and it controlled the finances of the state. Decisions of the *Sejm* required the concurrence of all its members. Failure to achieve unanimity on any question not only led to dissolution of the assembly but also invalidated all decisions previously reached at that particular session. The use of the unanimity rule (*liberum veto*) paralyzed the functions of government.

The first reforms of the system were introduced in 1768. The *liberum veto* could no longer be used in economic or judicial questions, or to dissolve the assembly and invalidate the decisions previously taken. After the first partition of Poland in 1772 a belated effort was made to strengthen the monarchy. On May 3, 1791, the *Sejm* adopted a Constitution which abolished the *liberum veto* and established a hereditary monarchy with wide powers. Parliamentary control over executive power was to be exercised through appropriate ministers, responsible to the *Sejm* who were to countersign royal decrees. The Senate was given a suspensory veto; legislation it rejected could be reintroduced in the next *Sejm* and promulgated without Senate approval if passed by the Deputies a second time. In addition to removing their control over the selection of the monarch the Constitution further restricted the power of the nobility by placing the peasantry under the protection of law and permitting the townsmen to elect representatives to the *Sejm*.

The final partition of Poland in 1795 erased Poland as an independent state, and the Constitution of 1791 was never implemented. It became, however, one of the major elements in Polish political tradition and helped preserve the ideals of constitutional government until the restoration of the Polish state in 1918.

THE INTERWAR PERIOD

In February 1919 a Chamber of Deputies, popularly elected the previous month and adopting the traditional name *Sejm,* convened to formulate a constitution for the new Polish Government. The central issue for the constituent *Sejm* was the question of executive versus legislative power. Debates on this issue were strongly colored by the emergence of Józef Piłsudski who held the allegiance of the military forces and had captured the imagination of a large segment of the population. Many conservative elements in the *Sejm* feared Piłsudski, both as a potential autocrat and as a potential social revolutionary. These fears were resolved by the creation of an executive on the French model: a chief-of-state, or president with ceremonial functions but without real power. The entire power of the state was centered in the legislature.

Next in importance was the issue of establishing a bicameral or unicameral legislature. Conservatives demanded an upper house, or Senate, as a check on the "rule of the mob." Socialists and left-wing peasant delegates contended that an upper house would 'be "ultra-conservative" and "clerical"—a body "representative of the landed classes."

The Constitution, as adopted in March 1921, represented a compromise. It established a legislature of two chambers: an upper house, or Senate, and a lower house which adopted the name *Sejm*. Both chambers were popularly elected. The Senate was denied legislative initiative; its function was limited to review of *Sejm* legislative acts, with power to suspend action if necessary. It could send to the lower house within thirty days amendments which the *Sejm* could reject by a vote of eleven twentieths of those present (one third of the *Sejm* constituted a quorum).

Constitutional limitations on the judiciary reinforced the principle of legislative dominance. Lawfully promulgated acts of the legislature were placed specifically outside the competence of the courts. The judiciary, appointed by the president "from among persons possessing the qualifications demanded by law," was an independent organ of government; judges, once appointed, could not be recalled.

The Constitution of 1921 could be amended by two thirds vote of the *Sejm* and Senate. Motions for amendment required the signature of one fourth of the total number of deputies and fifteen days' notice. Provision was also made for the convocation of the National Assembly, a joint session of the *Sejm* and Senate, every twenty-five years to reconsider the Constitution—a procedure taken from the Constitution of 1791. A simple majority of the National Assembly could modify the Constitution.

The provisions dealing with the rights and duties of citizens reflected the same need for compromise that characterized the sections dealing with the structure of government. A broad range of civil rights, including habeas corpus, freedom of religious practice, immunity from search without warrant, freedom of the press, were enumerated. The sections dealing with the rights and privileges of labor, however, were balanced by clauses protecting private property.

An electoral law (July 29, 1922) provided for a *Sejm* of 444 deputies and a Senate of 111. Contested elections were to be decided by the Supreme Court. Within the all-powerful *Sejm*, the parties of the Right (see chap. 6) established a loose coalition which was able to block legislation. Representatives of the Center and Left were divided among a multiplicity of political parties. As a result, the minorities, representing almost a third of the population, held the balance of power. Political fragmentation within the *Sejm* led to general disillusionment with parliamentary democracy. Among the populace mounting economic crises were associated with the inability of the government to function effectively.

Dissatisfaction with the government culminated in the coup by Józef Piłsudski in May 1926. Piłsudski marched on Warsaw, and, in the face of the support given his forces by the workers of the city, the government collapsed.

The new government, contrary to the fears of the constitutionalists, did not at first attempt to abrogate the constitutional forms but made every effort to adhere to them; it insisted, for example, on the formal resignation of the former government. Equally contrary to expectations was Piłsudski's attempt to consolidate his position by seeking the support of business and landed interests. Proclaiming a program which called for freeing both the army and the conduct of foreign affairs from considerations of party politics, and demanding an end to political factionalism, Piłsudski won the allegiance of much of the population.

In August 1926 a limited constitutional amendment was adopted. The president was given the power to dissolve the legislature with the consent of the Cabinet (the Council of Ministers). He also was empowered to issue ordinances with the effect of law.

The progressive decline of the political parties after 1926 was reflected in the increasing strength of Piłsudski's "Nonparty Bloc of Supporters of the Government" (Bezpartyjny Blok Współpracy z Rządem—BBWR) and the use of administrative pressure to effectively limit the free exercise of the electoral process (see chap. 6). The forces opposed to parliamentary government achieved their aims in the Constitution of 1935, adopted under circumstances raising questions as to its legality. Despite the government's failure to adhere to the requirement of fifteen days' notice of introduction, as stipulated in the Constitution of 1921, and the lack of a sufficient majority to pass the measure, the Constitution of 1935 was promulgated with a show of adherence to constitutional form.

Under the new Constitution, the center of power was shifted from the legislature to the executive. Article 31 explicitly stated that "the functions of governing the State do not belong to the *Sejm*." The president was given full power to dissolve the parliament. In addition, going far beyond the generally agreed areas of reform, the president was invested with powers that included decisions to make war and conclude peace; the right to appoint or dismiss the prime minister, name a candidate to succeed him; appoint his successor in time of war; the right to appoint or dismiss the commander-in-chief and inspector general of the armed forces; the right to appoint or dismiss one third of the members of the Senate.

The Constitution of 1935, although assuring citizens "the possibility of developing their personal capabilities, as also liberty of conscience, speech, and assembly," declared: "It is the duty of each generation to increase the power and authority of the State by its own efforts." The rights of a citizen to "influence public affairs" were to be "estimated according to the value of his efforts and services for the common good" and "in case of resistance [to the aims of the State, as expressed in its laws] the State applies means of compulsion." Opposition parties were not abolished by law, but they were prevented from active participation in government. Under a new electoral law, electoral commissions appointed by the state chose the candidates for the *Sejm*. The major opposition parties boycotted the elections that were held under the new Constitution.

People's Democracy

WORLD WAR II AND AFTER

During World War II the Polish government-in-exile functioned under the Constitution of 1935, but with a provision which rejected any form of dictatorship or oligarchic rule. Inside Poland the Polish "underground state" found itself challenged in 1942 by the Communist attempt to organize an underground movement divorced from the London government-in-exile. The withdrawal of Soviet recognition from the *émigré* government in April 1943 (see chap. 10) had been preceded in July 1942 by the Communist rejection of the Constitution of 1935 in favor of the 1921 Constitution. The Moscow-oriented group based itself on the 1921 Constitution for two reasons: the action provided a dividing line between the London and the Lublin groups, and there was propaganda value to be found in rejecting the authoritarian Constitution of 1935 in favor of the more democratic document of 1921.

After the war the Communists declared their Home National Council (Krajowa Roda Narodowa—KRN) an "interim parliament," with its speaker, Bolesław Bierut, as president. A referendum in June 1946 (see chap. 6) abolished the Senate and established a unicameral legislature. In February 1947 there was promulgated a "Little Constitution" which claimed the Constitution of 1921 as its "politico-juridical basis."

Under this "temporary" Constitution of 1947, the executive was composed of the president, the Government (Council of Ministers), and a Council of State—an innovation in modern Polish government. The unicameral legislature was still called the *Sejm*. A system of "independent" courts was to exercise judicial authority.

Unlike the Constitution of 1921, the "Little Constitution" did not include a statement of rights. A separate "Declaration of Rights" was promulgated but its provisions were qualified in terms reminiscent of the 1935 Constitution:

> The abuse of the civil rights and liberties for the purpose of overthrowing the democratic form of government of the Republic of Poland shall be prevented by law.

The period of temporary constitutional organization came to a close in 1952, when the Constitution now in force was promulgated.

THE CONSTITUTION OF 1952

In mid-1951 the *Sejm* appointed a constitutional drafting commission which included "leading representatives of political, professional, and social organizations as well as representatives of science, culture, and art." The draft constitution was published by the Polish press in January 1952, and the government called for nationwide discussion in order to "elicit suggestions, corrections, and comments from the broadest people's masses." Adopted in its final form on July 22, 1952, the Constitution differed very little from the January draft; only minor changes had been made, in wording rather than in substance.

The first of the 91 articles defines Poland as a "state of people's democracy," not yet a "socialist state" of the Soviet type. The fact that Poland was considered to be in transition accounts for the major divergence between the Polish Constitution of 1952 and its model, the Soviet Constitution of 1935: the Soviet Constitution describes a state declared to have reached the stage of "socialism" and governed by the principle "From each according to his ability, to each according to his work"; the Polish Constitution states only that the Polish People's Republic "gives increasing practical effect" to this principle.

The first two chapters of the Constitution include fourteen articles which state the political, social, and economic bases of the government. Power is said to belong to the "working people of town and country," exercised through their representatives elected to the parliament, the *Sejm,* "on the basis of universal, equal, and direct suffrage by secret ballot." The basic principles of the electoral law are set forth in Chapter VIII (Articles 80 through 88). All citizens over the age of 18, except for the insane and those "persons deprived by Court decision of public rights," are eligible to vote, "irrespective of sex, nationality and race, religion, education, length of residence, social origin, profession, or property." All citizens over the age of 18 are eligible to stand for election to the People's Councils (the organs of local government), and every citizen over the age of 21 is eligible for election to the *Sejm*. Members of the armed forces are accorded all electoral rights. The candidates for the *Sejm* and the People's Councils are nominated by "political and social organizations in town and country," although the procedure for nominating as well as the electoral and recall procedures, "are established by law" (see chap. 6).

The Constitution says that the Polish People's Republic "ensures a continual rise in the level of prosperity" and "secures the development and continuous growth of the productive forces of the country through its industrialization" by means of a planned economy. The transition in social organization is also clearly stated:

> The Polish People's Republic . . . places restriction on, gradually ejects and abolishes those classes of society which live by exploiting the workers and peasants.

In regard to the peasantry, the government "protects the individual farms of working peasants," while giving "special support" to the development of "cooperative farms"—in reality, collective farms of the Soviet type—through the establishment of state machine stations and "state credits on easy terms." In regard to the workers, the Constitution states that "work is the right, the duty of, and a matter of honor for every citizen."

The second major section of the Constitution, Chapters III through VI, deals with the organization of the state apparatus (see chap. 8). The *Sejm,* the unicameral legislature, is declared to be "the highest organ of State authority." Its actual role is not clearly defined—it "passes laws and exercises control over the functioning of other organs of State authority and administration." Immunity is granted deputies; one deputy, elected for a four-year term, is provided for every 60,000 inhabitants. The *Sejm* must hold at least two sessions each year.

The executive of the Polish People's Republic is a dual one. A Council of State, elected by the *Sejm* from among its members, functions as the "head of State," and serves as an interim parliament between sessions of the *Sejm*. It has the authority to "issue decrees with the force of law." It also is responsible for convoking the *Sejm* and is the only body specifically empowered to lay down "universally binding interpretation of laws." The "supreme executive and administrative organ of State authority" is the Council of Ministers, responsible to the *Sejm* collectively and individually. In theory, the Council is much like a Cabinet in a western European parliamentary system. In practice, however, it functions in the same fashion as does the Council of Ministers of the Soviet Union (see chap. 8).

Local government, under the Constitution, is vested in the People's Councils, which have a dual responsibility—to the Council of State and, through their presidia, to the Council of Ministers. The details of composition and operation of the councils are established by law.

Chapter VI of the Constitution deals with "the Courts and the Public Prosecutor's Office": "Organization, jurisdiction, and procedure of the Courts are established by law." The courts serve as "custodians of the political and social system of the Polish People's Republic." The judges and "people's assessors" (lay judges) are elected according to law, while the members of the Supreme Court, "the highest judicial organ," are named by the Council of State for five-year terms. Judges are declared to be independent, and defendants are guaranteed the right to legal defense. The Public Prosecutor's Office is charged with "safeguarding the people's rule of law," and supervises "in particular, the prosecution of offenses endangering the political and social system, security, and independence of the Polish People's Republic." The Constitution does not define the limits of jurisdiction or the scope of activity of the Public Prosecutor's Office; these are to be determined by law. The prosecutor general is responsible to the Council of State, while the subsidiary organs of his office are specifically declared to be "independent of local organs."

The fundamental rights and duties of citizens are set forth in the twenty-three articles of Chapter VII. Article 1 restates the "transitional" nature of the Constitution, declaring that the "Polish People's Republic . . . strengthens and extends the rights and liberties of the citizens." Each of the subsidiary articles, dealing with such "rights" as health protection and education, is qualified by such a phrase as "effect is being given to this right on an increasing scale" or "this right is ensured on an increasing scale." The range of rights and duties is comprehensive and includes declarations of the full equality of women and ostensible safeguards against discrimination on national, racial, or religious grounds. While "freedom of conscience and religion" is guaranteed to citizens, the Constitution also states that nobody may be coerced "to participate in religious activities and rites." Freedom of speech, press, assembly and inviolability of person, home, and privacy of correspondence are also guaranteed. In addition, "citizens have the right to approach all organs of the State with complaints and grievances," and officials "guilty . . . of displaying a soulless and bureaucratic attitude toward citizens' complaints and grievances will be held responsible."

The concluding two chapters of the Constitution describe the coat of arms and colors of the state and declare Warsaw its capital. The procedure for amending the Constitution is stated; theoretically, only the *Sejm* may amend, by a two thirds vote of its members, but this provision has not yet been put to a test.

Prospects

Popular pressures stemming from the dissatisfaction produced by the disparity between constitutional provisions and the practice of the Communist government increased throughout the period of attempted Sovietization. In April 1956 the government itself recognized the depth of feeling on the issue and admitted that:

> Without a doubt too large a part of the legislative process took the form of issuing decrees. The *Sejm* was called for short, too short, and too infrequent sessions, and under these conditions it had to limit itself to endorsing decrees without being able to analyze and discuss them fully.

An attempt to revitalize the constitutional basis of the state was a major plank in the October 1956 program of the Gomułka leadership. A resolution adopted by the Eighth Plenum of the Central Committee of the PZPR in the same month stated:

> The Party will strive to create both political and legal conditions in which the *Sejm*—the supreme organ of power in the people's democratic State—shall be able fully to execute its basic constitutional task. Legislative work should be concentrated in the *Sejm*. The *Sejm* must fully exercise its constitutional right to all-embracing control over the work of the government.

Up to the autumn of 1957 the major changes have been a reduction in the power of the secret police and an increase in the activities of various *Sejm* committees and subcommittees. Debates on the Constitution have centered on the need for formal amendments to distinguish more clearly the functions of the *Sejm*, the Council of Ministers, and the Council of State. An attempt is being made to secure constitutional safeguards against the previous practice of "legislation by decree" by both Councils at the expense of the *Sejm*. Once again the issue of executive versus legislative control is being raised.

The present limits of reform established by the government indicate that any major changes will be of form, rather than in the leading role of the Party. Many Polish intellectuals, however, apparently feel that the Gomułka government has not gone far enough. They continue to hope for constitutional and democratic government as it is practiced in the West. Their dissatisfaction with a system in which the policy-making core remains outside the constitutional framework is a source of continuing tension in Polish political life.

STRUCTURE OF THE GOVERNMENT

THE BASIC FRAMEWORK OF THE POLISH GOVERNMENT IS CLOSELY and consciously modeled after that of the USSR: the unicameral parliament, the *Sejm,* corresponds to the Supreme Soviet of the USSR; the Council of State to the Presidium of the Supreme Soviet; the Council of Ministers, with its Presidium, to the same units in the Soviet government structure.

The government of Poland, like that of the Soviet Union, serves as the administrative machinery of the Party. The Party has insured its control over the government structure through an interlocking directorate—the placement of top Party members in key government positions—and through an independent hierarchy of control which parallels the government at each level. The Party in Poland, however, is not monolithic, all-pervasive, all-powerful, united doctrinally and programmatically. Until very recently it controlled with the help of the Soviet Army. Today, it controls by balancing off various pressure groups, many of which are not contained within the Party itself.

The Russians introduced into Poland the cumbersome and complex system utilized to govern the vast Soviet Union—a system which has not been accepted readily by the Poles. The system has built into it a great overlapping of functions and a blurring of lines of authority and jurisdiction. There is little coordination of the functions of different agencies covering the same field. In Poland the Council of State and the Council of Ministers exercise control over the same areas, issuing regulations and orders that are in some cases repetitive, in others contradictory. On the lower levels the result is administrative indecision, buck-passing, and jurisdictional squabbling. Administrative indecision is somewhat overcome in the Soviet Union by punishment and threat of punishment for failure to act to fulfill the Plan, but that goad has been blunted in Poland.

Thus, the government structure which has been imposed upon Poland is Soviet in form but tends to be Polish in practice. It is a structure designed to extend lines of governmental-Party control into every area of life, a move which the Poles have resisted. In the Polish view the bureaucracy is top-heavy, and since "Polish October" there has been a continuous reduction both in the size and the complexity of the government bureaucracy. The Party, at the same time, has relinquished much of its day-to-day operational control over governmental administration.

Polish officials evidently find it extremely difficult and distasteful to work without having clearly defined areas of authority. There has thus been a shift away from overlapping control lines toward some measure of local autonomy. This streamlining operation has also produced a great deal of intra-governmental and inter-Party jockeying for political control and influence. The need of the moment, however, is to make the administrative structure viable so that a modicum of social order and regularity can be maintained.

Perspective

In trying to create an efficient administration the Poles are handicapped by a lack of practical administrative experience. For a century and a half, while the political systems of other European countries were developing under the stimulus of rapidly changing conditions, Poland was partitioned—giving the people little chance to take part in the everyday functioning of a government—and the ensuing interwar period was too brief to compensate for that long period.

PARTITIONED POLAND

Under the partitioning powers the Polish people developed a strong dislike and distrust of governmental bureaucracy. The peasants were particularly hostile to the local officials with whom they had direct dealings and blamed such officials for their ills far more readily than higher authorities. When they were emancipated from serfdom, they tended, for example, to regard the tsar, the emperor, or even the provincial governor as a personal benefactor. On the whole, however, they were apathetic and restricted their political activity to the everyday problems of life raised in the village councils.

It was the gentry and the urban intellectuals who struggled with the three alien administrations, alternately trying opposition, "organic work," and opportunistic compromise. As members of the parliaments of the partitioning powers they usually acted as a united minority group ready to cast their supporting vote in exchange for some concessions. Occasionally, as in the Russian Duma, they cooperated with the more liberal non-Polish elements in the hope of obtaining political advantages for Poland.

RUSSIA. With the establishment of the Congress Kingdom in 1815, the Russians permitted the Poles a certain measure of self-government for a very short time. The Congress Kingdom had its separate administration, its own army, and was given a constitution. After the uprising of 1830 the concessions were nullified and the Congress Kingdom was incorporated into the Russian state. The inefficiency and corruption of the Russian bureaucracy was intensified in the Polish area by the low caliber of the public servants sent there by the Russian Government.

The manipulation of the courts by the tsarist police left the Poles with little respect for any form of legal order. The necessarily conspiratorial nature of much of Polish life in the Russian section heightened this disregard for normally organized public life. Defiance and opposition to foreign administration went beyond dissatisfaction with a disorderly and dishonest bureaucracy; it became identified with the struggle for national independence.

PRUSSIA. In its first ninety years of administration Prussian Poland presented a marked contrast to the area under tsarist domination. Though there was almost no opportunity for Poles to take part in the government, the Prussians and Germans did send a body of efficient and incorruptible officials to administer the area. Education was relatively widespread, for a time in the Polish language as well as in German, and some land reform which benefited the small farmer was accomplished. The Polish gentry in this area showed a sense of responsibility toward the peasants and were instrumental in laying the foundations of a number of native Polish banking and agricultural cooperatives.

The relatively liberal Prussian policy was designed to win the support of the Poles against Russia. With the rise of Bismarck in the late nineteenth century, however, the Poles were hard pressed by German immigrants and by the open attempts to turn Poles into Germans. Nevertheless, the experiences of the earlier period had created a spirit of cooperation and respect for a well-run and efficient government.

AUSTRIA. In the administration of its empire Austria tempered centralized control with the use of locally recruited officials, who served in both the imperial and the provincial administration. A small group of Poles thus gained experience in administration on levels as various as sheriff and prime minister. After 1867, Austrian Poland was granted a large measure of self-government, including a provincial parliamentary assembly. There was also a special ministerial post in Vienna for Galician (Austrian Poland) affairs.

Polish was the language of all administrative departments except the army, and there was little organized effort to suppress Polish culture. A divide-and-conquer technique rather than outright oppression was used by the Austrians to keep under control the subject nationalities of the Hapsburg empire. They set the Ruthenians and Poles against each other and did everything in their power to maintain the wide gulf between the Polish gentry and the Polish peasants. The gentry came to be identified with the Austrian administration, and it alone reaped the benefits of cooperation with the Hapsburg government. Neither the Austrian nor the Polish officials made any effort to ameliorate the position of the peasants.

Although the Austrian administration of Galicia bequeathed to interwar Poland an experienced group of government servants, it left the people of the area with a suspicion and dislike for a bureaucracy identified with upper-class conservatism.

THE INTERWAR PERIOD

The early interwar government inherited the complex administrative and attitudinal accretions of the partition period. With the creation of an independent Polish state many Poles felt that the restrictions imposed by the partitioning governments would all but disappear. At a time when the new Polish Government was in a precarious situation both internally and externally, some Poles confused liberty and independence with license and irresponsibility.

One of the most difficult tasks was to unify the three sections of the country. In many instances—in local government, for example—the forms established by the previous administrations were left untouched. In others, such as codification of the laws, drastic changes were made, though the task was not completed until shortly before the outbreak of World War II.

The problem of adequate administrative personnel was serious. Since the most experienced administrative personnel came from Galicia, Poles from other areas tended to be excluded from administrative posts. This situation made cooperation between former Russian, Austrian, and Prussian Poles extremely difficult, creating misunderstandings and mutual suspicion.

In theory the Constitution of 1921 gave the country a democratic, representative government. Under the terms of the electoral law of 1922, parliamentary deputies were elected by universal franchise on the basis of proportional representation. In order to curtail the number of small parties in parliament, national lists were drawn up from which seats were allotted to parties only if they had deputies elected from at least six districts. This measure did not achieve its purpose; during the early years as many as eighty political parties were represented in parliament. Most of these joined in various alignments, but cabinets frequently were unable to obtain the support of a coalition strong enough to be effective. Until 1930 the parliament was characterized by the inability and unwillingness of the various parties to cooperate and a reluctance to subordinate partisan and personal interests to the national welfare.

Following the Piłsudski coup in May 1926 a series of decrees curbed the power of the legislative branch of the government. The most important, issued on August 2, 1926, gave the president the right to dissolve at will both the lower and upper houses of parliament; during their suspension he was empowered to issue decrees having the force of law. The struggle between the executive and parliament continued until the 1930 elections when a parliament subservient to Piłsudski took office.

The Constitution of 1935 formalized the structure and function of the government which had been operating in fact since 1930. In it wide powers were granted the president, virtually making him a dictator and the parliament a powerless debating society. In 1935 also a new electoral law reduced the size of the lower house by half and transferred the right of nominating candidates from the parties to new electoral colleges controlled by the government.

Both constitutions entrusted the actual functioning of the government to a Council of Ministers composed of members of the Cabinet and the prime minister. The prime minister directed the activities of the government and laid down the general principles of state policy. The prime minister, the Council, and the individual ministers had the right to issue regulations, to implement statutes and decrees of the President of the Republic, and to supervise agencies at the local level. To assist the prime minister there was also a Presidium of the Council of Ministers.

Under both constitutions the organization of the judiciary was much the same (see chap. 7); nominally, it was as independent in 1935 as it had been in 1921, but in fact the Piłsudski and post-Piłsudski governments exercised considerable control over the courts. The President of the Republic appointed the president of the Supreme Court, and the Ministry of Justice had wide latitude in the removal and appointment of judges.

In establishing local administration the new Polish Government generally followed the pattern set by the partitioning powers. There was little effort to unify the systems of the three sections, as this was considered impractical and undesirable. In time, however, with the centralization of power in the hands of the President of the Republic, the governors, as his agents, became the focal points of power and control in the provinces.

In general, through the various government appointed officials, local government was well centralized. The Ministry of Interior was the central executive authority over the various local executive offices, and during the rule of Piłsudski and his followers the president had considerable control over all local organs, without any appreciable change in the structure that had been established for local affairs as early as 1921.

Thus, during the interwar period, with little change in the formal structure of government, Poland was transformed from a potential representative democracy into an authoritarian state. In contrast to the periods which were to follow, however, state control was limited to the political and economic spheres and the government made little attempt to interfere with the non-political, everyday life of the people.

FOUNDATIONS FOR THE PRESENT GOVERNMENT

The foundations for the present government were laid during World War II by Polish Communists both in occupied Poland and in the USSR. Poland's liberation by Russia insured the political success of the Moscow-oriented and Moscow-directed Poles against the government-in-exile in London. The breakoff of diplomatic relations in April of 1943 between Soviet Russia and the government-in-exile precluded any possibility of that government's assumption of power in post-World War II Poland. At the end of 1943 delegates from a number of leftist groups in German-occupied Poland formed the Home National Council (Krajowa Roda Naradowa—KRN). In July 1944 Polish exiles in Russia who, under Soviet auspices, had organized the Union of Polish Patriots joined the Home National Council. In December 1944 the KRN established at Lublin the Polish Committee of National Liberation, which functioned as a government in areas of Poland liberated by the Soviet army. The KRN accepted the Constitution of 1921 as the basis for its power and functioned as a parliament with Bolesław Bierut as Presidium president and head of state. During the December 1944–January 1945 session of the KRN its Presidium permitted the inclusion of some acceptable non-Communists in forming the temporary government of Poland. At the same time the KRN was extending its influence into the countryside through people's councils. The support of these "spontaneously" created local councils gave the KRN further basis to claims of legitimacy and served as a source of control on the local level.

On January 5, 1945, the Soviet government recognized the new provisional government of Poland, while the United States and Great Britain still maintained official relations with the government-in-exile in London. The future of the Polish government was settled at the Yalta Conference in February 1945. The Lublin Poles were to include in their government democratic leaders from Poland and from among Poles abroad. The Polish Provisional Government of National Unity was to hold "free and unfettered" elections as soon as possible. The new government was overwhelmingly dominated by the Lublin Poles, who held two thirds of the Cabinet posts, among them the key Ministries of National Defense, of Public Security, and of Industry, Food, and Trade.

When the elections were finally held in January 1947 there was little question as to the outcome. The pre-election measures of intimidation and repression through the Communist-controlled Ministry of Public Security and the confusion in the listing of the Peasant Party candidates on the ballot assured the Communists of an overwhelming victory without resorting to falsification in tabulating votes.

After defeating Mikołajczyk and his Polish Peasant Party, the Communists then moved to merge their own Polish Workers' Party with the strong Socialist Party. The merger was effected in December 1948 and the Communist-led Polish United Workers' Party (PZPR) could then turn to the task of transforming Poland into a Communist state (see chap. 6).

Like previous administrations, the regime in Poland was faced with the problem of inadequate personnel. While it could be sure of having completely loyal and politically reliable people in the top governmental and administrative posts, the cohesion found, for example, in the Yugoslav Communist Party was lacking among Polish Communists. They were divided into the Moscow-trained group and those who had worked in the underground during the war. The former, who returned to Poland with the Red Army, were immediately given important positions, but the very top posts went to men such as Bierut, Gomułka, and Marshal Rola-Zymierski, who had been active in Poland during the war. Other administrative personnel came from the non-Communist ranks; many of these had worked initially with the government during the period of coalition and remained because of intimidation or for economic reasons. Still other personnel was incorporated from the ranks of the Socialist Party when it was merged with the Polish Workers' Party. Further help came in the form of Soviet "advisers," technicians, and military personnel.

By holding key government posts, the PZPR maintained undisputed control of the government. The policy of the Party became the policy of the government. The long-range economic Plans, for example, were first adopted at a Party Congress, then presented to the

Sejm, which passed them as law. Many other resolutions of the Central Committee of the PZPR were in the pre-1956 period similarly made law by the rubber stamp of the *Sejm.*

Central Administration

The Polish governmental structure, modeled on that of the Soviet Union, is highly centralized. All power radiates from the central administration, whose loci are the Council of State, the Council of Ministers, and, in theory, the *Sejm.* Control over Poland is strictly exercised from Warsaw, and the real guiding force behind the government has been the Politburo of the Polish United Workers' Party.

Some vestiges of interwar structure remain (see chap. 7). The *Sejm* is based on the parliament of prewar Poland, and many of the forms of local government, including the basic subdivisions, have been retained from the previous administration. At lower levels of the administration there are Poles who served in the prewar government.

THE COUNCIL OF STATE

The Council of State, elected by the *Sejm* from among its own members, is in theory the supreme legislative organ. At the apex of the hierarchy of people's councils, it has most often initiated legislation in the *Sejm.* It shares its theoretical control and its membership with the Party and the Council of Ministers. Thus, members of the Council of State are not only high Party functionaries but also hold the highest government offices. The membership of the Central Committee of the Party has always been represented on the Council. The vice-speakers of the *Sejm,* who are members of the Council, have usually also occupied some other important posts. One of the vice-speakers has always been president of the Supreme Court, another has been chairman of the Special Commission for Combating Corruption and Economic Abuses. The president of the Supreme Audit Office was not only a member of the Council of State but also commander in chief of the police force. Today, Władysław Gomułka is the First Secretary of the Party and also a member of the Council of State. The speaker and three vice-speakers of the *Sejm* have a particularly important role as members of the Council of State, for the Council can rely on them to successfully maneuver through the *Sejm* all resolutions and decrees.

This interdependence of the Party, the government, and the legislature has insured the Communists absolute control of the government structure. A man who is at one and the same time a member of the Council of State, the Central Committee of the Party, and president of the Supreme Court can be quite sure that any Party directive concerning the judiciary will be passed as a decree by the Council of State and approved by the *Sejm*.

The Council of State's most important functions as the collective head of state are the issuance of decrees during the intervals between the sessions of the *Sejm* and its overlapping control over the local councils. In the past the *Sejm* sessions were so brief that the Council actually acted as the main legislative body, its decrees automatically approved by the *Sejm*. The Council calls elections to the *Sejm* and also convokes it. It performs various functions attributable to a head of state such as the appointment to certain civilian and military positions, ratification and denunciation of international treaties, and the granting of pardons. It can declare war and introduce martial law. In its work it is accountable to the *Sejm;* this provision, a mere formality in the past, has been increasingly respected since October 1956.

THE COUNCIL OF MINISTERS

The Council of Ministers is the decision-making center of the administrative organization. It coordinates the activities of the individual ministries and their subordinate agencies, prepares drafts of the state budget and of the national economic plans prior to presenting them to the *Sejm,* and directs the work of the presidia of the local people's councils.

It is headed by a chairman of the Council, whose functions correspond to those of a prime minister, and a deputy chairman. Members include the heads of the ministries and the chairmen of commissions and committees. According to the Constitution, the government is elected by the *Sejm* or by the Council of State when the *Sejm* is not in session. In practice the *Sejm* was presented with a prepared list of the government for confirmation. Until the formation of the new government after the elections in the spring of 1957, the Council of Ministers had been composed of members of the National Front only. The new government included a few non-Party portfolios as well, but the most important were still entrusted to top Party leaders.

The ministries themselves cover every aspect of Polish political, economic, social, and cultural life. There is a particular preponderance of ministries dealing with economic matters. From the original four economic departments of the Lublin Committee, twenty-six ministries had developed by the end of 1953. Today, even after various mergers, half of the ministries are concerned with the national economy; they include such highly specialized portfolios as Meat and Dairy Industry, Chemical Industry, and Iron and Steel Industry (see chap. 15).

Each ministry has under it a number of central administrative boards, along with various departments. Executive orders are conveyed directly to a central board, and the departments act merely in an advisory capacity. A central board's function is to plan, supervise, and coordinate the activities of its subordinate enterprises or units.

The chairmen of various commissions, such as the State Planning Commission and the Special Commission for Combating Corruption and Economic Abuses, also play an important role in the Council of Ministers. These two commissions exercise great control in the economic sector of the country, the first in the formulation of the plans, the second as a special police enforcement body. There are many other committees and advisory commissions composed of various experts, set up on a permanent or an *ad hoc* basis to deal with special problems; there is, for instance, a Commission to Study the Problem of Reforms in Government Administration.

The Presidium of the Council of Ministers has a coordinating and directive function. Of particular importance is the role it assumed when the Economic Committee of the Council of Ministers was dissolved. The Presidium now determines basic economic policy, approves and prepares economic plans and legislation. It issues instructions for the execution of the state economic plan, and on the basis of this outline the ministries elaborate further plans for the departmental level (see chap. 11; chap. 15).

The relationship of the Council of State and the Council of Ministers in the governmental structure is such that the functions of the two overlap considerably. Both have authority and control over some of the same areas, and the lines of authority are very hazy. Confusion is particularly great in the economic sector and in matters concerning local government. Since each Council can issue orders and regulations, a vast collection of these has resulted. In many instances when orders are issued the necessary machinery to implement them is not provided. In other cases orders and regulations are in direct conflict. It has been particularly difficult for the lower administrative levels to determine what directive to follow and to ascertain to whom they are responsible—for instance, the local councils come under the Council of State, and yet the presidia they "elect" are responsible to the Council of Ministers.

THE SEJM

According to the Constitution the *Sejm* is the highest organ of the state and expresses the will of the people, but until the election of January 20, 1957, it was little more than an instrument for Party propaganda. Its deputies are charged with representing and upholding the interests of the "working people of town and country." Convoked at least twice a year, it initiates legislation and debates on the decrees of the Council of State.

For each session the *Sejm* elects a number of committees which concern themselves with various problems at hand, such as the budget, judicial reforms, and education. Until recently these committees had done little more than approve government policies. Since October 1956 they have exhibited considerable independence and, by their activity, have strengthened the position of the *Sejm* in the state.

Deputies to the *Sejm* are responsible to their constituents and it is their duty to report back to them on their work. They enjoy certain privileges—such as immunity from arrest and prosecution without the consent of the *Sejm* or, if that body is not in session, of the Council of State. They receive financial remuneration, but only during the sessions of the *Sejm* rather than for the four-year period for which they have been elected.

One deputy is elected for every 60,000 inhabitants. The list of candidates for the national elections, however, is drawn up by an electoral committee of the Front of National Unity under the control of the PZPR. Up to early 1957, voters were not offered a choice of candidates and considerable pressure was applied at the polls to secure "approval" of the single list of names sponsored by the regime. The January 1957 elections were conducted without intimidation, and a voter could freely strike any name off the ballot. In subsequent by-elections, to fill vacancies, the people were given for the first time the opportunity to choose between opposing candidates, though the selection of candidates was still controlled by the Front of National Unity.

THE JUDICIARY

The Supreme Court, according to the Constitution, is the highest judicial organ in Poland. Below the Supreme Court are the provincial and district courts. There are no circuit courts. There are a number of special courts and boards, such as the courts martial and the various boards for the settlement of economic disputes. Although the Constitution provides for an independent judiciary the Party and its ideology have been the main factors in determining the administration of justice. One of the general rulings of the Supreme Court issued for the guidance of Polish courts states:

> Interpretation of the law should not be concerned with the literal meaning of the law, but should aim at the realization of its social purpose and take into consideration that it is an expression of the will of the broad social masses.

The Supreme Court supervises the function of all other courts. It is the highest court of appeal and in some cases also acts as a court of first instance. Its members are elected by the Council of State for a tenure of five years. It consists of a number of divisions, including criminal, civil, and military, which sit in benches of three or five justices. In special instances, such as the reconsideration of rulings of the divisions or in certain criminal cases, the entire membership of the Supreme Court sits as a body.

The provincial and district courts are elected by their respective provincial councils. Following the Soviet model, they are composed of both regular judges and lay judges—the latter with legal training. They are courts of first instance, although the provincial courts also act as courts of appeal for the district courts.

Of particular significance are the special courts and boards. In the past, courts martial had wide jurisdiction over civilian matters; since October 1956 their function seems to have been limited to the administration of military justice and to espionage cases involving civilians. Because of the importance of the national economic Plan, all matters connected with it were entrusted to special courts, thus removing much of the litigation from the regular court system. The Economic Arbitration Commission is the most important of these and acts as a supreme court in litigation concerned with the national economic Plan. In its decisions the Commission is guided by "the principles of the legality of the People's Poland and in accordance with the provisions and directives of the Economic Plan."

The government is the largest employer in Poland, and labor disputes today constitute one of the most important aspects of litigation (see chap. 12). These disputes are dealt with by Enterprises Arbitration Boards composed of four members—two representing management and two the workers. The object of these boards is not so much to render a judicial decision as to effect a compromise between the conflicting parties.

The Constitution states that "judges are independent and subject only to law." But until recently political qualifications have been far more important than legal training. According to a former Minister of Justice, "the judge must cooperate with the government and understand and know how to realize the policy of the Party in every case." Because of a lack of judges with a "true democratic or socialist legal consciousness," it was considered necessary that part of the judicial function be performed by "lay judges," laymen elected by the people's councils on a basis of political desirability.

The over-all supervisory power in the Polish judicial system is vested in the prosecutor general (also referred to as attorney general).

He is appointed and recalled by the Council of State and is responsible to it for his actions. He has a hierarchy of field officers who are directly responsible to him and are independent of any local authority. The prosecutor general's jurisdiction extends over the entire government apparatus and the political and economic life of the country. He sees to it that in the everyday administration of justice "the laws are correctly and uniformly applied by all courts." He also initiates the interpretation of laws by the Council of State and supervises the actual implementation by the courts of policy established by the Council. He has far-reaching control over the courts. He can reopen a case on motion to the Supreme Court on his own initiative if he feels that the case has not been decided in keeping with the law. He has the power to designate in which court a case is to be tried. He can initiate legal proceedings in a civil suit and either uphold an action which has been abandoned by the suer or withdraw it against the suer's wishes. Out-of-court settlements can be reversed by him. In criminal cases, although he is a party to the trial, he conducts the preliminary investigation and decides its outcome.

Local Government

Local government and administration in Poland are based on a series of subdivisions, each of which has its own popularly elected people's council. The present subdivisions follow closely those set up in interwar Poland. The lowest administrative units are the town and the rural district (*gromada*). The latter is composed of several villages and usually includes a population of about 3,000. The next major subdivision is the *powiat,* the rural and urban county. The largest is the *województwo,* or province. Poland is divided into 17 provinces, plus two cities, Warsaw and Lodz, that have provincial status besides being capitals of the provinces of the same names.

In general, the local people's councils are similar to the soviets of the USSR. When they were first organized in 1944, however, certain traditional forms were preserved. With the reorganization of local administration in 1950, the centrally appointed provincial and executive officials, among the last remnants of the old administration, were removed. Today their function has been taken over by the presidia of the people's councils. Elected by the councils, the presidia act as a collective executive.

The people's councils are part of the hierarchy of power headed by the Council of State, but their presidia are responsible to the Council of Ministers. According to the provisions of the law of 1950, the councils are the agencies of authority of the central government. The most important functions of the councils as agencies of the central government are collaboration in strengthening the defenses of the state, maintenance and enforcement of public order, and implementation of the national economic plan. In theory, the people's councils can enact their own economic plans, pass their own budgets, determine local taxes, and supervise other social, economic, and political activities. In the past, however, their functions have been very limited. In all their work the councils are closely supervised by the Council of State, and their plans must fit within the framework prescribed by the Council of State, the Council of Ministers, and the State Planning Commission. The Council of State can annul any decision of a people's council; it can also dissolve the council. In addition to being under the rigid control of the central government, each council and its presidium is subordinate to the one on the next highest level. Decrees or resolutions of one presidium or people's council can be declared void by the council or by the presidium directly above it. Decrees and enactments of the provincial councils can be suspended by the Council of Ministers pending a decision of the Council of State.

Trends

The government structure in Poland has been under severe criticism since the Seventh Plenum of the Central Committee of the PZPR outlined a program of administrative reform in July 1956. In October 1956, speaking at the Eighth Plenum, Władysław Gomułka again brought out the problem of "liquidation of the so-called administrative overgrowths." For several years excessive bureaucratization and centralization have created severe problems for the proper functioning of the Polish governmental structure. In particular, minute and detailed day-to-day management of the governmental administration by the Party had led to great inefficiency and obstruction.

In discussing the problems left by the Stalinist regime, Gomułka blamed the breakdown of public administration on the old system of parallel organizations—official public officeholders, and behind them the Party secretaries who actually governed on all levels. Public officeholders, he went on to say, "held the rubber stamps, but the decision to apply or withhold the stamps was made by the Party secretary who corresponded to the official in question." All decisions were made in Warsaw and were implemented by the Party secretary acting behind the façade of the public official. A corollary to this problem was the need for experienced and competent personnel; since many of the men who had held office were nothing more than "rubber stamps," they had never learned to exercise authority. Gomułka agreed that the problem could not be solved simply by removing all Party secretaries, for then the government bureaucracy would be incapable of action and ignorant of the basic elements of public administration. Thus, the Party leaders argued in favor of maintaining their controlling position until efficient and responsible civil servants could be trained. Furthermore, although by January 1957 a large number of minor Party officials were being removed from positions of authority, Gomułka continued to stress that the Party should remain in the role of a "political mentor" to the government and administration. The emphasis now is on persuasion rather than dictatorial methods—an attempt to diminish the appearance of command without relinquishing political power.

Premier Cyrankiewicz in a speech before the new *Sejm* criticized the administration for its excessive size, uncoordinated activity, and countless conflicting decisions, regulations, and orders. In an effort to streamline and coordinate the administration, the Commission to Study the Problem of Reforms in Government Administration was formed; it is to try to improve the state apparatus, reduce its costs, coordinate the organizational work, and decentralize some authority. An important move in this direction was the merger of ten economic ministries into five and the elimination of three central administrative agencies. Considerable reduction in the numbers of administrative personnel on the lower levels has also been made.

Changes in top-level personnel have been few. Of the many Stalinists fired in October 1956, most have since been reinstated in their jobs. This turn of events has caused both bewilderment and resentment among intellectuals and supporters of Gomułka, who are concerned that the reinstatement and shifting around of the Stalinists may mean a sharp detour on the road to democratization. As expressed in a comment of *Trybuna Ludu,* the official Party newspaper: "Are these changes of jobs or changes of policy?"

Since the elections in January 1957 the parliamentary debates have been lively, and an attempt is being made to restore to the *Sejm* the powers granted it by the Constitution (see chap. 7). Gomułka, in his speech before the Eighth Plenum last October, stressed the importance of creating the political and legal conditions which would guarantee the *Sejm* its rightful position in the governmental structure. Certain minor reforms have been introduced and others have been proposed. How far Gomułka's proposals will be carried out will depend on the success with which the *Sejm* can actually challenge the power of the Council of State and the Council of Ministers.

In regard to the judiciary, the Central Committee of the PZPR has envisioned the following reforms: further strengthening of the prosecuting organs; extension of effective supervision by the Prosecutor General's Office over investigatory work of the citizens' militia and public security organs; consolidation of the independence of the courts and the raising of professional qualifications of the judges. Various legal measures for strengthening the independence of judges have been in preparation since early 1957. A number of committees have been set up to study the problems of prison reform, codification of laws, and the question of rights and guarantees of citizens before the law. Within the next two years new drafts of all the major codes are to be prepared by the codification commission. Another important proposed reform concerns an extension of the right of appeal against administrative decisions. At present the system of complaints gives some protection to citizens but not the right of a direct appeal to a superior court.

Since "Polish October" there has been particular agitation for reform of the local councils. At the Seventh Session of the Provincial People's Councils local government was severely criticized as having accomplished nothing. Members of village councils have complained bitterly that their function has consisted of nothing more than registering births and deaths. The people's councils have been accused of inefficiency and apathy, of being completely paralyzed by administrative confusion and bureaucratic red tape. Because of insufficient authority, they have failed to help implement the national economic plans at the lower level. Whatever the criticism, at the core is always the problem of centralization and overlapping authority. One member of a county council declared that "centralism has murdered the people's councils."

The problem of administrative overlap is partially one of adjusting the position of the councils in the national hierarchy of power. At present they are under the control of both the Council of Ministers and the Council of State, in addition to being supervised by the Party. Reforms have been suggested which would cut at least one of the governmental control lines and put the councils under one central agency. One outcome of such a shift—elimination of the Council of Ministers' control over the council presidia—might throw more power to the *Sejm*.

Many reforms have also been proposed to grant more power to the councils. The Seventh Plenum of the PZPR proposed that the councils be given the authority granted them by the Constitution to manage directly all aspects of the local economy as well as educational and cultural affairs. In granting broader economic powers it is hoped that the councils will be more instrumental in carrying out the provisions of the national economic plan.

The PZPR itself has been criticized by council representatives for interfering in their function. In many cases in the past the PZPR has in effect appointed council members and their presidia.

The great agitation for reform in the structure of government has been a strong indication that today people in Poland can at least complain about the regime and attempt to do something about their grievances. Administrative change in Poland, like the process of democratization, is qualified, however, by the supremacy of the PZPR and its unswerving determination to maintain its power.

DIFFUSION AND CONTROL OF INFORMATION

AS IN OTHER SOVIET SATELLITES, THE COMMUNIST REGIME IN Poland after World War II attempted to bring all the means of communication under their control and to promulgate information and propaganda designed to further their goals. From 1949 to 1954 they were able to exercise relatively tight control over the information available to the public, and in theme and style their propaganda was on the whole indistinguishable from that in the USSR. Since Gomułka's return in October 1956 the Party has continued to propagandize and exhort the populace toward Communist goals, but it has attempted to make its output more palatable by widening the limits of debate and adopting more colorful western techniques of presentation. Today the information available to the Polish people through the various media of mass communication is by far the closest to factual accuracy, the most diverse in subject matter, the liveliest in form, and the most daring in the presentation of divergent points of view of any to be found in the Soviet satellites. The change has been gradual; beginning soon after the death of Stalin, it gained momentum after the Twentieth Congress of the Soviet Communist Party, and reached its peak during the summer and autumn of 1956. Nevertheless, except for the months between the Poznan uprising in July 1956 and the end of that year, freedom of expression and the press as known in many of the countries of western Europe and in the United States has not existed in postwar Poland.

The Party uses the mass media to influence public opinion in support of a socialist system and the policies and practices adopted to attain it. For the most part such control is exercised indirectly: the Party makes policy and issues directives, but operational controls are imposed by government organizations and regulatory agencies dependent on the Council of Ministers. Most of the control agencies have subordinate offices responsible to provincial and local government authorities. In effect, however, the Party and the government are synonomous: personnel control provides a link between policy and operation, and through its power to appoint and remove officials, the Party sees that its policies are carried out.

News, information, and rumor also are spread with little restriction by word-of-mouth; rapidity depends largely upon importance and intrinsic interest. During the earlier years of Communist control there was a widespread fear of informers, and great care about whom one talked to. Listening to foreign radio programs was permitted but dissemination of the information so acquired was prohibited. After the death of Stalin fears decreased and today there is little or no restraint on what is talked about or with whom.

In 1955 a number of discussion clubs were organized among students and young intelligentsia, mostly in Warsaw. Political in orientation, "clubs of the young intelligentsia," as they were collectively known, took an active part in the social, literary, and artistic ferment of the post-Stalin years. One group formed among the staff of the editorial board of *Trybuna Ludu;* an associated press agency called Mamy Tego Dość (We've Had Enough) was formed. Another group among the staff of *Po Prostu,* was called Krzywe Koło (The Crooked Circle). For a short time these organizations had a central coordinating organization aligned with the National Front, but for the most part they have operated independently. Just how many of the clubs are still active is not known; Krzywe Koło still exists but seems to have become something of a social club.

Perspective

After Poland was re-established in 1918 as an independent nation, information media, particularly the press, expanded rapidly and, with certain exceptions, without government control. Radio broadcasting began under the auspices of a stock company in which the government owned 95 percent of the shares but the press was largely privately owned. By the mid 1930's the newspapers represented a wide scope and range of interests; published in Polish, Ukrainian, German, Yiddish, Hebrew, Belorussian, and even in French and English, they represented many shades of opinion. Daily, weekly, monthly, and quarterly periodicals included those devoted to technical, scientific, social, cultural, and religious subjects as well as those designed solely to entertain. Book publication followed a similar pattern of range and expansion.

In September 1939 Poland had 46 press agencies, 2,850 periodicals appearing in over 200 towns, 8 radio stations in operation with about 27 subscribers per 1,000 of population, and 2 more stations under construction. Despite the extensive damage and destruction of World War I, about 35,000 libraries, mostly in schools, could count some 21 million books.

The 1921 Constitution prohibited censorship of the press and guaranteed all publications access to the mails, unrestricted circulation throughout the country, and freedom to publish the findings of learned investigations and research. But after the press law of 1926 made the owners and directors of publications legally responsible for the material they published, the government began to limit the freedom of the press. Prepublication censorship was never imposed, but the government could force the withdrawal of an offending article or confiscate entire issues of newspapers or periodicals of which it disapproved. The government interfered seldom and little, however, with material published on nonpolitical subjects. The press continued to expand until the German invasion.

After 1939 the German Government confiscated all printing establishments and banned the publication of Polish newspapers in the territory it occupied. The eastern territories occupied by Russia became subject to the law of the Soviet Union, but the underground press continued to issue a great deal of material—printed, mimeographed, or even hand-copied—ranging from news to poetry.

Control of Public Information

Although the 1945 Constitution guarantees the right of freedom of expression, that right is to be exercised within the limits of the "interests of society" and the Party has always reserved to itself the right and the duty to define those interests. For a few years after the expulsion of Gomułka from his Party secretary post for "nationalist tendencies," all media of information were forced into submission to the Stalinist formula. But dissent was not stamped out either in the Party or among editors, writers, and artists. After 1954 the "thaw" was more noticeable in Poland than in other Communist countries. As noted, the present policy of the Gomułka government is to allow almost complete freedom of expression, except for criticism of the USSR and any challenge of the supremacy of the Party.

PARTY CONTROLS

The Party's control of information media has been almost entirely indirect. The publications of the Central Committee and policy directives have set the "line." Controls are imposed by placing loyal Party members in key positions and giving them the power to hire and fire other personnel.

ORGANIZATION. Party organizations which have direct responsibility for setting policy have varied in name and duties, but their function has remained constant. In October 1956 the following sections of the Secretariat of the Central Committee were most directly concerned with control of the mass media of information: Propaganda; Radio, Press, and Publications; Culture and Science; and Organization (see Chart, Polish Agencies For Control of Information Media).

Of these the Propaganda Section was the most important, for it gave general direction to the Party propaganda policy and its directives affected the operation of all the other sections, even those charged with supervision of various industries. The Radio, Press, and Publications Section, though not responsible to the Propaganda Section, elaborated the general directives in their particular application to the media and to the organs of censorship. The Culture and Science Section supervised the libraries administered by the Ministry of Culture and Arts. The Organization Section supervised the publications of the Party and other organizations. The Party is at present in the process of reorganization and many of its functioning sections have been abolished. Many of the information functions may now be centralized in the Propaganda Department that was formed in December 1956.

In July 1957 the establishment of a Commission of Publishing was announced, its members to be chosen from the Party apparatus, experts in the field, and editors of leading periodicals and newspapers. The permanent secretary of the Commission is a full-time employee of the Propaganda Department, providing continuous liaison. As customary in Polish administrative practice the Commission is advisory, and decisions will continue to be made in the Department. Its function is to study the problems of publishing and to make recommendations. It seems likely that one of the areas of study is organization of the Party's propaganda activities.

PERSONNEL APPOINTMENTS. Since October 1956 the most die-hard Stalinists have been removed from Party and government posts, while others have been assigned to less influential positions. As with all agencies of the central government, the chairmen of the committees which control the operation of publishing, radio, television, film production, and censorship are appointed by the Prime Minister with the approval of the Council of Ministers. Generally, such in-

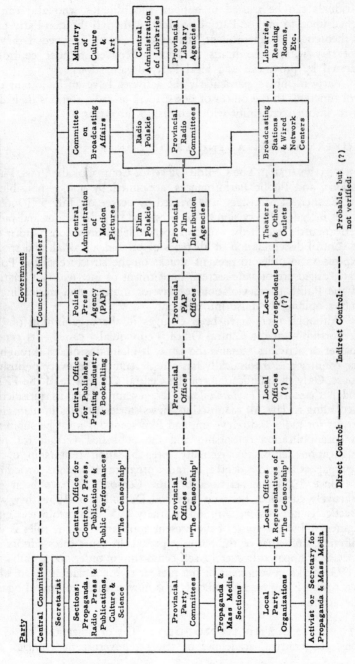

POLISH AGENCIES FOR CONTROL OF MASS MEDIA OF INFORMATION, OCTOBER 1956

Party

Government

Central Committee

Council of Ministers

Secretariat

Sections: Propaganda, Radio, Press & Publications, Culture & Science

Central Office for Control of Press, Publications & Public Performances "The Censorship"

Central Office for Publishers, Printing Industry & Bookselling

Polish Press Agency (PAP)

Central Administration of Motion Pictures

Film Polskie

Committee on Broadcasting Affairs

Radio Polskie

Ministry of Culture & Art

Central Administration of Libraries

Provincial Party Committees

Provincial Offices of "The Censorship"

Provincial Offices

Provincial PAP Offices

Provincial Film Distribution Agencies

Provincial Radio Committees

Provincial Library Agencies

Propaganda & Mass Media Sections

Local Party Organizations

Local Offices & Representatives of "The Censorship"

Local Offices (?)

Local Correspondents (?)

Theaters & Other Outlets

Broadcasting Stations & Wired Network Centers

Libraries, Reading Rooms, Etc.

Activist or Secretary for Propaganda & Mass Media

Direct Control: ——— Indirect Control: - - - - Probable, but not verified: (?)

dividuals can be trusted to appoint subordinates who also can be relied upon to impose Party discipline. Although the non-Party press is theoretically "independent," its editors may be removed if they do not stay within the limits of Party directives. Similar control is exerted by provincial and local Party organizations.

Party members, particularly the activists, have an important control function. In the offices of newspapers or radio stations their duty is to insure conformity with censorship directives.

GOVERNMENTAL AGENCIES OF CONTROL

CENSORSHIP. The Central Office for Control of the Press, Publications, and Public Performances, appointed by and responsible to the Council of Ministers, was created by decree on July 5, 1946. Its duties included supervision of the press and of publications and public performances within the range of specific legal provisions; and it was to control dissemination of all types of printed, pictorial, and spoken expression in order to prevent attacks on the structure of the Polish state; disclosure of state secrets; impairment of international relations of the Polish state; violations of law or morals; and misleading of public opinion by false information.

Although there have been changes in the organization of "the Censorship"—as the Central Office is colloquially called—its general charter of activities remains the same. It maintains offices throughout the country and theoretically has a representative in every publishing house. Only the publications of the Central Committee of the PZPR, and perhaps only *Trybuna Ludu*, are exempt from its jurisdiction. According to law, all manuscripts, news stories, articles in magazines, scripts for radio and television, and film scenarios must be submitted for prepublication censorship and the published version for postpublication censorship. Actually, prepublication censorship of the newspapers and, to a degree, of radio programs is seldom carried out.

Since 1954 the activities of "the Censorship" have been progressively curtailed; between July and December of 1956 they were practically nonexistent. Around February 1957 censorship was again tightened, but the spirit of the present application of the rules is very different from that of the Stalinist period. In some cases editors and publishers apparently exercise self-censorship in order not to embarrass the Gomułka government in the present trying situation. Even when censorship is imposed by officials it is now possible to appeal against the action.

LICENSING AND MONOPOLY. The organizations, trade unions, cooperatives, academies of science, government agencies, and

Party organizations engaged in publishing must obtain licenses and submit to detailed central regulation and supervision. Licenses are issued by "the Censorship." An application must include details about the nature of the planned publication and of its financial plan, as well as a statement of willingness to act in accordance with central publishing plans.

Set up by law in 1951, the Central Office for Publishers, Printing Industry, and Bookselling supervises all book and periodical publication and develops the over-all publishing plan, which includes technical requirements of costs, prices, sales, size of editions. In the autumn of 1956 the agency was accused of undue interference with the choice of subjects for publication, of causing excessive time to be taken in publication, and of faulty distribution methods. In November the chairman stated that the Committee was being decentralized and that administrative control would be replaced by that of agencies concerned with the organizations of public opinion—the institutes, learned societies, and professional and public organizations. He further stated that he had proposed that the Central Office be abolished as an independent agency and its curtailed functions be transferred to the Ministry of Culture and Arts. Whether the proposed decentralization has in fact become effective or whether the Central Office has been transferred is not known at present.

OTHER CONTROLS. Under a decree of September 1946 censorship of correspondence, radiotelegrams, and radio conversations with foreign countries was abolished. It was necessary, however, to take letters addressed abroad to the post office unsealed for currency inspection, since sending currency out of the country was prohibited. In late September 1956 this last requirement was abolished, and both ordinary letters and registered letters may now be put sealed into post boxes. Incoming letters and packages were and still are subject to customs inspection. So far as can be determined, there has been no censorship of internal mail.

Newspapers and Periodicals

In comparison with the number of newspapers and periodicals published during the interwar period, the size of the the postwar press is small. Recent expansion, however, has been rapid. In the spring of 1957 the catalogue issued by the government's newspaper and periodical distribution agency (Przedsiębiorstwa Upowszechniania Prasy i Książki "Ruch"—Ruch Enterprise for Popularization of Press and Books) contained 972 listings including 46 dailies, 186 factory newspapers, 80 provincial papers, 96 scientific periodicals, 198 economic, technical, and agricultural periodicals, 33 sports papers, and 23 periodicals published by various religious organizations. Since October 1956 so many new publications have been started and old ones discontinued that even the Poles find it difficult to keep up with the changes.

Polish circulation figures refer to the number of copies printed rather than sold. Until recently, the press was heavily subsidized and the announced printing could not be interpreted as an index of real distribution. Unsold copies are known to have run as high as 40 percent of those printed. Apparently, the Party press had a much higher rate of return than the illustrated non-Party newspapers and periodicals. Since October 1956 the government has attempted to make the press self-supporting; prices have been raised and the number of copies drastically reduced. Some of the newspapers have begun to publish the number of copies printed for each issue, and it is probable that these figures now are reasonably close to the actual circulation.

As soon as the Lublin government was established it set out to reorganize the Polish press on the Soviet model. Since all printing presses were in its hands, it was able during the first years to enforce conformity to its rules. At first, tentatively, writers were permitted some leeway in the choice of subjects. If they wrote about politics, however, they were not allowed to be critical of the new government or of the Soviet Union. Gradually, controls were tightened and the mechanisms and requirements of censorship were established. Between 1948 and 1953 there was little in the selection of material, treatment, and general tone to distinguish the Polish press from that of the other satellites and the USSR, or one Polish paper from another. Only the locale of the news and its concern with certain peculiarly national or regional problems marked the press as Polish. Otherwise it extolled the virtues and accomplishments of the socialist system, excoriated the system's enemies at home and abroad, and sought to gain adherents to the theories of socialism and the policies and practices of the Party. The relation of events to such goals, rather than their timeliness or newsworthiness, was the main criterion for publication. The press was doctrinaire and didactic and, to the Polish people, exceedingly dull. But the government was determined to make the people read its newspapers and periodicals, for a time requiring students to spend stated periods in reading rooms. Subscriptions to certain newspapers were obligatory and newspapers often were read to assembled groups.

After the death of Stalin greater variety in style and subject matter gradually appeared, along with increasing, though still limited, divergence of opinion. In August 1955 the weekly literary review *Nowa Kultura* (New Culture) published Adam Wàzyk's "Poem for Adults" (see chap. 21), which, though denounced by the Politburo of the Central Committee of the PZPR, was acclaimed by many writers and Party activists. *Po Prostu* (Simply Speaking), a political-cultural weekly, was founded in 1955 by a group of young intelligentsia and soon became an outlet for increasing criticism of the government and Party leadership by elements that were to force the political changes of October 1956. In the period between the Poznan rebellion and the end of 1956 the press was almost entirely free of effective restraints; open expression of political opinion ranged from advocacy of a return to "Stalinist" policies to complete rejection of socialism and the Party.

Since the beginning of 1957 the Party, under the leadership of Gomułka, has reinstated its control of the press but has allowed and encouraged diversity of expression on almost all subjects except criticism of the Soviet Union, advocacy of the rejection of socialism, or challenge to Party leadership. The new policy of forcing all newspapers to be self-supporting has affected content and treatment by making it necessary that they have public appeal.

For the most part, news today is reported quite promptly. The amount of objective reporting has greatly increased. For example, *Trybuna Ludu* (The People's Tribune), the organ of the Central Committee of the PZPR, reported the findings of the United Nations Committee on Hungary with practically no explicit editorial comment. The July meeting of the Socialist International in Vienna, which under former policies would have been the subject of a blistering attack if reported at all, was factually reported, with only one editorializing device—the insertion of "so-called" before the name of the organization.

Various devices are being used to make the papers more interesting to the people. Human interest stories now are frequent and "cheese-cake" is occasionally included. The interview technique is often used. *Życie Warszawy* (Warsaw's Life) one of the leading papers of the capital, has a regular column—entitled "Excuse Me, Only Three Questions."—in which three questions on timely topics are put to visiting leaders from foreign countries and to Party and government officials and others. Public opinion polls on a variety of important problems and controversial subjects are taken and reported. Photographs are more frequent and some advertising is allowed.

Although these general trends apply to the entire press, certain differences in degree reflect the division of the press into Party and non-Party organs. For the most part the division relates to the function and sponsorship of the various newspapers and periodicals and does not concern the degree of control or the mechanics of operation;

except for *Trybuna Ludu* and possibly some of the other publications of the Central Committee of the PZPR, all newspapers, periodicals, and books are subject to the same censorship authority and bound by the same operating rules.

THE PARTY PRESS

In an article in *Trybuna Ludu* for May 29, 1957, Jerzy Morawski, a member of the Politburo of the Party, made an authoritative and relatively precise definition of the current functions of the Party press. As a particularly important and sensitive link between the Party and the masses, he stated, the Party press should take an active part in achieving the goals of socialism. In so doing, it must take up difficult and unpopular matters whether the readers are pleased or not. Its chief attention should be

> . . . concentrated on . . . convincing the working people of the equity of the socialist way of development, as the only road of progress, independence, and the improvement of the standard of living of the working masses.

More specifically, he defined as the primary task of the Party press making a knowledge of economics more general among the masses and the Party activists and placing

> . . . on a new realistic ground the problem of the participation of the working class in the administration of factories and . . . [to] develop participation of the peasant in economic self-government.

In setting the limits of permissible criticism for the Party press and the non-Party press, both of which had in previous months engaged in lively discussion of the definition of the "Polish road" and the role of the Party in charting it, he said:

> We also believe that newspapers and periodicals should also display their own initiative, they should put forward new ideas, should develop a discussion on problems which *can be discussed*. We do not want our press to propagate *erroneous views, contrary to the Party line*. But not every search for new solutions in matters in which the *Party did not adopt a stand* can be considered an error.

> We do not want unjustified and unjust criticism, but on the other hand we do not want a stifling of criticism to be tolerated, where the criticism is just and justified. A criticism like that is necessary.

Whether or not the Party press actually provides the realistic and constructive assistance now being asked of it, the path in that direction is being charted by the writings and public statements of Gomułka and other Party and government leaders. They have consistently set forth, with a clarity and bluntness unknown in Poland for many years, the harsh, unpleasant facts of the economic situation of the country and the unavoidable difficulties and problems which face the government and the people. Although the Party press does not attempt to appeal to the public with the methods used by the non-Party press, it is now attempting to reach the people by factually reporting specific, practical explanations of the Party's plans and actions.

The most important Party newspapers and periodicals are published by the Central Committee of the Party (see Tables 6 and 7). Its authoritative paper is *Trybuna Ludu,* which to a certain degree serves as a model for the rest of the Polish press but is not copied as *Pravda* is in the Soviet Union. Less definitive, but perhaps as important, is *Polityka* (Politics), the weekly journal of the Gomułka faction of the PZPR; it specializes in the political, economic, and social problems of Poland as well as international economic affairs. *Nowe Drogi* (New Ways) is the Party's chief theoretical journal. Various other publications are directed toward special groups—peasants, youth, and the activists.

Trybuna Ludu is fairly typical of Polish newspapers, except that it carries more Party interpretation of events and official news than other papers do, particularly those of the non-Party press. A rather high proportion of news of general interest is also carried. It has six pages in its daily edition, eight on Sunday. (Four pages are more usual for other papers.) There is no editorial page but editorials or reports of special importance appear in the upper left corner of page one.

Provincial and many country and local Party organizations have their own publications, which generally follow the pattern set by the central organs, although the lower Party organizations seem to have considerable authority and responsibility for their own newspapers. Press control does not stem directly from the central control bodies; it is imposed by the provincial control committees and local Party secretaries. Generally, an editorial board supervises the work of the editor and his staff.

THE NON-PARTY PRESS

Newspapers and periodicals of the non-Party press (see Tables 6 and 7) are published by diverse organizations, including government departments, trade unions, the Church, political parties, and groups of individuals, and represent a wide variety of interests. Although subject to licensing requirements and censorship they are except in political affairs allowed considerable freedom of expression. Hardest hit by current censorship are such publications as *Po Prostu, Nowa Kultura, Życie Warszawy,* and *Szpilki* (The Pins); these not only were critical of the "Stalinist" regime but vigorously expressed views about the direction the Party and the new government should take in following a "Polish road to socialism." A number of "liberal" editors were dismissed from their posts and "revisionism" is being suppressed, but so far as is known no papers have been closed and criticism and discussion continues to be vigorous within the prescribed limits. Some news stories have been purchased directly from West European news agencies, but the frequency and extent of this practice is not known.

The range of the nontechnical and nonprofessional publications in Poland is illustrated by a few of the new publications. *Świat i Polska* (The World and Poland), first issued in February 1957, is a weekly publication of a rather high intellectual level essentially interested in articles and commentaries on international affairs and Poland's role in the "consolidation of the idea of cooperation and peaceful relations between nations." It includes articles by specialists and foreign journalists on world economics, foreign trade, and activities of international organizations; some issues are to be published in foreign languages. In February 1957 *Przygoda* (Adventure) also appeared; Poland's first comic periodical, it featured the "Wild West," space travel, philately, crossword puzzles, and competitions. The issue was sold out immediately. Contests and competitions seem to be very appealing to Poles young and old: in May 1957 two other publications, both fortnightly, were announced. One of them, *Rozrywki* (Recreation), is to be entirely devoted to crossword and other types of puzzles, word games, and the like. The prizes offered included savings books for as much as 3,000 złotys and an excursion abroad for the most consistent winner during a three-month period. The Association of Polish Journalists issues *Szaradzista* (Charade Game) which features various kinds of riddles and "intellectual entertainment." *Filipinka,* addressed to teen-agers, contains in addition to competitions a cultural section, short stories, and advice on fashions. *Zwierciadło* (The Mirror) is addressed to women, with articles on such subjects as cosmetics, dress design, travel, and birth control.

In recent months a number of newspapers and journals which formerly were official organs of government departments and organizations have changed in status. *Nowa Kultura,* formerly the organ of the Writer's Union, is now called "independent," although still edited and published by the same men. *Żołnierz Wolności* (Soldier of Freedom), formerly published by the Ministry of National Defense, is now published by the Polish Army. The significance of such changes is not known. They may be a part of the general reduction of the bureaucracy undertaken by the Gomułka government.

POLISH PRESS AGENCY

The Polska Agencja Prasowa (Polish Press Agency), known as PAP, was established by law in September 1945 as the official and sole press agency of the country, responsible to the Council of Ministers. PAP collects foreign and domestic news and distributes it to government offices, newspapers, radio stations, and state institutions. It also publishes government organs, including the official gazette of laws— *Monitor Polski*—and maintains a publicity and advertising service. With headquarters in Warsaw, PAP has branch offices in the larger Polish towns and correspondents throughout the country. It has permanent offices and correspondents in ten foreign capitals—Berlin, Budapest, London, Moscow, New York, Paris, Peiping, Prague, Rome, and Sofia—and plans to station correspondents in Belgrade and Hanoi.

PAP maintains mutual exchange agreements with Tass, Reuters, and Agence France-Presse (as of 1957 news from the latter two was being used largely for information within the organization rather than for promulgation). It also has exchange agreements with a number of national eastern European and Asiatic agencies. The PAP daily service averages some 25,000 words, of which about 40 percent concerns foreign news.

Through its virtual monopoly over the gathering and domestic distribution of foreign news, as well as its domestic resources, PAP has acted as an agency of control as well as dissemination. Its censorship functions were particularly apparent, before October 1956, in the distribution of foreign news: in addition to its selected releases to the mass media, it published a special bulletin, referred to as the "inner bulletin," which was circulated only to high government officials and Party leaders and was classified as confidential. The bulletin dealt only with foreign news, giving a prompt and fairly complete coverage of important events, articles, translations of speeches, agreements, documents, and the like. After October the confidential classification of the special bulletin was dropped; reportedly its transformation into a weekly digest of foreign news available to public subscription is being considered as a means of compensating for the shortage of foreign newspapers.

Radio and Television

ROLE AND ORGANIZATION

The Polish Radio, Polskie Radio, is operated by the Committee for Broadcasting (Komitet do Spraw Radiofonii), which is responsible to the Council of Ministers. The manufacture, installation, and maintenance of radio and television equipment are, however, under the jurisdiction of the Ministry of Communications. This division of authority has been subjected to considerable criticism in recent months. Consolidation under the Committee for Broadcasting Affairs has been suggested, but so far as can be determined no change has yet been made.

The technical duties of the Committee, as outlined in a 1951 law, are to promote and develop the country's radio and television services; to establish the broadcasting station network; to negotiate international broadcasting matters; to issue licenses for construction, operation, and possession of radio and television receiving and transmitting equipment; to supervise programs, organization, and management; and to finance enterprises and their operation of radio or television equipment.

By law, Polskie Radio is the voice of the government. In practice, it speaks for the Party, a role which was emphatically restated by government and Party leaders after October 1956 during the controversy about the part to be played by the mass media under the new regime. Since early 1957 various steps have been taken to improve the content and presentation of the programs on radio for the Party considers it second only to the press as a propaganda medium.

Radio has two sources of revenue—a license fee charged owners of all sets, including wired speakers, and a government subsidy.

BROADCASTING AND RECEPTION

Broadcasting in Poland is of three types: radio, wire, and television. Polskie Radio operates at least 13 long-wave and medium-wave transmitters, with a total power of 790 kilowatts, 10 short-wave transmitters totaling 264 kilowatts, and 1 FM transmitter. Most broadcasting is from Warsaw; some of the regional stations are little more than relay stations for Warsaw programs. The Five-Year Plan (1956–60) provides for increasing the power of transmitters but not for building new ones. An unknown number of transmitters which previously were used to jam incoming foreign broadcasts are being converted to normal broadcasting stations.

Although listening to foreign broadcasts has never been prohibited, and was quite open during most of the postwar years, a number of transmitters in Poland formed part of the Soviet jamming network. In October 1956 workers in these stations requested the government to stop jamming operations. When such orders were not immediately forthcoming workers in several stations, including an important one in Katowice, went on strike. In November the government announced that it was converting all of the jamming stations to regular operations in order to answer criticism "with argument, not noise." No Polish station is now engaged in jamming, although Russian military transmitters on Polish territory may be.

Approximately 3,700 centers transmit radio programs to loudspeakers and wired receivers in such institutions as state farms, agricultural cooperatives, factories, hospitals, clubs, schools, as well as in private homes. Some 14,500 villages are included in the wired network, but not all rural areas are covered.

The radio audience has increased rapidly and Polskie Radio estimated the number of radio listeners in 1956 at 14 million, about half the population. In 1955 about 3 million Poles owned radio receivers or subscribed to the wired network—about 109 per 1,000 population as compared to 47.6 in 1949 and 26.5 in 1939. On the basis of these figures, there are now probably about 3.8 million owners and subscribers. Some 55 percent of the receivers in use in 1955 were tube receivers, 45 percent loud-speakers or radio headphones (see Table 8). The government has been trying to increase both domestic production and importation of receivers, and to improve the quality of wired reception.

Radio sets have been in short supply since the end of World War II when few survived the confiscation policies of the Germans. For a number of years coupons which could be obtained only from trade union organizations were required before a prospective buyer could get his name on a waiting list for a receiver. Whether this regulation is still in effect is not known, but, so long as it existed, farmers had great difficulty in buying sets. Waiting lists are reported still to exist.

In March 1956 there were two television stations, one in Warsaw, the other in Lodz. A third was scheduled to begin operation in Poznan in April and another near Katowice in December. According to plan, the Katowice station will have a power range enabling it to cover nearly all of Upper Silesia; it is to be connected by cable with Warsaw and, it is hoped, with Moravská Ostrava in Czechoslovakia, thus linking with the European television network. Stations in Gdansk and Szczecin are also being planned. All the stations use imported equipment, chiefly British and French.

Official sources estimated that there were about 10,000 television receivers in use in 1956, with an average of 8 viewers per set. Viewers are concentrated around Warsaw and Lodz.

PROGRAMING

Polskie Radio's broadcast time is divided as follows: verbal, 19.3 percent; "verbal-musical," 33.7 percent; musical, 39.1 percent; other, 7.9 percent. Musical programs are predominantly classical, but folk and lighter music as well as jazz are broadcast. Content of the verbal broadcast closely resembles that of the press. Speeches, open letters, and comments of Party and government leaders are broadcast in full, but little use is made of "live" broadcasts or tape recordings of the speeches. At the height of the Stalinist era many of the programs were uninteresting to most Poles—reports on accomplishments and failures of government programs, "inspirational" talks designed to whip up enthusiasm for socialist competitions, campaigns against "speculators," "hooliganism," and alcoholism. But a writer in *Przegląd Kulturalny* (The Cultural Review; November 1956) maintained that the Polish radio has

> to an important degree broken with the customary "empty talk" in its political and literary work, becoming, together with television, the field of interesting theatrical, musical, and artistic experiments and also of broadcasts on subjects of social interest.

The degree to which such a change has actually taken place cannot be determined, but a number of innovations in programs have in fact been introduced during the last year or so. Literary programs and discussions of music, art, and the theatre are frequent. Recordings of "authentic conversations" in factories, villages, and schools are used, and sessions of the *Sejm* and plenary sessions of Party committees are taped for broadcast. Important international documents are presented in dramatic form.

In June 1957, Warsaw Radio announced that it was initiating a new feature, "On the Warsaw Wavelength," which would broadcast taped recordings of opinions, proposals, and complaints of the "man on the street." Microphones were to be placed at pre-announced points in the city and citizens were invited to express their thoughts. "Wave Length 49," originally a special feature designed to combat "enemy propaganda," now deals more with domestic social and economic problems and frequently consists of talks with state and Party leaders on problems of current interest.

The Office of Studies and Program Evaluation of Polskie Radio is using public opinion polls to discover audience preferences and to report on public reactions to controversial problems. In April 1957, as part of a campaign to counteract discrimination against students who requested exemption from religious instruction (see chap. 5), there was a program of discussion and comment on a nationwide poll concerning the problem of tolerance. Similar polls are to be taken bimonthly in the future and although such programs contain Party line propaganda they deal more realistically and meaningfully with current problems and events and are cast in less hackneyed and bombastic form than in the past.

Polskie Radio also broadcasts talks for teachers as well as daily programs for approximately 28,000 schools equipped with receivers. These programs supplement the school curriculum and are approved by the Ministry of Education; they serve all classes in the elementary and secondary schools. Special programs for nursery schools are given twice a week. The Free University of the Air has over 200,000 student listeners.

In 1956 Polskie Radio transmitted programs in 14 languages, among them English, French, Italian, Spanish, German, Serbo-Croatian, Yiddish, Greek, Russian, and Polish, for a total of some 61 hours daily. In contrast to the themes broadcast abroad in the early 1950's, there is no urging of emigrants to return home or suggestion that they act as dissident groups in the countries of their residence. Realistic reports of conditions in Poland and frank accounts of problems are disseminated. Emigrants are urged to act as "unofficial ambassadors of the Polish cause." During the negotiations over United States aid to Poland, in the spring of 1957, broadcasts to the Poles in America urged them to support the Polish request by exerting influence on their congressmen and the American public.

Books

PUBLISHING

There are several hundred book publishing houses in all parts of Poland. The most important are in Warsaw, among them the State Publishing Institute (Państwowy Instytut Wydawniczy—PIW), Publishing Cooperative for Cultural Publications, "The Reader" (Spółdzielnia wydawniczo-oświatowa—"Czytelnik"), Book of Knowledge (Książka i Wiedza—KiW), "Our Book-Shop" ("Nasza Księfarnia" —NK), Iskry, Pax, Instytut Wojekowy, Państwowe Wydawnictwo, and "Popular Science" (Wiedza Powszechna). Państwowy Instytut Literacki, a very active firm, is located in Cracow. All Polish publishing houses are highly specialized: some concentrate on children's books, some on books for teen-agers, others on dictionaries, political books, science, art, fiction, or nonfiction.

All publishing is regulated by the government through the Central Office for Publishers, Printing Industry, and Bookselling, and all publishers depend upon the Central Publishing Administration (Centralny Urząd Wydawniczy) for allocation of paper and printing facilities. Many houses are operated by government agencies, some others are directed by academies of science or professional organizations.

During 1956, according to PAP, 9,874 titles were published,

generally in large editions, for a total of close to 143 million copies. Among these were 1,039 fiction titles (20.9 million copies) 346 children's books (23.9 million copies), 321 titles dealing with agricultural subjects (2.8 million copies), and 762 technical titles (3.5 million copies). For a population of some 28 million such a volume of publication is extremely high. More titles but small editions were planned for 1957. Most titles are original Polish books. The majority of translations are from Russian; only a few from French, German, and English have been available, and they are generally books which were first published in the 1920's and 1930's.

A great deal of the published material has been heavily weighted with propaganda. Fiction was forced into the mold of "socialist realism" (see chap. 21), textbooks, particularly those in history and economics, expounded Communist interpretation and theory; the writings of Marx, Lenin, and Stalin were issued in large editions. There are indications of change. Restrictions on literature have been reduced. New histories which are to accord with fact are being written. There are more and more varied translations and imports of western publications are increasing. It has been announced that the Ministry of National Defense will publish such works as J. F. C. Fuller's *Second World War,* Dale O. Smith's *U. S. Military Doctrine,* Heinz Guderian's *Panzer Leader,* De Gaule's *Memoirs,* and Eisenhower's *Crusade in Europe,* as well as a series of works on the participation of Polish military units in the campaigns in the West.

The government has consistently tried to stimulate the reading of books. An interwar Polish publisher estimated that whereas before World War II about 15 percent of the population read books now about 50 percent do. Book publishing is heavily subsidized and prices have been kept very low—estimated to be about equivalent to the price of the less expensive paperback of the United States or even lower. There has recently been considerable effort to make publishing a self-sustaining industry. With the relaxation of control on selection of titles, it is hoped that production will more closely reflect the desires of the people and that sales will increase.

DISTRIBUTION

Book stores and stalls abound in Polish cities and are found throughout the country. Many are operated by Dom Książki (Home of the Book), an organization which also handles distribution and conducts such activities as book fairs to stimulate distribution.

Libraries, nationalized in 1946 and placed under the administration of the Ministry of Culture and Arts in 1951, have been given an important role in the over-all plan for molding public opinion.

Controlled by the Ministry's Central Administration of Libraries, the system includes public libraries, school libraries, scientific collections, bookmobiles, and small collections placed in reading rooms of organizations and enterprises. The bookmobiles supply books ·and periodicals to places of work, hospitals, collective farms, private homes, and so on. In 1955 there were about 4,000 libraries with 58,216 branches, and 28,900 other library outlets; they contained some 22 million books and were used by over 3 million readers.

Until quite recently the library collections were restricted to titles by approved authors and heavily weighted with Marxist-Lenist theoretical works and propaganda material. Such restrictions apparently are being withdrawn. New titles will be available and many formerly banned titles are being put back into circulation. Warsaw radio has announced that in February 1957 libraries in Wroclaw had begun putting back into circulation such formerly prohibited books as the works of Trotsky, political literature of the interwar period, including Piłsudski's writings, various Polish and foreign books on the occupation and postwar years, among them Winston Churchill's memoirs, the fiction of Zofia Kossak-Szczucka, Zygmunt Nowakowski, and Juliusz Kaden-Bandrowski, and *Grimm's Fairy Tales.*

Films

Production and distribution of films in Poland are controlled by the Central Administration of Motion Pictures (Centralny Urząd Kinematografii—CUK) which is responsible to the Council of Ministers. Its operating agency is known as Film Polski—FP. Domestic production of films has been relatively small and artistic and technical standards have been rather low, though a few films have won prizes abroad (see chap. 21). According to official statistics, 204 motion pictures were produced in 1955, only 9 of them full-length features. Of the 195 short feature films, 82 were newsreels, 27 were puppet films, cartoons, and popular scientific shorts, others were educational. Imported films numbered 115, most of them from the USSR, Czechoslovakia, and East Germany; French, Italian and English films are, however, the most popular and are being shown in increasing numbers.

In 1955 there were 2,672 cinemas in Poland: 1,434 permanent installations in urban areas, 953 in rural areas, and 285 touring theaters. Sixteen-millimeter projectors and educational films are available from the library of the Polish Film Institute, a section of Film Polski. The number of cinemas is far from sufficient to meet the demands of the people, and long queues are reported as common.

Information from Abroad

Radio broadcasts probably are the most important means of contact between Poland and the West. Foreign broadcasts have been popular, and many are beamed directly to Poland in the Polish language. The programs of the British Broadcasting Corporation aim to present objective, world-wide news coverage; the Voice of America presents news coverage and features designed to give information about America. Radio Free Europe seeks to keep alive hopes for an eventual liberation from Soviet domination. Radio Liberation supports the overthrow of Soviet communism.

The most important reason for listening to foreign broadcasts appears to be the desire to get factual, unbiased news of the world and of Poland, which many listeners believe cannot be obtained from domestic news sources. The desire for entertainment—music, drama, and other features—also plays a part. Among a sample of 108 Poles who defected to the West in 1951 and 1952, strong anti-Communist feelings and a belief that liberation would come from the West underlined the motivation for foreign radio listening. They wanted to learn what progress was being made toward that end, when the day would come, what the future of Poland would be; they also sought information that would discredit the Polish regime. Radio Madrid had a large following because of its vigorous anti-Communist stand. In more recent years Radio Free Europe has gained a sizable audience for much the same reasons.

Books from western countries as well as from the USSR and the satellites are being imported and distributed through the International Book and Press Clubs. The *New York Times* and *Life* magazine are on sale and other publications are to be made available shortly. Increasing numbers of Poles are traveling in Europe and America and reporting freely on their visits; more foreigners are visiting Poland and talking freely with the people. United States participation in the trade fair in the summer of 1957 was the first American activity in Poland, other than diplomatic representation, since the close in 1948 of the office of the United States Information Service.

Attitudes toward Information

Until the grip of propagandistic conformism began to loosen, eager as the Poles were for information, their general reaction to the press and to the verbal content of the mass media was that of boredom. Repetitiveness of propaganda themes and lack of variety in style, tone, and presentation contributed to the general lack of interest.

Musical programs on the radio were popular but there was a wide-spread feeling that too much Russian music was played. Although many avoided political and economic news, confined their reading and listening to sports, entertainment, occupation news, and food-price announcements, a large majority of the people were exposed to various media, either under compulsion or of their own volition.

The changes in the content of newspapers, periodicals, and radio since the October 1956 events have had great effect. Writers, editors, and producers enthusiastically joined the controversy over the new policies during the months of freedom from censorship, and, even though they are again subject to official restrictions, there is still latitude for individuality and variety, and less distortion of fact. The public has responded with an increased demand for newspapers and periodicals. The new radio programs are provoking great interest and many comments from listeners.

FOREIGN RELATIONS

THE POLISH STATE WAS DESTROYED AT THE END OF THE EIGHT-eenth century by the pattern of political relationships that emerged in Europe with the rise of Russian and German (Prussian) power. Poland's independence after World War I was made possible by the simultaneous collapse of Germany and Russia and rested on the ability of other powers to preserve and defend the order created at Versailles. The revival of German and Russian might during the 1930's and the inability of the League of Nations to protect the *status quo* led once more to the destruction of Poland as a political entity. Subsequently, as a result of the distribution of power established in Europe at the end of World War II, Poland became a Soviet vassal.

Polish foreign policy today is little more than a function of the world-wide power balance of which the USSR and the United States are the main weights. Poland cannot display any great independence in foreign relations as long as the Soviet Union is able to maintain a continuous position of preponderance in eastern Europe. Further, Poland is economically dependent upon the USSR and the Soviet bloc (see chap. 16). But by taking advantage of existing weaknesses, tensions, and struggles—both within and outside the Communist bloc—the Polish Government can within limits pursue its national interests.

Since Stalin's death in 1953, Poland has attempted to free itself from total subordination to Soviet policy. With the return of Gomułka in October 1956 the government demanded that the USSR treat Poland as an "independent, sovereign state." This meant, above all, respect for its independence in internal affairs. The Gomułka government has been attempting to strengthen its internal position by seeking closer, independent ties with other Communist countries resisting strict Russian controls, notably China and Yugoslavia. It has also encouraged an increase in political, cultural, and economic contacts with non-Communist nations and is seeking their support, in addition to that of the USSR, for Polish claims to the "western territories" —the former German lands incorporated into Poland after World War II.

In all of this, however, Gomułka, the Party, and the government have the fate of Hungary before them. Gomułka has at all times been careful to insist that maintenance of the Soviet alliance and continued membership of Poland in the "socialist commonwealth of nations" must remain the bedrock of Poland's foreign relations. While the Soviet leaders have relinquished many controls over Polish domestic affairs in favor of indirect pressure and influence, the Gomułka government is acutely aware that the USSR is not likely to tolerate the existence of a fully independent and potentially hostile Polish state.

Interwar Poland

In January 1918 President Woodrow Wilson called for the establishment of an independent Polish state. In June 1918 Britain, France, and Italy issued a declaration stating that the creation of a united Poland was a condition of a just peace. On November 11, 1918, the official date of the creation of the Polish state, the armistice agreement required the Central Powers to evacuate all occupied territory, including Poland.

The boundaries of the new state were to be determined by the peace conference. Poland's political leaders were divided on the issue. One major group led by Józef Piłsudski demanded the historical eastern frontiers of 1772 which would have included in Poland large Ukrainian and Belorussian areas and populations. Others felt that such demands could not be fulfilled, or, if realized, would create major problems of overextension, and minority difficulties which would only weaken the new state. The United States, under the Wilsonian principle of self-determination, wanted a Poland the boundaries of which would include only Poles, insofar as this was compatible with the creation of a viable economic entity. France, the traditional "friend" of Poland, sought a "bulwark against Bolshevism" and a deterrent to a revived Germany.

The Treaty of Versailles and subsequent plebiscites in Silesia gave Poland almost all of the territory formerly under German (Prussian) administration. East Prussia remained German, but a Polish corridor to the sea cut it off from Germany proper, and Danzig was made a Free City under the administration of the League of Nations. The remaining boundaries were more difficult to settle. The League determined the Czech boundary in 1920 to the satisfaction of neither party.

The boundary with Lithuania and the eastern boundary were settled on Polish initiative. Marshal Piłsudski led the newly organized Polish army against the Russians in an attempt to return to the boundary of 1772 which would have placed most of the Ukraine within the new Polish state. The Russian counteroffensive was turned back, with the support of the French, in the suburbs of Warsaw. The eastern boundary was finally settled in 1921 by the Treaty of Riga, which divided Belorussia and the Ukraine between Poland and Russia. It was not until 1923 that the Poles secured international recognition of the gains resulting from the military campaign against Lithuania and which placed the city of Vilna and its environs within the new Poland.

The settlement of frontiers by diplomacy and force, regardless of ethnic considerations assured tension in Poland's future foreign relations. Polish insistence on maintaining the western boundaries, bringing a sizable German minority within the Polish state, was to prove a fatal source of conflict with a resurgent Germany. Territorial demands on Poland's other neighbors, most prominently the Czechs, served as another source of rivalry and dispute.

In the early years after World War I Polish foreign policy was characterized by active participation in the League of Nations and by close cooperation with France. France came to Poland's aid in the critical days of 1920; and it helped Poland equip and organize its army, sending instructors and officers and granting loans for the purchase of military material. France saw Poland as her main ally in the east: a strong Poland would replace tsarist Russia as the watchdog on Germany's eastern frontier. In 1921 the Franco-Polish Treaty was signed providing for mutual consultation on matters of common interest and in the event of an attack; the treaty was supplemented by a military convention signed in September 1922. Another alliance, directed against Soviet Russia, was signed with Rumania in 1921 as the Polish state attempted to buttress its security through a series of bilateral agreements.

While Poland participated in the League of Nations and theoretically subscribed to the principles of collective security, it steadfastly refused to enter any multilateral arrangements with its immediate neighbors, reserving the right to act independently, particularly in the case of Czechoslovakia.

The French alliance remained the cornerstone of Polish relations until 1925 when France and Germany reached an agreement on their boundaries. The failure of the agreements to mention the eastern borders of Germany, while guaranteeing the inviolability of the Franco-German and Belgian-German frontiers, left many Poles feeling they were "sold down the river." The Soviet-German Treaty of 1926 increased the sense of danger. Once more the Poles were faced with the possibility of a German-Russian "concert." The threat seen in the Soviet-German agreement was made even worse by the feeling that French policy had bought security on the Rhine by giving the Germans a free hand in the east.

The year 1926 brought domestic as well as international crisis. The coup of Józef Piłsudski (see chap. 2) produced a basic reorientation in Polish foreign policy. Among factors which combined to create a sense of crisis were: the growing awareness of French weakness, especially after 1930; the continuing German demands for revision of its eastern boundaries; the specter of a renewed German-Russian *rapprochement* directed against the Polish frontiers; the tensions created by the Polish treatment of the minorities, especially the German, Ukrainian, and Belorussian (see chap. 4); and the continuing dispute between Poland and Lithuania over the Polish seizure of Vilna.

Under Piłsudski and his successors—the "regime of the colonels" —from 1932 until the invasion of Poland in 1939, Polish foreign policy was directed primarily by Colonel Józef Beck. Basing himself on "historical lessons," Beck tried to make Polish policy independent of both Germany and Russia by balancing the pressure of one against the other. A nonaggression pact with the Soviet Union was signed in 1932. In 1934 a similar pact was signed with Germany.

The attempt to pursue an independent policy by achieving a balance between Germany and Soviet Russia proved impossible. Poland's range of action was too restricted to allow her to shape the course of international relations in interwar Europe. The rise to power of Germany and of the Soviet Union returned Poland to a situation analagous to that of the eighteenth century. France was obviously weak; neither France nor Britain would take effective action to limit either German or Russian power; no nation appeared willing to risk war to save Polish boundaries. Moreover, the "regime of the colonels" could not really play off Russia and Germany against each other because it feared above all the specter of Bolshevism.

During the Munich Conference of 1938, which confirmed the Polish Government's suspicion of French and British policy, Beck exploited Czechoslovakia's weakened position by demanding the Teschen (Cieszyn) area. The Czech Government reluctantly acceded. Soon, however, Poland itself was faced with Hitler's demands for Danzig and an extraterritorial route across the Polish Corridor.

While Europe awaited Hitler's next move, British policy changed. On March 19, 1939, the British proposed to France, Russia, and Poland a joint declaration voicing determination to resist further Nazi aggression against any European country. Beck rejected the proposal because Russia had been brought in. Two days later Neville Chamberlain, the British Prime Minister, announced in the House of Commons that, in the event of an attack Britain would support Poland. On March 31, Beck declared that Poland would assist Britain under the same circumstances.

On April 28 Hitler denounced the German-Polish nonaggression pact. Beck's answer to Hitler was that Poland did not consider the 1934 nonaggression pact with Germany exclusive, citing German agreements with Slovakia and Italy, and Poland's own pact with Rumania and France; in addition, he maintained that Hitler had no cause for unilateral abrogation of the treaty because the Polish-British guarantee did not constitute a threat to Germany.

The worst fears of the Polish regime were realized in August 1939 when the Ribbentrop-Molotov pact was announced. In September the German armies crossed the Polish frontier and quickly swept over the Polish plain. The German invasion from the west was soon followed by a penetration by Soviet troops to an approximation of the Curzon Line. The German-Russian "concert" had again destroyed a Polish state.

World War II

The Polish government-in-exile (see chap. 2) served during the war as a symbol of resistance to the Axis powers, but its role in international affairs was slight. The fate of Poland remained in the hands of greater powers.

The German invasion of the Soviet Union in 1941 forced a *rapprochement* between the Polish government-in-exile, resident in London, and the Soviet Union. General Władysław Sikorski, Prime Minister and Commander-in-Chief, and the Soviet Ambassador in London signed an agreement on July 30, 1941, by which the USSR formally repudiated the Ribbentrop-Molotov Pact of 1939. No mention was made of Polish frontiers, the issue that was to split the *émigré* Poles. The Soviet Union ordered the release of all Poles held on Soviet territory either as prisoners of war or civilian internees. In August a Polish-Soviet military agreement was signed providing for the organization on Soviet territory of a Polish army, under the command of General Władysław Anders, to fight under the operational command of the Red Army. The difficulties faced by both Poles and Russians in the organization of the Anders' army increased the mutual distrust. In July 1942 Stalin agreed to the evacuation of the entire Polish force from Soviet territory.

The Russians began openly to pursue their own Polish policy; they disregarded the pleas of the Americans and British for allied unity. In January 1943 the Soviet Government announced that all Polish deportees remaining on Soviet soil would be treated as Soviet citizens; in February a call was issued to Poles still in the Soviet Union to join the military force being organized under the command of Colonel (later General) Zygmunt Berling.

The Crisis in Soviet-Polish relations reached its climax in April 1943. German reports of the discovery at Katyn of the mass grave of several thousand Polish officers massacred by the Russians caused the Polish government-in-exile to ask for an investigation by the International Red Cross. Moscow broke off diplomatic relations with the Polish government in London.

The British Government supported the Soviet demand that the Curzon Line be the basis for determining the Polish-Soviet border. After the November-December Teheran conference Winston Churchill increased pressure on the Poles to accept the Soviet position, but they remained adamant insisting upon a return to the pre-1939 frontiers.

In December 1943 the Russian army crossed the 1921 boundary, and the establishment under Communist auspices of the Home National Council (Krajowa Roda Narodowa—KRN) was announced. In January 1944 the Polish government in London tried to restore diplomatic relations with the Soviet Union and called on its underground forces in Poland to cooperate with the Red Army against the Germans. The Soviet Union rejected the Polish overtures on the ground that the Red Army was not yet on what it considered Polish soil.

The Red Army crossed the Bug River in July 1944. The establishment of the Polish Committee of National Liberation (the "Lublin Committee") was announced the same month. The Red Army, now on what the Soviets considered Polish territory, turned over the civil administration of the liberated area to the Lublin Poles. Stanisław Mikołajczyk, who became Premier in the Polish government-in-exile in June 1943 after General Sikorski's death, opened direct negotiations with the Soviet Union in Moscow in July 1944. Under heavy Soviet and British pressure, he accepted the Curzon Line as the basis for determining the eastern boundary. Failing to win over his colleagues in London, he resigned and was succeeded by the strongly anti-Soviet Socialist Tomasz Arciszewski. The London government-in-exile continued to insist on the 1921 boundaries.

In January 1945 the Soviet Union formally recognized the Lublin

Poles as the Government of Poland. The repeated objections of the United States, in which the British concurred, produced a major split in the policies of the members of the wartime Grand Alliance. At the Yalta Conference in February 1945 the Soviet Union confirmed its previously announced position that "the problem of Poland is inseparable from the problem of security of the Soviet Union." The task of the Conference was to find a solution to the Polish question that would meet the need to maintain the alliance, continue the war, and insure a stable peace. A new Polish government was to be created to replace both the Soviet-recognized "Lublin" government and the government-in-exile recognized by the United States and Great Britain. The Yalta decision called for a Polish provisional government which could "be more broadly based" because the western portions of interwar Poland had been liberated. The Lublin government was to "be reorganized on a broader democratic basis with the inclusion of democratic leaders from Poland itself and from Poles abroad." The new government was pledged to hold as soon as possible free and unfettered elections on the basis of universal suffrage and secret ballot. Once the government had been formed by such a free election, diplomatic relations with it would be established by the United States, Great Britain, and the Soviet Union.

The Conference Communiqué further declared that the three Powers "consider that the eastern frontier of Poland should follow the Curzon Line, with digressions . . . of five to eight kilometers in favor of Poland." Polish losses in the east were to be compensated by "substantial accessions of territory in the north and west," but "the final delimitation of the western frontiers of Poland should . . . await the peace conference." The reorganization of the Polish government was to be supervised by a commission of Soviet, British, and United States' representatives.

In April 1945 Mikołajczyk, who with his fellow Peasant Party members had withdrawn from the London government-in-exile, endorsed the Yalta decisions, including the boundary settlement, and declared "close and lasting friendship with Russia to be the keystone of future Polish policy."

In June 1945 the Three-Power commission agreed on the list of Poles to be invited to Moscow so that the Poles themselves might solve the problem of the composition of the new government. The representatives from the Communist-sponsored Warsaw (Lublin) government included the President, Bolesław Bierut; the Prime Minister, Edward Osubka-Morawski; and Władysław Gomułka, then Secretary-General of the Polish Workers' Party (Communist). Four additional leaders from within Poland but not associated with the regime were also included. The *émigré* Poles were represented by Mikołajczyk; Jan Stańczyk, Socialist and former Minister of Social Welfare and Labor in the government-in-exile; and the leader of the Polish Seamen's Union of Britain. No member of the London government was invited. While the government which emerged from the Moscow conference included Mikołajczyk and three other new members, it left the Communists and their left-Socialist allies in control with 16 out of the 20 posts. On July 5, 1945 this government was recognized by the United States and Great Britain; recognition by Czechoslovakia, France, Sweden, Norway, Switzerland, and Canada soon followed.

Postwar Poland

During the period of consolidation before 1948 the Polish Government retained a limited degree of independence in foreign policy. The dominant factors determining Polish attitudes, however, were the memory of the horrors of the German occupation and an awareness of the strength of the Soviet Union, reinforced by the presence of Soviet troops within the country. An additional influence upon Polish attitudes and policies was the fact that the Soviet Union alone of the Powers had recognized the Polish western boundary.

The Yalta Communiqué had declared that Polish territorial acquisitions at Germany's expense in the north and west would make up for losses in the east. But at the Big Three meeting in Potsdam in July and August 1945 the United States and Great Britain refused to recognize as final the Polish western boundary on the Oder-Niesse line; they insisted that the final determination of the Polish-German frontier should await the peace settlement with Germany.

Poland's major problem was reconstruction. Financial assistance through UNRRA and through United States' credits was sought and received. Increasing communist control over the country became obvious in 1947 when Poland refused an invitation to the Paris conference to discuss Marshall Plan aid. The Polish economy was tied to that of the Soviet Union and the country became dependent on Soviet economic policy (see chap. 16). In the autumn of 1949, Poland joined with the other Communist states in denouncing Yugoslavia and abrogated its three-year-old treaty with Belgrade. During the same period the leadership of the PZPR was purged of its "national" element.

Most Poles realized that the unsettled issue of the western boundary made dependence on the USSR necessary. Their memories of the German occupation tempered anti-Soviet feeling, but objections to

Warsaw's subservient role in international affairs played a part in the general feeling of resentment against the attempted Sovietization of Poland. During the period from 1948 to the return to power of Gomułka the Poles felt isolated, especially from the cultural centers of western Europe. They resented the subordination of the Party to the Soviet leadership, the "colonial" status of their country proven by the below-world market price of exports to the Soviet Union (see chap. 16), and the stationing and movement of Soviet troops in Poland with no Polish control. One of the demands in the reassertion of Polish identity, which culminated in the Eighth Plenum of the Central Committee of the PZPR (October 1956), was for "restoration of initiative" in foreign policy.

The October Plenum marked a break-through for the Party and, hence, for the government. The election of a Political Bureau without prior consultation with Moscow and the inclusion in key positions of elements purged earlier for opposing Soviet policy ended the direct control of the PZPR by the Communist Party of the Soviet Union. Soviet control of the army was ended, Soviet members of the security apparatus were removed. Nikita Khrushchev, First Secretary of the Soviet Communist Party, and Soviet Premier Nikolai Bulganin rushed to Warsaw, but the PZPR leadership was united in rejecting the Soviet leaders' demands for reconsideration of the changes; they insisted on a redefinition of Polish-Soviet relations. The Poles agreed to remain within the "camp of socialism" and the Soviet military security system, but, in return, relations between Poland and the Soviet Union were to be conducted on a basis of independence and respect for Polish sovereignty.

In November and December 1956 Poland formalized its gains in a series of agreements with the Soviet Union. The agreements covered settlement of the Polish "indebtedness" to the USSR resulting from the previous pricing system; guarantees of economic aid; repatriation of Poles still detained in the USSR; and arrangements to govern the stationing of Soviet troops on Polish territory.

Since 1956 the Polish Party and government have been pursuing a course more independent of Moscow's than that of any other Communist state except Yugoslavia. The PZPR has established close contacts with the Communist Party of China and, more significantly, with the Communist Party of Yugoslavia. The desire for closer contacts with the West, especially with France and the United States, is also being satisfied. A broad cultural pact with France has been signed. In July 1957 the first shipment of grain from the United States arrived in Poland, under the terms of an economic agreement negotiated in Washington earlier in the year. The Polish Government has established economic, cultural, and political relations with nations outside of the Communist orbit on an increasing scale. It has not hesitated to champion causes, such as that of Israel, which the Soviet Union continues to denounce.

In regard to the Soviet intervention in Hungary, Poland has taken a position closer to that of Yugoslavia than of the Soviet Union—condemning the first intervention but supporting the second as an unfortunate but necessary step. Poland has also begun to pursue a more independent policy in the United Nations. On November 9, 1956 it voted for the Austrian relief resolution, which the Soviet Union opposed, and in February 1957 it joined with Yugoslavia in introducing a resolution on United Nations aid to underdeveloped countries. The government has repeatedly emphasized, however, that the alliance with the Soviet Union, including Poland's continued membership in the Warsaw Pact, is "necessary for Poland to exist."

While the Soviet alliance marks one set of limits for Polish foreign policy, one over which Poland has little control, a second factor which is given equal prominence by Polish spokesmen is the question of the western boundaries. The Poles recognize that the question of the Oder-Neisse line is directly connected with the general issues of the "cold war." The refusal of the West German government, which is supported by the United States, to accept the present boundary—recognized by the Communist East German government in June of 1950—continues to be the major specific issue for the Polish Government in international affairs. In general, present Polish policy is apparently directed toward creating areas of support, especially in economic and political spheres, to balance the dominant position of the USSR.

BASIC FEATURES OF THE ECONOMY

THE COMMUNIST GOVERNMENT OF POLAND WAS FACED WITH the basic economic problem of the interwar period—how to industrialize a predominantly agricultural, overpopulated, and largely underfed country. The problem was compounded, however, by Poland's relations with the USSR. In the interwar period industrialization, then also initiated and directed by the state, was carried out by Poles for Poland. After 1945 Polish industrialization proceeded under Soviet direction and in the main was carried out in the interests of the Soviet bloc.

Under the law, Poland today has a "mixed" economy. The industrial base and most large enterprises have been nationalized and are part of what is termed the "socialized sector." The right to establish new industrial or commercial enterprises within the "private sector" is guaranteed under the law but such activities have in fact been restricted in a number of ways (see chap. 15), with the result that they play a nominal role except in agriculture.

Accelerated industrialization has changed the character of the Polish economy so that the country is no longer predominantly agricultural. In 1938, 38 percent of available capital and labor went to industry, 62 percent to agriculture; in 1953, 72 percent went to industry, only 28 percent to agriculture.

Paradoxically, the over-all economic problem posed by forced economic growth has been further intensified in Poland by the lack of an effective and all-pervasive control apparatus. It was largely by means of such an apparatus that the Soviet Union was able rapidly to build up its vast economic strength with little regard—at least until fairly recently—for popular discontent. But in Poland, for example, there has been nothing approaching the Soviet collectivization drive of the early 1930's and even at the height of the Polish Government's efforts "socialized" agriculture never encompassed more than a fraction of the recalcitrant peasantry. This relative lack of control over the agricultural sector has resulted in recurrent food shortages, which in turn have contributed to inflation.

Following Soviet practice, Poland now has a centrally planned economy. Practically all important means of production, transportation, finance, and trade are collectively owned, principally by the state but also, with varying degrees of direct state control, by municipalities and cooperatives. The major exception to state ownership or control is provided by the agricultural sector—between 80 and 90 percent of tillable land remains in private hands.

In the Soviet system, prices are determined not in the market place but by the central planning authorities; in Poland economic planners have been little influenced by consumer needs. Following Soviet practice they have kept the prices of consumer goods high, relative to those of investment goods and raw materials, so as to restrict consumption and make more resources available for industrialization. But planning also involves controlling wages—the major source of effective consumer demand in any Soviet-type economy. Here Polish planners have not been successful, mainly because wage increases in excess of planned goals are constantly being granted as workers' pressure overrides state financial controls on industrial enterprises. "Planned" inflation thus has been a constant threat to Communist Poland's economy.

Increased foreign trade and economic aid could remedy some of these difficulties while at the same time permitting continued industrialization and healthy growth of the economy. Before World War II Poland relied on western markets for supplies of manufactures and of raw materials for its industries, in return for which it exported agricultural products, coal, and timber. But incorporation into the Soviet orbit has meant severance from the West, and Poland has had to rely on the Soviet Union for deliveries of iron ore and essential heavy machinery. Deliveries and financial aid from the USSR have been subject to calculated delays and capricious interruptions, and trade relations with the West could not be increased to the point where imports would restore the imbalance between wages and goods.

The economic burden resulting from Poland's efforts to industrialize on the Soviet model has fallen on the urban workers rather than the peasants. Most of the peasants appear to have reached a level of comparative comfort, essentially because of their stubborn and successful resistance to government controls. The workers, now a substantially greater proportion of the population than before the war, have seen their standard of living fall drastically and can find small hope for improvement in the foreseeable future.

Still unable to bring the agricultural sector under control or to successfully enforce the strict labor discipline considered necessary to increase productivity in consonance with ambitious economic goals, plagued by incompetent planning and inefficient administration, the government in late 1956 found that the entire economic program had to be transformed. That transformation appears to be in the nature of a holding operation aimed merely at keeping the economy going and heading off further political explosions. Fundamental improvements in living standards in line with the expectations of the people are unlikely to come soon. Although economic salvation may lie in re-establishing closer contact with the West, political realities, including the ever-watchful presence of the Soviet Union, make a basic realignment, for the time being at least, virtually synonymous with national suicide.

The problems now besetting the Polish economy are to some extent carry-overs from previous periods. The effects of partition (see chap. 2) not only slowed down economic, political, and social development but also complicated economic unification of the new independent state established in 1918. Each of the three parts of the country had been incorporated into a separate economic organization, with a different set of civil, commercial, and fiscal laws, a different monetary system, and membership in different customs unions. Transportation systems had been layed out to unify each of the three Polish areas with the territory of one of the occupying powers rather than with one another. World War I had left the country severely damaged, and early efforts at unification and reconstruction were interrupted by a new war against the Soviet Union in 1919.

Under these circumstances direct governmental involvement in the economic life of the country after unification was practically mandatory. Various controls affected almost every sector of the economy of the new state, and although controls disappeared after the Soviet-Polish War (1921), the state continued to participate in several operations either too large or too risky for private capital and private initiative.

Poland inherited from the partitioning powers a number of state-owned factories, railways, forests, mines, banks, and fiscal monopolies. In view of the prevailing scarcity of capital, it seemed preferable to leave those enterprises under state management rather than let them revert to private ownership. From about 1928 the state gained even more influence in the economic sphere, owing both to the prevailing uncertainties in world markets—to which Poland as a primary producer was particularly sensitive—and to the onset of a world economic crisis.

World War II brought widespread devastation but postwar territorial changes were, on balance, not to the disadvantage of the Polish economy. The areas ceded by Poland to the USSR in the east were not heavily industrialized—with one third of the total prewar population they accounted for only one eighth of total prewar industrial employment; except for petroleum they had no important mineral resources. By contrast the German territories acquired by Poland in the west were heavily industrialized, especially in Upper and Lower Silesia and around Szczecin (Stettin) on the Baltic. Extensive war damage, however, prevented immediate utilization of existing productive capacity, and Poland's limited supply of skilled labor and technicians was inadequate to replace the transferred German working force. Population transfer and war damage also disrupted the agricultural production of the region.

In terms of potential mineral production the largest gains resulting from the territorial shift were in coal, coke, lead, and zinc (see Table 9). The former German area added only between six and seven billion tons of coal reserves to the estimated sixty billion tons in prewar Poland, but lead and zinc ore deposits were doubled. There also are increased production possibilities for nickel, chromium, copper, uranium, arsenic, and low-grade iron ore. Other mineral gains include asbestos, quartz, and slate, as well as clays for ceramics. The salt deposits within the postwar boundaries appear adequate for Poland's domestic needs, but a major part of the requirements for potash and oil products will have to be met by imports and, in the case of petroleum products, by synthetic production.

Installed electric capacity was nearly doubled by the transfer, and as of 1946 the new territories were already supplying about 28 percent of the total electric power output. Important heavy and light engineering industries, cement works, and glass and ceramic plants were acquired.

Economic Policy and Practice

Although comprehensive economic planning along Soviet lines began as early as 1946, the Polish Government at first was concerned with emphasizing the differences between economic and social conditions in postwar Poland and the situation of the Soviet Union in the late 1920's. While trying to adjust to the territorial changes and to rehabilitate the economy, the government also had to consolidate its position politically and therefore found it useful to formulate the essentially political doctrine of the "Polish road to socialism."

In economic terms the doctrine meant the adoption of a program of relative gradualism rather than a Stalinist economic program of ruthless collectivization and control through terror. Collectivization was to be achieved at a rate geared to peasant attitudes, which were to be reshaped by propaganda. In the industrial field priority was given to heavy industry, but by Soviet standards the pace adopted was leisurely and labor discipline relatively mild.

By 1949 the political situation had changed. The Soviet Union was exerting ever-increasing pressure to make Poland's economic development conform to Soviet rather than Polish needs, irrespective of the human and economic costs involved. In the Six-Year Plan (1950–55) the Polish Government quit the "Polish road" and set out to "construct the bases of socialism." In essence this meant "socialist" industrialization on the Soviet pattern—the fastest possible increase in production of capital goods, minerals, and electric power and the systematic reduction of consumer goods output. Full attainment of initially set targets would have meant an overspecialization in heavy industry utterly unsuited to the needs of the country, but the original goals were not attained. Even during the first years of the Plan downward revisions were forced by economic circumstances and adverse internal political and social reactions. With the return of Gomułka came a reversion to the "Polish road" and a formal revision of economic policy, the ramifications of which can as yet be only dimly discerned.

NATIONAL PLANS

The Three-Year Plan (1947–49) was concerned primarily with economic reconstruction and the increase of industrial production rather than with reshaping Poland's industrial base. By and large, planned goals were met, but because of increasing difficulties in importing industrial machinery from the West, some targets in the production of capital goods were not met. By the end of the Plan total industrial production exceeded the prewar level. In agriculture, to which a relatively small proportion of available resources was devoted, total production was lower than before the war, but given the country's smaller postwar population per capita agricultural production actually was higher. In return for industrial imports from the West and the USSR, Poland had to provide (in addition to coal) large quantities of food products, especially meat, irrespective of domestic requirements. This meant a curtailed food supply for the increasing numbers of urban workers.

The Six-Year Plan (1950–55) was not adopted until July 1950, six months after it should have gone into effect. The delay was caused by successive upward revisions of goals under Soviet prodding. Initial goals in industry were nearly doubled, and in anticipation of more widespread "socialization" of agriculture, targets in that sector also were raised. By greatly expanding capital goods production, the Polish Government wholly subordinated economic considerations to political aims. The industrial base was strengthened but agricultural output lagged far behind that of industry, partly because of low priorities for farm machinery and chemical fertilizers, partly because of effective peasant resistance to collectivization. In 1953 some of the planned goals for heavy industry had to be revised downward and adjustments made in the investment program in favor of agriculture, consumer goods industries, and housing construction.

Three groups of industrial districts were recognized by the Six-Year Plan (see chap. 15). The first was the old industrial center including Upper and Lower Silesia and the area around Lodz, where more industry would create undesirable congestion. Katowice Province was scheduled to decline somewhat in relative importance but to remain the chief industrial area. New establishments were to be located outside the limits of the coal basins. A similar development based on mineral resources and avoiding excessive nonproduction investment was scheduled for the Walbrzych and Dzierzoniow districts. Lodz, the largest textile center, was to have a broader industrial base to counteract excessive specialization.

The second industrial district, including Cracow, Czestochowa, and Opole, was to be expanded. The Cracow district was second only to Upper Silesia in magnitude of investment under the Plan. A considerable expansion of the industrial center around Czestochowa was based on previously existing metallurgical and metal goods industries. Expansion at Opole on the upper Oder was chiefly of the cement industry, which also was based on local raw materials. An increase was registered in various manufacturing activities in and around Warsaw, and shipbuilding and related activities were increased at the industrial port cities of Szczecin, Gdansk, and Gdynia.

The third group of districts comprised centers in which industrialization was to be initiated; it included the Konin and Klodawa regions, where industrialization was to be based on local deposits of lignite and potassium. Progress in the area has not been notable. The same holds true of the entire eastern part of Poland for which the Plan foresaw development of industry based on agricultural raw materials, food processing, metal products, textiles, and other light industries.

On balance it would appear that changes since the beginning of the Six-Year Plan have not been as great as the government would have wished, although the areas outside the three most highly industrialized provinces—Lodz, Katowice, and Wroclaw—increased their share of total industrial employment from 37 percent in 1949 to about 50 percent by 1953. This trend appears to have continued in more recent years. Warsaw and surroundings seem to have gained most of the light industries.

Among the guidelines for the Six-Year Plan was a provision for:

The deepening and consolidation of mutual economic relations and cooperation based upon the principles of socialist solidarity and mutual assistance, leading to the broadest possible development of productive forces on the basis of the economic plans of Poland, the Soviet Union, and the People's Democracies.

Poland's adherence to the Council for Mutual Economic Assistance (Rada Wzajemnej Pomocy Gospodarcze—RWPG—also known as KOMEKON or the Molotov Plan) was thus made a keystone of economic policy.

Under the current Five-Year Plan (1956–60) the government is trying to reconcile the realities of the economic situation with ultimate political objectives. Investment in the machine-building and mining industries is to be increased; but here, as in other industries, new projects are to be curtailed and maximum use made of existing capacity. In the power industry, for example, only one third of allocated investment is to be spent on new installations, with the balance to be used to develop existing plants. The change reflects the government's recognition that a breathing spell in forced economic development is mandatory, given the present inflationary situation.

"Maintenance of market equilibrium" remains the most pressing economic problem. This bit of official Polish jargon refers to the need for balancing the population's income—swollen by successive wage increases and widespread profiteering—with a supply of consumer goods. The new Plan calls for holding the line on wages and producing more consumer goods. Part of the production is to come from re-established private handicraft industries, while private trade outlets are to distribute these goods at the retail level. For the time being, however, the major effect of these moves has been an increase in black-market activities.

A Fifteen-Year Plan to run from 1961 to 1975 is now reportedly in preparation. In imitation of the current Soviet model it is to stress "decentralization [of the economy] while maintaining the necessary coordination."

STATE PLANNING ORGANIZATION

From 1945 to September 1950 the economy was directed by the Economic Committee of the Council of Ministers, which supervised the State Commission for Economic Planning (Państwowa Komisja

Planowania Gospodarczego—PKPG), called until February 1949 the Central Board of Planning. The chairman of the Commission also served as chairman of the Economic Committee of the Council of Ministers, which was composed of fourteen economic ministers, the ministers of National Defense and Public Administration, and two vice-chairmen of PKPG. The Committee determined basic economic policy, approved economic plans, prepared economic legislation, and supervised performance under the plans. When it was abolished in September 1950 the Presidium of the Council of Ministers took over its policy-making and coordinating functions; its other duties were assumed by the PKPG.

The PKPG was subordinated directly to the Presidium of the Council of Ministers. Its organizational structure was based on that of the Soviet Gosplan, and it had a much wider scope of activity than its predecessor, the Central Board of Planning. It was responsible for drafting national economic plans (annual and longer-range); for investment plans and combined financial plans of the enterprises in the socialized sectors; utilization of the potentialities of the economy and prevention of imbalances in the development of particular branches; control and coordination of all divisions of the state administration; and supervision and execution of economic plans at all levels. In the realm of technological development PKPG's responsibility included control of the execution of the plan for technical progress; organization and methods of production control; patents and trademarks; norms and standards; development of inventions; and rationalization of economic processes.

By 1956 the State Commission for Economic Planning reportedly was the largest governmental office in Poland, employing about 1,800 persons in over 30 separate departments. Poles had come to regard it as the symbol of a bureaucracy so bogged down in paper work that it had lost sight of reality. Ministries and directors of departments resented its interference with their work. Suggestions for change and reform were inevitably initiated by the ministries and, just as inevitably, were resented by PKPG. There were constant disagreements between the ministries and PKPG concerning the allocation of investment funds and the setting of production quotas.

Early in 1956 increasing importance began to be attached to plans and projects formulated by lower echelons. Some ministries were freed from the need to seek PKPG's approval for every decision in the field of organization, planning, and the use of funds. The role of central industrial boards (see chap. 15) and factory managers in determining ways of organizing production and of using allocated funds was also somewhat broadened.

After the upheaval of October 1956 the PKPG was stripped of

its supervisory functions in matters of economic administration and reduced to approximately half its former size. At the same time a Council of Economic Affairs was established under the Council of Ministers; the Council serves as a policy-making and advisory body for the PKPG.

The scope of central planning is itself changing. The guiding principles now being affirmed involve the combination of central planning with the widest possible autonomy for enterprises, initiative from below, and "democratic control by the masses." The ultimate functions of the reorganized PKPG are still uncertain, pending maturation of various plans for reshaping the economy. Similarly, the functions of the provincial economic planning commissions are still not clearly defined.

PLANNING PRACTICE

The Six-Year Plan was prepared by the PKPG and its regional offices. With the growth of the socialized sector the scope of economic planning expanded steadily. Beginning in 1950 the whole apparatus of central and local governmental administration was gradually drawn into the preparation and execution of the annual national economic plans. Increased efforts were made to translate the national or regional goals into definite tasks for particular producing, transport, marketing, and financing units. Planning teams, whose task is not only to plan but also to see that the annual plans are properly executed, were installed in all government departments, in the provincial and district people's councils, and in major enterprises.

The evolution of planning methods was beset by many technical difficulties, particularly the lack of trained personnel, and by the passive resistance of large groups of the population. By 1952 a procedure for annual plans had evolved. Following the general goals of the Six-Year Plan, but also taking into account previous experience and the directives of the Party, the PKPG prepared detailed directives for the given year. The directives, when approved by the Council of Ministers, were broken down among industries and provinces, finally reaching the individual enterprises. Based on these instructions, tentative annual plans were prepared, first by the producing, trade, and transport units, subsequently by all planning teams at the various levels. The PKPG had to digest all the plans and coordinate them into an over-all plan, which became law upon approval by the government and passage through the *Sejm*. The plan was then subdivided and passed down the ladder again to the enterprises, which had to adjust their detailed operational plans accordingly.

In practice the planning system was extremely cumbersome. Planning personnel, poorly trained and with little experience, had to work with preliminary plans originating at the lowest administrative level. The planning teams at the intermediate levels also lacked experience and they simply summarized proposals coming from the enterprises and the people's councils and, finally, subdivided the goals which were passed down from the PKPG. The planning units of the individual enterprises did not receive copies of the final plan until the middle of the plan year; they had to operate during the first half of the year on a preliminary plan which subsequently was adjusted to meet the requirements of the over-all final plan. The PKPG had great difficulty fitting each individual enterprise plan into one internally consistent, coherent plan. When finally broken down again into enterprise plans, the plan often had little relation to local needs or production possibilities.

Since April 1953 changes made in the planning process have shortened the procedure and have placed major responsibility for preparing the annual plans on the planning teams of particular ministries and the provincial people's councils. Preparatory work is more strongly emphasized. Detailed directives no longer go down to the producing units. The units also have been relieved of the duty of preparing the annual preliminary plans; instead they submit, through the people's councils or directly through their central boards, current statistical materials and any suggestions they may wish to make. On the basis of these factual materials and the general directives, tentative plans are compiled by all ministries and the people's councils, then reconsidered by the Presidium of the Council of Ministers, with technical assistance from the PKPG.

To overcome the difficulties involved in central planning of activities of numerous small undertakings in agriculture (predominantly in private hands), industry, handicrafts, and trade, the Polish Government has placed strong emphasis on so-called territorial planning (*planowanie terenowe*), which has been assigned to the provincial and county people's councils. The territorial economic plans embrace territorial small industry and handicrafts, agricultural production (except large state farms), local transport and communications, most of the retail trade, the purchasing program of farm products, operation of restaurants and canteens, social and cultural facilities, public utilities and housing.

Planning commissions, attached to the people's councils, have been organized both at the provincial and district levels. In addition to permanent staffs (seven to ten persons at the provincial level), these commissions since late 1952 include some of the local political and economic leaders.

Most of the planning commissions have failed in the tasks assigned them. Aside from inadequate experience and training in planning techniques, there were shortcomings reflecting the people's councils' "marked lack of appreciation of the importance of territorial planning." Specialists of planning commissions also have been used for purely administrative tasks. Many cases are reported of ministers who, confronted with the weakness of the territorial planning units, decided matters that ought to have been planned locally.

Economic Prospects

Central to Poland's economic difficulties is its low agricultural and industrial productivity. In order to raise productivity the government must provide incentives for peasants, workers, and salaried employees. The major incentive would be consumer goods, now priced out of reach of most income groups. It will take time, however, to convert industry to consumer production. During that time prices will continue to rise, there will continue to be a lack of incentives and a general build-up of political pressure.

In agriculture the government has made a short-term adjustment by officially putting an end to forced collectivization. Peasants are now allowed to buy land and implements freely and are no longer burdened by compulsory deliveries and discriminatory taxation. As a result there has been some improvement in the food situation, but unless more consumer goods are made available in the countryside, and soon, the peasants will not find it worth while to keep up the present level of production.

A profound change in Poland's industrial structure is needed if more goods are to be provided. In the new Five-Year Plan the government is trying to redress the imbalance between heavy and light industry. The speed with which the shift can be accomplished will depend on the extent to which Soviet demands on the Polish economy can be scaled down and on the amount of capital equipment Poland can import, largely on credit, during the transitional period. Even while the shift is taking place Polish industry will have to be more productive, which calls for better planning and management, stricter work discipline, and, above all, resistance to wage increases while the present shortage of goods lasts. Imports of consumer goods may alleviate the situation somewhat, if foreign countries are willing to accept Polish exports or to extend credits, but they cannot alone furnish sufficient goods to help establish long-term economic stability.

ORGANIZATION AND USE OF MANPOWER

SINCE 1945 THE INDUSTRIAL LABOR FORCE HAS MORE THAN doubled in size, the most rapid rate of increase occurring during the Six-Year Plan (1950–55). Well over half of Poland's total labor force is now employed in industry—in contrast to the overwhelming predominance of the peasantry during the interwar period. The majority of new workers have come from the farms; they are largely untrained, unaccustomed to the use of machinery and the discipline of factory work with its emphasis on regularity and constant effort.

In the early postwar years the economy was able to use a great deal of unskilled labor, but Polish industry now has all of that kind of labor it can absorb and suffers from a severe shortage of skilled and educated workers. Unskilled labor still, however, pours into the cities from the countryside. The inability of the economy to absorb these unskilled migrants has contributed to the serious unemployment in urban centers.

The major problem in both agriculture and industry is how to increase worker productivity. In agriculture the government has resorted to incentives and training. Agricultural work has such low status, however, that the peasant youths trained by the government for agricultural work have refused to return to the countryside. The productivity of Polish industrial labor has always been comparatively low, and since the war it has not kept up with industrial growth. This situation is due to a number of factors, including the traditionally negative attitude toward work (see chap. 22), resistance to a Russian-directed government, inadequately trained personnel, and inefficient planning and management. The government is attempting to provide more thorough training and better equipment and methods and to carry out a program combining material and psychological incentives. Wage increases are being given where possible, but not fast enough, so far, to prevent work stoppages. More consumer goods are to be made available, which should reduce prices and provide an incentive to the workers. The workers have also been given more responsibility and a chance to participate in decisions affecting their work. As yet, however, these measures have produced few results.

The trade union movement has had a greater development in Poland than in any other country of eastern Europe except Czechoslovakia. With roots in a highly developed craft guild organization, the development of trade unions began in the 1870's and proceeded rapidly and legally in the Austrian and German areas, illegally in the Russian areas. By 1918, when Poland was re-established as an independent state, industrial and agricultural unions were in a position to take an active part in the drive for labor and social legislation.

During the interwar period Polish trade unions developed a strong class and political orientation in the French and German tradition. They were concerned with a higher standard of living, better working conditions, and other benefits for workers, but they fought for these goals primarily in the political arena rather than at the bargaining table with individual employers. Class interests were directly related to political groupings in the interwar period—and remain so today—and the majority of union members belonged to the Socialist Party, which acted as the political vanguard of the unions.

Union leaders directed their activities toward influencing government legislation not only because of their sociopolitical base but also because the government was the largest single employer in the interwar period. While the unions suffered setbacks from the economic depression and from the political restrictions imposed on them by the government in the mid 1930's, they had approximately 1.6 million members in 1939.

In contrast to the relatively free trade union tradition in Poland, established communistic theory and practice regards trade unions as "transmission belts" for Party indoctrination and regulations—instruments to enforce the rule of the state rather than economic and political bargaining agents for the workers. The Polish Communist government slowly changed the traditional function and role of the unions until, by 1950, union structure and leadership matched Soviet models. The rank and file, however, remained racalcitrant, resorting to passive methods of resistance—absenteeism, slow-downs, and noncooperation with the rules of "labor discipline." The regime was plagued by scattered strikes and finally by open resistance at Poznan in June 1956.

These signs of worker discontent forced a basic change in Party theory. In July 1956 the chairman of the Central Council of Trade

Unions gave official sanction to workers' demands that the trade unions again function as defenders of the rights of the workers rather than as an arm of the government. This principle was part of the policy espoused by the Gomułka group, and in the following months the workers rallied to the group's support. In November 1956, at the meeting of the Ninth Plenum of the Central Council of Trade Unions, the policy was put into practice. The delegates, some of whom had been seated in spite of the attempts of the presidium of the Council to exclude them, rejected the official agenda, forced an un-scheduled accounting of the previous year's activities, and elected as chairman a close associate of Gomułka to replace the "Stalinist" who had held that position.

In another development, which followed closely on the events at Poznan, workers in a number of enterprises began to organize workers' councils to take part in management. This movement was in-fluenced by German syndicalism of the 1930's, the Yugoslav experi-ence, and the brief activities of some Polish workers in operating industrial plants between the German evacuation and the arrival of Russian forces. The movement was a literal interpretation of the constantly reiterated Communist slogan "The worker is master of the factory." Supported by Gomułka, workers' councils were given legal standing as part of management by the Statute on Workers' Councils passed in November 1956 by the *Sejm.*

Though the law was fairly specific in providing safeguards for the councils against pressure from management, their role is still in the process of definition. On one hand, the government has taken the firm position that they cannot be allowed to undermine either "one-man" direction of plant operations or freedom from central planning of production. On the other hand, some matters, such as wages, which were formerly the concern of works councils, have been placed under the purview of the workers' councils.

The unions and workers have won other concessions: the govern-ment has relaxed the rules of labor discipline and focused the duties of the state Labor Arbitration Boards on the enforcement of manage-ment's compliance with the labor laws. While the government has recently (August 1957) issued stringent new regulations in regard to absenteeism, it has given workers greater participation in manage-ment. It has stated clearly, however, that it does not intend to abdicate its over-all control.

Interwar Labor Force

Throughout the interwar period Poland was one of the least in-dustrialized countries of Europe. Approximately 60 percent of the population depended upon agriculture for a livelihood. Neither urbanization nor emigration, both of which involved sizable numbers of people, resulted in any significant changes in the occupational structure of the country by 1939.

Agricultural underemployment was widespread; it has been estimated that between 30 and 60 percent of the rural population could have been removed from the land without appreciably reducing agricultural output. Poverty was common throughout the country and acute in the central and eastern areas. To augment their incomes many farmers worked as seasonal laborers in Germany and Latvia or as hired laborers on the larger Polish estates. Thousands of others emigrated until that became increasingly difficult with the establishment of the quota system in the United States (1925) and the onset of the world-wide economic depression. Urban unemployment was a growing problem—the manpower for industrial expansion was available, but unused.

Postwar Labor Force

In 1950 about 53 percent of the occupationally active population was engaged still in agriculture, a decrease of some 10 percent from 1931. In nonagricultural employment, the largest increase during the 1931–50 period was in industry and the manual trades—from 11 to almost 18 percent. Employment increased slightly in construction, transportation, communications, trade, and other occupations (see Table 10). With the initiation of the Six-Year Plan, calling for rapid industrialization, the rate of labor transfer from the agricultural sectors of the economy was accelerated. Almost a million workers entered industrial employmnt between 1945 and 1955.

Before 1950 the changes were primarily the result of territorial shifts following on World War II. Most of the area acquired from Germany included good farms largely cleared of their German populations, and highly industrialized areas in which only a small nucleus of skilled personnel were allowed to remain. Both absorbed much of the excess population from the central areas of Poland, as well as many repatriates from other countries (see chap. 3).

Excepting heavy industry, transportation, and communications, which are entirely subsidized, nearly all economic activities are carried on in both socialized and private sectors. In 1950 only some 5 percent of those engaged in agriculture were employed in the socialized sector —on state farms or in the various types of collective farms (see chap. 14). The vast majority (94.7 percent) consisted of private owners, members of their families, and a very few hired employees.

proved technology also contributed. Since 1949, however, gross industrial output has gone up faster than individual productivity. The Five-Year Plan which went into effect in 1956 calls for greater industrial and consumer output, but with capital in short supply production increases depend on improved worker productivity rather than on expansion of plant capacity. The government now is concentrating upon improving training methods and offering high incentives to workers who produce in excess of the Plan.

Unemployment

Although there had been indications for some time that the number of job seekers in various Polish cities had been increasing, the problem of unemployment was not officially recognized until the early summer of 1956.

Po Prostu, the newspaper of the young intelligentsia, reported on June 6, 1956 that unemployment had risen from about 5,000 in 1950 to 51,000 in June 1956. Four days later it published an article stating that these figures were much too low, since they represented only those workers who had registered with employment bureaus—the majority of jobseekers tended to register as a last resort. The Bureau of Labor Reserves was quoted as accepting 306,000—six times the number registered—as a realistic figure. Other newspapers and magazines published similar figures and estimates, including reports that in some places one third of the working force was without employment. There was a general demand that the government give immediate and careful consideration to the problem.

The various factors contributing to unemployment in Poland were outlined in August 1956 at the Seventh Plenum of the Party and have been discussed in official and semiofficial sources since that time. They include: (1) the low level of real wages which has forced many women to seek jobs in order to augment family income; (2) the failure of the vocational education system to turn out an adequate number of well-trained personnel; (3) the location of productive facilities away from areas of surplus labor; (4) the sharp reduction in the number of government employees; (5) the reduction, during 1956, in the size of the armed forces; and (6) the policy of eliminating mall workshops and cottage industry. Various steps to remedy these conditions taken during 1956 have been intensified by the Gomułka buernment.

The speeches and resolutions at the Seventh Plenum emphasized wou he government should encourage the formation of new handiwere prkshops and "cottage industries" and create conditions in which they could operate profitably. This shift from the previous official policy, directed toward the elimination of the private sector of the industrial economy, was explained as an attempt to increase production of consumer goods. But the need to solve the problem of unemployment was also admitted; the government raised to four the number of hired workers a private craftsman was allowed to employ and made it easier to get craftsmen's licenses and workshop permits. The press subsequently reported large increases in applications for both. It is doubtful, however, whether such a development will absorb significant numbers of the unemployed since socialized industry plays such a predominant role in both manufacturing and service and is likely to continue to do so.

The main center of Polish industry will continue to be the Wroclaw-Katowice region where there are shortages of labor and housing. A similar situation exists in most cities, particularly those in such areas as Silesia, that have a rapidly expanding industry. The government is unwilling to force the transfer of surplus labor into labor-scarce areas without first engaging in a large-scale building program so the migrants will not be forced to live under harsh conditions. Similarly the government has abolished the forced assignment of vocational graduates.

Reductions in the size of the bureaucracy since June 1956 also have swelled the number of job-seekers. Although the total number of employees involved has not been announced, it is sufficiently large to cause the administration to set up special organizations to assist in relocation and retraining. The number of registered unemployed "intellectuals" increased by 5,000 in Warsaw during the first month of the reductions. Some sources have charged that many of the "paper pushers" were untrained and unqualified for their jobs and that their transfer to manual work in industry and agriculture would actually result in improved occupational assignment. Whatever the facts, it is unlikely that white-collar workers will look with favor upon reemployment as manual or even skilled labor in industry and agriculture.

Many of the young men released from the army had received no vocational training either before being called up or during their service; consequently, they too lack qualifications for anything but unskilled labor. A large number of the unemployed women, between 60 and 80 percent of those seeking jobs, are in a similar situation: many are looking for work for the first time, are relatively new to the urban scene, and have had no work experience except in agriculture.

Among the graduates of vocational and technical schools many are experiencing difficulties in finding jobs either because their training was inadequate or in a specialty for which there is little demand; others often are unwilling to take jobs because of the lack of housing in areas where employment can be found.

It is reported that young men and women who wish to acquire specialized training find it difficult to obtain admission to vocational schools. In a situation which includes critical shortages of skilled man-power, large-scale unemployment, and the necessity of increasing productivity of labor, improvement in vocational training would bring reasonably quick returns.

Development of Labor Organization

THE GUILD TRADITION

Guild organization of craftsmen and artisans was adopted by Poland from western Europe, particularly Germany. Reaching their height of power and influence in the prosperous years of the fifteenth and sixteenth centuries, the guilds continued to wield considerable in-fluence on the industrial development of Poland through the nine-teenth century—long after French, German, and English guilds had disappeared. They controlled the quantity, quality, and prices of products produced by their members. In partitioned Poland most manufacturing, most services, and some food processing were in the hands of the guilds. Though the guilds have disappeared, consumer goods production and some trade union organizations in modern Poland show the influence of guild organization.

UNIONS IN INTERWAR POLAND

The cradle of the Polish labor movement was in Austrian Galicia, where it developed under legal authorization. Some of the unions preserved such guild characteristics as apprenticeships and a limited membership. Others, among them the unions of miners, railroadmen, and municipal workers, were industrial unions with a large member-ship, and after 1919 these became the mainstay of the labor move-ment. The workers in the German areas were absorbed into German trade unions. In Russian areas, however, where labor organizations were illegal, the unions were allied with political organizations; they operated clandestine schools and were generally concerned with political reform.

In 1918 most of the trade union organizations in the formerly separated regions formed a federated Central Committee of Labor Unions (Centralny Komitet Związków Zawodowych—CKZZ). A number of white-collar unions as well as some "Christian Trade Unions" remained outside the CKZZ, which nevertheless dominated the Polish labor scene.

The usual organization was on an industrial basis, with all workers in a given branch of industry belonging to the same union. Within each industrial union was a hierarchy of organizations extending from the local units through regional and provincial to the national level. The members or delegates at each level elected by secret ballot the officials and delegates to the next higher. With few exceptions, membership was open—dues and initiation fees, if any, were low; unemployed workers were recruited into special unions.

Among the more powerful organizations were those of the railroadmen, miners, chemical, metal, textile, and municipal workers; most of the industries employing these workers were owned by the government. This group of unions succeeded in obtaining relatively favorable economic conditions for their members and operated schools, clubs, and other recreational facilities. The Atheneum Theater and the orchestras of the railroad union achieved nationwide fame.

Agricultural unions in Galicia carried out strikes as early as 1902. A sizable proportion of the agricultural labor force consisted of *fornals* or *bandos*—landless peasants hired with a yearly contract to work on the large estates—whose lot was even harder than that of the part-time and seasonal agricultural laborers who hired out to supplement the income from their own land. With the encouragement and direction of the Polish Socialist Party (PPS) in the interwar period, these unions spread to the rest of Poland. Their strikes, especially in the early 1920's, were greatly feared by the landowners.

All Polish unions stressed their nonpartisan character and admitted to membership all workers without regard to political affiliation. Nevertheless most of the members were Socialists and the PPS exerted decisive influence on the affairs of the unions. It acted as their political arm and took the lead in the promulgation of labor legislation. Trade union leaders often were the PPS representatives in the *Sejm*.

The pressure exerted by the unions through the PPS made Poland a leader in the field of labor legislation: hours were limited to 8 daily and 46 weekly; special regulations governed the employment of women and minors; health and safety standards were adopted; and social insurance—including sickness and disability benefits for workers and their families as well as old age pension—was provided (see chap. 17). The unions were given the exclusive right to bargain collectively for both union and nonunion workers.

In 1926 the Piłsudski government attempted to split the labor movement by requiring all workers in state-owned enterprises to join the government-sponsored Association of Labor Union (Zrzeszenie Związków Zawodowych—ZZZ). The ZZZ lost much of its influence following the depression of the 1930's during which its own members went out on strike, but the independent unions also lost many members. During the 1930's the government was increasingly hostile to organized labor and the PPS. Labor regulations of the previous decade were not enforced or were openly abrogated by the government; managers of the social security funds who had previously been elected by the unions, were replaced by government appointees.

While many of its accomplishments were swept away, the Polish trade union movement in 1939 could still count as members approximately 25 percent of the working force. Through it Polish workers in both agriculture and industry had acquired considerable experience in organization as well as a tradition of independent trade unionism.

Labor Organizations Since 1945

ORGANIZATION

Lacking the political strength to embark upon an immediate reorganization of unions to make them fit the Soviet model, the Polish Communist regime temporarily permitted the unions to function much as in the interwar period, freely electing their delegates and officials within each industrial union and sending representatives to the Central Council of Labor Unions. Communists did, however, infiltrate much of the top union leadership. But once the period of economic reconstruction was officially over and the Polish United Workers' Party (PZPR) had consolidated its power, President Bierut announced that the unions were to function as "the basic transmission belt of the Party to the non-Party masses."

The new Trade Union Act passed by the Communist-dominated *Sejm* in July 1949 reorganized the trade unions on the principle of "democractic centralism" as practiced in the Soviet Union. Nominally, union organization remained the same, with separate industrial unions organized on local, provincial, and national levels and united in the Central Council of Labor Unions—CRZZ. Functionally, the entire organization was changed. Instead of coordinating the affair of all unions, the CRZZ became the highest policy-making body of the union structure; actually it simply received and passed on the decisions of the Party. All other union bodies were responsible for enforcing these decisions, over which they had no influence or control despite the "elections" that were still held on the local level and the "approval"—unanimous—of policies by the workers.

Officials of various individual unions, as well as the rank- and file-members, continued to express considerable opposition to the destruction of union independence and the changing role of the unions. By such means as purges and the introduction of "reliable" officials through rigged elections, the Party tightened its control until by 1950 the unions had become organs of the government rather than representatives of the workers.

Since October 1956 the unions have recovered a measure of autonomy in handling some of their problems and establishing policy. The CRZZ has been reduced in size and function and is to become once again a coordinating body for its member unions. Officially, the activities of all unions are to be "concentrated on safeguarding the interests and living conditions of workers and employees." At the same time, however, the unions are to continue to see to "the strict observance of labor legislation and collective agreements in enterprises" as well as struggle for "a correct attitude by trade unionists to the production tasks of their enterprises." The determination of wages is still a power reserved to the government. In May 1957 the Central Committee of the Party called for "proper direction" of the lowest union units, the works councils, by Party teams.

WORKS AND WORKERS' COUNCILS

The basic unit of trade union organization in Poland has been the works council (rada zakładowa), elected by both union and non-union workers in a given plant. During the interwar period the works councils functioned to protect workers, support the programs of their higher echelons for labor legislation, serve as checks upon management's fulfillment of collective agreements and obedience to the law, and render a variety of social services to its members. Their participation in management was restricted to personnel matters.

During the latter years of the interwar period the councils were almost completely suppressed. They were revived during the German occupation as clandestine organizations of subversion and resistance. Later, in the wake of the retreating Germans, they were also instrumental in protecting and putting back into operation various enterprises thus assuming managerial functions for a short time.

Shop committees (rada oddziałów) were established in 1945; they are often called works councils and in general their functions were to be those of the prewar works councils, but there were certain extensions of their supervisory role over management in both private and state enterprises. According to law, a shop committee was elected by vote of all the employees in every establishment employing more than 20 workers. The role of the committee was to represent the workers' interests in all matters concerning personnel, including work regulations, overtime, leave, promotions, demotions and firings, cooperation with government agencies in enforcing health and safety regulations, and the establishment and direction of social and cultural activities.

With the tightening of Communist control after 1948, shop committees and unions had in fact no influence upon management policy, working conditions, or wages. The shop committees became organizations through which the government and the Party threatened and cajoled the worker to increase production. Violations of collective agreements and labor law by management were generally ignored.

Expressions of worker discontent increased after the death of Stalin in 1953, and the government was forced to attempt some palliative measures. In November 1954 labor inspection was reinstituted in an attempt to reduce the flagrant violation of existing labor laws by management. In February 1955 enterprise funds, to be used for welfare benefits and bonus awards, were extended to all plants rather than just to favored industries. In May of the same year labor discipline laws were softened.

The Poznan riots in June 1956 made it clear that these revisions were not satisfactory. Open demands for worker participation in the planning of production and management of factories were frequent. In a number of factories workers' councils (*rada robotnicza*) were organized.

In August 1956 the Central Council of Trade Unions attempted to take account of these new developments within the existing organizational framework. They drafted a law, never enacted, which gave the works councils a role in the distribution of enterprise funds and in the development of production plans. During the summer and fall, however, newly organized workers' councils, frequently under the leadership of young Party activists, bodily threw out a number of Party-appointed managers.

In October 1956 Gomułka threw his support to the workers' councils, as distinguished from the union works councils. In November the *Sejm* passed the Statute on Workers' Councils which provided that they be elected by the secret ballot of the entire working force of a given plant, that no more than one third of the council members might be persons in administrative or managerial positions, and that members might not be fired during their term of office. No mechanism for dissolution of the councils by higher authority was provided. The plant manager, appointed by the appropriate economic ministry, is to be an ex officio member of the council but both he and his assistant are barred from the chairmanship. He must report his actions to the council and execute council resolutions. He may, in emergencies, take action for the council provided that he subsequently gains its approval. In cases where the council and the plant manager disagree about whether an action of the council violates the law, higher government authorities, the exact agency is not known, are appealed to for a final ruling.

COLLECTIVE AGREEMENTS

During the interwar period, collective agreements could be concluded only by trade unions or federations of trade unions on one hand and by employers or their organizations on the other. Many agreements were negotiated on an industry-wide basis. A collective agreement automatically superseded any individual agreements which might be in effect, and no item in it could be modified until its date of expiration. Agreements covered wages and working conditions and applied to all workers whether or not they belonged to the union.

In the postwar period, however, collective agreements were reoriented toward increasing production. As in the Soviet Union, they were not arrived at by bargaining but were drawn up by the appropriate economic ministry and the officials of the union in accordance with the over-all production plan. "Approval" by the workers was a foregone conclusion. Wages, pensions, and other benefits were excluded from consideration; they were set by law. The agreements consisted of promises on the part of workers to fulfill and overfulfill their production norms, to engage in socialist competition, to work for extension of the piecework system and the Stakhanovite movement, and to comply with labor discipline. Individual earnings were thus tied to the fulfillment of the production plan set up by higher authorities and collective agreements became an instrument for regimentation and propaganda.

ARBITRATION BOARDS

During the interwar period the supervision of the labor laws was the responsibility of a corps of labor inspectors (set up in 1927) under the jurisdiction of the Ministry of Labor. They also acted as mediators in relatively minor types of disputes, but their essential duty was that of enforcing laws designed to protect the worker. The settlement of most labor disputes was in the hands of special labor courts composed of a professional judge and four lay judges—two representing the unions and two management—selected from lists submitted by the respective organizations. Arbitration was employed to settle collective grievances and was mandatory in disputes endangering national economic interests.

In 1945 the labor courts, which had ceased to function during the German occupation, were re-established. Mechanisms for arbitration were also expanded; shop committees were given initial responsibility, and all cases which could not be settled within the enterprise were sent to District Conciliation and Arbitration Boards attached to the offices of the district inspectors of labor. In 1950 the labor courts were abolished and labor cases placed under the regular courts but few cases have actually been tried by them.

As the organization of labor along Soviet lines proceeded, Enterprise Arbitration Boards were established with jurisdiction over all labor disputes except those concerning housing or involving higher managerial positions. A board consisted of four members, two representing labor and two management. Decisions had to be unanimous and were taken in "the interests of the working masses and the welfare of the national economy." Thus a compromise, assumed by the unanimity rule, between the interests of production and workers' rights was practically required. Since production was the overriding concern, workers' interests generally received little consideration. Only in rare cases did the Arbitration Board declare that it was unable to reach a decision, thus allowing the worker to take his case to the courts.

New labor legislation was introduced in late 1956. One bill provided for labor inspectors to be attached to the provincial councils of the unions. They are to check for violations of the labor laws by management and are empowered to impose fines upon employers who illegally dismiss workers, delay payment or make illegal reductions of pay, withhold legitimate allowances, or refuse to carry out decisions of the Arbitration Boards—now called Commissions. Another bill also extended the jurisdiction of the Arbitration Commissions to practically all management-labor disputes. Members of the Commissions, previously appointed by the government, now are to be elected by the workers. Dismissal of a worker member during the time he serves on a Commission or for three years thereafter is expressly prohibited. The general effect of these two bills is to extend the legal safeguards of workers' interests; whether or not they actually do so in practice is not known.

MASS EDUCATION

During the interwar period the unions had engaged in a certain amount of indoctrination of their membership in the theory and practice of trade unionism and in Socialist Party principles. In the postwar period mass indoctrination of workers in "the revolutionary spirit and Marxism-Leninism" became one of the primary functions of the unions.

Though some indoctrination was carried on in places of work during or after hours, mass education was carried on largely in the Culture and Recreations Halls (*świetlice*) through a program of lectures, classes, library facilities, meetings, and various forms of entertainment. An official survey made in October 1951, however, reported that only 20 percent of all union members took advantage of the cultural and educational offerings of the unions.

SOCIAL SERVICES

In 1945 a social security system, similar to that of the interwar period, was established; it included disability and sickness benefits, insurance, pensions, and so on (see chap. 17). Funds for such allowances are financed by industrial profits rather than, as in the prewar period, through joint payments by workers and employers. Administration of the funds was originally placed in the hands of the shop committees, but in 1950 it was transferred to management with only nominal supervision by the shop committees; this arrangement led to considerable worker dissatisfaction—expressed in open charges of mismanagement of funds and of discrimination in benefit awards.

As part of the general relaxation following the death of Stalin the unions were given greater responsibility in the administration of benefits. In addition they operated such various services for the workers as nurseries, cafeterias, housing, and laundries.

Regulation of Labor

While the labor laws of the interwar period were primarily designed to protect workers from exploitation by management, after 1946 their main function was to give the government control over the distribution and use of the labor force. Regulation became the prerogative of the state rather than the result of compromise between management and labor.

COMPULSORY JOB ASSIGNMENT

On January 8, 1946 all males between 18 and 55 years of age and all females between 18 and 45 years were required by law to register for "socially useful work." There were a number of exemptions from labor duty, however, and the law was used primarily to recruit skilled and professional personnel. Two years later all young men and women between 16 and 21 years of age were required to undergo vocational and ideological training as well as preinduction military training in "Service for Poland," a paramilitary organization. Young people in this age group could be drafted for labor three days per month or for a continuous period of six months. The avowed purpose of this Act was to train cadres for the socialist sector of the economy; actually, it provided the government with a large pool of labor which could be assigned to specific tasks as the need arose.

In 1950 two bills were passed which further extended controlled assignment of labor. Under the provisions of one, professional and skilled workers in certain categories could be frozen in their jobs for a period up to two years by action of the Council of Ministers. The other made work at assigned jobs compulsory for graduates of secondary vocational and general schools for periods of three years, beginning immediately after graduation. Similar assignment of graduates of the higher schools was made obligatory some time later.

The job assignments program and other devices to freeze key workers on their jobs—such as permission being required from an employer before a worker could resign—were largely ineffective in reducing labor turnover and in directing personnel where it was needed. "Service for Poland" and compulsory assignment of graduates were abolished in the fall of 1956. Maldistribution of labor remains a problem of considerable dimensions.

LABOR DISCIPLINE

Absenteeism has been a serious problem in Poland, but one which was not attacked by legal regulation until 1950. The Labor Discipline Law passed that year, although not as severe as that of the USSR, provided punishments for repeated absence and tardiness—a code never previously applied in Poland. Workers more than 1 hour late or late 20 minutes to an hour more than twice a year, without valid reason, lost a day's pay; "valid reasons" for absence were extremely limited. For 3 days of absence during a year, 2 days' pay was deducted for each day of absence or the worker could be transferred to a job with lower pay. "Willful and persistent violations of work discipline"—absence of 4 or more days during a given year without adequate reason—would bring the worker before a court. Conviction carried a punishment of reduction in pay of 10 to 25 percent for a maximum of 3 months during which a change of jobs was prohibited. Administration of the sentence was the responsibility of the plant management. Failure to punish workers made the management subject to heavy fines or imprisonment. The law also authorized certain rewards for exemplary behavior. Workers who had irreproachable attendance for 3 years were awarded honary titles, orders, decorations, and cash prizes.

Enactment of these laws was not accompanied by a significant decrease in absenteeism. By May 1955 mounting evidence both of this failure and of worker discontent with the arbitrary fashion in which managers administered the laws forced a reorganization of the system. The unions were made the principal agencies for the enforcement of labor discipline, and the cumulative period for unexcused absence from work was reduced to 3 months. Thus a worker could be absent 12 days in the course of a year without running the danger of criminal penalty. A few months later "comradely" courts were set up as part of the local union organizations to take disciplinary action in addition to managerial action.

In September 1956 the law on work discipline was abolished and the workers' councils were given responsibility for the development of a disciplined labor force. Press reports indicate, however, that absenteeism is increasing and "loafing" on the job is prevalent. New work regulations provide that absentees will receive two warnings; if these are not heeded, fines and demotion to lower work classifications will be applied. In aggravated cases, dismissal without the usual three months notice is the final measure. So far, some 1,500 miners have been dismissed.

"SOCIALIST COMPETITION"

High pressured Soviet-style rivalry between workers, shops, and enterprises to increase production did not begin in Poland until 1948. The trade unions had sponsored certain competitions in industry and for such specific reconstruction jobs as clearing rubble and debris from the ruined cities. Competitions between youth brigades had been staged since 1945.

With the organization of the Central Competition Committee in 1948 the pressure of "socialist competition" was intensified through the unions. Shock workers, like the Soviet Stakhanovites, became leaders and norm setters. The pressure put on the workers kept them under constant physical and psychological strain. When existing production norms were exceeded this was generally taken as evidence that they had been set too low. Those who consistently exceeded the norms were given, in addition to monetary rewards, priority in housing and in accommodations in vacation resorts, preferential care for their children, tax reductions, and a variety of medals and titles—all awarded with considerable fanfare.

The Gomułka government is apparently not relaxing the pressure of continued competition. "Practical" production pledges were part of the celebration of May Day in 1957. Workers' councils are being urged to discuss their pledges with their membership and to set and undertake goals with "a feeling of responsibility." The goals of the competition have, however, been shifted to a promised improvement in the standard of living of the workers.

HOURS OF WORK

Postwar statutory provisions governing hours of work generally followed those of the interwar period. With certain exceptions, the official work week is 46 hours—8 hours daily on weekdays and 6 hours on Saturday. Shorter hours are provided for pregnant women. The minimum working age is set at 14 years; youths between the ages of 14 and 18 are to combine work and vocational training. Night work by persons under 18 is prohibited. Provision is made for the reduction of the work week in certain dangerous and unhealthy industries. A proposal for a 6-hour day for all who work under unhealthy conditions was under consideration early in 1957 but, so far as can be determined, has not been put into effect. A two-week vacation with pay is set by law. Rates for overtime are from 50 to 100 percent higher than basic rates.

The administration of the work week law has been far from strict, and violations have been frequent. Vacations have been denied, extra hours have been required at regular pay rates, and women and youths have been forced to put in more hours than are legal at jobs in which they are supposedly protected. One device for avoidance of the regulations has been the "voluntary" request of workers that overtime for a specified time be considered part of the 8-hour day in celebration of special events. Underlying the frequent abuses of power by management has been the fact that wages have been so low as to force many workers to work extra hours at regular rates in order to attain a bare subsistence.

WAGES AND PRODUCTION NORMS

In interwar Poland pay varied considerably from industry to industry. Such strong unions as those of the printers, the tile makers, the miners, and the chemical workers gained relatively high wages for their members.

In the postwar period the government has set wage rates in accord with the production goals of the economy. Piece rates, rather than hourly rates, have been widely used. Production norms for each job are the standard against which worker performance is measured. Failure to meet the norm results in loss of pay; overfulfillment brings rewards, both in higher pay—according to a scale of rates for production over the norm—and in a wide variety of awards, bonuses, and honors. There are also wide differentials in rates within and between industries.

Production norms for an individual worker are geared to the planned production of his plant. Considerable pressure is placed upon management to meet the plan, and management in turn places pressure upon the workers to increase their production. The most usual method of arriving at individual norms is to average the production of all workers over a certain period. Lately, the government has been attempting to use time and motion studies in order to set more precise norms. Once established, a norm is subject to upward changes on the basis of the production of individual pace setters. Fulfillment of the norm is a prerequisite for receiving the minimum pay rate for each job.

There had been few general wage increases until the summer of 1956 when a number of increases fixed minimum monthly wages at about 500 złotys per month for production and administrative workers; general wage scales were also increased. Further increases were granted to miners, transportation workers, and certain specialists early in 1957. The government is apparently attempting to eliminate progressive piece rates and to substitute fixed wages so as to avoid what it calls the "race" for the fulfillment of production norms; the emphasis will now be on the quality of production as well as on quantity.

The wage increases have not, however, met the demands of the unions and the workers' councils. The government has stated that further increases will be possible only if there is an increase in productivity and that under existing conditions there is no money for higher pay, but it has mentioned the possibility of a "thirteenth month's pay," as a premium for those plants whose profits exceed the amounts specified in the plan. The responsibility for making this premium a reality is placed upon the workers' councils and their success in improving the efficiency and productivity of the plants.

Forced Labor

Forced labor, as a means of political coercion or legal punishment on a scale to constitute an important factor in national economic projects, was introduced by the Polish Communist government after World War II. At its peak in 1952 the system made use of approximately 150,000 laborers, but by 1956 the number had dwindled to an estimated 50,000.

In Poland, as in other European satellites, the objectives of the forced labor system were patterned closely after those of the Soviet Union—the direct removal of known political opponents, the establishment of terror to intimidate the rest of the population, and the use of prisoners for large economic projects. But from the beginning there were noteworthy differences in the scope and use of forced labor in Poland as compared to that of the Soviet Union or the other European satellites. The Polish Government, apparently doubtful that it could effectively terrorize the whole population or hesitant to make the attempt, relied on the system to help maintain a minimum of order through coercion and to assist the free labor force in meeting the requirements of the economic plans.

In contrast to the system of the USSR and other European satellites, forced laborers in Poland generally work at jobs in collaboration with free labor, and most of them receive pay comparable to that of free laborers. Persons sentenced to forced labor by the former administrative procedures could be sentenced to no more than the maximum of two years.

Reductions of forced labor sentences may be won for surpassing work norms. Generally forced laborers have played the role of shock brigades, especially in the mines, setting the pace for free laborers. The Polish Government has tended to stress the economic rather than the strictly political character of the system, even though a majority of the sentences have been for alleged political offenses, and although forced labor, in relation to the total free work force, has not played a really significant role in the over-all economy. By general Polish standards camp conditions have varied from miserable and inhuman to fair, but on the whole they have been moderate enough to permit a more efficient use of the forced laborer than is the case, for example, in the Soviet Union.

It is questionable whether the forced labor system is a major source of popular disaffection. Compared to the system existing under the German occupation the present system is mild. Furthermore many Poles are able to compare from direct experience the far more inhuman forced labor system in the Soviet Union with the more benign Polish form. It is noteworthy that even with the relatively free criticism of existing conditions that takes place under the Gomułka government, little or no criticism of forced labor as a whole has been heard.

FINANCIAL SYSTEM

THE POLISH BANKING SYSTEM HAS BEEN ORGANIZED TO MAIN-
tain tight financial discipline in the execution of the national economic
plans and thus serves as an instrument of economic control. In practice,
however, control by the banks has been ineffective.

Through manipulation of credit and currency the government has
attempted to stave off and control the basically inflationary tendencies
of the economy. Monetary reforms also served the political purpose
of hitting at those groups, largely peasants and private speculators,
who had amassed relatively large sums of money with which
they were bidding up prices of available consumer goods. The credit
program of the banks also had discriminatory political features
aimed at expanding the socialized sector of the economy at the expense of private enterprise.

The tax system and the state budget are two more of the many
means used by the Polish Government to promote its political
objectives as well as to fulfill its economic plans. The tax program
is a device for siphoning off excess purchasing power and thus reducing
the inflationary threat; it has served as a way of progressively eliminating remnants of private initiative in urban as well as rural areas;
and it has been manipulated, not very successfully, to provide incentives
for the realization of specific production goals. The consolidated budget
is made a tool of national economic planning by subordinating to it
all financial plans. The government's policy has been to channel the
financing of most economic activities through the state budget, and
to strike a balance with planned revenues.

Despite its apparent inefficiency when compared to the allocation
of resources to production and distribution via the price mechanism,
the Polish (Soviet) financial system has the advantage of rapid ac-
commodation to the planners' objectives. The entire postwar period
has been characterized, however, by both open and disguised inflation

despite repeated attempts at control through rationing, price control, monetary reforms, and revisions of prices and wages. Given the conflict between the preferences of the population and the demands of the planning authority, all but the strongest controls are circumvented by the consuming public and the independent producers.

The Polish Złoty

Upon the liberation of Poland during 1944–45, four different kinds of currency were in use: reichsmarks, in the formerly German area; occupation złotys issued by the German authorities of the so-called General Government of Poland; Soviet rubles; and the notes of the Polish National Bank, printed in Moscow and issued by the Lublin government beginning in October 1944. From 1945 the occupation złoty was converted on a 1-to-1 basis, up to a maximum of 500 złotys per person, for the new złoty notes of the Polish National Bank. Remaining amounts of occupation złotys had to be deposited in blocked accounts, which could only be released by special permission of the Ministry of Finance. Reichsmarks were similarly exchanged but on less favorable terms, varying from the 1-to-1, with an upper limit of 300 reichsmarks in Bialystok, to 1 złoty to 2 reichsmarks, with a limit of 500, in the remaining provinces. This conversion drastically reduced the stock of money in circulation and made it possible for the government to finance a major part of its early postwar requirements simply by increasing note circulation in line with the expansion of goods production and of services in the economy.

Poland's second postwar monetary reform, introduced by legislative action on October 28, 1950, was motivated by the resurgence of inflationary forces after a period of relative stability between the last half of 1947 and 1949. Under this reform the unit of currency on October 30, 1950, became the new złoty, defined as being equal to 0.222168 grams of pure gold. All wages and incomes from labor, pensions and stipends, as well as prices for goods and services, were recalculated on the basis of 100 old złotys to 3 new złotys. Money in circulation was subject to exchange at the ratio of 100 old złotys to 1 new złoty. All savings kept in banks, savings institutions, and in The National Savings Fund were recalculated at the same ratio as prices and wages. But deposits in excess of 100,000 złotys, a relatively modest sum at that time, were subject to conversion at less favorable rates. Private debts were validated at the 100 to 3 ratio, but the debts of small and medium peasants to the so-called "village rich" were converted at the 100 to 1 ratio. Thus the reform discriminated against the wealthier peasants, persons holding cash reserves, and the remnants of the urban middle class. The regime expected that the prospect of similar reforms in the future would discourage the population from accumulating spendable funds that, when finally used, would have an inflationary effect by bidding up prices of scarce commodities. This expectation has not been fulfilled.

The new złoty, like the old, remains an internal currency. Although defined in terms of gold, it is not freely convertible into gold or foreign exchange at a rate equivalent to its declared value. The law which introduced the monetary reform prohibited the possession of foreign exchange, gold coins, gold, and platinum, except for "useful articles," without the permission of the Polish Foreign Exchange Commission. It also raised the punishment for illegal traffic in these items to include the death sentence; trial is to be by summary court.

As of February 11, 1957 the Polish Government introduced a special exchange rate—24 złotys per United States dollar—to be applied to a wide range of transactions, including purchases by foreign tourists, Polish travelers abroad, diplomats, and missionaries, and to all types of travel costs, telecommunication services, pensions and earnings, legacies, authors' rights, fees for professional services, income from property, public donations, etc. The exchange rate of 4 złotys per United States dollar remains the official rate and will continue to be applied to foreign transactions in merchandise trade and to services connected with such transactions. The demand for dollars, on the other hand, has been so great in Poland that the black-market rate has been reported at times as between 100 and 300 złotys per United States dollar.

Effective May 1, 1957 the Polish złoty was devalued by one third in relation to the Soviet ruble. The new exchange rate is 1.50 złoty per ruble, whereas previously the złoty and the ruble had been at par. This move, which reduces the overvaluation of the złoty in terms of the ruble, has no effect on foreign trade transactions inside the Soviet bloc since such trade is carried on in terms of special units of account and does not involve currency or gold settlements (see chap. 16).

The Problem of Inflation

The first postwar currency reform reduced monetary circulation by about two thirds and cut the purchasing power of private cash balances to one third their former values (prices were converted at 100 to 3; cash was exchanged at 100 to 1). In 1945 and 1946 the government also tapped excess purchasing power by heavy taxation, internal loans, sales of abandoned and German property, and disposal of

UNRRA supplies. Inflation, however, was still fed by deficit financing, which amounted to 16 percent of budget revenues in 1946, as well as by the granting of short-term and medium-term credits by the banks, which were not yet committed to regular financial planning. In late 1948 rationing was abolished altogether and inflation became open, as prices for food and textiles rose in state stores and on the gray market.

As a result of the inflation between 1946 and 1950 the peasants were able to accumulate sizable cash balances. This impeded the government's policy of class warfare and the allocation of credits in agriculture. A series of measures was passed—regulating and limiting private trade, subjecting cooperative organizations to the discipline of central planning, and expanding the network of socialized trading establishments. The outcome was the virtual elimination of private enterprise in trade. The currency reform of October 1950 served to diminish the liquid reserves of the peasantry and other groups of the population.

The enormous investment in industry at the outset of the Six-Year Plan (1950–55) required an increase in nonagricultural employment of more than half a million persons, most of whom were recruited from the countryside. This had an adverse effect on the output of the agricultural sector, especially on such labor-intensive products as meat, milk, and vegetables. At the same time there was a drop in labor productivity, due to the influx of unskilled labor into industry. To maintain the planned rates of increase in heavy industrial products and chemicals, production of consumer goods was allowed to lag.

The bad harvest of 1951 and the heavy slaughter of cattle in that year made the situation even more dangerous. Fewer consumer goods were available to match the increased earnings of workers and peasants, and another round of inflation ensued. In August 1951 special commissions were established to deal with "speculation" and to remedy these "temporary supply difficulties" (see chap. 15). Meatless days were decreed, and in September 1951 rationing of certain foodstuffs was reintroduced; the rationing was extended in December and again in March 1952.

Rationing was again abolished in January 1953. At the same time, however, the prices of formerly rationed goods were raised and open-market prices were somewhat reduced. The government felt it had finally brought cash balances held by the population to a "desirable relationship" with current incomes, so that purchasing power would be proportional to the individual citizen's contribution to the "national effort." In this way no person who had accumulated purchasing power at a time when his contribution was valued on a different, more favorable scale could enter the market and make off with goods destined for the "more efficient" workers or for the elite.

All these reforms, however, could not put an end to inflationary tendencies in the economy. In March 1957 it was reported that the strong pressure for higher wages, combined with a fall in production and a reduction in grain and potato deliveries, had accelerated the inflationary trend. The prices of food and other consumer goods have risen disquietingly. Pay raises in 1956 and 1957 have affected about 4,200,000 persons. The average monthly wage of workers outside coal mining rose from 1,093 złotys in February 1956 to 1,347 złotys a year later. In that period the average wage of a workman rose by 241 złotys, of an engineering or technical worker by 294 złotys.

In the hope of narrowing the gap between the amount of money in circulation and the amount of goods on the market, the government has increased the importation of consumer goods (see chap. 16). It has also tried to halt inflationary trends by refusing to consider any claims for wage increases unless they are linked to increases in productivity.

Total peasant income was expected to increase from 32.1 billion złotys in 1956 to nearly 40 billion in 1957, largely as the result of larger purchases of agricultural products by the state trade organizations at free-market prices, as well as of smaller compulsory deliveries at regulated prices. A March 1957 law canceling some 9 million złotys in accumulated claims of workers and employees may defeat the effect of incentives on increasing industrial production—and thus create further inflationary tendencies.

The Banking System

Although private banks were predominant in Poland during the early years of the interwar period, the world depression brought about increased governmental financial intervention. By 1938 the field of long-term credit was almost completely controlled by state institutions, and private banks frequently had to seek aid from the state banks even for short-term credit operations.

One of the steps necessary for financial planning of the Polish economy after World War II was a reform of the banking system to enable the state to plan the total volume and distribution of credit. The first development in January 1945 was the establishment of the Polish National Bank (Narodowy Bank Polski—NBP), which was granted the exclusive right to issue notes and was made responsible for regulating the country's credit structure. At the same date the National Economic Bank (Bank Gospodarstwa Krajowego), later reorganized as the Investment Bank, was re-established to finance the long-term needs of the economy. Also re-established were the State Agricultural Bank (Państwowy Bank Rolny), the Postal Savings Bank (Pocztowa Kasa Oszczędności), the network of Communal Savings Banks, with central offices at Warsaw and Poznan, the prewar Central Bank of Agricultural Cooperatives (Centralna Kasa Spółek Rolniczych), and the "Społem" Bank, a central union of consumer cooperatives. The last two were merged in 1946 to form he Bank of Cooperative Economy (Bank Gospodarstwa Spółdzielczego) with 300 branches and main offices in Warsaw and Poznan.

The only privately owned banks to be resurrected were the Bank of the Association of Cooperatives (Bank Związku Społek Zarobkowych) and the Commercial Bank (Bank Handlowy); these in effect were nationalized, since the government owned 80 percent and 50 percent of their respective shares. The Polish Bank of Social Welfare (Bank Polska Kasa Opiecki) was still formally a stock corporation, but its entire capital was owned by the Postal Savings Bank.

Banking reforms carried out in October 1948 and March 1951 tended mainly to strengthen the hold of the National Bank and its branches upon state enterprises through "control by the złoty." The Act of 1948 also eliminated the last relics of private banking, concentrating all domestic banking activities into the following institutions: the Polish National Bank; the State Investment bank (Bank Inwestycyjny) which channels budget grants to the socialized economy and supervises investment, capital repairs and amortization; the State Agricultural Bank, which handles both long- and short-term financing of private and socialized agriculture; the State Municipal or the Communal Bank (Bank Komunalny) and its branches, which take care of the short-term credit and investmer⁻ needs of the communal economy; the Bank for Handicraft and Commerce (Bank Rzemiosła i Handlu), which served the credit needs of small industry, handicrafts, and trade, and supervised urban credit cooperatives; and the General Savings Bank, replacing the Postal Savings Bank.

Additional measures to reconstruct the Polish banking system on the Soviet model culminated in a revised decree concerning the banking reform. Issued on June 4, 1951, this decree subordinated the banking system to the supervision of the Ministry of Finance. Three categories of banks acquired the exclusive right to carry on banking activities in Poland; the state banks, banks in the form of joint-stock companies, and village credit cooperatives.

From 1948 until the beginning of 1957 the trend was toward greater concentration of investment. The Bank for Handicraft and

Commerce was liquidated in March 1951, and the Communal Savings Bank in January 1952; their functions were taken over by the Investment Bank. By 1953 the Investment Bank was financing 92.5 percent of all investments, the rest, mainly for the benefit of agricultural collectives, being financed by the Agricultural Bank.

BANKING INSTITUTIONS

The state banks are independent legal entities and operate on commercial principles, using their earnings to cover their expenditures. The highest level of the state banking system is occupied by the Polish National Bank. Each state bank is headed by a director who independently manages the activity of the bank and is responsible for it.

The Polish National Bank is entrusted with the regulation of money and credit circulation and handles foreign transactions. Currency notes may be issued only by this bank, and these constitute legal tender in Poland. The volume of bank notes to be issued is limited by the decisions of the Council of Ministers. According to the decree establishing the bank, the amount of money in circulation must always be secured by, and thus should vary with, the holdings of gold, foreign exchange, trade bills, collateral for loans, and the obligations of the state treasury. Although gold and foreign exchange were included in the backing of the currency established by the decree, their relation to the volume of circulation was not indicated, and in practice they have been used chiefly to settle foreign claims. In effect the złoty was established without external connections and can be managed by the Ministry of Finance through the National Bank according to internal requirements.

Other functions of the National Bank include preparation of cash and credit plans for the national econom., the plan for foreign exchange, and other financial plans requested by the Minister of Finance. It is to execute these plans in its own competence and to control execution of the plan by other banks and economic units. The bank finances the national economy within the framework of the credit plan by granting credits to production units and other banks. It controls the economy of the units it finances, and that of other units as designated by the Ministry of Finance.

It also services the state budget—which includes both central and local budgets—and cooperates in the control over the budget expenditures. It organizes and executes settlements between enterprises, institutions, and organizations, and watches over the observance of principles of sound financial management.

The Investment Bank finances investments except in sectors serviced by specialized institutions such as municipalities and agriculture. It also exercises financial control over the enterprises that receive investment funds.

The Municipal Bank finances and controls current operations in the communal economy, which, defined by the Ministry of Finance, includes such institutions as public utilities and similar installations. It finances investments and capital repairs in this area and exercises control similar to that of other banks.

The General Savings Bank functions as a central savings institution accumulating individual savings and carries out activities connected with money transfers by means of checks. Table 13 shows its operations between 1953 and 1955. Noteworthy is the small size of demand deposits in comparison with total savings deposits.

In late May 1957 the head of the General Savings Bank announced that savings deposits at the General Savings Bank amounted to over 3.5 billion złotys. In the first four months of the year alone 1.2 billion złotys had been deposited, and the number of savings accounts had increased to 5.3 million. There were also some 18,000 school savings groups, to which 1.5 million children belonged. In all, some 7 million people were taking part in the savings movement. The average deposit was over 600 złotys, but—not counting 2.5 million dormant deposit accounts—the actual average deposit per book was about 1,000 złotys. (The dormant accounts are those with balances of between 5 and 20 złotys to which nothing had been added in some time.) The average deposit per wage earner—rather than depositor—was about 500 złotys. A new type of deposit book has recently been introduced, which entitles the depositor, in lieu of interest, to participate in a drawing for special premiums that include motorcars and motorcycles. There were about 57,000 "motor-car premium books," and the bank had 57 cars set aside as prizes.

There are two joint-stock banks which are controlled through shares held by the government and by the organizations they service. One of these is the Commercial Bank in Warsaw which deals in certain types of foreign transactions. The other, the Bank of the Polish Welfare Fund, formerly under the Postal Savings Bank, handles remittances from abroad. Both are under control of the Polish National Bank.

The State Agricultural Bank functions as the financial, organizational, and auditing head of the rural credit cooperative system. Credit cooperatives have served the needs of farmers in surrounding townships and have acted as auxiliary organs of the Agricultural Bank.

Prior to 1948 the rural savings and loan cooperatives were independently operated by their members and granted inexpensive loans. By decree of October 25, 1948, most of the rural credit cooperatives either were abolished or nationalized, and those that remained in existence were not allowed to grant private loans to peasants. Since October 1956 the rural loan cooperatives have been made the cornerstone of the newly-proclaimed program of "agricultural self-government" (see chap. 14). They are now to provide short and medium-term credit to individual peasants and rural craftsmen as well as to members of "producer cooperatives."

FUNCTIONS AND OPERATION OF BANKS

The National Bank and other specialized banks not only act to distribute and control the credit and investment funds granted to the various sectors of the economy but also control all planned financial transactions. The National Bank, for example, is directed to supervise each enterprise's financial plan, taking into account all the contracts signed by the firm for the delivery of raw materials and the sale of products. The officials of the bank's branches are also detailed to expand and improve the cost accounting of socialized plants and to see that working funds are neither squandered nor left idle.

This "control by złoty" is exercised through numerous directives issued by banks, ministries, central boards, and trusts to the enterprise. These directives lay down the maximum level of inventories to be maintained by plants producing a given product, or prescribe the number of workers that may be employed. Plant managers argue, however, that if they were to follow these numerous and complex directives to the letter their initiative would be severely curtailed, and that in some cases compliance would mean a drop in production.

While the banks have been given a great deal of supervisory power, more than in the Soviet Union, they cannot always exercise their power to withhold wage payments or credit to plants violating financial discipline. The withholding of funds by the banks is tantamount to foreclosing on or bankrupting an enterprise, which would throw the workers out of jobs and make it impossible for the production plan to be met. The bank can report the situation to the ministry controlling the plant or to the committee on state control. Rather than close the plant, the agencies may simply fire the plant manager and release new credits to get production up to the desired level. The plant staff itself may bargain with the bank representatives, or it may appeal to its ministry. Often the responsible ministry will free the enterprise from the sanctions imposed by the financial authorities, even before analyzing the causes of the violation, so that the wages of large groups of workers will not be withheld for an extended period. Thus, violations of work norms, of wage regulations, and of planned employment levels have been and continue to be widespread.

While the banks are concerned with making the enterprises financially solvent and profitable, the plant management regards profitability as less important than meeting all possible contingencies and fulfilling the plan. Since supplies are often erratic, the plant will constantly pressure the bank to release credits for building up "above-norm" inventories.

The control of credit by the banks is based on the assumption that the financial plan of the enterprise, handed down by the responsible ministry, adequately meets normal operating requirements. Actually, there have been frequent complaints about the undiscriminating formality of planning and its failure to set tasks in keeping with the real ability of enterprises. The basic technical and economic indices appear to be based on averages rather than on the special circumstances of each enterprise. Thus, one enterprise may exhaust its working capital sooner than foreseen and, unless it is granted credit, can throw others off their schedules. The prevailing incompetence of the professionals in the financial offices has also been a source of complaint.

The State Budget

The state budget is prepared by the Ministry of Finance, which, assisted by the Ministry of State Control, supervises its implementation at all levels of the economy, down to the individual enterprise. The government presents the budget to the *Sejm,* which usually approves it with but minor changes.

The scope of the budget has been progressively expanded over the postwar years as the government's control over and manipulation of the economy increased. Following a resolution by the Council of Ministers on April 17, 1950, the state budget became the central financial plan for the entire economy. The budget must finance the "national economy," social-cultural outlays, national defense, public security, the judicial establishment, and the political and economic administration. State enterprises are provided with investment capital and supplementary working capital from the budget, and intermediate industrial organizations (see chap. 15) receive their funds from the same source. Enterprises actually engaged in the production of goods, however, are expected to operate as economically self-sufficient units, covering their expenditures from sales and meeting temporary requirements for additional working capital by borrowing from state banks.

Since 1951 the state budget has also included the complete budgets of the local governments, the social insurance program, and various social funds. Because of these and other changes which made the 1951 budget about twice as large as that for 1950, direct comparisons of budgets before and after 1951 are misleading.

EXPENDITURES

Appropriations to finance the "national economy" have become steadily more important in postwar budgets, increasing from about one fourth of total budget expenditures in 1947–48 to more than half in 1953 and the following years (see Table 14). Expenditures for the national economy go to finance most new capital investment, provide working capital to expand production in existing enterprises, and cover the operating losses in state enterprises. Investment grants account for the major part of national economy financing from the state budget; bank credit and other investment funds play a very small role. Since the investment plan controls outlays from all sources, not much attention is paid to the distinction by source of funds within the plan, even though some funds may be earmarked for special purposes. The investment plan is governed by the over-all tasks of the national economic plan.

The next largest category of expenditures in the state budget goes for social and cultural services, which are an integral part of the national economic plan and are designed to assist its execution by training a skilled labor force, freeing women for industrial work, and shaping desired attitudes.

Increases in appropriations for national defense lagged behind increases in total outlays from 1947 to 1949, but from then on rose sharply, especially between 1951 and 1952.

Despite Poland's current economic difficulties, the 1957 budget foresees a 1.4 percent increase in total outlays, with social and cultural expenditures 24 percent higher than in 1956. Capital investment and defense expenditures, on the other hand, have been significantly reduced, the latter being set 15 percent below the 1956 planned figure —a cut greater than in any other of the eastern European countries. Table 15 shows the changes in the relative size of major expenditure items for 1955 to 1957.

REVENUES

Approximately 70 to 80 percent of total revenue is now derived from the socialized sector of the economy; only a small part comes from the private sector or directly from the population. This contrasts with 1937–38 when direct taxes amounted to approximately 35 to 40 percent of state revenue, or a little more than the revenue from government-owned monopolies. Following World War II direct taxation gradually decreased until 1951, from which time it has been about 10 percent of the total revenue, roughly the same proportion as in the Soviet Union.

Most of Poland's revenue comes from indirect (turnover) taxes usually imposed as a percentage levy on the wholesale price of consumer goods. This sales tax, as well as the planned profit, is included in the price paid by the consumer.

Revenues from the socialized sector are derived from three main sources: turnover taxes, gross profits earmarked for contributions to investment, and profits taxes (see Table 16). Some taxes are levied for the central budget (the turnover taxes and the profits tax, the income tax and the land tax), others for the budgets of local administrative units (principally taxes on real estate and fees for licenses on business). Customs revenues are relatively unimportant since all foreign commerce is under direct state control (see chap. 16).

At times the state has also levied special nonrecurring taxes. In 1945, for example, men in the 18–55 age group exempted from military services were specially taxed; revenue was also collected through a capital levy with rates from 15 to 75 percent on wartime profiteering. Another nonrecurrent levy was the so-called "National Tribute" (*Danina Narodowa*) of November 11, 1946, destined for the reconstruction of the reacquired territories. Exacted at rates varying from 0.5 to 15 percent of an individual worker's monthly salary, receipts from this tax were included in the state budgets for 1947 and 1948 and amounted to 37.5 billion old złotys (348 million new złotys)—or three times the anticipated return.

INDIRECT TAXES. *Turnover Tax.* Taxes on the turnover of goods and services accounted for more than one third of the total revenues of the Polish budgets from 1947 to 1950; with the transition to Soviet-type budgets in 1951, the proportion increased substantially.

Turnover taxes are levied on transactions by both the private and the socialized sectors; rates in 1946–48 ranged from 1 to 10 percent for most categories, but were significantly higher on such consumer goods as wine, 10 to 35 percent, beer, 22 percent, playing cards, 50 to 75 percent. The relative magnitude of these rates does not appear to have been changed in recent years. Following the Soviet model, producer goods in general were taxed at lower rates than consumer goods, a practice reflecting the regime's preoccupation with industrialization.

By varying the turnover tax on specific commodities the regime can exercise control over resource utilization and influence the final output of the industries concerned. The rate on petroleum products for example, was set relatively high (10 percent) in comparison with coal (4 percent) presumably in order to limit the use of liquid fuels which must be imported in large quantities (see chap. 15).

DIRECT TAXES. *Income Tax on Wages and Salaries.* The wage and salary tax is levied progressively on earnings and employers are directed to withhold it from the employee's salary or wage. Rates in 1953 ranged from 0.9 percent in the lowest category to 23 percent in the highest with earnings in the highest tax category about 10 times as great as in the lowest. A taxpayer supporting more than 2 children is allowed a 25 percent reduction of the computed tax; for more than 4, 50 percent; for more than 6, complete exemption. Childless married persons and unmarried persons over 25 are required to pay from 10 to 20 percent more than the basic tax. Persons who earn wages or salaries from literary, artistic, and scientific activities enjoy preferential tax treatment.

General Income and Profits Tax. The following types of income are subject to the general income and profits tax: (1) royalties from literary, artistic, and scientific activities; (2) profits of handicraft enterprises employing less than three persons; (3) profits of other handicraft and commercial enterprises, and certain agricultural organizations; (4) professional fees received by physicians, architects, and engineers; (5) income from real property and investments.

Each of these groups is taxed differently. The basic schedule as of 1951–52 was that of group 3, with rates varying from 5 percent on income between 3,600 and 4,200 złotys per year to 50 percent on income in excess of 162,000 złotys. Reductions from this basic rate were provided as follows: 20 percent for the first group, 25 percent for the second, and 10 percent for the fourth. For the fifth group, however, the rate increased by 25 percent. A surtax with rates varying from 4 to 30 percent in March 1952, was levied on incomes in excess of 10,800 złotys. As in the case of the wage-and-salary tax, reductions were allowed for dependent children while childless taxpayers paid an additional levy. State enterprises generally paid one half of their profits as tax, and in no case could the rate fall below 10 percent.

Land Taxes. Receipts from land taxes are divided between central and local authorities. Revised every year, the land tax is a typical example of an economic-political weapon aimed at a specific group —in this case the wealthier peasants. In 1949, for example, rates ranged from 2 percent—on farms with an income equivalent up to 1,000 kilograms of rye through 13 stages up to 18 percent on incomes equivalent to over 2,500 kilograms of rye. Farmers joining producer cooperative farms (see chap. 14) were granted tax reductions amounting to 30 percent on the land to be placed in collective use. Collective farms paid at rates set near the minimum. In 1953 the tax rate on the income of private farms ranged from 10 to 48 percent, while the rate on the more highly socialized collective farms was 3.5 percent and on the less highly socialized, 4.5 percent. Members of Joint Tillage Associations were taxed at the same rate as individual farmers but received a 30 percent reduction of taxes on land included in the joint effort.

In 1951 rates were graduated according to the potential yield-value of the land. An average farm of 12 to 14 acres was expected to pay 19 to 22 percent of a computed yield-value of 25,000 to 35,000 złotys. The owner of such a farm either could pay cash or deliver about 500 kilograms of grain at a nominal price set by the state. The peasant could also sign "voluntary" agreements with the government's purchasing agencies to deliver certain products at prices higher than the forced deliveries but lower than the free market price (see chap. 14).

Payments in cash and in kind allow the government to siphon off a substantial part of the "excess profits" of the peasantry and to some extent influence production. It is not clear, however, whether these taxes were sufficient to preserve the relation between urban and rural incomes desired by the government. In November 1953 President Bierut complained before the Central Committee of the Polish United Workers' Party that during the Six-Year Plan, although industrial production had far outpaced the very modest gains of agriculture the real income of peasants had increased faster than that of the urban workers.

OTHER SOURCES OF REVENUE. Payments by state enterprises into the budget include amortization allowances, surpluses in price equalization funds (see chap. 15) and excess working capital. Other sources of revenue include the proceeds of domestic and foreign loans (see chap. 16) and deposits of insurance organizations. These are considered current revenues, rather than liabilities, as they would be in, for example, the United States—a fact that relates to Polish claims of balanced budgets. Since 1949 income from these sources has amounted to only 1 percent of total budgetary revenue.

National Savings Fund. Between 1948 and 1950 compulsory saving accounted for approximately 4 percent of the central budget revenue. Since 1950 it has probably declined in relation to the greater scope of subsequent budgets. According to the 1948 law establishing the National Savings Fund (*Powszechna Kasa Oszczędności*), those required to make deposits into the fund were individuals and private enterprises subject to income or wage-and-salary taxes and having an income exceeding 240,000 old złotys per year, and those subject to the land tax and having an income exceeding the equivalent of 600 kilograms of rye. Deposits earned interest or yielded premiums at rates determined by the Ministry of Finance. Depositors were permitted to withdraw annually 5 percent of the balance of deposits as of the end of the preceding year. Greater withdrawals were allowed in the event of death in the family, maintenance of children in school away from home, and floods, droughts, or similar disasters.

Public Loans. Immediately after World War II, Poland suspended its prewar financial obligations, and no provisions have since been made to resume regular payment of the prewar debt. Under the present regime a method of debt management was developed based on public loans and resembling that of the Soviet Union. The loans had a dual purpose: to provide the government with funds for immediate postwar reconstruction and development of the country's industrial potential, and to alleviate the danger of inflation by reducing the amount of money in circulation.

On December 31, 1945 the government launched a "premium loan for the reconstruction of the country"; it was secured by the "whole immovable and movable property of the state" and was to be repaid by 1969. At the end of the subscription period a total of 4.7 billion złotys worth of bonds had been placed, or over 50 percent more than the government's target of three billion złotys. There were no interest payments but subscribers could win premiums if the serial numbers of their bonds came up at periodic drawings. Compulsory subscriptions to the loan were based on a sliding scale based on social groupings, and citizens' committees were authorized to prescribe higher quotas for persons in favorable financial circumstances.

On June 18, 1951 a second loan, the "National Loan for the Development of Poland's Strength," of half a billion złotys was floated. The bonds were to mature in 20 years. Although the regime stressed the voluntary nature of this loan, actually it was compulsory; minimum subscription quotas were assigned to all groups of the population according to their earnings.

The Tax Burden

Many of the taxes which affect the urban worker are hidden in the price of the goods he buys. While there have been complaints over such direct taxes as the income tax, compulsory savings, and the like the worker has been more concerned about the shortage of consumer goods and high prices.

The peasant, though burdened by both direct and indirect taxation, has been able to feed himself and his family, if not well, at least adequately. According to unofficial calculations something like half the money which went into the villages in 1951 remained in the hands of the peasantry even after taxes had been paid because of the sheer lack of goods on the shelves of village stores.

There can be little doubt that as long as the peasant stays on his own farm he has more ways at his disposal than the industrial worker of evading taxes and the forced accumulation of capital. In extreme cases he slaughters his cattle and stops cultivation; he may also increase beyond the figure calculated for him by the planner the amount of produce earmarked for family consumption, or he may sell his surplus in the black or gray market (see chap. 16). Since 1953–54 delivery and tax-evasion has become a mass phenomenon in the countryside, a practice so widespread that the peasant has little fear of the consequences.

In a speech on January 7, 1957 Gomułka promised that peasants with up to two hectares of land would be exempt from compulsory delivery quotas, grain-delivery quotas for other peasants would be reduced by about one third, delivery payment for compulsory deliveries would be doubled. Urban workers (who have fewer opportunities and devices than the peasants to evade tax payments) have not, however, been promised any tax relief.

AGRICULTURAL DEVELOPMENT

THE BASIC PROBLEM OF POLISH AGRICULTURE TODAY IS HOW TO adequately feed a growing industrial population. While in 1931 nearly 61 percent of the Poles obtained their livelihood from agriculture, less than 46 percent do so now. By pulling people off the land into the cities, industrialization has caused increasing demands to be made on the remaining agricultural workers. The problem was inherited from the interwar period but it has been intensified and complicated by war losses and destruction, boundary shifts, stepped-up industrialization, government mismanagement, and peasant resistance both to collectivization and discrimination against private farmers.

A series of land reforms, begun in the middle of the nineteenth century by the three partitioning powers and continued after each of the two world wars left marks on the countryside which recent readjustments have only partly removed. During the interwar years Polish farms were small and worked by more people than they could comfortably support. Most of the small farms lacked even the simplest machinery and except in Poznan and Bydgoszcz provinces agriculture suffered from a lack of capital. Farmers seldom could afford to buy synthetic fertilizers and the sharp decrease in livestock herds during World War II reduced the supply of organic fertilizers, causing a further decline in productivity.

In the newly acquired western territories farming as practiced by the Germans was far advanced and yields were correspondingly higher, but war damage in that region was severe, and the Poles who replaced the Germans were forced to rebuild many of the farms. Increased investment and improved farming practices may permit the region to regain its prewar level of productivity. Although the Communist regime initially took direct control over large portions of this land without putting it to productive use, recent developments indicate that the situation will be corrected.

The Communist drive towards collectivization of agriculture has been less successful in Poland than in some of the other European satellites. Even after a dozen years of Communist rule private farming remains the backbone of Polish agriculture. Collectives and state farms account for barely one sixth of the agricultural land. Moreover, the productivity of the socialized sector is far lower than that of individual peasant farms, irrespective of size.

Industrialization in Poland has been more at the expense of the worker than the peasant. During and immediately after World War II, when foodstuffs were at a premium, Polish peasants actually enjoyed a privileged position. Individual peasant farming has retained much of its importance, despite discriminatorily high taxes in the late 1940's and compulsory deliveries of agricultural produce decreed in late 1944 but eliminated in 1946. The government has made it possible for many young people to leave the farms and find employment in the cities, lessening the pressure on the family-size farm and reducing the traditional tendency to subdivide holdings into excessively small units. It has further improved the position of the private farmer by providing higher market prices, as well as bank loans and equipment.

Compared with the prewar period, however, production of most agricultural products still lags. In line with Communist preoccupation, industrial crops have a better production record than food crops. The 1956–60 Five-Year Plan provides for a 25 percent increase in agricultural production, including 27 percent more livestock but even if this goal is attained Poland will have to import at least a million tons of grain by 1960 to cover increased consumption demand and ensure fodder for livestock.

Land Reforms

BEFORE WORLD WAR II

Land reforms began in the nineteenth century with the emancipation of the serfs, first in the Prussian provinces, then in Austrian Galicia, last in Russian Poland. Enacted by the partitioning powers as a device to weaken the economic and political influence of the landholding gentry, they did not particularly improve the peasant economy. Individual peasant holdings shrank, since inheritance laws permitted almost limitless subdivision of land, and by 1918 there existed a multitude of holdings smaller than five acres side by side with very large estates. Poland addressed itself to agrarian reform primarily as a defense against the extremes of action taking place in adjoining Soviet Russia, but little was accomplished. During the crisis caused by the Russian counterattack into Poland in the summer of 1920 a reform bill was rushed through the *Sejm* providing for the immediate parcellization of large properties with a minimum compensation to the owners. With the defeat of the Russians, however, the whole matter was shelved. Only at the end of 1925 was another bill passed by the *Sejm:* parcellization was to take place on installments. Many large farms were exempted from the law, and dispossessed landlords were allowed full compensation. Much land, however, already had changed hands through private sale, passing to peasants who would till it themselves. During the depression of the early 1930's the big land-owners had to sell very large areas in lieu of unpaid taxes.

Nearly 8 million acres were transferred from large estates to smaller holders during the 20 years of the interwar period. By 1939 only one seventh of the arable land in Poland was still in the hands of the big landlords. Of over 45 million acres of arable land more than three fourths was by 1929 composed of farms of less than 120 acres; by 1939 the portion was six sevenths. Nevertheless, the number of landless peasants was still high and holdings of under 12 acres were far more numerous than all other types of holdings.

The larger farms were concentrated in the onetime Prussian provinces where many estates were still owned by Germans; the battle against parcellization here involved political issues. Many of these farms, however, had subsidiary industries such as breweries, tanneries, etc., which exempted them from the land reform law. The level of production per acre in the provinces east of the Vistula was uniformly only about half that of those to the west. In the south-central region, where overpopulation was worst, food production was not sufficient even for local needs. There, and in a few other districts, the privations of the depression years were extreme.

AFTER WORLD WAR II

Expropriation of the remaining large landholdings and distribution of the land to peasants were an important part of the Communist program in the initial postwar period. The land reform decree of September 6, 1944 abolished the economic base of the landlord class by ordering the expropriation of all properties exceeding 247 acres and those comprising more than 123.5 acres of arable land. In addition all land belonging to German nationals or to collaborationists was to be confiscated and added to the land pool created ostensibly for distribution to the peasants. In the "old territories" of Poland some 7.9 million acres were expropriated, but only about 3 million were distributed: 48 percent to former farm hands, 18 percent to landless peasants, the remainder to existing small and medium-sized farms to increase their acreage. In addition about 623,000 families were settled in the "recovered territories," either on individual holdings or on settlers' cooperatives.

This change converted the land from one undesirable form of administration to another equally undesirable: the former farm hands were left with holdings too small to provide a living and, in spite of land addition, the former small holdings were still not large enough to be economically adequate. To slow the process of parceling land the government withheld title deeds to new owners and kept for itself considerable land, some of which it converted into state farms.

An abrupt change came in 1948 after the Soviet break with Tito. On the heels of the Polish Government's resolution condemning Tito's farm policy, Hillary Minc, the "economic tsar," announced the government's desire to collectivize Polish agriculture. It was to be a slow process, entirely "voluntary." The peasants were to be given a choice of three (later four) types of producer cooperatives involving various degrees of resource pooling—from a loose association for the joint use of machinery to a form of collective whose members were to pool all their land and equipment.

In 1949 the government owned about 90 percent of the forest lands but only 10 percent of the agricultural land. Nearly two thirds of the peasant farms were still less than 25 acres, while only about 8 percent of total peasant farm acreage was in farms of 50 acres or more. This situation allowed the state simultaneously to wage class war against the richer peasants, and to organize the poorer peasants into production cooperatives under state control.

In the beginning the peasants looked with favor on the land reform and the liquidation of the estates. But after about two years it began to appear that the private farmer was actually far worse off than in prewar times. He had to contend with high obligatory deliveries exacted by the state at low prices, discriminatorily high taxes, and a low priority in investment allocation.

By the end of 1953 the government had adopted policy revisions which provided more incentives and better technical services, but the basic framework of continuing socialization and high compulsory deliveries was retained. Furthermore while prices paid by the government for obligatory deliveries rose somewhat, the movement of industrial prices against the farmer continued. In mid-1955, for example, for 100 kilograms of rye in the Bydgoszcz area farmers were being paid 60 złotys, an amount with which they were able to buy only 10 loaves of bread. Because of high delivery quotas, peasants had run out of their own grain by the time spring came; they were unable to buy bread because of the general food shortages and they were also unable to buy necessary clothing and other consumer goods.

As a result of such hardships some peasants have left the land and gone to work in factories. Others manage to resist the government's policies by various subterfuges, for instance, by holding on to such produce as eggs, butter, and milk which can be exchanged for tools and fertilizer or sold at high prices on the black market; or by lending each other missing quantities of produce to fulfill delivery quotas. Many sons and daughters working in industry send part of their wages to their parents to help them until conditions change.

Despite the new agricultural policy announced in January 1957 in a joint statement by the Central Committee of the Polish United Workers' Party (PZPR) and the Executive Committee on Agriculture Policy of the United Peasant Party (ZSL), many of the hardships and peasant reactions to them continue. In part, the revisions have been imposed upon the government by the peasants themselves, who, encouraged by increasingly liberal pronouncements, have been slowing down compulsory deliveries, delaying tax payments, and disbanding collectives—8,000, in the two months following the October 1956 Plenum.

With a view to making the sparsely settled western territories more attractive, the new policy provides that peasants are to be given the opportunity to acquire state lands there. The limit on the size of farms is 37.1 acres of arable land. Uncultivated land held by the state will be leased for at least 8 years to individual producers.

The agrarian structure of the country has not been improved by postwar land reforms. Motivated by political considerations rather than by economic rationality, land reform and settlement have hampered the governmental policy of rapid industrialization. The present land structure prevents agricultural production from keeping pace with the requirements of rapid industrial growth. The predominance of small farms with low productivity, making a relatively small contribution to commercial supplies, has not been altered.

The Land

CLIMATE AND SOIL

Interwar Poland, though a predominantly agricultural country, had neither rich soils nor a climate exceptionally favorable for agricultural production (see Map, Land Utilization in Poland). The new boundaries, however, include territory in which the moderating influence of the Gulf Stream is more pronounced and in which the seasonal and daily variation in temperature is less disadvantageous. The variety of the crops that can be grown is wide, though not as wide as in western or southern Europe. The choice for vegetable and fruit

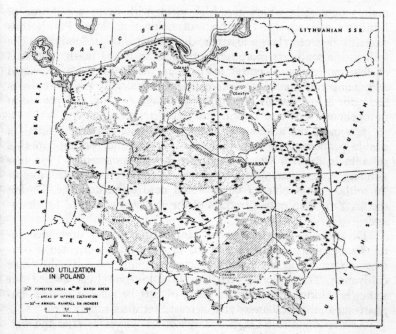

LAND UTILIZATION IN POLAND

FORESTED AREAS   MARSH AREAS
AREAS OF INTENSE CULTIVATION
—30″— ANNUAL RAINFALL (IN INCHES)
0   50   100
Miles

production is more limited than, for example, in Germany, Czechoslovakia, and Hungary, and with less assurance of a satisfactory yield. Corn, soybeans, grapes, and peaches can be grown in the southern part of the country, but the risk of failure is high. A fairly short growing season for the whole country keeps yields down and makes for a sharply fluctuating demand for farm labor over the year. Cattle can be kept outdoors only about five months of the year. Seasonal variations in milk and egg production are high. Late spring frosts often damage crops, particularly vegetables. Early frosts in the fall are a threat to potato and sugar beet harvests.

January mean temperatures vary from 30.2 degrees F. in the west to 24.8 degrees F. in the east. The period of frost lasts from two to three months in the west and about one month longer in the east. July mean temperatures vary from 62.6 degrees F. in the north to 68 degrees F. in the south. Temperatures may depart widely from these averages: cold as severe as 63 degrees F. below zero has been known, and summers may bring dry, hot spells lasting three to four months.

The richest black soil and loess in southeast Poland were lost after the war to the Soviet Union. The land acquired in the west has mainly light soils, which give high yields with heavy application of fertilizers and advanced methods of cultivation. Most Polish soils alternate between clays and sands, the latter being predominant. The soils in the south are more fertile than those in the north. The soils of the northern and central lowland are largely podsols associated with temperate forest regions; deficient in calcium and phosphates and with a low humus content, they require manure and plowed-in nitrogenous crops and stubble for satisfactory yields.

Erosion is not a major problem, but despite moderate rainfall a sizable proportion of soils needs draining because of impermeable subsoils. In the new western territories it was estimated in 1946 that although water conditions were comparatively well regulated, almost 10 million acres of crop lands would need some drainage. During the Six-Year Plan only a fraction of the area was scheduled for drainage.

Diversity of farm operations ranges from highly developed intensive farming in western Poland, strongly market-oriented, to extensive farming in the eastern reaches, tending towards subsistence cultivation. The regional variations in cultivation were evened out somewhat during the interwar years, in part because of greater emphasis on animal husbandry and increased fertilizer supply.

As a result of shifts in boundaries and populations after the war, the ratio of arable land increased about 5 percent and the newly acquired areas were almost twice as productive as the ceded areas. If the regime had been able to maintain prewar levels of production within the new boundaries, the total output of Polish agriculture would already exceed the total prewar production, with per capita output becoming even greater. But the prewar level of total output has not yet been reached.

CROP DISTRIBUTION AND PRODUCTION

Grains, of which rye is the most important, covered two thirds of the harvested area in pre-World War II Poland, and their share in the immediate postwar period was only slightly smaller (see Map, Crops and Livestock in Poland). After 1949, however, both their relative importance and their share in the harvested areas decreased. In 1953 the value of harvested grains amounted to only 33 percent of the value of total plant production, as compared to 42 percent in 1949. The decrease of the area under grain is the result of an acreage increase in sugar beets, hemp, flax, and other industrial crops. While these products are needed, low grain production in the former German areas and increased urbanization has forced Poland, once a grain exporter, to import grain, particularly wheat. The new Five-Year Plan

Crop and Livestock in Poland

(1956–60) calls for a 20 percent increase in grain production over 1955.

Potatoes, the second most important single crop after rye, account for about 17 percent of the total harvested area. Oats are the third largest crop. The predominance of rye, potatoes, and oats is explained by the fact that these crops are better suited to poor soil than wheat, barley, or sugar beets. Oil-bearing crops have been introduced only recently. The area under corn has been expanding. Where corn cannot fully ripen, it is cut early and either fed to animals as green fodder or used as silage for winter feeding.

The principal changes in land utilization caused by the shift in boundaries were reductions in orchards and gardens, meadows and pastures, and an increase in the ratio of arable land to the total area.

The areas Poland acquired in the west featured large estates, and the agriculture used more advanced methods and had a higher level of capital intensity than in the area ceded to the Soviet Union.

Prewar yields of the principal grains, potatoes, and sugar beets for Poland in prewar boundaries were slightly higher than those of the ceded eastern provinces. The former German areas, however, averaged a yield about twice as great as that of Poland as a whole in wheat, barley, oats, and approximately one and one-half times as great in rye, potatoes, and sugar beets.

In taking over the former German farms, the Poles faced initial disadvantages in the extensive wartime destruction of buildings, equipment, livestock, and draft power. They also had new techniques to master in order to attain the prewar output in the new area. Nevertheless, the outlook for per capita production in Poland now is more favorable than in prewar days because of the much reduced population.

Trends in per acre yields of the principal crops have not varied greatly since before World War I despite the fact that the Six-Year Plan envisioned increases of 20 to 40 percent. Heavier application of fertilizer, better seed, and a higher level of applied agricultural science were expected to be the factors making possible the projected gains. The gains were not envisioned as uniform for the whole country, but as distributed between a gain over prewar yields in the eastern central areas and a loss in the western provinces, particularly in the newly acquired territories.

Return of fallow lands to production made possible modest gains from 1947 to 1949, but after that period there was much less scope for expansion from that source. The Six-Year Plan therefore had to rely primarily on higher yields per acre to achieve scheduled production goals. By the end of 1953 production was officially reported at about 10 percent above 1949. Since it was evident by then that the projected ultimate goal could not be reached, the Plan was revised so as to provide for a 20 percent rather than a 50 percent over-all increase. Although there were production increases in 1955 and 1956, partly due to favorable weather conditions and the government's new policies towards the farmer, the revised goal was not achieved. Production still remains substantially below the prewar level.

Organization of Agriculture

After ten years of Communist rule and pressure, more than 75 percent of Polish farmland is still in private hands. In contrast to the tactics used in the Soviet Union, where the regime did not hesitate to wage a brutal civil war against the peasantry in order to achieve collectivization, Polish officials have moved very gingerly.

In 1955 state farms and collectives (or "producer cooperative farms") together accounted for somewhat more than a fifth of the total agricultural area and for about 14 percent of total agricultural output. More recent exact figures are not yet available, but the Polish Government has noted that since October 1956, only 2,000 collective farms remain out of a total of 10,000. Not only are private farms responsible for the bulk of agricultural production, but the value of output per hectare is about 20 percent higher on private farms than on collective farms (see Table 17).

The new agricultural policy, announced in January 1957, emphasizes the free development of individual farms. Property rights are to be clearly defined and observed; "the feeling of ownership" is to be strengthened; and all restrictions are to be removed regarding ownership, leasing, and purchase and sale of land. Liberal provisions are also made for leasing state lands to individual producers, especially in the western areas.

Individual peasants and collective farmers will henceforth be allowed to buy all types of agricultural machinery. The peasants formerly were dependent upon state-run Village Machine Centers; the State Machine Centers, which formerly serviced collective farms only, are now to lend support to private producers as well.

Private farming is also emphasized in another sector. The Peasant Self-Help Association (ZSCh) advocated in early October that dairy plants be given back to the peasants and run as "profit-making" concerns under cooperative managements. Witold Mierzejewski, chairman of the ZSCh in Poznan Province, declared in an interview that peasants are the rightful owners of the dairies and that after the dairies were nationalized in 1950 "we have seen the growth of a tremendous bureaucracy in all phases of dairy farming." Before nationalization the average establishment employed 4 to 5 people, but since then the number has gone up to 15 or 16. Moreover, with the recent abolition of compulsory milk deliveries, dairy plants under state operation were no longer assured of their milk supply.

PRIVATE FARMING

Polish peasantry has been officially classified into three groups, according to ownership of land: (1) poor or small peasants, owning parcels of land up to 12.4 acres, who comprised not quite 60 percent of the total number of farmers in 1950; (2) medium peasants, holding from 12.4 to 37 acres, who comprised about 30 percent; and (3) the "village rich" or kulaks, owning farms larger than 37 acres, who made up the remaining 10 percent.

As a result of redistributions of agricultural land, the kulaks' share in the nation's farming operations has dropped appreciably. According to official estimates, there existed in mid-1956 about 120,-000 kulak farms (as against 180,000 in 1950), accounting for about 4 percent of all individual farming in the country. Despite the relatively small percentage, kulak farming remains of considerable importance in terms of both agricultural productivity and commodity production. In 1952 farms of this type provided about one quarter of production of bread grains, and four years later the percentage had not been materially reduced.

The number and efficiency of the larger independent farms have varied by region. Apart from the reacquired western territories, where kulak farming was never of great importance, there existed at the end of World War II two major types of kulak farmers. The first, encountered in the midwestern region (Poznan and Bydgoszcz provinces), had relatively large landholdings, highly developed agricultural techniques, and extensive machinery. Hired labor played an important part in their operations. The second type was related somewhat to the Russian kulak farmers of precollectivization days. Operation of their farms was relatively little advanced, steady hired help was rare, and tenancy relationships of various forms prevailed. This type existed largely in the east and south (Białystok, Warsaw, and Lodz provinces).

The moves instituted by the regime toward socializing the agricultural sector of the economy affected the midwestern kulaks more severely than the southeastern, impairing their erstwhile high level of cultivation by discriminatory allocation of inadequate supplies of seed and fertilizer and by limited access to machinery. The labor force on these midwestern farms had been predominantly hired help; their tendency to drift to the industrial centers contributed to the reduction of agricultural output in the region. Furthermore, the norms for compulsory deliveries were generally higher in the Poznan-Bydgoszcz region than elsewhere, because of the generally higher level of cultivation. Meeting the higher norms, however, called for more extensive use of equipment than was allowed by the regime, and the decline from the earlier level of production was severe. Finally, local officials were often inclined to force liquidation of these farms instead of merely reducing their size.

In the eastern provinces, where farm poverty is far more widely spread than in the midwest, class antagonism between poor and wealthier peasants is strong. The Poznan kulak, on the other hand, is far more cooperative and "loyal" to the government in terms of fulfilling his obligations. Accordingly, conflicts of kulaks with their generally well-paid farm workers and also with the poorer farmers in the area are reported to have been relatively infrequent.

Even before the October 1956 reforms the regime had advocated a more flexible and lenient policy towards kulaks, since it realized their importance to Polish agriculture. "Loyal" kulaks were to be relieved of their burdensome and discriminatory obligations and to be accepted as an integral part of the countryside. Under the 1957 Plan this policy has been continued. The kulaks' grain delivery quotas will be decreased, and they will be allowed to sell more on the free market. The state-controlled price of produce and livestock will be raised, and the supply of agricultural machinery to private farmers will be increased at the cost of some decrease in deliveries to the state farms. There is little doubt that the government's attitude toward the nationalization of the land has undergone a fundamental change.

COLLECTIVIZATION

Collectivization is intended to increase government control over what is produced and to ensure efficient collection of obligatory produce deliveries. State ownership of Machine Centers, control of the supply of fertilizer, and manipulation of the flow of industrial consumer goods to the village stores provide some leverage to influence crop production and collection; while a differential taxation policy (see chap. 13), administered on a class basis, serves to undermine the position of the well-to-do peasants.

Four types of state-approved cooperative farms were introduced in postwar Poland. Ranked in increasing order of socialization, they are: (1) Land Tillage Associations; (2) Agricultural Cooperative Associations; (3) Agricultural Production Cooperatives; and (4) Agricultural Cooperative Collectives.

All types of collective farms require a stipulated minimum of communal labor from their members. Use of hired labor by the collective is generally prohibited. In a Land Tillage Association, the least socialized form of collective, all means of production brought into the association, including the land, not only belong to the member but also remain in his individual possession and are pooled only for certain periods of the year. In the other three types of cooperatives, farmlands are continuously pooled, though members do not lose the right of ownership to the land they brought into the organization when they joined—or were forced to join. The only piece of land each household has for its own use, however, is a garden plot of 0.75 to 2.5 acres on which pigs, chickens, and two cows and their calves may be kept. The return from cooperative farming varies according to the stringency of organization, from a mere expense-sharing in Land Tillage Associations to the Soviet-type system of workday unit payment in the more socialized collectives.

To accelerate "voluntary" collectivization of peasant argiculture, various subtle forms of compulsion have been applied to make the peasant "aware of the superiority" of the system. Official spokesman have in fact acknowledged instances of "violation of the voluntary principle" tantamount to outright coercion. In theory, the cooperative elects its own administration from among its members and the general assembly is the highest authority. All producer cooperatives are members of a central union of agricultural cooperatives which instructs and watches over the members.

The state has fostered the formation of the more highly collectivized cooperatives by assigning to them certain lands without charge. Members of the fourth type are completely absolved of paying off to the state the indebtedness arising from their acquisition of land under the land reform and settlement programs. The other types have received similar but correspondingly lower dispensations.

The statutes of the "highest order" producer cooperative provide that the basis for distribution of income among members should be the number of workday units put in by each member. Each operation on the collective is defined in terms of workday units. All work performed is supposed to be calculated in these units, taking in account the qualifications, difficulties, and economic importance of the particular tasks. Planning authorities have published tables of standard norms of work for converting factors for different kinds of work. Premiums are given for doing more than one's daily work norm.

The work on the farm is usually carried on in brigades. The composition and size of brigades vary constantly, because members take time out to work on their individual plots and in some cases even in nonagricultural employment outside the cooperative. According to one report (*Nowe Drogi,* February 1954), about one fourth of the members in industrialized or densely populated districts had outside employment not related to farm work.

One major weakness of the collective system in Poland is the lack of experience of the chairmen and their executive committees in running such complex, and frequently quite large, enterprises. Some of the officials possibly have been given a special short course in agronomy or sent on a brief tour of the vast collective farms in the Soviet Union, but neither this cursory instruction, nor the supervision and control exercised by State Machine Centers, the Peasant Self-Help Association, the Party, and local National Councils guarantees efficient management.

Another major difficulty is that the collectives are not real cooperatives. Most of the peasants joined under pressure, hence try to take as much and give as little as possible. They devote the greatest possible attention to their individual garden plots and animals. Collective chores are considered to be ancillary employment or a way of obtaining fodder for privately owned livestock. In many cases members have not surrendered to the cooperative the livestock and equipment they originally declared as their contribution; the private plots around the homesteads are often much larger than permitted in the regulations, and hogs, cows, and horses above the limit established by the farm statutes have been kept for personal use. These infractions have been facilitated by the lack of stables for collectively owned livestock, so that both a peasant's own animals and those of the collective would be kept on the household plots. This may explain why the building of proper collective livestock enterprises has been delayed by the peasants even though the authorities have proffered help. Animals have often been secretly slaughtered and sold on the black market, and there have been cases of leasing of parts of the collective's land to private farmers.

Executives often fail to call a general meeting of the members, thus violating the collective statutes and violating the provisions for self-government. The most important problems of the collective are usually decided by a small group composed of the chairman, the local Party secretary, the Executive Committee of the County National Council, and any Party members who may belong to the collective.

From the very beginning the regime pursued collectivization in a circumspect manner, especially in comparison to the program in the other satellites of eastern Europe. The Six-Year Plan for agriculture set no precise goals for the extent of collectivization but merely referred to a "considerable" advance. Even up to the end of 1953 the progress of collectivization appears to have been extremely slow. The census of December 1950 still listed nearly 3.3 million individually owned farms, almost exactly the same number as in 1931 —the intervening land reallocations compensating for the decrease in peasant-cultivated area. The agricultural producer "cooperatives" of various types contained probably no more than 50,000 peasant families on July 1, 1951, when the total number of collectives was reported to be 3,054. In July 1952 President Bierut admitted that the number of "cooperatives" was "more or less at a standstill," with only 308 collectives added during the year. Only about 2,000 of the total number of the "cooperatives" were of the "highest" type, which is similar to the Soviet kolkhoz; the majority of these were in the reacquired territories, where new settlers depended considerably on government guidance and assistance.

From 1953 on there has been a definite drop in the formation of collective farms. Between 1952 and 1953 the number of collectives increased by 3,146 from 4,904 to 8,050, involving about 200,000 peasant families and about 7 percent of available farmland, but in 1954 only 1,662 new collectives were formed and in 1955 not more than 251. Three-hundred-twenty-three collectives were dissolved in 1955. In some provinces—Lodz, Lublin, Bialystok, Olsztyn, Szczecin, Opole, and Katowice—an absolute decrease took place.

Beginning in 1955 restraints on operations of collective farms were progressively loosened. Although the collectives differed greatly in efficiency and productivity, it had become established practice, for example, to fix a universal "minimum payment" for the workday unit. Not all collective farms were able to pay that national minimum and meet their other obligations, such as taxes and repayment of credits to the state. By juggling accounts and countenancing delinquencies, these farms in effect were able to extract from the state an indirect subsidy in addition to other preferential aid already granted. One such preference involved the supply of fertilizers, of which the average collective farm in 1954–55 used twice as much as individual farmsteads per hectare of arable land. Despite this advantage, the average yield of the collective sector was appreciably smaller than that of the private sector.

Gomułka in his speech of October 20, 1956, called for new guidelines to be established for cooperative farming. Basically sound farms were to be assisted with repayable investment credits. Other sorts of state grants were to be abolished. The cooperatives which had only a poor chance of development and whose operations were conducted at a loss were not to be granted credits, and Gomulka suggested that their members be given a chance to consider dissolution of the organizations. He intimated that the major problem would be the repayment of state credits granted in the past to such cooperatives. According to the charter governing cooperative farms, a member upon resigning from a cooperative is supposed to receive from the cooperative in kind or in value of grain, the capital he put in and a parcel of land on the outskirts of the cooperative farm of the same value as that he originally contributed.

In view of the resentment of the peasants who had been pressed into a cooperative or collective farm, the dissolution of these establishments was bound to be far from orderly. Stealing of produce has been widespread. While the regime foresaw the dissolution of inefficient cooperatives only, many others seem to have taken the opportunity to quit socialized farming. In many provinces a rush toward dissolution was reported, with members saying in effect, "Let us dissolve our cooperatives before it is too late." One difficulty encountered upon dissolution has been the division of buildings; cowsheds for 100 cows and sties for 200 pigs were, for instance, quite unsuitable for use by an individual operator. Similar difficulties attended the transfer of land. The hurriedly drawn-up legal regulations that were intended to make for a more orderly transfer apparently have been hard to implement and will probably remain a source of internal disturbances for some time to come.

Because of the peasants' restored confidence and their sizable cash holdings, land prices have risen sharply, reflecting the increased demand for farmland. Livestock prices have also risen. Prices of horses, for example, in December 1956 were reported some 50 percent higher than in 1955, and the price of pigs in some instances had reportedly doubled.

The government appears to be exploring various ways of coping with the difficulties. One idea finding wide acceptance in official circles is the transformation of cooperatives of a higher (more collectivized) type into cooperatives of a lower (looser) type, something permissible in the past in theory but never put into practice. Another suggestion, voiced in late 1956 by Zygmunt Garstecki, chairman of the Central Board of the Peasant Self-Help Association, concerns formation of grange-type "Agricultural Circles," which as "trade and social organizations will constitute the basic element in peasant self-government." This suggestion was taken up in January 7, 1957, by the Joint Directive of the PZPR and ZSL, and it may point the way toward a new indirect approach in the socialized sector.

STATE FARMS

Agricultural planning is being applied in its most direct form to the state farms. They operated under the direction of the Central Administration of State Farms, which in April 1949 became the Ministry of State Farms. The aims of the state sector in Polish agriculture, according to a statement by Hillary Minc in August 1948, were:

1. To serve as a socialist basis in agriculture and contribute to the food supply of the population—about 15 to 20 percent of the grain, and 7 to 10 percent of the meat supply.
2. To assist peasant agriculture by supplying improved plant varieties and animal breeding stock, assist neighboring small farms with available agricultural equipment, and participate in educating the villages in agricultural science.
3. To serve the individual peasant farms as a model of large-scale modern, socialist, mechanized farming and stimulate the transfer of small and medium peasants to collective farming.

These aims have remained essentially unchanged. In furthering the goal of increasing the marketed share of state farm production, the wage system was changed in favor of cash payments on April 1, 1950, to eliminate allowances in kind. Housing for workers, shelter and feed for their livestock, fuel, and a plot for gardening are still being furnished, however. State farms are regarded as the "highest" form of socialist agriculture and get priority in the supply of equipment, fertilizers, and trained personnel.

The performance of state farms, however, has remained below expectations. Although they occupied in 1953 about 12 percent of agricultural land, they accounted for only 9.2 percent of agricultural production. No improvement was visible in more recent years. Bad management is the major difficulty. Insufficient supervision by administrative officials, theft of building materials, and falsification of payrolls and records appear to be quite common.

Other difficulties appear to have been rooted in unsatisfactory working conditions. A new collective agreement for state farm workers, effective March 1957, includes the abolition of norms, the institution of fixed wages, a more liberal vacation policy, and increased allocations of fuel and grain.

Under the agricultural policy announced in January 1957, state farms are to operate on the principle of profitability and are no longer to depend upon government subsidies. This will require a rise in the prices paid by the government for their products. Labor shortages on state farms are to be overcome by better working conditions as well as participation in the state farm's revenues and management through workers' councils. Professional, not political, qualification is to be decisive in the selection of state farm managers. Of particular interest is the proposed transfer of inefficiently cultivated arable land of state farms in the western territories to private producers, since "it may yield better results if cultivated by them."

STATE MACHINE CENTERS

From the beginning of the postwar era the government made great efforts to supply agriculture with the means of production. Producers, however, were not to be in direct control of mechanized farm equipment. Only state farms were allowed to have all types of equipment of their own. Private farms were deprived of any large machines they might own and were forbidden to buy new ones. For technical services, private farms as well as collective farms have had to rely on the State Machine Centers (POM)—the number of which rose from 30 in 1949 to 416 in 1954—and on the state-controlled Village Machine Centers (GOM)—which numbered 2,718 in 1954 but in 1957 were being done away with. Until recently new machinery supplied by the state has gone exclusively to these two organizations and to the state farms. Manual implements, however, could be bought by all producers.

The POM could enter into contracts for servicing noncollectivized peasant farms, but only if groups of owners signed contracts agreeing to raise the same crop—a first step in the direction of collective work. A POM now serves an entire district and operates 10 to 40 tractors. The extensive network of community or village machine centers, originally set up as cooperative centers connected with the distributive outlets of the Peasant Self-Help Association, have been serving private individual farms.

In 1955 over 26,000 tractors were on state farms and about 19,000 were owned by POM. Only 2,000 were operated by GOM. According to official 1956 figures, about 86 percent of POM operations were performed for collectives, 8 percent for state farms, and only 6 percent for private farms. The rates payable for services of the machine centers were discriminatory—collectives paid less than private farms, and private farmers according to the size of their farms. Payments were frequently in kind, providing another source of government acquisition of agricultural commodities.

With respect to the cooperative farms, the POMs were to provide technical assistance as well as politico-economic guidance. In theory the POMs also were to furnish professional assistance in the formulation of financial and production plans. In practice, however, the assistance never seems to have reached the level desired by the state. As early as March 1951, POMs were criticized for being too passive in extending technical aid to collectives and of neglecting their political task of converting individual farmers to collective farming. To remedy the defect, political departments were added to the POMs to propagandize the countryside more intensively and to assure more complete implementation of the regime's economic aims. In October 1953, however, President Bierut still found reason to criticize the POM's inadequate support of cooperative farms in such matters as fulfilling work contracts on time, introducing up-to-date agricultural methods, and effectively pursuing political tasks.

The POM, because of its continuous contact with the collectives, is held responsible for efficient performance and work discipline in the collectives. With the representatives of the local people's councils, the POM is also expected to supervise the annual accounting, the purpose of which is to keep collectives from squandering their seed and fodder reserves by increasing the distribution of income in kind among members and to prevent delay in repayment of credits granted by the state.

The new agricultural policy announced in January 1957 provides that individual peasants and collectives will be allowed to buy all types of agricultural machinery. Village Machine Centers are being disbanded and their equipment sold to the collectives, peasant co-operatives, and private farmers. Collectives will continue to enjoy priority in the purchase of machines, as well as preferential treatment in other respects. The State Machine Centers are to lend more support to private producers and will no longer supervise the work of the collectives. The Centers are now required to operate according to the profit principle rather than rely on state subsidies.

DELIVERIES TO THE GOVERNMENT

OBLIGATORY. All sectors of agriculture are subject to compulsory deliveries of produce to the state. With the introduction of the Three-Year Plan in 1947, the government proceeded to weld the agricultural sector more firmly into the framework of national economic planning. At first the state expanded its network of socialized trading establishments and at the same time restricted and stifled private trade. It was hoped by such indirect methods, including the setting of attractive prices for industrial crops and dairy products, to channel agricultural surpluses according to the government's desires. By the end of 1949 procurement of grain and meat was completely in the hands of state agencies and the cooperative distributive network.

The land tax was re-established in June 1947, according to a graduated schedule of farm production, with farms producing less than the equivalent of 49 metric quintals of rye exempted from the tax. The tax, expressed in terms of rye equivalents, is reassessed every year (see chap. 13).

By 1951 the agricultural collection goals provided for in the Plan were not being reached. The peasants had found means of circumventing officially designated channels for grain sales and were withholding grain from the market. In June 1951 the regime decreed the compulsory sale of grain at state-set prices, in amounts regulated by norms which varied according to the various conditions governing yields. In 1952 compulsory deliveries of grains were established as a permanent feature of state control over agriculture, within the framework of an over-all plan. Until recently nondelivery of the obligatory quota was punishable by administrative action, with steep fines and jail sentences ranging up to three years.

In order to assign delivery quotas, the government has established schedules for converting farm areas throughout the country into uniform "accounting hectares." The delivery quota in a given locality is allotted so that the levy per hectare increases in proportion to the size of the farm. Under the most steeply progressive schedule worked out under the 1951 decree, the smallest farms were obliged to deliver 0.7 units of grain per hectare, whereas the largest farms—25 hectares (62 acres) and up—were being charged with 11.3 units. Similar assessments were established for meat, milk, and potatoes.

The government revised its schedules of compulsory deliveries of animal products in December 1953 to encourage livestock production and to bring the quotas in line with past performance. Some relief was given to owners of very small farms and to various forms of collective or cooperative farms. Broader exemptions were established for families holding less than two hectares of farm land. Quotas were reduced on certain classes of poor land. A wider range of substitutes for the specified deliveries was permitted, and certain exemptions were allowed for peasants raising breeding stocks under contract with the state. The major "concession" was a promise that in 1954–55 the delivery norms would not be increased, thus permitting the peasants to sell their surplus in excess of obligatory deliveries at more attractive prices.

In the fall of 1955 the government began to relax the strictness of its policy against peasants who failed to fulfill their delivery quotas. Although no major change in the 1953 law was made, in certain cases penalties for nondelivery were postponed. The new provision applied to widows with children under 14, peasants who had no helpers on their holdings, farmers over 65, and chronic invalids. Fines could be rescinded when the accused met his quotas in full. By the end of 1956 compulsory deliveries were again in arrears in all sectors. Grain deliveries were reported in deficit by more than 400,000 tons, and potatoes by about 500,000 tons. Livestock deliveries were also behind schedule. Apparently some of the difficulties were due to the peasants' expectation that the system of compulsory deliveries would be revamped if shown to be sufficiently nonfunctional.

The peasants' expectations were borne out. In early 1957 the total amount of grain required to be delivered from the 1957 harvest was cut by one third and the price per quintal doubled. This reduced the ratio of free market prices to prices for compulsory deliveries from 4:1 to 2:1. For very small farms (below five acres of arable land) compulsory deliveries were abolished completely. The progressive quotas for medium and large farms have also been reduced. Compulsory milk deliveries were abolished as of the beginning of 1957, and other compulsory deliveries, such as potatoes and livestock, have been reduced. Even these reduced quotas have not, however, been met by the peasants.

CONTRACT. Contracting for grain and livestock production remains an important element of Polish agricultural policy. Certain crops, such as sugar beets, oil seeds, and some meat products, are entirely on contract. For others, the government contracts over and above what it receives from the tax in kind and from payments made by the farms to the State Machine Centers. In the case of industrial crops the government contracting organization provides a great deal of technical direction, aid, and supervision during the entire period from soil preparation to harvest. As work on a crop progresses, the state agency pays advances to the farm. Prices paid the farms for a given crop depend in part on quality, but also in part on the degree to which the farm succeeds in exceeding the originally planned delivery total or the planned yield per hectare. Bonuses for high excess deliveries rise sharply. Contracting farms also receive needed industrial goods at very low prices. The entire emphasis in making contracts is on providing farmers with the maximum income stimulus to increase both production and the sphere of contract sales to the government; thus, contract prices paid are very close to the going market prices.

The number of commodities covered by state contracts rose from 4 in 1945 to 60 in 1951. In 1952 crops grown under contract covered approximately 14 percent of the area of spring planting. Among the more important crops for which the contracted area was increased in the past few years were sugar beets, oil seeds, fibers, and potatoes. Contracting of livestock was increased appreciably in 1954.

Modernization of Agriculture

MECHANIZATION

In the first part of the postwar period there was a serious lack of many kinds of production equipment and supplies, especially draft power, fertilizer, farm implements, seed, and insecticides. Almost all of the tractors existing before the war on present Polish territory (seven eighths of which was in the former German territory) had been destroyed. UNRRA assistance of nearly $76 million in equipment and supplies was an important factor in the recovery of production in 1946–47.

Polish postwar economic plans set high targets for the output of tractors and other farm supplies. But, following the Soviet model, over-all investment in agriculture had a much lower priority than industrial investment, and in the course of the Six-Year Plan the priority was further reduced. A reversal of the trend took place for the first time in 1953, when the Polish Government established higher priorities for the agricultural implement industry. By 1955 there were 47,000 tractors and the number of other farm machines had increased. Polish agriculture still derives 75 percent of its draft power from horses, as against nearly 100 percent in 1938 and 93 percent in 1949. Expansion in the stock of farm equipment consisted primarily of replacement of obsolescent horse-drawn equipment and the expansion of tractor-drawn implements. The draft plan for 1957 provides for an increase in agricultural investment of 20 percent over 1956. Mechanization, however, demands trained personnel, and there have been many complaints in the past year about the lack of basic agricultural training.

FERTILIZERS

The Polish soil, poor in organic and mineral nutrients, requires relatively large quantities of manure and commercial fertilizers to maintain an adequate level of fertility. The great difference in crop yields existing before the war in the German parts of the present territory and in the old Polish provinces was partly due to the difference in the use of fertilizers. In 1938, for example, the grain yield per hectare (2.47 acres) in the German sector was 19.1 metric quintals, as against 12.3 in the Polish sector; the respective yields for sugar beets were 311 and 221, and for potatoes, 168 and 125. The corresponding consumption of chemical fertilizer (per hectare in terms of pure nutrient) was almost ten times greater in the German sector than in the Polish sector.

The extensive destruction of livestock herds during and after World War II and the resulting deficiency in manure supply have not yet been made up. By 1954–55 the level of fertilizer consumption had reportedly reached approximately 92 percent of the prewar level, but distribution of fertilizer has been discriminatory, with private farms receiving less than half the amount of fertilizers (per hectare of sown area) supplied to collectives and state farms.

ELECTRIFICATION

Under the postwar Plans, Polish villages are being gradually electrified and supplied with electric motors and other equipment, particularly items for collective use. In 1948 each farm having electricity consumed on the average about 244 kilowatt hours—barely enough for light alone. Relatively slow progress of electrification was achieved under the Six-Year Plan, and the goal of the Plan—the electrification of between 55 and 60 percent of all farms—was not realized.

As of January 1957, 16,000 villages are reported to have electric current. By the end of the Five-Year Plan (1960) 81,250 villages, comprising 56 percent of the countryside, are to be electrified.

Livestock

Mixed crop and livestock farming, rather than specialized grain farming, has been the rule in Poland. This type of agriculture has met the need for manure and for animal draft power, and was favored by the abundant labor supply in rural areas. Before World War II farms of less than 124 acres, while covering less than 80 percent of all agricultural land, had over nine tenths of all cattle, pigs, sheep, and goats. Even now there is more livestock per hectare on individual small farms than on large state or collective units. Over-all production of livestock in Poland, however, was relatively low before the war, in comparison with western Europe, and it still appears to be below the level which prevailed in the present Polish territory before the war (see Table 18). War losses were particularly great in livestock. According to an official Polish estimate, losses were as follows: horses—2,776,000 or 75 percent of prewar numbers; cattle —8,541,000 or 60 percent of prewar; pigs—6,434,000 or 80 percent of prewar.

Before the war, Poland was one of the largest horse breeding countries in the world. The light type of horse, less useful for deep plowing than the Belgian or Danish horse, was most common, as it was adapted to small farm units and could be used for transportation as well as farm work. The horses found in the reacquired territories and those imported by UNRRA are of a heavier type.

Cattle raising was of great importance before the war, accounting for over a quarter of the gross income of farms of 5 to 123.5 acres. Dairy cattle prevailed; they are now even more dominant because the all-purpose cattle of what was formerly southeastern Poland now belong to the Soviet Union. Average annual milk yields per cow before the war were between 1,400 and 2,000 kilograms. Yields were always higher on the Polish territory that was not ceded, but, after war losses and the effects on herds of malnutrition and disease, rebuilding of stock and of its productivity has been proceeding rather slowly.

Hogs and sheep increased much faster after the war than did cattle, and the composition of the livestock population has changed accordingly. In 1938 there were, for each 100 head of cattle, 71 pigs, 32 sheep, and 37 horses. In 1955 the respective figures were pigs, 138, sheep, 53, and horses, 34.

Conditions for hog raising are favorable. With the rapid development of the bacon industry in the early 1930's and later the production of tinned hams for export, hogs became a major enterprise on middle-sized and larger farms. Supported by the government and encouraged by a strong demand for meat, hog breeding expanded after the war. In 1953 the number of hogs (9.7 million) was higher than before the war on either old or present territory.

The numbers of sheep fluctuated during the interwar period, but even when herds were at their peak they could only supply about one fourth of the requirements for hides and wool. Peasants and high-landers in the Carpathian Mountains kept sheep mainly as a source for homespun materials. The high prices of wool, due to increasing domestic demand and import restrictions after 1948, created favorable conditions for extending sheep breeding. The 1955 target under the Six-Year Plan (3.8 million) was exceeded in 1954, and more than double the number of sheep are now being raised as compared to prewar.

Goats have been particularly popular among workers, especially miners, in the reacquired territories. This appears to be one reason why the goat population recovered first—reaching nearly double the prewar level in 1948.

Polish postwar policy has fostered the development of animal production by various means, including high market prices; the payment of premiums for deliveries in excess of contracted amounts; the giving of priorities for the purchase of scarce industrial articles to those who deliver livestock to state procurement agencies; tax reductions for raising pigs; and honors and decorations for efficient producers. In December 1953 the 1955 goals for livestock were changed from the Six-Year Plan figures, downward for cattle and upward for pigs and sheep. Since a given number of cattle may be presumed considerably more valuable than the same number of either pigs or sheep, the reduction of the goal for cattle by about 1.5 million head far outweighed the 0.45 million increase for sheep and 0.25 million for pigs.

In November 1955 the annual quotas of compulsory meat and milk deliveries by collectives were reduced. Collective meat deliveries were to be cut by 15 kilograms for each piglet kept for breeding; milk deliveries were reduced by 300–400 liters for each calf kept for breeding and 400 liters for each calf sold to the state. The provisions were intended to prevent a further decline in livestock breeding on collective farms.

Forestry

About one fifth of Poland's land surface is forest area (the figure for Europe as a whole is one third). The value of the forests as a natural resource is second only to coal. Forest land capable of producing crops of industrial woods and almost entirely accessible is approximately equal to the forest area of Louisiana. Overcutting before and during World War II, however, greatly depleted the growing stock and on about 15 percent of this productive forest land eliminated it completely.

The forests are predominantly coniferous, and Scotch pine occupies about 75 percent of the forest areas. Broadleaf "hardwood" forests were once much more abundant in Poland than they are now. Peasant preference for firewood from broadleaf trees and the tendency in forest management toward pure even-age stands of coniferous trees have led to the virtual elimination of hardwood stands. The influence of systematic silviculture has been strongest in the forests of the western territories, where it has been practiced for more than 100 years.

The total forest area of approximately 18 million acres includes about 2 million acres of swamps and other land capable of producing only small amounts of firewood. Of this total, approximately 15.3 million acres are state forests (as compared with 8.2 million in 1937), and about 2.7 million acres are private forests (as compared with prewar holdings of 14 million).

Poland has productive forest area of 0.67 acres per capita, equaling that of France. A timber exporter before the war, Poland must now husband its forest resources to meet existing and future needs. Heavy timber exports in the interwar years, largely of unprocessed wood, not only depleted timber resources but also hampered orientation of wood-using industries toward the domestic market. Since the war, lumber, plywood, and wood-pulp production has been greatly expanded.

Poland depends chiefly on railroads for timber transportation outside the forests: about 75 percent of the wood output is transported by rail between stump and ultimate consumer. Since the country's extensive inland waterways were severely damaged during the war, water transportation is much less common now than it used to be.

Ship supplies and tanning extracts are important forest by-products. Formerly Poland imported most of its supply of these commodities, but the state is now trying to free itself from dependence on foreign sources.

Fishing

In terms of employment (4,450 marine fishermen and 22,000 shore workers) Poland's fishing industry occupies a relatively minor place in the country's economy. But in view of the population's low meat consumption and generally low purchasing power, the 80,000 tons or more of fish landed annually are extremely important. Aware of the need for protein in the national diet, the government has been expanding the industry and attempting to increase the per capita consumption of fish.

Since the end of the war the regime has assumed complete control over the sale and distribution of fishery products and has taken charge of the development of fishing and packing facilities. At the end of 1952 nationalization was still in progress; the remaining private owners of boats and gear were gradually being forced out of operation by confiscatory prices, taxes, and other discriminatory practices.

Before World War II Polish fish exports were small and 75 percent of the fish consumed domestically, mostly salted herring, was imported. Increased postwar production has made imports less important, although established domestic preference for salted herring, especially among the peasants has necessitated continued large imports of this low-priced product. Poland has begun to export fish in sizable quantities.

The marine fisheries have expanded almost continuously during the past 25 years. In the 1920's only a small marine catch was taken from nearby coastal waters, but thereafter the catch increased rapidly because of intensified coastal operations for sprat and the expansion of North Sea herring fishery. Coastal operations, temporarily suspended during World War II, were resumed in 1945, and the following year fishing in the North Sea and trawling for cod in offshore Baltic Sea waters were expanded. Since 1952 Polish fishermen have been trawling in the Barents Sea.

The country's extensive fresh-water lakes and rivers have been consistently productive, although no data on the quantity of fish caught are available. Pond-raised fish also play an important part in domestic food consumption.

INDUSTRIAL DEVELOPMENT

SOLUTION OF MOST OF POLAND'S PRESENT ECONOMIC PROBLEMS depends upon its ability to build up industry and find both favorable foreign markets for its products and foreign sources of needed raw materials. Between the two wars industrialization was retarded by a lack of foreign markets, a very small internal market, and the lack of investment funds to finance new technical development. In the post-war period these obstacles have been compounded by a series of economic measures which benefited the Soviet Union at the expense of the Polish economy and by the imposition of Soviet industrial practices ill-suited to Poland's needs.

From August 1945 until November 1953 coal deliveries to the Soviet Union, at a fraction of the world market price and in disregard of Poland's internal needs, were a constant drain on the economy (see chap. 16). In 1946 private industries were nationalized or subjected to discriminatory rationing of raw materials. In 1947 and 1948 private trade was crushed by controls and prohibitive levies. From 1948 on, the Polish economy was clamped into a system of Soviet-type centralized planning, although psychological and natural differences between Russia and Poland made Soviet institutions particularly difficult to apply to Poland. For example, the narrow base of natural resources in Poland called for a system that would promote economical use of raw materials, but the incentive system actually adopted in effect put a premium on material waste. Further, the extreme administrative centralization and bureaucratic overlap along Soviet lines has not been the most efficient method of operations for Poles, whose experience in business management would have warranted more scope for initiative—especially since the Polish industrial and business class was relatively more important than the corresponding class in prerevolutionary Russia.

Soviet patterns were superimposed indiscriminately on all sectors

Polish Industrial Centers

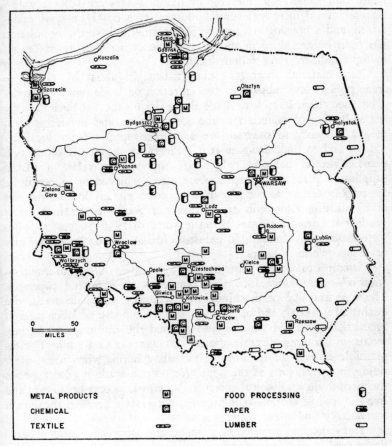

METAL PRODUCTS	M	FOOD PROCESSING	
CHEMICAL	C	PAPER	
TEXTILE		LUMBER	

of the Polish economy and the Six-Year Plan laid the groundwork for an ambitious industrialization program. At the cost of enormous investments, estimated at more than 30 percent of national income, the Plan was successful in its main goal: the output of producers goods, according to official statistics, nearly tripled between 1950 and 1955. During this period nonagricultural employment rose by more than 60 percent; 45 percent of all investments went to industry, 9 percent to agriculture, and 10 percent to housing, primarily in the large industrial centers. (See Map, Polish Industrial Centers.)

The adverse effects of rapid industrialization at the expense of consumer production and of the workers in the factories are now being felt. Relative to the cost of living, wages are still very low despite several increases; rural buildings have not been well maintained, and a housing crisis exists in the cities, where the population has risen by one third in six years; efficiency and quality of output in light industry have fallen drastically.

Raw material shortages, initially brought about by restrictive trade policies and subsequent concentration on trade with the Soviet orbit (see chap. 16), were made worse during the Six-Year Plan by the siphoning of materials to the Soviet Union and by the government's tendency to overestimate available supplies from local resources and to underestimate requirements for ambitious production plans. Material balances, which are supposed to relate available supplies to Plan requirements, were often achieved on paper only. Shortages were made good by drawing down already low inventories or by shifting allotments from consumer goods to the investment goods industries. Sometimes, as in the winter of 1955–56, coal supplies were so short that many light industries had to shut down temporarily or reduce working hours.

Attempts to combat waste by relating planned outputs to inputs— "norms"—were vitiated by the complexity of industrial processes. The type and age of machines, the frequency of repair needs, the quality of materials and of products, and the amount of labor used in production remained variable and affected the consumption of materials to an unpredictable extent. Producers found more or less plausible excuses for ignoring or exceeding norms when some overriding incentive, such as the bonus for output, made it advantageous for them to do so. Physical controls also failed, in part because of the live-and-let-live attitude that prevails in relations between the Polish bureaucracy and plant managers.

Transportation services, equipment, and labor have been wasted. Prices used in transactions among socialized enterprises were equalized all over Poland and made to include costs of rail delivery. Thus there was no incentive to cut down on transportation costs. Bulky materials such as coal have been consumed in excessive quantities even where local substitutes like peat are available. All important equipment is supplied by the state without charge—"paid for" only through amortization charges based on inordinately optimistic estimates of the life of the equipment. There is thus no incentive for enterprises to forgo acquisition of laborsaving machinery; yet such machinery could well be dispensed with in a country where labor is still relatively cheap and capital is scarce.

The system also has tended to stifle technical innovation. Invention is poorly rewarded and attention has focused on Soviet techniques. Funds have often been wasted on research that had already been done abroad. In the early 1950's, for example, a license was purchased from the Soviet Union to manufacture electric locomotive motors of a type produced in the United States and in Italy in the 1920's and subsequently discontinued in all countries, including the Soviet Union. Inefficiency and backward technology is exemplified in another landmark of "industrialized Poland," the Zeran automotive works near Warsaw. Started in 1951, the works had a theoretical annual capacity of 50,000 cars, but its 6,000 workers have never put out more than 7,000 cars of all types per year, or an annual average of 1.1 cars per worker. (At the Chevrolet plants in the United States some 90,000 workers produce 1,947,000 motor vehicles a year, an average of over 20 cars per worker.) The car itself is a copy of the Soviet Pobeda, using a 4-cylinder engine of 1938 design, and the model has not been substantially changed since its first run.

There is constant concern about Soviet reactions to present and future reforms. Poland's economic dependence provides the Soviet Union with substantial political leverage. A large number of Polish industrial plants were designed with a view to processing Soviet materials. Cutting off Soviet ores would virtually close down Nowa Huta, for example, and cause substantial unemployment, with resulting increase in internal political difficulties. Many other industrial plants are similarly dependent on the Soviet Union or the Soviet bloc for critical materials, supplies, and parts.

Interwar Industry

Before 1914, apart from the Galician oil field and the Silesian and Lodz industrial districts, there were some scattered factories in Poland but virtually no industrial areas. During World War I existing industry was largely destroyed.

By the outbreak of World War II Poland had become a moderately industrialized country—20 percent of the population derived its livelihood from industry. There was a marked divergence in the degree of industrialization, however, between the areas west and east of the Vistula River: the western area contained the industrial centers of the Silesias, Czestochowa, Lodz, and Warsaw. It was in part to correct this undesirable distribution that plans were made for developing the Central Industrial District.

During the interwar years there had been a considerable development of state capitalism modeled somewhat on the Italian and Austrian patterns. By 1939 approximately a million nonmilitary persons were working for the government. The Polish state owned and controlled assets valued at some 4 billion złotys, including about 100 industrial complexes comprising over 1,000 establishments—the most important industries in the country. The armament industry was entirely state owned, as was approximately 80 percent of the chemical industry, 40 percent of the iron industry, and 50 percent of the rest of the metallurgical industry. The state also owned all commercial aviation lines, all railways, over nine tenths of the merchant marine, as well as the largest forests in Central Europe. It had a monopoly on alcohol, matches, tobacco, and salt.

As the country's major entrepreneur, the state took an important part in economic planning, including the establishment of the Central Industrial District in 1936. The District, embracing the greater part of the triangle formed by Warsaw, Cracow, and Lvov (Lwow) was to fit into a fifteen-year economic plan to correct the imbalance between agriculture and industry.

The Central District was an area of some 60,000 square kilometers with a population of about 5.5 million. It was one of the most impoverished areas in the country, with an estimated rural overpopulation of nearly half a million and correspondingly low living conditions. It did have, however, great potential natural wealth, and it formed a naturally balanced economic unit. Around Kielce were rich mineral deposits, the Lublin region was eminently suitable for agriculture, and the Sandomierz region for processing industries.

The development of the District was undertaken by the state in partnership with private enterprise. Apart from the erection of large-scale armament industry, the state set out to equip the region with communications—road, rail, and water—and a power grid for electricity and gas. Industrialists were granted locational advantages and financial assistance. Private capital flowed into the region, and a number of "mixed"—state and private—enterprises were established.

Imports of industrial raw materials and machinery for the District greatly strained the country's balance of payments: advancing industrialization cut into available export surpluses and the problem of obtaining foreign raw materials and machinery became increasingly acute. The resulting establishment of foreign exchange restrictions, import quotas, restrictions on consumption, and other state controls made a significant part of the economy subject to government planning.

Hand in hand with state capitalism for Polish industry went widespread cartelization under government control. With the exception of textiles, every important industry was organized into a cartel. Cartelization prevented the operation of free-market forces which would have driven high-cost enterprises out of existence and concentrated production in low-cost plants. Competition therefore was not allowed to destroy relatively inefficient plants. To that extent cartelization preserved capital and maintained industrial employment, in a country in which capital was critically short.

The interests of consumers were not, however, left at the mercy of unregulated cartel policies. In interpreting cartel legislation the government put great stress on maintaining economically justifiable prices. The Ministry of Commerce and Industry could dissolve any cartel it considered harmful to the public interest or economically unjustifiable, and it made ample use of this power. In both the planning and regulatory phase of industrial activities state control in pre-World War II Poland thus was exceptionally important.

Postwar Industry

As Poland was liberated the Soviet-sponsored government took over communications and large- and medium-scale industry; in early 1946 it legalized the acquisitions by formal nationalization. During the course of the Three-Year Plan (1947–49) the economic measures taken by the Communist government reflected its political aims. This period saw the limitation of private business enterprises through licensing, taxation, and government regulation and the extension of state control over all phases of industrial activities. The cooperative sector was subjected to centralized planning and control, and handicraftsmen were regimented into state-controlled associations. At the same time, the financial sector was transformed into a tool of the central planning authorities.

NATIONALIZATION

By the law of January 3, 1946, the Polish Government formally nationalized the industrial base and most large enterprises. State ownership, the law asserted, was necessary "to permit planned reconstruction of the national economy, to assure the country economic sovereignty, and to raise the level of general welfare." The state assumed ownership, without compensation, of all enterprises that had belonged to or been controlled by the government or the citizens of the German Reich and the former Free City of Danzig (Gdansk). It also took over certain types of enterprises, paying for them with state bonds: the specific list of enterprises and industries to be nationalized included mines, oil refineries, electric power stations, gasworks, waterworks, foundries, transport and communication facilities, and all sorts of light industries, including food and textiles. Enterprises not specifically designated had to employ fewer than 50 workers per shift in order not to be nationalized. Under the law, the Council of Ministers could raise the 50-worker limit for industries that were little mechanized, or "of a pioneer or seasonal" character, or which produced "articles not widely used." Any enterprises wholly or partly owned by local governments or cooperatives also were exempt from nationalization.

THE PRIVATE SECTOR

A separate law defined the private sector as those industrial and trading enterprises not affected by the stipulations of the nationalization law. According to the law, anyone had the right to establish a new industrial or commercial enterprise, subject to "fulfillment of legal requirements."

These two laws thus laid the basis for a "mixed economy" resembling that of the Soviet Union of the mid 1920's. But the private sector in industry and trade had at best a narrow field for development, one that could be narrowed still further by the withholding of concession permits or by the exigencies of planning. A tightening occurred as early as October 1947, when the government established compulsory registration of all persons engaged in the conduct of industry and certain professional activities. A registration fee was levied, ranging from 10 to 30 percent of the gross income from professional services, and from 6 to 22 percent of turnover in the supply of materials, or a combination of the two. The fee increased progressively with the size of the turnover. Socialized enterprises, including cooperatives, were exempt from the fee.

A further squeeze on the private sector was the requirement that private enterprises belong to state-directed associations. By 1950, 19 associations had been formed; thus the state in effect directed and controlled what private industry remained.

These various pressures resulted in the decline of the share of total industrial production originating in the private sector. In 1946 the share amounted to slightly less than 9 percent of the gross value of industrial output excluding handicrafts; by 1950 it had fallen to 5 percent, by 1953 to less than 1 percent. Since the latter part of 1956 this trend has been reversed, but available data are not adequate for an assessment of this development.

COOPERATIVES

The cooperative movement was one of the outstanding features of the economy of interwar Poland. By the end of 1937 there existed approximately 14,000 cooperative societies, divided about evenly into agricultural and consumer cooperatives, with a membership of over 3 million. The consumer cooperatives also engaged in minor manufacturing.

The agricultural cooperatives were organized into the Union of Agricultural Cooperatives of the Polish Republic, with a membership of 1,645,000 in 5,497 societies, as of 1938. The consumer cooperatives, consolidated in 1926 into the Union of Consumer Cooperatives of the Polish Republic (Społem), had at the end of 1938 a membership of 395,630 in 1,886 societies. The national minorities had their own societies (see chap. 16). As of 1939 there were in the smaller towns and villages 3,700 small credit-cooperative societies known as Stefczyk Banks and about 1,600 larger cooperative banks. These societies brought into action local funds which otherwise would not have been used productively—a particularly important function in view of the shortage of capital in Poland. They also distributed loans from the state banks and the public funds placed at the disposal of agriculturalists. The manufacturing cooperative societies (such as the dairy cooperatives) created new opportunities for the utilization of agricultural raw materials.

In 1948 the cooperative movement was reorganized to render it responsive to centralized planning and control, and in 1949 it was integrated into the national economic Plan as part of the socialized establishment. This subordination of the cooperative sector was accomplished by a pyramidal structure of central boards topped by the Central Cooperative Union (Centralny Związek Spółdzielczy—CZS). The administration of the union enforced economic discipline over central boards and lower level organizations. The authority of government ministries extended directly to the activities of the cooperative central boards and the subordinate cooperative units. Financial discipline of the cooperative sector closely paralleled that of the state enterprises.

Initially, the cooperatives were assigned a twofold role by the Communist regime. As instruments of class war, they were to collaborate with nationalized enterprises in crowding out large-scale capitalist elements in both the city and the village; as a form of socialist economy, they were considered the most efficient means for socializing small business and eventually transforming it into large business.

As can be seen from Table 19, the cooperatives have a very important share in the total economy and function largely in the consumer sector. There are current indications that their share in total production may be increased.

BASIC INDUSTRIAL POLICIES

In order to provide the resources necessary to expand production capacity, Polish economic plans designated a large and increasing percentage of the growing national product for investment and a declining percentage for consumption. In addition to the role of new investment and increased employment in the expansion of output, Polish planners also placed great emphasis on raising the level of worker skills, providing incentives to production workers, introducing better plant layouts and other rationalization measures, and utilizing production equipment more intensively.

Since January 1946 the gross value of industrial output has exceeded the corresponding indices for agriculture and transportation, and that of producer goods production has exceeded all others. The share of machine-building in gross value of the output of large- and medium-scale industry increased from 7 percent in 1937 to about 10 percent in 1949 and 14 percent in 1955. The output of socialized construction enterprises showed similarly high rates of increase. Under the Six-Year Plan the 1955 production goal for machine-building was over three times the 1949 output.

Polish planning for location of industry (see chap. 11) unlike the less refined Soviet practice has recognized the real costs associated with the production and distribution of goods and services. An example of rationality in the selection of an industrial site is provided by the new metallurgical combine, Nowa Huta, near Cracow. Selection reportedly was governed not only by technical considerations relative to terrain, water resources, and similar factors but also by economic considerations of the cost of transporting both raw materials and finished products. The presence of a reservoir of manpower in the vicinity and the proximity of Cracow were additional elements in the selection of the construction site. The political element, however, was not neglected. It was expected that the predominantly conservative tendency of the region would be altered by placing a new and growing community, planned and given preferred treatment by the government, close to tradition-laden Cracow.

The first two postwar plans also recognized the economic limitations imposed by capital requirements, supply of materials, and the uncertain possibilities of expanding the skilled and unskilled labor force in selected localities. Thus, expansion of existing facilities, rather than new construction, was generally held to be a less costly way of increasing production.

Structure and Organization of Industry

The experience of the Soviet Union provided the principal model for Polish planners. Polish economic policies and major goals are established by the Polish United Workers' Party (PZPR); it then becomes the task of the central economic agencies (see chap. 11) to translate these objectives into over-all plans specifying production goals, distribution of the national product, and other means for achieving the goals.

The central economic agencies also administer the economic program. This entails elaborate coordination of the various economic activities, supervision of socialized enterprises, regulation of the private sector, and enforcement of various restraints on the population.

EXTERNAL CONTROLS ON THE INDUSTRIAL PLANT

ECONOMIC MINISTRIES. Under the Polish Committee of National Liberation, which began to function as a government in July 1944, there were only four economic departments: Agriculture and Agrarian Reform; National Economy and Finance; Labor and Social Welfare; and Transports, Ports, and Telegraphs. Within about a year this number was doubled. By the end of 1953 there were 26 ministries concerned primarily with the administration of the national economy. In addition, certain economic functions were carried out by a number of noneconomic ministries, and there were many central offices and special commissions (responsible directly to the Council of Ministers, the Council of State or the State Commission for Economic Planning—PKPG).

The Council of Ministers in defining the sphere of activity of the new industrial ministries specified the particular industries within the jurisdiction of each new ministry. The Ministry of Light Industry for example, as of 1949, included in its scope of activity the textile, clothing, leather, wood, match, paper, minerals, and printing industries. For each of these, the Ministry was responsible for economic planning and investment policy; direction of activities of subordinate state, state-cooperative, and state-administered enterprises; the direction and supervision of the industrial activity of central offices of cooperatives, state-cooperative central offices, and individual cooperatives; arbitration among subordinate agencies; manpower problems; research operations. The functions of other industrial ministries are similarly specified.

THE MINISTRY OF FINANCE. The Ministry of Finance is directly responsible for comprehensive financial planning, supervision, and audit of the accounts of various establishments in the socialized sector. Much of the control function of the Ministry is performed by the banking system, which is subordinate to it (see chap. 13). In the industrial sphere the Ministry of Finance is responsible for examining the financial plans and transactions of socialized enterprises, controlling the legality and correctness of their expenditures, and setting norms for the elaboration and execution of the cash and credit plans.

In order to fulfill its tasks of audit and financial control over state institutions, socialized enterprises, and social organizations receiving state financial aid, the Ministry is authorized to carry out financial inspection and to make complete audits. It may issue whatever orders are necessary to correct financial practices, and in special circumstances it can suspend the financing of institutions violating financial regulations.

THE MINISTRY OF STATE CONTROL. Legal provisions concerning the execution of state control over the socialized economy underwent a series of modifications culminating in the law of November 22, 1952, which, among its other provisions, established the Ministry of State Control. This Ministry is responsible for the supervision and control of all organizations in the socialized sector. It carries out its tasks both on a planned basis and by occasional checks either upon request of other government agencies or on its own initiative. Representatives of the Ministry are authorized to examine the accounts and other relevant documents of the controlled units and to gather other needed information. When violations of regulations or state policy are uncovered, the Ministry can report the incident to the supervisory organization of the unit in question, requiring remedial action to be taken within a stated period. Criminal offenses are referred to the public prosecutor. The Ministry itself may take administrative action against lesser violations.

CENTRAL INDUSTRIAL BOARDS. The organization of state enterprises and intermediate administrative bodies has been changed from time to time, but, since there has never been a complete overhaul, there now exist widely diverse organizational forms (see Chart, Organizational Pattern of Industry in Poland).

Initially, the central boards, which coordinate large- and medium-scale enterprises, functioned as departments within a ministry, but by resolution of the Economic Committee of the Council of Ministers in October 1946 the boards became self-contained state enterprises. The state enterprises comprising a central board were grouped in branch, or branch-territorial, associations. In December 1950 the central boards were shifted back to administration by the ministries. Each board within a ministry administratively combines enterprises in the same or related type of activity, on a national or regional basis depending on the number of enterprises within the branch or activity.

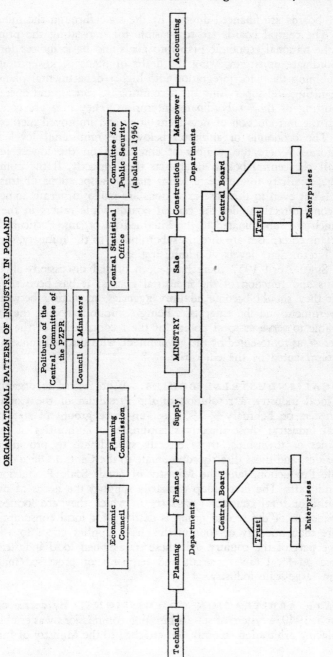

ORGANIZATIONAL PATTERN OF INDUSTRY IN POLAND

Politburo of the Central Committee of the PZPR

Council of Ministers

Economic Council

Planning Commission

Central Statistical Office

Committee for Public Security (abolished 1956)

MINISTRY

Departments: Technical — Planning — Finance — Supply

Departments: Sale — Construction — Manpower — Accounting

Central Board

Trust

Enterprises

Central Board

Trust

Enterprises

The boards are financed directly by the state through the ministries.

The central boards are responsible for translating the principles of the national economic plan into goals and basic indices for their subordinate units; reviewing the drafts of plans of lower units and combining them for integration into higher departmental plans; and organizing and supervising the accounting, statistical, and operational reporting of their subordinate enterprises. They also are concerned with the introduction of new technology and improved methods.

The economic organization below the ministerial level is not uniform. Where the number of enterprises on the lowest level is small, the central board administers them directly. If the number is large, auxiliary intermediate forms such as associations or trusts are used, but even in this case exceptions are made to permit some units to come directly under the central boards while others in the same branch are subordinated to the intermediate organs. Particularly important enterprises are directly subordinated to the ministry, omitting all intermediate levels of administration.

Since April 1957 there have been official discussions about the status and function of the industrial boards; it has been suggested that they should become advisory agencies, mediating between the government and the enterprise. Being semipublic bodies, they would be able to serve as focal points for the reconciliation of the general interest, as represented by the government, with the particular interest, as represented by the enterprise.

LOCAL INDUSTRIAL BODIES. With regard to organization of local industry, a resolution of the Presidium of the Council of Ministers on February 3, 1951, set up three groups of state-owned local industry: those directly subordinate to authorities of municipalities or townships; those directly subordinate to provincial authorities; and those directly subordinate to the Central Office of Small Scale Production, later the Ministry of Small Scale Production and Handicrafts. The first group primarily supplies the needs of municipalities or rural counties (*powiats*) in which they are located; the production of the second group is destined for local consumption in more than one city or county; the third supplies goods to all or a large part of the country. All these state-owned local industries are based on local raw materials and remnants of processed materials from large-scale industry.

STATE ARBITRATION COMMISSIONS. By decree of August 5, 1949, a system of state arbitration commissions was established, replacing arbitration commissions attached to the Ministry of Industry and Trade. Their function is to resolve disputes between units in the state-owned sector of the economy. A particularly important activity is the mediation of interplant agreements, for the planned supply of goods and services, and of disputes arising out of these agreements. Interplant agreements, introduced by the law of April 19, 1950, are patterned on current Soviet practice. Their purpose is to develop a coordinated system of supply and procurement which would assure punctual performance of economic plans and make more efficient the cooperation of economic units in planned tasks. The obligation of concluding planned agreements extends to nearly all the socialized sector, including the state-cooperative organizations and the cooperative central boards.

General agreements are concluded first between higher-level economic units, which specify which subordinate units of the agencies concerned will be contract partners. The agreements stipulate kinds and qualities of goods and services, date of delivery, prices, and so on. The arbitration commissions may be called upon to settle precontract differences as well as in cases of breaches of such agreements.

SPECIAL COMMISSION FOR COMBATING WASTE AND ECONOMIC SABOTAGE. Created in 1947, the Special Commission was charged with enforcing price-control regulations. Its subordinate organs were authorized to sentence violators of price regulations to a maximum of two years in labor camps, without resort to the courts; they also investigated and prosecuted violations of legal regulations which threatened the economic life of the country, especially theft of public property, corruption, bribery, and speculation. In addition, the Commission was authorized to enforce economic discipline over the compulsory associations for private industry.

As part of the reform of the judicial system in 1950, the Office of the Public Prosecutor was endowed with supervision over the legality of activities of units of the national economy and thus took over some functions formerly carried out by the Special Commission. The precise present functions of the Commission are not known.

INTERNAL CONTROLS ON THE INDUSTRIAL PLANT

THE PARTY AND TRADE UNIONS. The formal machinery of administration is essentially an instrument of control to insure the execution of the policy of the Polish United Workers' Party (PZPR). As in the Soviet Union, the Party enjoys exclusive power in the formulation of economic policy.

At the enterprise level, the Party secretary (see chap. 6) supervises every facet of operations, including plan fulfillment and record keeping. He also has advisory functions in management—to increase efficiency, expand production, and maintain labor discipline.

The chairman of the works council—the trade union organization at the enterprise level—is generally a Party member and is concerned with the enforcement of labor discipline and increasing productivity of the workers. In addition he is responsible for certain aspects of the workers' welfare (see chap. 12).

Party organizations have been criticized for overstepping the limits of their functions and taking over the functions, prerogatives, and responsibilities of the enterprise manager, thus undermining the principle of one-man management. In any case there can be little doubt that the proliferation of organs of internal controls, with the concomitant heightening of the administrative burden, gives rise to tensions and possibly results in various sorts of maladministration.

MANAGEMENT OF THE ENTERPRISE. A system of one-man management was introduced for all state-owned enterprises by a resolution of the Economic Committee of the Council of Ministers on May 12, 1950. This system endows the manager at every enterprise level with power and responsibility for managing—within the dictates of the economic Plan—the unit or sector placed under his supervision. Theoretically, he has limited scope for independent determination of the internal organization of the enterprise and even less discretion concerning what and how much is to be produced. Initiative is supposed to be confined to devising schemes for cost reduction and increased output within the framework and limitations of the plant's economic plan. In practice, however, the range of discretion of managers has been much greater than the legal provisions suggest, because the planning procedures and controls are relatively new and imperfect and managers have been forced to cut corners and improvise when plans go awry.

In November 1956 workers' councils (see chap. 12) elected in a given plant were assigned joint responsibility with the manager for all phases of the plant's operations. For the time being the manager and his staff thus have become, at least in theory, the executive organs of the workers' council. It is still too early to appraise the effect of this development on managerial efficiency.

"EXPERIMENTING ENTERPRISES." Evidently hesitant to embark upon sweeping changes during the present economic crisis, the government created early in 1957 a special Commission to study the many suggestions for management improvement put forth by individual workers and workers' councils. If a seemingly worth-while suggestion involves changes "beyond the competence" of the minister concerned, the enterprise may, with the consent of the Prime Minister's Office, be given the status of an "experimenting enterprise."

The experiments may involve methods of fixing prices and of fixing wages, organization of supplies and sales, rates of interest on fixed and circulating capital, planning of production, use of amortization funds, and so on. Once an enterprise is given the status of "experimenting," it is exempt from the existing financial regulations to the extent necessary. To avoid a profusion of such enterprises, they may not normally exceed 5 percent of the total number of enterprises under a given ministry.

INDUSTRIAL PRICE FIXING AND COST ACCOUNTING

The Council of Ministers has primary authority to set prices, but it may delegate its authority in certain instances to ministries, the State Planning Commission (PKPG), the presidia of local people's councils, special price commissions, or central industrial boards. According to official policy, prices at which goods and services of state enterprises are sold on the domestic market should, in general, cover costs and provide revenues for financing state expenditures.

After a succession of experiments in industrial pricing methods, the government in 1954 adopted a system of "factory prices." These prices correspond to the Soviet-type of "wholesale prices of enterprises," which represent the difference between the sale price of a given product and the turnover tax (see chap. 13) applicable to it. The use of these factory prices for planning settlements between enterprises and for cost accounting had been only partially carried out by mid-1956, and the government has not enforced industry-wide acceptance.

Lack of uniformity in pricing procedure has compounded another serious deficiency of Polish economic planning—the failure to operate with a set of prices which adequately reflect current costs. Use of prices which do not reflect relative scarcity or oversupply of a particular commodity leads to failure on the part of enterprises to produce the right assortment of goods. Plans of enterprises are generally set in quantitative terms, but when there are differing varieties or qualities of goods for which it is administratively impossible to specify required output in sufficient detail, targets are set in terms of the total value of a whole range of commodities. Since prices of individual goods tend to be fixed and are not related to their scarcity, there will be certain commodities within the range whose current costs are high. By concentrating on these high-cost commodities, plants can overfulfill their value targets and earn premiums over basic earnings, while at the same time producing a completely inappropriate assortment of goods.

The inadequate pricing system also makes difficult the rational allocation of investment funds among various industries. The same price for two commodities produced by different industries would conceal different degrees of scarcity, so that an increase in the output of one resulting from increased investment would not necessarily give an indication of increased productivity. This impossibility of comparing productivity of investment in various industries has tended to make the allocation of industrial investment funds a matter of political bargaining rather than of economic calculation.

Since prices do not reflect scarcity, a shortage, must first be recognized by the planners. There may be considerable delay in this, since there are no "automatic" price increases to signal the shortage and it takes time for the planning decision to filter down to the enterprise level. Allowing enterprise managers to fix or suggest prices would obviously do away with much of this difficulty.

INCENTIVES

BONUS TO PLANT MANAGERS. The bonuses paid by the state to plant managers increase rapidly according to output, particularly if output surpasses the plan. They also serve, however, to encourage production gains at the expense of cost reductions. Controls on material expenditure and requests by higher authorities to save materials run against the self-interest of the managers and hence are not heeded. The bonuses, averaging over 70 percent of the base pay of the managerial staff, make it profitable to hoard materials or use them to turn out little-wanted items "above plan." Meanwhile, other firms may have to cease or curtail operations for lack of even small consignments of these same materials. As these deviations multiply, the over-all performance of the economy tends to become skewed.

THE PLANT FUND. The Plant Fund was established in February 1950, on the pattern of the Director's or Enterprise Fund in the USSR. Superseding previously existing profit-sharing arrangements, the Fund is used to finance cultural, social, and housing investments serving the needs of the workers in the given enterprise and also supports an incentive system to reward outstanding employees.

Initially, the quotas of the plant's profit to go into the Fund were set at 1 to 4 percent of planned profit and 10 to 30 percent of overplan profit. On July 1950 the Economic Committee of the Council of Ministers reset the percentage contributions at 2 percent of planned and 15 percent of overplan profits, for enterprises under the jurisdiction of the Ministries of Mining and of Heavy Industry, and at 1 percent and 10 percent, respectively, for all other state enterprises. In March 1951 the rates of contribution from overplan profits were revised in line with the importance that planning authorities attached to various industries: mining, 30 percent; heavy industry, 20 percent; and light industry, 15 percent; the rates of contribution from planned profits were raised to 4, 2.5, and 2 percent, respectively.

The individual enterprise is allowed to establish the Fund only in the event that it fulfills or overfulfills the plan of production as a whole—in terms of volume as well as of product mixture—and attains at least the planned profit. In allocating the Fund to various uses, the plant management is expected to spend at least one half for above-plan investments for cultural and social purposes and for workers housing, about one third on promoting competitions to raise output and improve quality, and one fifth for premiums for individual employees. As the total income of the Fund cannot exceed 3 percent of the plant's annual wage bill, the amount of money available for incentives, aside from organized competitions, will not be more than about one half of one percent of the wage bill of the enterprise having a Plant Fund.

These incentives schemes have not been successful. Premiums for 1946 were paid to the central boards only in 1948 but were not distributed to the individual enterprises. As late as March 1949, the premiums for 1947 had not even been approved. In 1950 only a small portion of state enterprises established Plant Funds under the new law.

RECENT CHANGES

Lately the trend has been away from detailed centralized planning. Enterprises are permitted to prepare their own technical, industrial, and financial plans, within the yearly or quarterly quotas set for each enterprise by the appropriate ministry. They may manipulate delivery dates but must still adhere to quotas fixed by the ministry. An individual plant may also set prices for commodities of minor importance which do not appear in the official lists, and it may accept production orders outside of the plan, provided that this does not interfere with the execution of plan targets.

In the field of investment the enterprise continues to be under the strict control of monthly or quarterly orders received from the authorities, although it has a somewhat greater scope for undertaking capital repairs without authorization in each case. The amortization fund of an enterprise may now be used, not only for repairs, but also for modernization of existing equipment and for purchase of new machinery if this is more economical than repair. Moreover, the enterprise is encouraged to purchase building materials produced by local and cooperative undertakings, rather than apply for deliveries from central stocks.

Enterprises have also been given more latitude in matters of internal organization. Directors can appoint department heads and decide upon the merger of existing departments or the establishment of new ones. Within the framework of the general wage scales and payroll allocations, they may manipulate labor norms, grant bonuses and extra payments for special tasks, and increase and decrease their specialist staff.

An enterprise is now free to sell its output to a state, cooperative, or private enterprise if the trading corporation to which it would normally sell has proved unwilling or unable to buy the articles within two weeks of their being offered. And the enterprise may sell to any interested purchaser unused or unnecessary machinery and equipment if the supervisory body does not issue contrary instructions within two months.

Natural Resources and Related Industries

Today, as during the interwar period, Poland's domestic sources of raw materials, with the exception of coal, lead, zinc, and lumber, have been inadequate to meet the demands of industry (see Map, Mineral and Power Resources of Poland).

The Silesian coal field, with an estimated potential output of 60 million tons a year, has been of fundamental importance in the industrial development of the country. Important deposits of lead, zinc, and silver also exist in the region. This major industrial complex between the Ruhr and the Donets Basin makes Poland of value to the Soviet bloc. Its huge coal reserves constitute a solid fuel base for Soviet eastern Europe. Since it is generally more economical to move ores and concentrates to the fuel base than to ship fuel to the ore source, the Polish metallurgical industry will probably continue to rely on foreign ores, particularly as the planned expansion of the country's inland waterways—a means of least-cost transport—is being continued.

COAL

Coal provides the main source of industrial energy for Poland and is the principal raw material for the expanding chemical and metal-

Mineral and Power Resources of Poland

lurgy industries. Coke production is adequate to meet domestic requirements, but the coke is not as hard as that produced, for instance, in the United States, Great Britain, or Germany, and disintegrates under heavy pressure. High-grade metallurgical coke has been imported from Czechoslovakia to meet special requirements.

Poland ranks as the fifth largest coal producer in the world. Its bituminous coal deposits are continental Europe's third largest, and rank sixth in the world. Total proven and probable reserves of the Upper Silesian Basin total about 108 billion tons, those of Lower Silesia 3 billion tons. The thickness of coal seams in the Upper Silesian Basin reaches a maximum of 55 feet, exceeding that of all other European deposits, and the average depth of workable deposits is generally less than that of British and German coal deposits. Probable total reserves at a depth not exceeding 4,500 feet are estimated to be 100 billion tons, or nearly 2 percent of the world's total coal reserves. The natural conditions for coal mining also are exceptionally good, explosions due to firedamp and coal dust being rare. The quality of Polish bituminous coal is generally high, though somewhat inferior to that of British or Westphalian coals. Most Polish coals are suitable for long storage, as well as for long-distance shipping that requires reloading for transhipment.

During World War II the Germans at first exploited captured Polish mines without regard to future maintenance. But when the virtual destruction of the Ruhr by Allied air forces focused German attention on Silesia a more rational approach to mining was required, and in 1943 over 91 million tons of coal were produced. This peak output, not yet surpassed, was accomplished essentially by increasing the number of workers—primarily forced laborers from Poland and other parts of Nazi-occupied Europe. Territorial adjustments after World War II left Poland with the German sections of Upper and Lower Silesia, but the eastern part of the Ostrava-Karvina field (Slask Zaolzianski), which Poland had received after the Munich agreement in 1938, was returned to Czechoslovakia.

After a short period of rapid recovery following the end of the war, under the Three-Year Plan the coal industry was unable to secure an adequate labor force and meet its commitments to domestic industrial consumers. Planned output targets had to be reduced and the coal shortage, unavoidable during the years of reconstruction of 1945–46, continued as one of the chief concerns of the regime during the Six-Year Plan.

Among the causes of the widening gap between coal demand and supply were the so-called "political coal exports" to the Soviet Union in exchange for Soviet deliveries to Poland of East German industrial commodities as reparations (see chap. 16). Poland's own industrial growth had rapidly increased demand for coal; coal consumption increased by 44.4 percent from 1949 to 1954, while coal output rose by only 12.3 percent. Both in 1937 and 1954, an almost equal share of the disposable output was diverted to industrial uses—about half of total production. The share consumed by public utilities and households remained constant, though per capita consumption rose from

155 kilograms in 1937 to 366 in 1949 and 537 in 1954. A higher proportion went into coke production. The change in consumption by railroads is not known.

On the supply side, the major problems were inadequate supply of labor, a low level of productivity due to inadequate investment, insufficient mechanization of mining operations, an excessively centralized administration, and inefficient price and cost structures. Further difficulties were added by the Six-Year Plan (1950–55), which called for the development of 11 new mines, with a total output capacity of 9 million metric tons, and established for the coal industry in 1955 the unrealistic output and productivity targets of 100 million tons and 1.7 tons per manshift.

The labor problem in coal mining appears to be increasingly responsible for the limited growth of production. Poor living conditions and inadequate housing, coupled with very low safety standards, have discouraged the needed influx of additional workers and boosted the rate of labor turnover. Inadequate training and supervision also affect this trend of rapid turnover; managerial dissatisfaction with individual performance often results in transfer or dismissal of workers. In 1953 nearly 83 percent of miners left their jobs. Constant pressure to meet planned goals, often resulting in workers "voluntarily" spending a Sunday in the shaft, is an added deterrent to staying with the job.

LIQUID FUELS

The areas ceded to the USSR after World War II had been the source of about two thirds of Poland's former petroleum productive capacity —about 350,000 tons of crude oil production out of a total 1938 production of 510,000 tons. Only by the end of 1949 did the producing areas remaining within Poland reattain their 1938 level of output. In 1938, Poland used about 400,000 tons of petroleum products. Postwar requirements have been much higher; for example, the Six-Year Plan goals for 1955 meant doubling the total number of tractors and other motor vehicles of pre-World War II Poland.

Poland's consumption of petroleum products in 1948 amounted to 19 kilograms per capita, or a total of 450,000 tons. On the basis of the 1955 targets under the Six-Year Plan, requirements for petroleum products were to have been raised four to five times the 1948 consumption level. While in 1949 domestic crude oil production supplied about one quarter of the petroleum products consumed, by 1955 the share of the domestic industry had dropped to about 10 percent. The output of refineries has grown somewhat but still does not meet the country's needs; in 1950 only 40 percent of the demand for refined products was met by Polish plants. In 1948 production of benzol (from distillation of coal) and of alcohol (from potatoes and sugar beets) filled about 10 percent of liquid fuel requirements.

Poland planned to import a substantial part of its petroleum requirements in the form of crude oil, since planned domestic capacity for 1955 was 530,000 tons, whereas planned crude oil output was only 394,000. Major portions of these imports were expected to come from the Soviet Union and Rumania, while specialized petroleum products and equipment were to be obtained from non-Soviet areas. Czechoslovakia and East Germany, with their synthetic liquid fuel industries and large engineering capacities, were expected to supply refinery equipment and to cooperate in the production of synthetic fuel and compressed natural gas.

Under the new Five-Year Plan existing refineries are to be expanded and modernized, with emphasis upon refinement of product rather than increase of output. Consumption of petroleum products by 1960 is expected to be double that of 1955.

ELECTRIC POWER

Production of electric power in Poland is based primarily on thermal (coal) generation, including use of coal dust at the mine site. Hydroelectric stations are being built primarily as appendages to the construction of waterworks and the regulation of rivers. According to present plans for increasing production, the Silesian coal basins would become the main centers of the electric power industry. Deposits of lignite at Konin, in central Poland, and lignite and peat in other regions would provide local sources of electric energy.

Poland's power production increased from 6.3 billion kilowatt hours in 1937 to 15.4 billion in 1954 and 17.8 billion in 1955. Between 1949 and 1955 output of electric power increased by 9.5 billion kilowatt hours. The target for 1960 is 29.5 billion kilowatt hours, an increase of 66 percent over 1955.

Large-scale industry and communications during the Three-Year Plan (1947–49) consumed over 80 percent of the electric energy produced, small-scale industry less than 3 percent, and households about 10 percent. No change appears to have occurred to alter this pattern appreciably.

METALLURGY

IRON AND STEEL. The expansion of the iron and steel industry is based primarily on Poland's abundant deposits of coal.

The country's iron ore reserves, estimated at 58.6 million tons probable and an additional 175 million possible, are located mostly in central Poland, near Czestochowa and southeast of Radom. Their metal content is relatively low, on the average between 30 and 40 percent. The gain in deposits from the territorial shift after World War II was insignificant.

Production of iron ores from domestic sources filled about 33 percent of Polish requirements in 1939, but only 15 percent in 1949; in 1955 this proportion came near 30 percent. Imports of iron ore come from Sweden and the Soviet Union, chiefly in exchange for Polish coal. Most of the ferrous alloys were likewise imported, but Polish production of these increased during the Six-Year Plan (see Table 20).

LEAD AND ZINC. With the exception of zinc and lead Poland's production of nonferrous metals is comparatively unimportant. Zinc and lead ores occur in the region near Kielce in central Poland, in the Upper Silesia–Cracow area, and in Lower Silesia. Before World War II, Poland exported zinc but found it necessary to import lead. Lead production reached 18,000 tons in 1937 (prewar boundaries) but fell to 11,300 tons in 1947. Since lead and zinc ores occur in compounds with sulphur, the production of these metals yields sulphur and sulphuric acids as valuable by-products. (Table 20 shows the increase in zinc production in the past two decades.) Poland has been importing lead and zinc ore concentrates, but in recent years, as exploitation of domestic lowgrade ores has increased, efforts have been made to bring about a gradual reduction of such imports.

URANIUM. Polish uranium deposits are situated in Lower Silesia. The richest mines are in the areas of Walbrzych (Waldenburg) and Jelenia Gora (Hirschberg); they are under Soviet control and heavily guarded. It has been reported that Gomułka brought up the subject of Polish uranium mines during his trip to Moscow in early 1957. The Poles may now receive treatment similar to the Czechs and East Germans: half-share in control and a "fair profit margin."

OTHER METALS. The Six-Year Plan aimed at the expansion of mining of copper-bearing ores. The production of electrolytic copper was expected to reach 25,000 tons annually by 1955, to satisfy an important part of domestic requirements. Disregarding profitability of operations, it was estimated that low-grade copper deposits of Lower Silesia could produce about 20,000 tons of metal a year.

In the immediate postwar period great emphasis was placed on the collection of all kinds of metal scrap. In 1948 state enterprises were designated as monopolies for all transactions in such metals. All holders of metal scrap were obliged, under risk of penalty, to safeguard the scrap in their possession and surrender it upon demand to the monopoly at state-fixed prices.

CHEMICAL INDUSTRY

Large deposits of such basic raw materials as coal, salt, gypsum, and lime favored development of Poland's chemical industry in the interwar years. The industry produced a wide assortment of basic chemicals, including caustic soda, calcium carbide, and sulphuric acid, as well as coal derivatives, soap, explosives, rubber goods, synthetic fibers, and fertilizers.

The addition of the chemical industry in the former German territories increased by one third the number of chemical plants in the postwar Polish economy. During the Three-Year Plan (1947–49) emphasis in the field of chemical production, as in every other industry, was on reconstruction of facilities damaged by the war. The Six-Year Plan (1950–55) sought not only to expand production of selected lines previously produced but also to introduce new products and processes. Production in 1955 was estimated at three and one half times that of 1949, more than twice the rate of expansion for Polish industry as a whole. Table 21 shows the development of some of the major products of the Polish chemical industry.

Other Industries

MACHINERY AND METAL PRODUCTS

Before World War II production of the metal products industry included railroad locomotives and rolling stock, machine tools, internal combustion engines, boilers, farm machinery, sheet metal products, and miscellaneous items. At the beginning of 1946 the nationalized sector comprised about 46 percent of the entire metal products industry, not including handicrafts (40 percent with handicrafts included). Subsequent growth of nationalized production, as reported in official statistics, is a reflection in part of the extension of the socialized sector, rather than an actual increase in output.

Before World War II the metal products industry in the reacquired territories was about half as large as that within Poland's prewar boundaries. Although extensive reconstruction was needed to repair war damage, this area even as early as 1947 produced 70 percent of total Polish output of freight cars, 30 percent of steel cables, 55 percent of precision equipment, and 48 percent of machinery.

Under both the Three-Year Plan and the Six-Year Plan great

stress was placed on expanded output of metal products. The goal for the industry—a 264 percent increase in the value of production between 1949 and 1955—was one of the highest set in the Plan and appears to have been exceeded. Under the new Five-Year Plan production of the machine industry is to be doubled.

Table 22 shows the increase in output of three important lines of the machine-building industry for selected years, including the goals for 1960 under the new Five-Year Plan. Increased output of machine tools obviously is significant for the industrialization of the country, but the excessively high goal under the Six-Year Plan appears to have undergone a realistic downward revision. The postwar assortment of the machine-building industry has steadily broadened. New Products introduced during the Six-Year Plan included complex machine tools, steam turbines, high-pressure boilers, mining machinery of various types, chemical equipment, agricultural combines, road-building machines, cranes, marine engines and pumps, electric locomotives and other transportation equipment, ball bearings, optical and precision instruments, electric motors, generators, and steel cables.

Polish design of machinery for agriculture, taking account of the typically poor service given to such equipment, is characterized by wide tolerances and rugged construction. In the immediate postwar period, German, Czech and Italian machines served as models, but shortly thereafter Soviet designs, production practices, and technical advice became more prominent.

CONSUMER GOODS INDUSTRIES

Under the Three-Year Plan per capita consumption, especially of such articles as food, textiles, clothing, shoes, and household goods was to be raised above the prewar level. The Six-Year Plan aimed to "raise the standard of living 50 to 60 percent," but a considerable part of this planned increase represented such intangibles as cultural and scientific activities and social services. Official claims to the contrary, the requirements of the population are still being met inadequately.

A great deal of criticism has been and is being leveled against the crude finish, bad quality, limited selection, and bad packing of goods; the disregard of consumer taste is also criticized. Since a large share of Polish manufactured consumer goods is exported (see chap. 16), production figures alone are no indication of consumer welfare.

Industrial consumer goods produced in Poland primarily include such everyday products as processed foods, beverages, wearing apparel, furniture, soap, tobacco products, and the more basic household equipment. Heavier consumer durables, such as passenger cars and washing machines, are produced only in small quantities (see Table 23).

Light industry is more evenly distributed over the country than is heavy industry; in some cases the raw materials required are found in many localities, in others the transport costs of raw materials to centers of fabrication are relatively small. Moreover, the saving on cost of delivery of the finished products to consumers favors local fabrication.

CONSTRUCTION

The performance of the Polish building industry lags badly behind the needs of the expanding industrial and urban areas. In 1954, for example, 6.3 million persons were engaged in nonagricultural employment—over half a million more than the number planned for 1955 (see chap. 12). The increase in new housing accommodations has not kept pace with this shift to the cities, and it is about four times slower than the natural increase of population.

The share of housing in total fixed investment increased from 7 percent in 1950 to 12 percent in 1954. In 1949 the outlay for housing amounted to 940 million złotys, while expenditure on schools, hospitals, and public buildings was 1.97 billion. In 1955 an estimated 4.6 billion złotys was spent for housing, with 3.6 billion being devoted to other types of nonindustrial construction. Targets for 1960 are a tenfold increase over 1955 in heavy reinforced concrete construction, a threefold increase in light concretes, and a doubling of brick and cement production.

Transportation and Communications

TRANSPORTATION

Poland does not have a balanced transport network; the western part of the country is much better provided with transportation than is the region to the east of the Vistula River. The system nevertheless appears adequate to meet the industrial needs of the country. Rail and road facilities have undergone a substantial expansion, the frequency of connections has been increased, and utilization of all transport media for passengers as well as for freight has increased significantly. The large seaports, however, are far from the Silesian industrial area, and the navigational possibilities of the Oder River and the Vistula have not yet been fully exploited.

RAILROADS. In contrast to the interwar period, reasonably good connections now exist to all parts of the country (see Map, Major

Major Railways of Poland

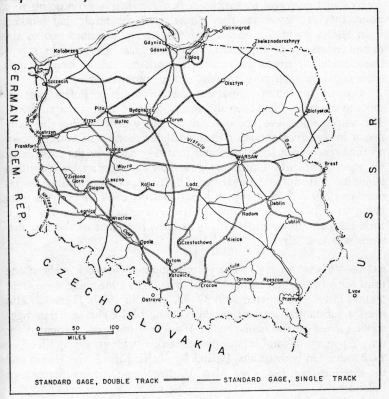

STANDARD GAGE, DOUBLE TRACK ═══ ─── STANDARD GAGE, SINGLE TRACK

Railways of Poland). Construction of rolling stock, however, has not kept pace with increased requirements. While railway passenger traffic has increased by 300 percent over 1938 and the length of lines in operation 23 percent, the number of coaches in 1951 was about one tenth lower than in 1938. The railroads, with fewer coaches, are carrying approximately three times as many passengers as before the war. The resulting discomforts have been a frequent source of complaints in the Polish press.

The increase in traffic since the end of World War II is a reflection both of the population shifts in the years immediately following the cessation of hostilities and of the steady migration of rural population to the urban areas—involving not only travel with a view to changing residence but also frequent journeys to the countryside to visit relatives left behind. Another important factor has been the great increase in vacation travel. Polish workers are now entitled to free travel to various resorts for their vacations; up to a point, they can go where they please, with the result that workers from Silesia go to the seaside and those from the north go to the mountain resorts of the south. Finally, a great many workers now live outside the towns and travel to work by rail—a trend that is encouraged by a 90 percent reduction on commutation fares.

One of the more significant improvements in Polish postwar railroad operations has been the speeding up of freight car turnover. This appears to have been accomplished by lengthening the daily run of locomotives, operating them at higher speeds, and cutting down on time spent on maintenance and repairs—that is, at the expense of the equipment's life. Utilization of freight car capacity, on the other hand, has left much to be desired. Official reports on loading operations in 1949 and 1951 revealed that in many cases freight cars were being used below 50 percent capacity. In general, there has been little modernization, and as of 1954 only 1 percent of the rail network was electrified.

ROAD TRANSPORT. The postwar highway network is about one third longer than that before World War II. In 1948 there were some 54,000 miles as compared with 37,800 miles in 1937. There has also been a substantial increase in the volume of freight and passenger traffic carried on the roads, but in 1954 road transport accounted for only 2 percent of total inland transportation, with an average haul of 11.2 miles. On both counts, Poland lags behind the Soviet Union and the satellite countries. (See Map, Highway and Airway Systems of Poland.)

In 1938, Poland had only 10 motor vehicles (including trucks) per 10,000 inhabitants; by 1949 that figure had increased to 31, owing to increased production and population shrinkage. Although there were General Motors and Fiat assembly plants in Poland during the interwar period, most cars were imported. In general, the country has continued to rely on imports, primarily from Czechoslovakia, Hungary, and the Soviet Union. During the Three-Year Plan preparations were made to develop Poland's own automobile industry. In 1955 the industry produced some 4,000 passenger cars and 12,500 trucks. Under the new Five-Year Plan passenger car production is to increase more than seven times and truck production is to be more than doubled. The major new automobile factory is the Zeran plant near Warsaw.

Inefficient operation appears to be a frequent problem confronting Polish road services. An industrial ministry, for example, in 1952

Highway and Airway System of Poland

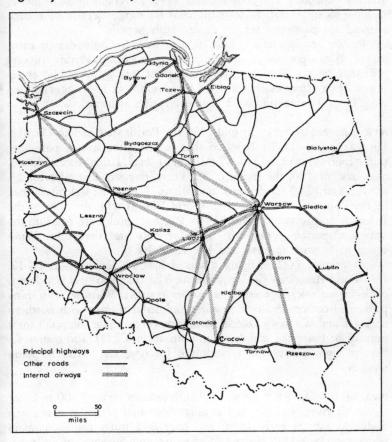

was reported to have a fleet of 1,500 trucks, but with only 2 employees in charge of maintenance. Many industrial enterprises estimate inaccurately the volume of goods to be carried, thus wasting available carrying capacity. The operational target for trucks is 600 tons per truck per year, but many enterprises are using less than 300 tons. There have also been problems with regard to the distribution of trucks. According to one report, only one fifth of all enterprises in the district of Poznan had 6 or more vehicles, whereas in other districts ministries and industrial concerns had so much rolling stock that they were using it on hauls far beyond the accepted limit of 31 miles.

Frequency of bus connections has been improved and the bus network expanded. Travel by bus is however extremely uncomfortable; in some localities trailers normally used for freight service have been adapted for passenger service during rush periods.

Private transportation, since it also includes horse-drawn carts, still occupies a position of some importance in Poland. Private truckers primarily operate vehicles withdrawn from service by public enterprises. Their activities are restricted by government licensing, and they work largely on contract with state enterprises at local jobs.

AIR TRANSPORT. In mid-1956 the Polish state airline (Polskie Linie Lotnicze—LOT) reported that it had increased its passenger traffic fourfold over the pre-World War II level. Using the 1938 level as a base of 100, the index of ton-kilometers stood at 550 for all services and 1,905 for domestic operations. The airline was established by the Polish Government after World War II with the help of the Russians, and service began in 1946. Plane schedules are tied into the state transportation network, flight arrivals and departures being timed to fit with railroad and bus schedules.

At present LOT is flying a mixed fleet of Soviet Il–2, Il–12, Il–14 and American C-47 equipment. The line also operates dozens of light aircraft. Domestic air routes connect Warsaw with nine provincial centers and link southern industrial regions with northern seaports, and Warsaw's Okecie Airport serves as a junction point for a number of European and east European airlines. LOT also operates a fleet of light planes for agricultural, forestry, and aerial mapping services.

INLAND WATERWAYS. Poland possesses about 3,100 miles of navigable rivers and canals, but only about half of this network was usable as late as early 1954, and only 685 miles constitute main waterways (see Map, Inland Waterways and Seaports of Poland). The Oder is navigable for 400 miles. Large vessels are able to use the Vistula only for about 125 miles, and there is no navigable connection between the Vistula and the industrial area of Upper Silesia. For the time being, therefore, the Oder is by far the most important of the two rivers, since it connects the southern, industrial part of Poland with the Baltic Sea and provides transportation for imported ores and other bulky raw materials. In 1948, for example, the Oder accounted for 62 percent of all waterway traffic.

Between 1948 and 1952, according to the latest available figures, total freight traffic on inland waterways increased from 657,000 metric tons to almost 2 million. Under the Six-Year Plan a number

Inland Waterways and Seaports of Poland

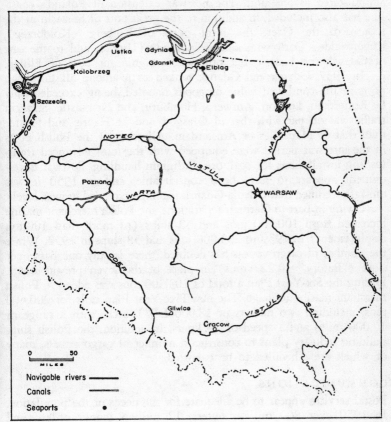

of important additions to the canal network were planned. The most important is the east-west waterway linking the Oder with the Bug River, which in turn is connected with the Dnieper through the Pripyat (Prypec) River. The project entails canalization of the Bug between Modlin and Brzesc (Brest Litovsk). With its completion, the entire waterway route from Silesia to the Soviet frontier will be navigable for vessels up to 250 tons.

MARITIME TRANSPORT. Before World War II, Polish territory included the modern port of Gdynia and the Free City of Danzig (Gdansk)—the latter joined to Poland by a customs union but politically independent of the Polish Republic. Since the war

Gdansk has been restored to Poland, and the two ports are now administered as one unit. The postwar extension of Poland's coast-line has also included, in addition to the great port of Szczecin at the mouth of the Oder, the local ports of Kolberg (Kolobrzeg), Rugenwalde (Darłowo), and Stolpmünde (Ustka), and to the east of Gdansk the historic but otherwise insignificant port of Elbląg.

In 1937, Gdynia and Gdansk ranked sixth among all European ports in the combined value of goods handled, being exceeded only by Rotterdam, London, Antwerp, Hamburg, and Newcastle. Szczecin traffic was on par with that of Glasgow and Le Havre, and greater than that of Marseilles or Amsterdam. All three of the Polish ports in the interwar period were equipped with the most advanced trans-loading installations for coal, ore, and grain handling. Postwar development appears to have been considerable, and in 1950 it was officially claimed that Gdynia-Gdansk loadings exceeded prewar levels.

Owing in part to German reparations, the Polish merchant marine increased from 100,000 tons and 52 ships (of more than 100-ton displacement) in 1939 to 233,000 tons and 58 ships in 1952. While the number of cargo vessels has doubled, there is only one passenger liner ("Batory," 14,227 tons) in place of the seven prewar liners. During the Six-Year Plan a total of 103,300 tons was added to Polish merchant marine tonnage. The new Five-Year Plan calls for 200,400 tons, including two tankers of 18,000 DWT each, with a range of 17,000 miles and a speed of 16 knots. In addition, the Polish ship-building industry plans to construct a number of cargo vessels, many of which are scheduled to be exported.

COMMUNICATIONS

Postal services appear to be adequate for the needs of the population. In 1950 over 800 million letters, 1? million money orders, and 7.2 million telegrams were handled. In the same year the telephone system handled almost 600 million local calls and 47 million long-distance calls. (For information on radio and television, see chap. 9.)

Trends

In a speech on January 9, 1957, Gomułka, discussing the difficulties facing the Polish economy, said:

> The first and at the same time the principal cause of our difficulties is the disproportion in the development of certain specific branches of the national economy, . . . in particular the disproportion between the productive capacity built in the course of the Six-Year Plan and the raw materials basis of industry, which is too scanty and does not per-

mit the full utilization of the created productive capacity without a substantial increase in raw material imports, as well as the disproportion between the development of industry and agriculture.

The roots of these difficulties lie partly in the past—as far back s the pre-World War I era when mines and other industrial plants f the future state were developed for the large national markets of ne partitioning powers, then were cut off from these markets after oland became independent. But new ills have arisen from policies f the Communist government.

The Five-Year Plan for 1956 to 1960 was approved at the end f its first year of operation. The Plan still concentrates on high nvestments in heavy industries, neglecting agriculture and housing. ut without actually scrapping the Plan, the Gomułka government ends to bypass it in order to solve economic problems as they arise. ome long-term projects are now being given up in favor of investments yielding quick benefit to consumers. Construction of factories s being reduced; if a projected factory would require heavier allotments of scarce raw materials than its output would be worth, it is not uilt. But the planners still aim at self-sufficiency in almost all types f machines and tools. Nevertheless, detailed calculations of profitaility and efforts to minimize costs are likely to assume far greater nportance than they did during the Six-Year Plan, when political onsiderations took precedence over all else in the selection of investent targets.

Cutbacks in the armament industry may also help to solve hortages in the domestic market. According to present plans, defense lants in the next three years will produce items for civilian use alued at 25 billion złotys, with production in 1957 worth 4.5 billion złotys. The yearly sales of these manufactures—consisting largely f agricultural machinery and such durable consumer goods as sewing nachines, motorcycles, and refrigerators—will amount to about 10 ercent of the total retail sales of industrial goods produced by the tate (see chap. 16).

These changes are rather far-reaching. There is some question as to ow the over-all plan targets may be kept internally consistent in the ace of apparently uncoordinated cutbacks of producer goods and ncreases in consumer goods. The Gomułka government, however, ppears to be fully aware of the problems besetting Polish industry nd determined to find appropriate solutions. Ultimate success or ailure is a matter, at the moment, of pure speculation.

DOMESTIC AND FOREIGN TRAD

SINCE THE POLISH ECONOMY SUFFERS FROM A PROTRACTED shortage of consumer goods, efficient allocation of the few good available assumes great importance—any failure in distribution make the consumer feel prevailing scarcities even more intensely. But th Polish distribution system is not efficient. Relatively few resources— equipment or trained personnel—have been devoted to the domesti trade network. The result has been very unsatisfactory execution o central distribution plans. Basic necessities are often unavailable.

The state directly operates or controls almost the entire wholesal and retail trade network. Trade channels have been organized alon, Soviet lines, under appropriate ministries with subsidiary administra tive organs responsible for filling the trade channels with a planne volume of goods, assorted and priced according to the nationa economic plan (see chap. 15). Despite formal control of the trad network, however, the black market obtrudes at practically every stag of distribution, reflecting the government's inability or disinclinatio to use full-scale coercion in order to achieve its economic goals Profiteering has pushed consumer goods prices to inordinately high levels. Incomes of consumers—wage-earners for the most part— have lagged far behind prices, and the general goods scarcity has bee most severely felt by the urban workers. The peasants, fending o collectivization and retaining control of critical foodstuffs, have bee better off.

Since October 1956 the Gomułka government has promised to pay more attention to meeting consumer needs and has encouraged private trade with the result that privately owned garages, work shops, bakeries, and clothing stores are springing up in the cities seemingly without regard to the availability of goods. No provisio has been made to supply these stores with goods from state enterprises

The crux of the domestic trade problem continues to be over-al shortage of consumer goods. The situation can only be improved if and when the Polish Government allows consumer needs to influence production plans and devotes fewer resources to turning out investment goods.

Since the end of World War II Poland has traded almost exclusively with the Soviet Union and countries of the Soviet bloc. Its major export, coal, has been sent to the Soviet Union at a fraction of world market prices. Polish industries have been dependent upon Soviet raw materials, some of which are returned to the Soviet Union as finished industrial goods. As a result of meeting Russian and Soviet bloc trade needs the Polish industrial structure has been imbalanced, the economy weakened, and the people subjected to prolonged hardships.

Poland is still dependent upon the Soviet Union for iron ore, manganese, copper aluminum, synthetic rubber, cotton, and bread grains. But since October 1956 it has pursued a more independent trade policy—curtailing its export of coal to the East and seeking markets and products in the West. It is attempting to obtain from the West materials it now receives from the Soviet bloc, as well as capital equipment, consumer goods, and foodstuffs; if industry is to be shaped to meet domestic needs, Poland must import these goods during the transitional period (see chap. 11).

To pay for imports, Poland must export. Coal and agricultural products—the major exports during the interwar years along with tiles and lumber—continue to be mainstays of present foreign trade with the West. But in both categories there are shortages due to technical inefficiency and low productivity. The export potential for finished goods is lowered by the predominance of heavy industrial products which Poland produces above competitive prices on the world market. Central planning of foreign trade lacks the flexibility necessary to respond to foreign needs and changes in export demand. Thus handicapped, Poland must rely on foreign credits over the next two or three years while reshaping its internal economic structure to suit its own needs.

The System of Domestic Distribution

During the first two years after World War II, there were three distinct sectors of domestic trade: (1) state trade, which provided supplies to state industries, marketed their products at the wholesale level, and operated a small portion of the urban retail trade outlets; (2) cooperative trade, active at both the wholesale and retail level, urban and rural; and (3) private trade, primarily at the retail level. Developments in that period included extension of the state network of wholesale and retail stores, liquidation of the autonomy of the cooperative distribution network, and the subordination of private trading enterprises to state policy.

The Three-Year Plan (1947–49) initially retained the three-sector system and envisaged the development of a more efficient marketing organization to be accomplished through training of personnel, construction of facilities, elimination of unnecessary middlemen, enforcement of price and profit margin regulations, and establishment of a more orderly and planned distribution of commodities in all three sectors. After cessation of UNRRA aid early in 1947, however, there was a sharp rise in the price of food and other basic consumer goods, whereupon the government felt compelled to discard its carefully laid plans and quickly assume control over all distribution facilities.

High taxes, control over most supplies, rigid regulations, and a licensing system constituted the major weapons used to shrink private trade and make it give way to the expanding state and cooperative trade enterprises. By 1949, 2,030 out of 2,573 wholesale enterprises were being operated by the state. Over 60 percent of the total volume of retail trade was handled by socialized establishments comprising 4,422 state and 39,596 cooperative stores. The cooperative sector itself was completely reorganized by the government in 1948 and transformed into a reliable tool of state policy and an instrument of direct planning under supervision of the Council of Ministers.

This program was continued under the Six-Year Plan (1950–55), and by 1951 private trade accounted for only 3 percent of retail turnover as compared to 45 percent in 1949. The remaining private traders were organized by the government into an association subordinate to the Chief Council of the Association of Private Trade and Services. Cooperative and state trade outlets continued to expand; by 1955 the state controlled and operated virtually all of the wholesale and retail network (see Tables 24 and 25).

ORGANIZATION

STATE TRADE. Trading enterprises established by the Ministry of Domestic Trade may be of two types: they may operate on the basis of the so-called "full economic account" (the Soviet type of profit-and-loss accounting), or they may be included in the state budget. As in other state enterprises (see chap. 15) the principle of one-man management has been generally adopted since 1950–51. Socialized trade enterprises at the various levels are obliged to conclude planned contracts with one another specifying the quantity, quality, and the time of delivery of goods. There is thus little room for salesmanship in the western sense.

The Ministry organizes its own establishments under Central Trading Agencies (*centrale handlowe*), Central Boards (*zarząd*), and Central Agencies (*centrala*). The Central Trading Agencies maintain warehouses and wholesale outlets in central locations throughout the country, from which goods are shipped to the various urban and rural retail establishments. Industrial users generally bypass these agencies, tending to purchase supplies directly from the producing ministry.

A number of model urban retail stores are operated by the Central Agencies themselves, but the bulk of merchandise sold in the cities passes through state-owned and state-operated general department stores, and that sold in suburban areas and workers districts through municipal retail stores operated by Central Boards.

COOPERATIVE TRADE. A salient feature of commercial organization in interwar Poland was the cooperative movement, comprising primarily agricultural cooperatives and consumer cooperatives (see chap. 15). The societies operated to benefit the small producer member and to eliminate the middleman's profits.

In 1937 there were approximately 14,000 cooperative societies with a membership of over 3 million. The majority of the urban consumer cooperatives were organized into the Union of Consumer Cooperatives of the Polish Republic (known as Społem), which at the end of 1938 had a membership of nearly 400,000 in 1,886 societies. There were some 3,700 rural consumer cooperatives. In addition, the national minorities had their own societies.

In the immediate postwar period cooperative organizations practically monopolized the purchase of farm products. The government reorganized them in 1947 when it transferred 6,000 privately operated markets to the cooperatives. At the same time the government organized 3,000 local (*gmina*) cooperatives to sell consumer goods to peasants and to purchase agricultural products. The local cooperatives were organized into district and provincial unions, and these into the Central Union of Agricultural Cooperatives of the Peasant Self-Help Association (Centrala Rolnicza Spółdzielni "Samopomoc Chłopska" —CRSSCh).

A second reorganization in 1948 embraced the whole cooperative movement and created a hierarchical, compulsory organization, the Central Cooperative Union (Centralny Związek Spółdzielczy—CZS). The CZS is the top cooperative organ, under government control. The relationship between the CZS and the CRSSCh is not clear, but the

CZS is responsible for seeing that cooperatives follow the directives of the government economic policy and the economic plans. Cooperative trade was thus included in the national economic plan beginning in 1949.

Cooperatives play a leading role in the marketing of nonagricultural products in the rural areas and have an advantage over urban retail outlets. In both areas supplies flow from wholesale houses which specialize in a single type of product which they purchase from state industries and distribute all over the country. In the countryside, however, an intermediate agency between the retailer and the specialized wholesaler offers a variety of products to the cooperatives on the retail level. Urban retail stores, whether state, cooperative, or private, must obtain their goods from the specialized wholesale agencies; they must, therefore, buy in a dozen or more state branch trade agencies instead of buying in one or two multibranch wholesale stores.

In rural areas the retail outlets are the local cooperative and village department stores; in the cities they are state units of the Urban Retail Trade and of General Department Stores, cooperatives, and some remaining individual retailers. The activities of the large department stores are subject to central planning, while urban retail trade is under the territorial planning organs of the people's councils.

Agricultural products are obtained mainly through the Peasant Self-Help Association, through its subordinate organs at the district and community levels.

The contracting and organizing of purchases of farm products are centrally planned in cooperation with the people's councils. A Central Office of Purchases and Contracting was established in 1951 to plan, organize, and supervise these activities. Grain, for example, is delivered to the State Grain Establishments which store and process grains. The small noncommercial and nonnationalized mills are strictly regulated with regard to clientele, the amount of grain they may mill for any individual, and the grade of flour they may produce. Other farm products go to the state food-processing industries.

In the cities wholesale trade in foods is carried on by the Union of Consumer Cooperatives; in the countryside it is handled by the wholesale organization of the Peasant Self-Help Association. Each wholesale unit supplies foods to a certain number of retailers; priority is given to establishments for communal feeding and to the socialized retail network before private retailers.

According to official figures, the Peasant Self-Help cooperative network had over 44,000 shops in 1956, as against 4,601 at the end of 1945. The number is expected to rise to 60,000 by 1960. The

Społem network in towns has 362 cooperatives, with over 3 million members, and runs 17,300 shops, 2,500 production establishments, 1,800 restaurants and canteens, and 1,200 craftsmen's workshops. Under the Five-Year Plan an increase of some 4,000 shops is anticipated as well as a considerable expansion of the restaurant and canteen network.

A union of housing cooperatives was established in December 1956, and by mid-1957 comprised 297 cooperatives of different types. In 1956, 3,500 rooms were constructed; by 1960, 151,000 rooms are planned.

The 3,487 work cooperatives have some 420,000 members and employees and run about 16,500 production establishments and 25,-000 craftsmen's workshops. They account for some 37 percent of the total production of clothing, 25 percent of the production of knitwear articles, and 32 percent of the production of furniture; as of mid-1957 they were the largest producers of luxury goods and medical equipment.

PRIVATE TRADE. While the socialist sector, including state and cooperative trade, expanded, the share of private trade in the total volume shrank. Under the law of June 2, 1947 the conduct of a trading enterprise or the professional performance of trading activity required prior permission from the proper industrial authorities, the final decisions on such permits resting with the Ministry of Industry and Trade. Following reorganization in February 1949, this function was transferred to the Ministry of Domestic Trade.

Coincidentally with the introduction of these permits a series of price control measures established control over wholesale and retail profit margins for certain categories of goods and services and set maximum prices for others. The Ministry of Industry and Trade established the maximum retail and wholesale prices on basic necessities, using for this purpose the established margins and an average of farm market prices reported at periodic intervals. It also established the maximum prices on goods produced by private handicraft, industry, and the socialist sector.

Government control and interference in domestic trade are not new to Poland. During the interwar period the government regulated trade in primary necessities such as foodstuffs, clothing, and fuel. Private enterprise in most fields required licenses, concessions, or permits. Cartels under government sponsorship introduced restrictions on production and marketing, and in some areas state monopolies totally excluded private enterprise or offered serious competition. However, the shopkeeping permits were readily granted. Most of the trade outlets in prewar Poland were very small units. In 1938, out of 374,153 retail shops in the country, 344,346 were one-man operations and nearly 60 percent dealt in foodstuffs. Most of the small shopkeepers were Jews. After the war, as Poles attempted to move into the trading field, considerable private dissatisfaction was generated by the government's policy against private trade.

As an outgrowth of the events of October 1956 private trade has been stimulated, but some of the new merchants are already under fire in the Polish press, either on ideological grounds or in the light of Polish tradition, which regards trade as a shady business (see chap. 2).

The Domestic System in Operation

PLANNING AND CONTROL OF TRADE

The Ministry of Domestic Trade supervises and directs all domestic trade, plans investment policy in the field of marketing, regulates supply and consumption, organizes the trade network, and controls its operation. It also acts as an umpire between individual trade enterprises, fixes prices for goods (except those whose price is fixed by the Council of Ministers), and determines the margin of gross profits to be made at different levels of the trading system.

The distribution of consumer goods is determined by the Ministry on the basis of quarterly quotas allotted to each province. Within these quotas the trade sections of the presidia of the provincial people's councils establish monthly allotments for the individual districts, while the trade sections of the presidia of the district people's councils determine the quantities of goods to be received by each community. Local political organs thus have a role in planning economic activities.

The volume and price of goods as well as the timing and direction of their distribution are all centrally determined. Central planning of trade is supported by regional planning at the provincial and district level. Plans for wholesale trade and activities of large department stores are made centrally. A major part of retail trade comes, however, under the regional planning of the Commissions for Economic Planning of the people's councils. These territorial plans must conform with the general directives of the central authorities. Retail trade under territorial (regional) planning is supplied from the centrally controlled wholesale agencies or from the territorial industrial and handicraft enterprises.

Control over the trade plans was first exercised by a special agency which worked under the Ministry of Domestic Trade and had trade inspectors on the provincial and district levels. The inspectors had the right to examine all books, documents, and physical facilities of trade enterprises and to take drastic steps if malpractice was discovered. In the fall of 1952 the functions of special controlling bodies within government departments were taken over by the newly created Ministry of State Control (see chap. 15).

The organs for enforcement of price control include authorities of the Ministry of State Control, Treasury authorities, courts, and the agencies of the Special Commission for Combating Waste and Economic Sabotage (see chap. 15), as well as an array of commissions for price control set up by local people's council from among representatives of labor unions, the Peasant's Self-Help Association, and the Central Cooperative Union. All these control organizations have the right to enter trading enterprises, verify inventories and records, and require full explanation of the transactions completed. Violators of price control regulations can be fined up to 5 million złotys or sentenced to up to five years in prison, or both.

This plethora of control organizations and the lack of coordination among them has vitiated attempts by the regime to bring order into a chaotic situation. To some extent it may even have fostered the abuses the organizations were designed to combat.

SHORTCOMINGS OF DISTRIBUTION

Distribution of food products has not been satisfactory since World War II. Because Poland benefited in the first postwar years from UNRRA aid, the ration system, differentiated to give priority to heavy industries, was gradually softened. Rationing of sugar, potatoes, *kasha* (cracked buckwheat), and bread was ended in 1948. Total abolition of rationing was to begin in January 1949, but was in part illusory. Ration cards for edible fats, for example, were replaced by priority certificates issued to "wage earners in densely populated industrial regions," and meatless days were observed in the large towns, a practice which has continued periodically to this day. Certificates for fats were discontinued as of July 1950.

A worsening of the food situation caused rationing to be reinstated in September 1951, first for meat, then for fats, soap, and sugar. In late 1951 a legal free-market sector was established in which prices were set deliberately higher than for rationed goods. The amount of available foodstuffs varied in relation to the quality of the harvests and to the degree of fulfillment of delivery obligations by the peasants. Food rationing was once more completely abolished in March 1953 with the official explanation that:

> . . . it has curtailed the free acquisition of commodities and thus stifled the economic stimuli necessary for raising the productivity of

labor, and thereby the output of industry and the standard of living. The system, moreover, contributes to waste and bureaucratism, fosters abuses in trade, and raises overhead costs.

Rationing no longer exists but indirect restrictions of various sorts remain in effect.

Under the coal distribution system of 1954, presumably still in effect, orders are taken and deliveries made twice a year, with payment required in advance. "Bloc stewards," chairman of citizen committees in charge of blocs of urban dwellings, distribute the limited amounts allocated by the economic Plan for internal consumption. Additional coal can be obtained at higher prices from coal dealers. This distribution system was designed to promote the use of local fuels such as peat and firewood in rural areas.

To purchase textiles after rationing had been abolished one had to be on a waiting list or stand in line in front of stores as soon as their stocks were replenished. To buy a bicycle and certain types of furniture one had to put one's name on another type of waiting list, this one controlled by the works council of a factory or some similar body—a system which reflected discrimination in favor of wage earners.

The rural distribution network was and still is generally neglected by the Polish Government. In 1952, of 40,000 rural communities, 15,000 had no stores; there has been no report of substantial additions since then. Where stores did exist, according to a Polish Press report in 1955, they were

. . . completely lacking in men's socks, cotton dresses, glass jars for canning fruits and vegetables, glass chimneys for kerosene lamps, plowshares, harrows, and other instruments. Only vodka is in plentiful supply and accounts for 35 percent of goods turnover.

The Peasant Self-Help Association, which runs most of these rural stores, can do nothing to change this situation, for it must follow the over-all economic policy laid down by the state, including a systematic undersupply of merchandise to rural stores. Polish trade also suffers from the already mentioned acute shortage of trained personnel.

SPECULATION

Given the shortage of goods, the unreliable and discriminatory manner in which they are distributed, and increases in worker and peasant incomes, it is not surprising to find a flourishing black market and wide-scale speculation.

A major source of goods for the black market sees to be within the state trade network itself. In Lodz, for example, a check by a control commission on state stores in 1954 found unexplained losses and deficits in goods and commodity wares of private production which were not entered on the books in about 80 percent of the shops. The number of people involved, including managers and sales attendants, was so large that authorities were able to demand only that deficiencies be made good and damages paid for; the employees were neither fired from their jobs nor prosecuted. Similar cases from all over the country are reported almost every day in the press.

There is a strong inducement for store employees to engage in such practices. Prices for commodities in the state stores often are set far below what the traffic would bear so store personnel frequently sell to a confederate an entire shipment of some scarce commodity at the state price; the goods are then resold at great profit on the black market. Similar activities are carried on by warehouse employees at both the plant and wholesale level.

Another source of supply for the black market, especially of such luxury goods as stockings, perfumes, lipstick, and coffee, has been gift parcels sent by relatives or friends abroad; recently high customs duties have somewhat limited this source, but such transactions remain an important source of income for some families.

These illegal activities are referred to, in the aggregate, as the "economic underground" (*podziemie gospodarcze*). Party members seems to be among the worst offenders. The government has attempted to stamp out such activities through special investigatory commissions, special legislation, and elaborate recording of the amounts purchased by each customer in a state store. It is illegal, for example, to

> corner articles in socialized trade for the purpose of profit; to sell articles originally bought in the retail network at prices above State prices; to sell articles above fixed State prices in shops; and to purchase and hoard articles in excessive amounts for profiteering.

But according to government officials the economic underground is so far-flung that law enforcement authorities cannot cope with the situation. At the local level most cases are ignored as either too widespread or too trifling.

The Pattern of Foreign Trade

After World War I Poland hastened to establish trade relations with its political allies and other countries in order to insure economic independence from her powerful neighbors, Germany and Russia (see chap. 10). Commercial treaties were concluded with Belgium, France, Italy, Rumania, Turkey, the United Kingdom, and Yugoslavia, as well as with Austria and Switzerland. Friendly economic relations were eventually established with Russia. In exchange for orders placed with Polish industries the USSR was granted import quotas and preferential duties on certain specified imports. A long tariff war with Germany had followed the period of preferential treatment of Poland made obligatory by the Treaty of Versailles; in 1934, however, a one-year trade agreement with provision for extension was signed.

Export activity was directed especially toward the Baltic and Scandinavian countries. As a result of the British coal strike of 1926 the Polish coal industry was able to obtain markets hitherto dominated by Great Britain. The progressive inflation which devalued the currency in relation to that of other countries artificially stimulated Polish exports. This boom, especially in foreign sales of Lodz textiles, ended in 1926 with stabilization of the currency at a relatively high exchange rate (see chap. 13).

In the following years foreign trade lagged behind the revival of domestic industrial production. Between 1928 and 1938 total industrial production increased by about 20 percent, whereas the volume of imports and exports decreased by about 25 percent each.

Before World War I nearly all of Poland's trade had been directed across land frontiers, and even by 1927 only about one fourth of its total trade (by value) was shipped through the port of Danzig; the role of Gdynia, Poland's other exit to the sea, was insignificant. Increasingly thereafter, partly as a matter of deliberate policy and partly as a consequence of the German-Polish tariff war, foreign trade was routed by sea. In 1938, 63 percent of total foreign trade (by value) was directed via the two Baltic ports; of the total, Gdynia had 48 percent, Danzig 15 percent. The port of Gdynia was constructed on government initiative and largely by public investment.

The world-wide depression brought an increase in government economic activity. To carry through the new policy of large-scale planned industrialization in 1936 there had to be significant imports of raw materials and machinery. Industrial raw materials accounted for half of Polish imports at this time; when added to the machinery and capital which had to be imported they threw a great burden on Poland's balance of trade. Increasing exports to pay for imports became even more difficult because the value of agricultural exports per unit quantity was far lower than before the depression. Overvaluation of the złoty also handicapped export trade severely. The government introduced currency control, placed all imports and exports under severe regulation, and suspended payment on foreign debts. It then negotiated bilateral agreements in order to balance exports and imports, country by country. By 1938 ten clearing agreements were in effect, covering about 28 percent of Poland's foreign trade.

After World War II Polish foreign trade was small in comparison with the volume of supplies delivered by UNRRA during 1945–47 —the most important external factor in the recovery of the Polish economy. The total program for Poland amounted to over $481 million, with about $171 million in direct aid to industry and agriculture. The over-all effect of that assistance was far greater, however, since food, clothing, and medical supplies increased the productive capacity of Polish labor—a partial substitute for imports of capital goods.

Between 1946 and the end of the Three-Year Plan in 1949, Poland, in addition to UNRRA aid, obtained about $675 million in loans and grants, chiefly from the West, including $90 million in credits from the United States. The total was more than Poland's 1949 imports, estimated at $632 million.

But increasing Soviet influence made orientation toward the West impossible. Early in 1947 Poland's request for a loan of $600 million from the International Bank for Reconstruction and Development was refused—about the same time that Poland refused to participate in the Marshall Plan. Shortly after came the complete integration of Poland into the Soviet bloc.

ORGANIZATION

Polish foreign trade has been a state monopoly since 1946—directly carried out by state agencies or by private and cooperative organizations on behalf of the state. By 1949 private enterprise was all but negligible.

A separate Ministry of Foreign Trade (Ministerstwo Handlu Zagranicznego—MHZ) was established in February 1949 with responsibility for financial and economic planning of foreign trade, conduct of trade negotiations, preparation of international trade agreements and supervision of their execution in liaison with the Ministry of Foreign Affairs and other interested agencies. It also directs state and cooperative enterprises producing primarily for foreign trade and supervises other enterprises producing export commodities. In cooperation with the Ministry of Foreign Affairs it establishes trade offices abroad and appoints commercial attaches.

Domestic activities relating to foreign trade are carried out by supply and sales offices under the central industrial boards for each industry (see chap. 15). Their activities are coordinated by the central administrative offices of the Ministry of Foreign Trade. Sales offices handle exports, supply offices deal with imports; both have representatives in foreign countries. Some of the many such enterprises are ANIMEX (Central Import and Export Office of Animal Products); CETEBE (Export-Import Central Trading Office of the Textile Industry); ELEKTRIM (Polish Foreign Trade Company for Electrical Equipment); IMPEXMETAL (Central Bureau for Iron and Steel); PETROL (Central Bureau for Mineral Oil Products); WEGLOKOKS (Central Coal Sales Bureau).

Such trade offices analyze foreign markets, seek out competitive sources of supply, arrange for transportation of goods (including suitable packing and insurance), set prices on goods sold so as to realize maximum profits while taking account of competition, assure payment for goods sold, and maintain liaison with production enterprises to see that the goods dispatched correspond to the conditions of the sale. Consular establishments, special trade missions, and trade delegations advise on prices, quality and assortment of exports to meet conditions on foreign markets.

The major difficulties experienced by the export offices relate to prices and the adaptation of goods to foreign requirements, the latter demanding a flexibility neglected in the national economic plans (see chap. 11).

The Polish Chamber of Foreign Commerce, an advisory body established in September 1949, facilitates the work of all foreign trade organizations, especially those involved with the Council of Economic Mutual Assistance. Before 1949 a similar role was played by the Chamber of Industry and Trade on behalf of private traders.

PLANNING

Foreign trade enters into the material and financial balances established in the plans for production, consumption, investment, and trade. Planned demands for raw materials, finished goods, and equipment that cannot be obtained from domestic sources form the basis of the import plan.

From the foreign trade goals established by the State Commission for Economic Planning (Państwowa Komisja Planowania Gospodarczego—PKPG), the Ministry of Foreign Trade prepares a list of the general assortment required for export. These requirements are included in the planning instructions passed on to the production ministries by the PKPG. The Ministry of Foreign Trade distributes quantitative goals for imports and exports to its central administrative offices. It also specifies levels of trade to be developed with each trading partner and the quantities of leading products to be traded. The central offices, as intermediate supervisory organs, elaborate the details of the plan in consultation with the trade officers of the central industrial boards desiring imports or providing exports.

The need for balancing trade relation in cases where credits could not be arranged led in the postwar period to the widespread use of long-term bilateral clearing agreements; such agreements provided a firmer basis for economic planning than short-term arrangements or completely unscheduled trade. Among the countries which have concluded long-term trade agreements with Poland, in addition to the Soviet Union and countries of eastern Europe, are Argentina, Italy, Switzerland, and the United Kingdom. The investment credits granted over a period of years against future deliveries of Polish goods constitute another factor that has served to facilitate the planning of foreign trade.

Prices received by Polish producers of exports and those paid by Polish industry for imports are to a large extent insulated from world market prices by means of special trade accounts and subsidies. Suppliers of export goods are paid internal prices which are generally lower than the foreign currency receipts obtained for the goods. In order to keep raw industrial material prices at a low level, the domestic "resale" prices for imported commodities are divorced from the prices paid abroad.

To balance foreign trade accounts, the state pays a subsidy to make up the difference between the import price and the resale price to the enterprise. The foreign trade accounts also receive profits from the resale of export commodities purchased at low prices from Polish industry. This system of accounting necessitates a conversion rate between the złoty and foreign currencies. The rate has primary significance for appraising the over-all results of foreign trade, but does not affect the production enterprises. In 1948 the conversion rate between the złoty and the dollar was 400:1 for foreign trade purposes, with other currencies being converted on the basis of this parity. Foreign payments, where required, were made in foreign currencies, the złoty being an internal currency (see chap. 13).

COMPOSITION

Imports of mineral products increased markedly in the postwar period, especially iron and manganese ores, petroleum products, chemicals including fertilizers, machinery and equipment including transportation equipment, and various precision equipment. Textile fiber, rubber, wood and paper products, metals and metal products, hides and leather, and grains and other plant products are other important items in postwar imports.

According to *Życie Gospodarcze* (May 1–15, 1950), the 1949

composition of exports (according to 1949 prices) was as follows: coal and coke, 46 percent; agricultural and food products, 20 percent; raw materials and semimanufactures, 17.8 percent; industrial products, 16.2 percent. This breakdown corresponds approximately to the most recent statistics on composition of trade as shown in Table 26.

Polish postwar export policy as formulated at the outset of the Three-Year Plan (1947–49) aimed at the export of highly processed agricultural products and certain manufactured consumer goods— even of items which were scarce on the domestic market—in order to acquire foreign markets or to re-establish prewar contacts. The most significant changes from the prewar composition of exports are (1) an increase in the export of transportation equipment, chemicals, and to a lesser degree textiles, and (2) the diminished importance of agricultural products and lumber. Coal and coke continue to consti- tute the major single item on the export list.

According to official data Poland's foreign trade in 1956 appears to have reached a total value of 7,503 million rubles, or 96 percent of the planned figure. Imports were 3,649 million rubles (97.9 per- cent of the plan), and exports 3,854 million rubles (94.9 percent of the plan). Although Poland still has a favorable balance of trade, failure to reach the 1956 export target appears to be making the repayment of foreign loans difficult. (Polish foreign trade statistics are given partly in złotys, partly in rubles, and partly in dollars. Before May 1, 1957, 1 złoty was equal to 1 ruble. The new rate is 1.50 złotys to the ruble; see chap. 13.)

In 1956 imports of capital goods were more than 10 percent below plan and amounted to only 918.6 million rubles, compared with 1,152 million rubles in 1955. The plan for the import of in- dustrial consumer goods, on the other hand, was exceeded by 67 percent. The plan for the import of raw materials for light industry (mainly cotton) was not fulfilled, but that for heavy industry was overfulfilled.

No major changes occurred in structure of exports between 1955 and 1956. A noteworthy development, however, was the doubling of the share of consumer goods in total imports.

GEOGRAPHIC DISTRIBUTION

The geographic distribution of Polish foreign trade in 1955 is shown in Table 27. According to the recent Polish-Soviet trade agreement the USSR will reduce its imports of Polish coal and coke and has canceled orders for cement and sugar. On the other hand it is supposed to provide such badly needed raw materials as iron ore, nonferrous metals, cotton, oil, and oil products.

Poland intends to become again one of the largest exporters of hard coal to western Europe and Scandinavia. An examination of coal production and consumption suggests that it could do so (see chap. 15). At the peak of its industrial production (1955–56) Polish industry absorbed some 36 million tons of coal; the total consumption was approximately 62 million tons. Assuming that industrial consumption of coal will decrease slightly in 1957–58 and that consumption by railroads and households will remain stable, the surplus may be in the vicinity of 30 million tons of a total output conservatively estimated at 92 million tons per year. Allowing for some stockpiling, the net amount remaining for export would probably reach approximately 26 million tons, of which Russia has already ordered 3 million tons. Thus Poland would be left with some 23 million tons of hard coal available for eastern and western Europe.

Economic Relations with the East

SOVIET ECONOMIC DOMINANCE

The Soviet bloc is the main outlet for Polish exports and a source of supply for Poland. Data is lacking, however, on the details of the relationship. There is no question that until October 1956 the USSR obtained from Poland some 8 million tons of coal per year at roughly one sixth of the prevailing world price. This type of exploitation started soon after the war when the USSR suggested the creation of a mixed Polish-Soviet company to work the Polish mines, with a fifty-fifty share of profits. The Soviet "contribution" to the company was to be the expulsion of Germans from the coal fields. When this suggestion met with strong opposition from the Warsaw government it was replaced by an "offer" to take "coal reparations" from Poland instead.

The Poles lay the blame for a major share of their economic difficulties on the unrequited exports and the one-sided industrialization program imposed on them by the Russians. In October 1956, Hillary Minc, former economic chief, told the PZPR Central Committee that when he went to Moscow in 1950 to discuss Poland's Six-Year Plan Stalin rejected the Plan as being designed primarily to establish "cheesecloth industries"—that is, industries to serve consumers—and demanded that war industries be constructed and that the program reflect Soviet import requirements.

An outstanding example of the extent to which the Poles are dependent on Soviet supplies is the Nowa Huta steel combine. The plant employs some 17,000 persons, virtually all of whom would be thrown out of work if the Soviet Union withheld iron ore supplies for one week. This dependence also applies to such other industries as shipping and textiles. Some Polish shipyards constructed since World War II can turn out only 4,000- to 5,000-ton vessels built to Soviet specifications for use on the Black Sea. The Poles say that these ships cannot be sold elsewhere. Readaptation of the yards would be costly and take a great deal of time. Many mills can work only with Russian cotton, which is traded by the Soviet Union for finished textiles. The Poles assume that the Russians will not send cotton if they stop buying finished goods. Since October 1956 all these supplies have been coming in fitfully, leaving some Polish plants operating almost on a day-to-day basis.

Some of these grievances may still exist but others seemingly have been assuaged for a time. Until quite recently no mention was ever made of the method of payment for Poland's "invisible" exports to the Soviet Union, among which the services of Polish railways in the huge traffic between the Soviet Union and Eastern Germany are of special importance. Neither was there any mention of how the Soviet debt to Poland on the German reparations account was settled. After the October 1956 upheaval the Polish Government asked the Soviet Union for a large amount of the uncollected East German reparations and for renegotiation of Polish-Soviet trade and economic agreements. The initial claim reported was $500 million. At the November 1956 meeting in Moscow, Poland's entire debt to the Soviet Union was canceled. This involved 2.4 billion rubles ($600 million at the official rate of exchange), apparently exceeding Polish expectations by some $100 million. The sum is roughly equivalent to the value of uncollected reparations due Poland combined with the value of the coal delivered between 1946 and 1953. Poland also received a 700 million ruble loan and a 2-year credit for 1.4 million tons of wheat. By the end of 1956 half of the grain had already been delivered; the USSR was reported to have agreed to deliver the balance at the rate of 200,000 tons monthly during the first half of 1957.

Another series of Polish-Soviet conferences was held in mid-May 1957. The Poles reportedly presented a bill for 300 million rubles ($75 million) for transit accounts due from the Soviet Union for postwar shipping of troops across Poland to and from East Germany. The Poles also requested increased iron ore shipments to put the Nowa Huta combine into capacity production. The Polish request for increased iron ore shipments is evidently under consideration. No exact accounting of Soviet shipments appears to be possible, however, since for many years the Russians did as they pleased and did not bother to notify the Poles. At the conference Khrushchev is reported to have told the Poles that he would not consider the transit account and that

Poland could not go on "milking" the Soviet Union and should "look elsewhere for aid since it had already found the path to another source" (namely, the United States). Second thoughts brought First Deputy Premier Mikoyan to Warsaw a few weeks later, reportedly with a view to placating the incensed Poles and assuring them that "the Soviet Union would study the transit account but would need time because it had been drawn up without Soviet participation."

POLISH-SOVIET TRADE

Two types of arrangements govern Polish-Soviet trade. Under the first, Poland pays for its imports fully and immediately by making counterdeliveries, in this way receiving iron ores, chromium, and copper (some 50 to 80 percent of total imports of these metals), about 50 percent of total imported cotton, and 100 percent of the imported nickel and manganese. Under the second arrangement, usually referred to as "brotherly aid," the USSR sells investment goods to Poland on credit. These credit transactions are small, having amounted to perhaps 3 percent of total investment under the Six-Year Plan. The terms are such as to make it hardly an investment credit in the usual sense. Deliveries are spread over a period of nearly ten years, but each shipment is to be paid for within five years, with repayment starting in the year following the first delivery. For some years about one third of the credit deliveries went to the Nowa Huta combine. The burdensome service of the investment credit, added to the requirements of counterdeliveries, drained the country of a constantly growing stream of goods, particularly rolling stock, machine tools, and other machinery as well as coal.

A comparison of actual exports to Russia in 1955 (before the change in Poland's foreign trade policy went into effect) with proposed exports under the new agreement indicates that Poland may have additional quantities of such commodities as coke, rolled steel, caustic soda, cement, and woolen fabrics to sell elsewhere (see Table 28). The export of ships, on the other hand, will remain at a fairly high level.

Poland's commitments in ships for Russia are still much larger than the Polish Government would like, inasmuch as early in 1957 Poland had to refuse Swiss and Swedish orders for the construction of tankers, along with a Swedish offer of a $3 million advance to enable the Gdansk shipyards to install the necessary equipment. Shipbuilding is being developed into a major export industry, and the new Five-Year Plan envisages the construction of 305 ships totaling 834,000 tons. Only 280,000 of the tonnage is destined for the Polish fleet; Russia's share, though reduced, is still very large, amounting to 452,000 tons. China is the second largest buyer, with an order for 90,000 tons.

TRADE WITH THE SOVIET BLOC

Trade relations within the Soviet bloc have been especially close since the establishment in 1949 of the Council for Economic Mutual Assistance (Rada Wzajemnej Pomocy Gospodarcze—RWPG—also known as KOMEKON or the Molotov Plan). It is responsible for guiding Soviet bloc trade in a uniform manner and caters to the interests of the USSR. All trade agreements between bloc members are submitted to the Council for approval and concurrence. There are also numerous triangular arrangements in which the Soviet Union appears as middleman and in which it can influence prices accordingly. Coordination of economic objectives within the Soviet sphere—one of the chief functions of the Council—seems to be effected primarily through long-term trade agreements covering the periods of the long-term production plans in each of the signatory countries—the Soviet Union, East Germany, Poland, Czechoslovakia, Hungary, Rumania, and Bulgaria. The official aims of the Council include exchange of economic experience, mutual exchange of technical assistance, and mutual aid with respect to raw materials, food, machinery, and industrial equipment.

In July 1957 it was reported that the seven eastern European satellites and the Soviet Union had completed an agreement for a multilateral clearing system—a major departure from the inflexible system of year-to-year bilateral agreements hitherto employed, under which actual surpluses and deficits among the countries could not be balanced off against each other. In a multilateral clearing system—like the European Payments Union in the West—surpluses and deficits among all member countries are settled periodically. The new system may give these countries, including Poland, greater maneuverability and flexibility in their relations with the Soviet Union. Despite the intensification of trade among the countries of eastern Europe, however, the volume appears to be rather small as compared to the level attained among most countries of western Europe. Poland reached the peak of its share in these exchanges in 1953 (see Table 29).

Economic policies being followed in eastern Europe with regard to the development of basic industries seem to run counter to the declared aim of these countries to develop a high degree of economic cooperation. Each of them has sought to achieve rapid increases in its own output of coal, electric power, and steel, although the resource endowment of the area would suggest some specialization of production. The autarkic policies also include the development of engineerng industries in each country. It is possible, however, for specialization to occur by types of output within broad product categories. It was planned, for example, that in 1954–55 Poland would produce all its requirements for medium tractors and a surplus for export against imports of other types of tractors.

Poland's 1957 imports from the Soviet bloc were expected to be about 25 percent higher than those of 1956, an increase of over 461 million rubles. Polish exports, however, were not expected to rise to the same extent and a sizable deficit is expected. This may be covered by Soviet credits for the purchase of 1.4 million tons of grain, while the remainder is to be met by a Soviet "technical help" interest-free loan of 100 million rubles. Trade with the Soviet bloc will probably amount to nearly 60 percent of Poland's foreign trade, more than half with the USSR.

The Poles have been dissatisfied with their trade with other Communist bloc countries. In December 1956 *Trybuna Ludu* stated, for example, that under the area's integrated planning Poland was obliged to export raw materials "characteristic of economically backward countries" and to import principally capital goods; "such an exchange does not correspond to Poland's interests."

The article cited a second grievance—that Czechoslovakia has acted as middleman for Poland, depriving it of foreign markets. Poland, for example, buys Brazilian coffee and Egyptian cotton from Czechoslovakia in return for coal and other valuable materials, instead of dealing directly with the producing countries. "Instead of winning new markets for our industrial products we are assisting our partners to do so." The Soviet Union, through the Council for Economic Mutual Assistance, supervises these relationships.

CZECHOSLOVAKIA AND EAST GERMANY. Poland's main trading partners among the satellites are East Germany and Czechoslovakia, providing about a quarter of Poland's capital goods imports, while Poland supplies them, as well as other satellites, with rolling stock, machine tools, and other machinery. Poland serves as the fuel reservoir for the satellite orbit, providing about 12 million tons of coal a year. Poland also is the bloc's source of zinc, but for its own aluminum supplies depends on Hungary. It gets a few other nonferrous metals from Bulgaria and Rumania, which also cover part of its demand for oil.

East Germany makes up a part of Polish deficiency in potash fertilizers. Poland has provided East Germany with foodstuffs at times of acute shortage such as in 1953. East Germany appears to be the only satellite with which Poland has a credit balance in commodity exchanges; to the extent that this account remains outstanding, Poland is financing the East German economy. Polish trade exchanges with the rest of the European satellite areas are probably balanced.

In the years after World War II, Poland became the most important supplier of coal to Czechoslovakia. A series of trade agreements between the two countries were concluded and various steps were taken to tighten economic relations. In February 1955 it was reported that Poland, Czechoslovakia, and East Germany were preparing to establish an economic production combination. Part of the plan was to give a share of control of the Polish Upper Silesian mining and industrial area to East Germany, which has suffered severely from being separated from this region. Czechoslovakia also was to be involved in the plan, with both countries receiving a definite percentage of the output.

Poland's economic collaboration with both countries was disrupted in 1956, however, because of Poland's refusal to supply needed coal. This refusal was a contributory factor in forcing the revision of Czech and East German economic plans for 1957. In the first half of 1957 economic relations between the countries were patched up again by the establishment of a Polish-Czech economic committee. In June it was announced that Czechoslovakia would invest the equivalent of 100 million rubles in a cooperative effort to exploit Polish sulphur deposits. Poland turned to this type of agreement after failing to interest western investors.

In March 1957 the governments of East Germany and Poland signed a trade agreement to increase their volume of trade in 1957 by 1 billion rubles. Figures for the total volume were not published at the time. East Germany undertook to ship machinery, chemicals, and precision instruments to Poland, in exchange for hard and soft coal, coke, machine tools, and goods. The agreement provided for further trade talks later in the year. Gomułka and other Polish leaders went to East Berlin in June in connection with this provision. In the course of the visit a declaration of amity was signed. It was implied that trade between the two countries also would be strengthened.

ASIAN COUNTRIES. In the Asian area Poland has had to make gift deliveries of machine tools, rolled goods, rolling stock, and other material for the reconstruction of North Korea. Poland also has assumed a heavy burden in its economic relations with China; up to two thirds of total ocean-going tonnage is tied up in Chinese trade. Polish exports of transport and industrial equipment to China are growing rapidly, and Poland has undertaken to deliver and construct complete plants there, starting with two sugar refineries. China reportedly has repaid, by counterdeliveries, only a small part of the Polish goods and services received.

Economic Relations with the West

In exchange for industrial goods, iron ores, and a few basic raw materials—mainly from overseas—such as rubber and wool, Poland has supplied the West principally with coal, food, and timber. The United Kingdom far outpaced all other western European countries as a market for Polish exports (see Table 27). Finland is a close runner-up, but the balance on Poland's Finnish trade of about $20 million a year has been offset by Finnish deliveries to the Soviet Union, in a triangular trade arrangement in which Poland was forced to participate.

Since exports to countries outside the Soviet orbit exceed imports, Poland has a currency surplus (estimated for 1952 at $80 million). The foreign credits accrue to a Soviet-controlled foreign exchange pool, presumably under control of the Council for Economic Mutual Assistance. From that pool the Soviet Union grants loans and otherwise provides for the currency needs of the satellites. Polish coal has been the greatest single foreign exchange earner of the Soviet bloc. At the time of the Korean war it brought in about $250 million a year; since then it has probably earned a third of that amount. Among the western countries, Sweden, France (less so after 1949), Finland, Austria, Denmark (also less so since 1949), and Italy have been the principal customers for Polish coal. Polish coal exports have been running into increasing difficulties, however, because increasing industrial demand at home has shrunk the exportable surplus. Poland also has been charging noncompetitive prices, which forced Sweden and Austria to cut down their purchases. Finally, the type of coal delivered was frequently of uneven quality and badly assorted.

Before World War II the United Kingdom was Poland's major trading partner, followed by Germany. Polish exports to the United Kingdom consisted mostly of lumber, lumber products, and agricultural commodities, whereas imports were primarily industrial goods, wool, and fish. After the war the old trading relations were renewed by means of trade agreements. Poland, whose export of foodstuffs generally had suffered a severe decline, actually increased its food exports to the United Kingdom but reduced shipments of other products. Wood and lumber exports fell off to practically zero by 1951. After the outbreak of the Korean war, British-Polish trade relations ran into difficulties, as the United Kingdom abided by the provisions

of the strategic trade controls of the Free World nations, taking ove
without appropriate compensation, for example, two tankers ordere
by the Polish Government. Poland, however, continues to maintair
an interest in trading relations with the United Kingdom. And the
United Kingdom, since it is being displaced by West Germany in other
world markets, may turn to eastern Europe as an outlet for its in
dustrial exports. In payment the United Kingdom would probably
take larger quantities of Polish coal, provided they could be made
available at or near world-market prices.

In comparison with the years before World War II, the composi
tion of Polish trade with West Germany also shows changes, es
sentially in Polish exports. Exports other than foodstuffs were sharply
cut, so that in 1952 they were only about half the volume of 1937
(46,000 metric tons as against 84,000 metric tons). But exports o
hogs, for example, were reported in 1950 to be twice as great as ir
1937—another example of the Polish Government's disregard of the
domestic food situation. There was a substantial decrease in the expor
of zinc and alloys and of raw materials, especially lumber and lumbe
products, which had figured importantly in exports to Germany before
the war.

Before World War II Sweden was an important trading partner
After the war, when reconstruction in Poland was badly in need o
raw materials and machinery, Sweden as a country not directly affected
by the war could supply the required commodities with the leas
delay. Sweden needed coal, and after two smaller trade and paymen
agreements it granted Poland a long-term credit of about $100 mil
lion for the purchase of investment goods in 1947. At that time a
settlement by Poland of confiscated Swedish property was arrived at
and Poland agreed to pay off the annual installments of this restitution
by means of coal deliveries. Until quite recently Sweden was the
largest western consumer of Polish coal, obtaining about 60 percen
of its coal from Poland. In addition to iron ore Sweden has been
providing Poland with ball bearings, generators, and various types o
machines which Poland was unable to obtain from other western
countries because of strategic trade controls. In consequence Sweden
has ranked first among suppliers of machinery to Poland.

Norway bought substantial amounts of Polish coal, but with the
rise in coal prices after the outbreak of the Korean War coal exports
to Norway fell off. Poland chiefly imported animal fats (including
cod-liver oil), fish, and hides from Norway.

Denmark also covered the major portion of its coal requirements
with imports from Poland. In 1951 Poland temporarily stopped coal
deliveries in reprisal for Denmark's refusal to ship American auto-

mobile parts in contravention of strategic trade controls—despite a Polish-Danish agreement for their delivery.

Through a series of trade agreements negotiated in 1957 with Britain, West Germany, and France, Poland has reportedly balanced its trade almost evenly between East and West, in contrast to the former two-to-one distribution. But trade with the West, like trade with the Soviet Union, will bring a radical improvement to the Polish economy only if large credits are granted. France has made a start, granting Poland a long-term credit of 10 billion francs, and Germany has advanced $9 million. The United States has granted the largest credit—although the Poles made it clear that they could accept no political strings—$95 million, which includes $30 million through the Export-Import Bank, to be repaid in dollars over a twenty-year period beginning in 1962, at 4.5 percent interest; of the $30 million, $4 million will be spent on coal-mining machinery, the rest on surplus farm commodities and transport costs. Another $18.9 million of the total credit will be used for the purchase of surplus farm commodities and is to be repaid in złotys at 24 to the dollar. The remaining $46.1 million is to be spent on surplus farm commodities and to be repaid in złotys; with this money Poland is to obtain 500,000 tons of wheat, 50,000 tons of cotton, 60,000 tons of soybeans, and 17,500 tons of fats and oils.

The economic plans that are emerging under the pressure of Polish popular feeling involve not only more moderate aims than the original plans patterned upon the Soviet model but also a change of direction in favor of consumer goods, housing, and agriculture. The change of plans in Poland has upset the Soviet attempt to bind the satellite economies together into an integrated whole under the guidance of the Council for Economic Mutual Assistance.

In the eastern European trading area Poland's greater independence is weakening Moscow's ability to direct the bloc as a whole and is pushing the other partners toward greater independence. Moscow evidently is aware of this threat. The chronology of recent Soviet-Polish economic relations would seem to indicate that the Soviet Government has moved rapidly with specific economic measures to facilitate the change-over to the Gomułka program. But the scope of the measures also shows the extent to which the Polish economy had been integrated into the eastern system, and how little room for maneuvering had been left to the Polish Government to deal in western markets. Not much room has been gained, and having practically exhausted its reserves of industrial raw materials and without any appreciable amount of western foreign exchange, the Polish Government may find it difficult to break away from the Soviet bloc.

PUBLIC HEALTH AND WELFARE

THE COMMUNIST GOVERNMENT OF POLAND ASSUMES RESPONsibility for and control of practically all activities which bear directly or indirectly upon the welfare of the people. Such responsibility and control conform with the Communist theory and practice of government. They were made necessary, moreover, by conditions after World War II and by the interwar precedent of government operation of a widespread social security system.

Many of the interwar public welfare benefits and agencies were retained and some were expanded. All, however, were brought under the control of the central government and subordinated to the Party-defined goals for rapid economic development of the country. The general welfare of the people was given little consideration. As a result the standard of living between 1948 and 1957 remained at a level little better than the barely adequate level of the interwar period.

The state of health is poorer and the standards of medical care are lower in Poland today than in western European countries, but marked improvements have been made since the end of World War II. In 1945 disease was widespread—dysentery, typhoid, and typhus in epidemic proportion. Already inadequate numbers of physicians and dentists had been greatly reduced by German extermination policies and by war casualties. Most sanitary facilities had been destroyed or crippled. Wartime living conditions and the starvation diet imposed by German policy had seriously undermined the health of the surviving population.

While the German retreat was still going on, the Polish authorities set out to promote a system of medical care capable of controlling disease and improving the health of the people. These goals continued to be a major concern of the government during the years of reconstruction. Considerable assistance was given by UNRRA, UNICEF, and private organizations outside the country and by the time the reconstruction period was officially declared ended in 1948 most of the emergency needs had been met, but major health problems remained.

Today, the nutritional level has at least reached the point of caloric adequacy. The diet is still lacking, however, in protein, vitamins, and variety. The death rate from all causes has declined to 11 per 1,000 in the towns, and infant mortality has also declined. Both rates are lower than they were in 1938 but considerably higher than in other countries. Tuberculosis and venereal diseases continue to present serious health problems. Sanitary facilities are being slowly extended and the people are being instructed in personal and community hygiene. Medical care, though inadequate, is more widely available than before the war.

Since 1950 the health system has been centralized along Soviet lines and made subject to over-all planning and control by the government and the Party. All medical institutions were taken over and all medical personnel became at least part-time employees of the state. The government viewed the provision of medical care as a means of increasing labor productivity rather than an end in itself. The health program has been hampered by inadequate funds, bureaucratic inefficiency, poorly trained and insufficient personnel.

The Gomułka government seems to be fully aware of the shortcomings of the present system and has promised corrective measures. Increased funds have been budgeted for public health. Reorganization and decentralization of the system have begun, and physicians are being given more independence. Pay and allowances of medical personnel are to be increased and the quality of training improved. Constraints of ideology upon medical research and practice are to be removed.

Such steps have long been desired by the medical profession and the public. But really significant improvement of the health services requires long-term investments and depends on improvement of the general economic situation. The standard of living is still so low that contagious diseases related to malnutrition cannot be effectively controlled. The eradication of many intestinal infections depends on better housing conditions as well as on improved sanitation, control of the carriers of infection, and increased use of vaccination and inoculation.

The Gomułka government came into power in 1956 with the support of a people whose tolerance of sacrifice, deprivation, and grueling work had worn thin. The new regime promised that the economy would be reorganized so that the people would receive greater

rewards for their labor, but although it has initiated actions designed
to raise the standard of living, the people remain far from satisfied

Agencies and Controls

During the interwar period many agencies were drawn into participation in public welfare activities—government ministries, organizations
of local government, business enterprises, trade unions, and various
citizens organizations. This kind of participation continues but under
the Communist government the activities of such agencies are defined
and supervised by the central authorities—a shift in pattern particularly
noticeable in regard to the trade unions and private organizations
The unions are restricted in the programs of assistance they can develop
for their membership and are required to perform certain functions
which they did not engage in during the interwar years (see chap
12). The private organizations are now independent in name only
and membership in them has ceased to be voluntary. For example
Caritas, the influential and widely known Roman Catholic charitable
organization, has been nationalized, and the Red Cross has become
in effect, a subsidiary of the government health agencies rather than
a cooperating agency. Moreover, the private agencies have been transformed into organizations for mass participation.

The Ministry of Labor and Social Welfare, the Ministry of Education, and the Ministry of Health handle the social welfare responsibilities of the central government. In general, they provide direction,
supervision, and the financial assistance beyond the means of the
operating agencies. The state provides complete financial support for
such special groups as veterans, civilian victims of war and of the
German occupation, and those suffering from such diseases as tuberculosis and venereal diseases. Industrial ministries are responsible
through their social divisions for promoting and supervising such
activities and programs as nurseries, canteens, recreation halls and
general recreation, housing, and the like; the factories under their
jurisdiction are responsible for providing many of these facilities for
their employees.

Local governments—up to and including the county level—are
the basic units for administration of social welfare and their public
welfare divisions coordinate their activities with those of semigovernmental agencies. Such activities have included communal feeding stations; distribution of clothing, fuel, and the like; provision of tools
and working materials; training and rehabilitation; day nurseries;
"mother and child" stations for counseling; material aid and direct
financial aid. County organizations provide residential institutions for

mothers and infants, orphaned children, the aged, and handicapped adults.

Trade unions conduct such activities as the distribution to their members of foodstuffs and other basic necessities; they promote various cultural, recreational, and social programs, provide vacation facilities, and give legal advice.

"Citizens organizations," provide social welfare assistance either as a primary or subsidiary function. They may operate children's homes, hostels, theaters, clinics, kindergartens, holiday camps and the like. The Polish Red Cross gives first-aid training to workers and youth; since 1955 it has been the official agency in negotiations with the West German Red Cross for the repatriation of Polish and German nationals and it is active in the resettlement of Poles who have returned. The Polish Women's League operates travelers' aid stations and homes for mothers and children. These and other semigovernmental organizations provide or operate all summer camps and clubs (*świetlice*), most playgrounds, nearly all the vacation homes, and a sizable proportion of the other public welfare installations in Poland.

Social Security

The present social security system is an extension of the program of the interwar Polish Government, which was one of the most comprehensive in Europe. It includes payment of benefits for sickness and maternity, industrial accidents, disability, old age and death, unemployment; it also pays family allowances, a new feature. During the interwar period the cost of benefits was shared by the employer and the employee, it is now borne entirely by the employer and the state, no direct payments being made by the worker.

Social insurance is compulsory for manual and white-collar workers, including those in both socialized and private industry, agricultural workers (covered by legislation in the 1920's but excluded in the 1930's), and collective farmers. As in the past, private businessmen and independent farmers are not covered. A much larger proportion of the population is covered by social insurance than before the war, largely because of shifts in the occupational structure of the country; the rural population, which is not covered by the law, has greatly declined, while eligible urban population has increased (see chap. 3).

Despite many similarities to the prewar system and certain nominal gains for the workers, the social security system has been thoroughly transformed to serve the government's economic needs and goals. The contributions required from private employers are larger than those from socialized industry. Workers in high-priority industries receive greater benefits. Benefit rates for manual and white-collar workers are now uniform, but, as before the war, those of the intelligentsia group receive additional benefits. The government may withhold benefits from any individual who lacks "political reliability," and special *ad hoc* arrangements are made by the Council of Ministers for individuals who have made contributions of "special merit to the cause of People's Poland."

ADMINISTRATION AND FINANCING

The interwar social security system lacked uniformity, largely because of the earlier differences in legislation and practice in the Austrian, German, and Russian areas. The cost of social security was shared by the insured and the employers, with the proportional contribution varying with the type of benefit. During the German occupation social security benefits were administered as part of the policy of discrimination against the Polish people. Germans received the full benefits of the Polish laws; Poles received only part of the benefits and at a reduced scale; and Jews were nominally entitled only to medical care and medicines. In actual operation, however, few Poles received benefits.

After the war the interwar system of social insurance was reinstated with two major changes—the assumption by the employer of the entire cost and the addition of family benefits. In 1948 the administration of all benefits was placed in the hands of the Ministry of Labor and Social Welfare. Gradually the system was remodeled through a series of decrees until finally the piecemeal revisions were consolidated and complete transformation of the system was accomplished in the Old-Age, Invalidity, and Survivors' Insurance Decree of June 25, 1954.

The general effect of the new law was to centralize the administration of all social insurance, unify the regulations, and remove distinctions between the white-collar worker and the laborer. The coverage applies to employees of the government, of government-owned and private enterprises, and of cooperative establishments; students in Party and professional schools, provided they were employed before enrollment; apprentices and workers in home industries. Pensions of employees of the armed forces, police, public security agencies, prison guards and their families, and employees of the Polish State Railways in certain categories (probably the security guards) are regulated by separate provisions. Persons employed in private enterprise who are related by blood or marriage to the owner are insured only against sickness and accident.

In February 1955 the trade unions were given responsibility for the administration of social insurance "with the exception of matters relating to pensions." Though details of the jurisdiction are not spelled out in the law, it presumably gives the unions direction of short-term benefits, such as medical and maternity payments and family allowances, and perhaps the certification of the eligibility of workers for pensions—a function performed after 1949 by the Social Insurance Institute, which was now abolished.

The administration of pensions was placed in the hands of the Ministry of Labor and Social Welfare, which works through the presidia of the provincial, district, and local people's councils. The rates of social insurance contributions of employers are to be fixed by the Council of Ministers, with the advice of the Central Council of Trade Unions, so as to cover the cost of operations. As has been the case since 1918, pension rates are established by law.

Contributions to the social security program have represented approximately 15 percent of the payroll of nationalized industry and between 21 and 30 percent of the payroll of private industry.

OLD AGE AND DISABILITY PENSIONS

Under the law of June 25, 1954 the pension and disability rate varies according to two categories of employment: (1) that which is underground or dangerous to the health of the employee, and (2) all other employment. The categorization of each occupation is left to the discretion of the Council of Ministers. Total employment time and the length of continuous employment in one establishment are also criteria for determining retirement time and the payment of extra allowances for both old age and disability benefits.

Retirement age, pension rate, and disability payments are based upon three categories of incapacity: (I) invalids completely incapacitated and requiring constant attention of another person; (II) invalids completely incapacitated but not requiring constant attention; and (III) those whose ability to work either in their profession or at a full-time job has been reduced but who are able to work part time or intermittently at less strenuous tasks.

Pensions are calculated on the basis of the average monthly cash pay received during the twelve months before retirement or disability, or a minimum of 1,200 złotys. Family allowances, which permanently affect the person's income, are included in the computation. It appears that the value of provided living quarters and of bonuses, premiums, and payments for production exceeding the basic norms used to be excluded from the income calculation. Since base pay is often a relatively small part of the total salary, the exclusion of extras greatly reduced the value of the pensions. This fact was recognized by the

Gomułka government, and, according to new regulations which are retroactive to July 1, 1956, remunerations in kind, such as allocations and accomodations, are now included in the base of calculations. Apparently bonuses and the like are still excluded, but there has been some effort to revise base pay schedules in order to reduce the high proportion of extras in the total wage. The two years preceding application for pension may now be considered in calculating average monthly rates.

The general effect of the regulations is to provide an extra incentive for workers in those industries such as mining and metallurgy which the government is especially interested in developing. The premiums for uninterrupted work are designed to reduce labor turnover, which has been a serious problem, and the requirements for length of work experience and the strict categorization of disability, with sharply decreasing benefits, exert considerable pressure toward keeping workers on the job to the limits of their capability for as long a time as possible.

Workers are eligible for old age pensions when they reach retirement age provided they are still employed or were released from their jobs at their own request not more than 2 years previously, and provided that the period of employment required for eligibility—25 years for men and 20 years for women—has been completed. If a worker reaches retirement age before completing the required period of employment, he becomes eligible for pension only when the employment period is completed. Retirement age for workers in employment category 1 ("dangerous, underground, or unhealthy occupations") is 60 for men and 55 for women; in category 2 (all other occupations) it is 65 and 60 respectively. It has been proposed that the retirement age be lowered, but so far as can be determined this action has not been taken. The monthly pension rate was formerly 50 percent of the calculated wage base for workers in category 1 and 40 percent for those in category 2; in September 1956 they were raised slightly, and a minimum of 260 złotys was established. The precise amount of the increase is not known, but the government admits that payments are still inadequate.

Workers disabled by accident or disease are paid disability pensions at rates varying from 30 to 100 percent of basic earnings, depending upon the degree of disability, its cause, and the category of employment (see Table 30). For group I disability, 300 złotys is the minimum pension. Eligibility for pensions for disability caused by nonindustrial accident or disease is dependent upon a period of employment which varies with age. One year of work is required for workers between 18 and 20 years of age, 2 for those between 20 and 22,

for those between 22 and 25, and 4 for those between 25 and
. Workers over the age of 30 must have worked for 5 years during
e 10 years immediately preceding cessation of employment. No
h requirements are needed to obtain benefits for job-connected
abilities.

RVIVORS' PENSIONS

vivors' pensions are paid to qualified dependents of workers who
 as the result of industrial accident or disease; they are also paid
en death is from other causes if the deceased had fulfilled the
rk-time requirements for receipt of a disability or old age pension
was receiving one. The basic monthly rate of the pension is 30
cent of the calculated wage base. An increment of 65 złotys is
led if there are two dependents, and 145 złotys if three or more.
the worker died as the result of work-connected accident or disease
additional 10 percent of the base pension is paid.

NSION SUPPLEMENTS

ecial supplements in addition to the regular allowances are paid
nonemployed pensioners (old age or disabled) and to nonemployed
ipients of survivors' pensions for children and other qualified de-
adents. They are comparable to the family allowances for workers
l are paid at the same rate. For each year of manual work in
ning establishments, pensioners are granted monthly supplements of
ween 1.25 and 11 złotys depending upon the cause and degree of
ability and the amount of the calculated wage base. Widows also
eive extra amounts for each year their husbands had done such
rk. Uninterrupted work since the liberation also provides the basis
 increments of 10 to 15 percent of pension for nonindustrial acci-
at or disease disability. Scientific workers are entitled to monthly
sion supplements of 50 percent of the pension rate, less supple-
nts for dependents, but not to exceed 100 percent of the pension
e. Special, unspecified supplements may be paid to both old age
l disability pensioners who have been awarded high distinctions
the government.

NERAL GRANTS

on the death of a worker covered by social insurance a funeral
nt is made, equal to seven times his weekly wage. In case of the
th of a pensioner, the grant is equal to three times the monthly
sion, minus the supplement for children. Upon the death of a
rker's dependent the funeral grant is equal to three times the in-
ed's weekly wage, while at the death of a dependent of a pensioner
 amount is 100 percent of the calculated wage base.

FAMILY ALLOWANCES

In 1947 payment of special allowances for dependents was added the prewar social security benefits. Since then the size of the gran has been changed a number of times; effective April 1957, they we raised to 165 złotys for the second child, 295 złotys for the thi and somewhat more for each subsequent child. At the same time t qualifying period was amended; instead of being required to wo 3 months at a job before becoming eligible, workers will now recei family allowances for every month during which they have work at least 20 days. Periods of sickness and training are counted as wor ing days.

UNEMPLOYMENT INSURANCE

So far as can be determined, the system of unemployment insuran operates today largely as it did when it was first enacted in 19. except that the contributions are now paid entirely by the employ In order to qualify for unemployment payments a worker must ha been insured for 26 weeks during the year, must be available f work, and must report to a government employment office for plac ment. He is then entitled to benefits of 30 percent of his avera weekly earnings, plus 5 to 20 percent additional according to t number of dependents.

SICKNESS AND MATERNITY INSURANCE

Complete, free medical care is provided by law for all workers a pensioners covered by social insurance. In addition, a worker w is forced to be absent from work because of illness is eligible for ca benefits amounting to 70 percent of his wages. If a worker witho dependents is hospitalized, he receives 15 percent of his wages; a m with dependents gets 50 percent of his wages. Miners' allowances somewhat higher; intellectual workers receive full pay, as they ha since before the war. Such payments last for 26 weeks (39 weeks tuberculosis); if the worker cannot return to work within that ti he becomes eligible for a disability pension. To be eligible for t cash benefits the worker must have been insured for 4 weeks prec ing the illness or for a minimum of 26 weeks during the precedi 12 months. In comparison to the prewar system, there are no ti limits on the medical care given to workers or their dependents, a the cash benefits are somewhat higher. The work time required qualify for cash benefits and the length of time they are paid acc with the original law.

Maternity benefits include full wages payable for 6 weeks bef and 6 weeks after confinement. A nursing allowance equal to liter of milk a day for 12 weeks is paid after the regular cash benefit ceases.

Diet and Disease

In 1938 average daily food consumption provided about 3,000 calories a day. In 1947 it fell to a bare subsistence level of 1,900 or less. In 1957, according to an official announcement, it had increased to an estimated 3,000 to 3,500 calories.

As in the interwar period, the Polish diet is high in starches and low in protein. Some vitamins and minerals are supplied by fruits and vegetables, which, however, are eaten only in season. Relatively little canned or frozen food is available in urban areas; food is preserved by drying, smoking, and salting. Peasants and most urban workers eat much the same food. Potatoes are the staple of the diet. Grains—predominantly rye and wheat, with some millet—are next in importance. Both potatoes and grain in some form are served at all meals—as soup, dumplings, noodles, porridge, or bread. Black rye bread is the usual fare; white wheat bread is generally reserved for very special occasions. Very small quantities of beef, pork, poultry, or fish are consumed, usually added to one of the starchy dishes. Evidently the peasants use little milk except in the form of sour cream and cheese. In urban areas milk is almost entirely reserved for the children and is in short supply. Eggs are generally reserved for special occasions. Vegetables, such as beets, cabbage, onions, and tomatoes, and fruits make up a small proportion of the diet.

The major health problems in Poland today are tuberculosis and venereal diseases, particularly syphilis. Since the war, health authorities have focused attention on them by campaigns which provide information and compulsory examination and treatment, as well as by expansion of hospital and treatment facilities, drugs, and medical staff. According to the Polish press, the tuberculosis infection rate has been reduced since 1953 but the mortality rate remains higher than in any other European country.

Before World War II the Polish Government, with the help of the United States, the League of Nations, and the League of Red Cross Societies, made considerable progress in controlling such diseases as smallpox, cholera, relapsing fever, dysentery, and malaria, but Poland still had in 1939 a high incidence of typhoid, paratyphoid, diphtheria, and epidemic meningitis, and the highest tuberculosis rate in Europe.

During the German occupation health conditions deteriorated rapidly. Semistarvation, the destruction of the public health system and sanitary facilities, and the concentration of large numbers of people in ghettos and concentration camps produced conditions highly conducive to the rapid spread of contagious diseases. Dysentery, typhus, and malaria reappeared in epidemic proportions. In 1945 there were 340 cases of typhoid fever per 100,000 population, an extremely high rate. The incidence of tuberculosis and venereal diseases, especially syphilis, also was high. Other infectious diseases were present at rates which made the development of major epidemics a distinct possibility.

Before the fighting ended the Lublin government had organized a health ministry and appointed an epidemic control commission. Through the commission's efforts, supported by assistance from UNRRA—which provided personnel and equipment for treatment and DDT for louse control—the typhus threat was brought under control within six months. Improvements in sanitation and fly control greatly reduced the incidence of dysentery. Nevertheless an epidemic of typhoid fever far worse than the one after World War I developed, but a large-scale vaccination campaign greatly reduced both the number of cases and the mortality rate. Malaria was largely brought under control by mosquito eradication and drug therapy.

The postwar government has released only infrequent and incomplete statistics on the incidence of diseases. Smallpox has been largely controlled through compulsory vaccination, but occasional outbreaks have been reported by the press. Outbreaks of endemic typhoid, typhus, and dysentery are common. Trachoma was known to be a serious problem during the early postwar years; it probably still exists.

Outbreaks of poliomyelitis have been reported within the last few years. Experimental production of vaccines began in 1955, and large-scale vaccination is to begin in the fall of 1957.

Diphtheria, scarlet fever, measles, and chicken pox are fairly common but do not constitute a major problem. Influenza and pneumonia are also reported. Brucellosis is prevalent; many of the cattle are infected and even in large urban areas pasteurization of milk is very limited. There is also some indication of an increase in heart disease and the psychoneuroses.

Little is known about the present state of sanitary facilities. Legal standards for food handling, water purity, etc., exist, and the government has sought to educate the people in the principles of sanitation. Following World War II, only 438 waterworks existed in the whole country—to serve a population of 23.6 million persons, over 7 million of whom lived in 1,091 cities and towns. Only about three fourths of the waterworks were at that time in actual operation, and even when operating to full capacity they fell far short of meeting full requirements. The Ministry of Health reported that 73 percent of the urban population was served by sewer systems. UNRRA estimated that construction of needed waterworks and sewers over a 45-year period at existing price levels would cost some $365 million in the cities and $400 million in rural areas.

Considerable improvement was effected by the removal of debris and the general reconstruction efforts of the first postwar years, but insufficient water supplies, shortages of sewage installations, and bad sanitary conditions in production enterprises and food shops continue to be major health problems.

Organization of Health Services

A 1928 decree outlining the functions of medical establishments and a 1939 law on the functions of the public health service are still the basic health laws of the country. The organizational changes made since World War II along Soviet lines have simply centralized the control and operation of the system in the hands of the government. The Polish health system differs, however, from the Soviet system in two significant ways: medical coverage is not universal (only about half of the population being eligible for free medical care), and the private practice of medicine and dentistry has never been prohibited. Today private physicians are being encouraged to establish their own organizations for group or cooperative practice.

ADMINISTRATION

The Ministry of Health controls all phases of the medical care system, including training and assignment of medical personnel, building and operation of hospitals, clinics, and first aid stations, manufacture and distribution of drugs and pharmaceuticals. According to a resolution of the Council of Ministers on January 10, 1953, amended in March of the same year, the Ministry was "temporarily" organized into three main divisions: the Cabinet of the Ministry; the State Sanitary Inspectorate; and five central boards—the Central Executive Board for Pharmacies, the Board of Trade for Medical Equipment, the Executive Board for Health Resorts, the Board for Production of Serums and Vaccines, and the Board for Disinfectants, Insecticides, and Rat Extermination. So far as can be determined, this arrangement is still in effect.

The Cabinet of the Ministry has 13 sections. Medical care is supervised and administered through 4 of them: Anti-Epidemic; Prevention and Healing; Combating Tuberculosis; Mother and Child Care, which has jurisdiction over nurseries, kindergartens, and school health programs. Education of medical personnel and the general public is the responsibility of the independent Section of Sanitary Enlightenment and of the Division of Education. Personnel matters, wages, and budgeted expenditures are handled through other divisions under the Cabinet. There is also a Division of Supply and Pharmacy, but the exact distinction between its responsibilities and those of the Central Executive Board of Pharmacies is not clear; apparently it is in charge of the operation of pharmacies and the distribution, rather than manufacture, of drugs and medical equipment.

The Ministry has an advisory Scientific Council "for the purpose of giving a socialistic direction to scientific investigations in the field of medicine." Its members are appointed by the Ministry from outstanding men in the medical profession. The Secretariat of the Council is part of the permanent organization of the Cabinet of the Ministry. The Council plans and evaluates medical research and advises the Ministry on personnel training, planning, and budgeting.

The State Sanitary Inspectorate has wide and detailed functions; it promulgates and enforces standards of hygiene and sanitation and levies penalties for violations. Its jurisdiction covers all levels of provincial and local administration, individual plants and workshops, and ships. Regulation of railroad sanitation, however, is under the direction of the Ministry of Railroads in consultation with the Ministry of Health. Substantively, the regulations of the Sanitary Inspectorate apply in such areas as food handling and preservation, sanitary standards of workshops, water pollution, housing, and disease control. Its major emphasis is disease prevention, and it directs the anti-epidemic action of all divisions of the health service. The Inspectorate is also responsible for the popularization of principles of health and disease prevention.

Local health organizations came under the control of the central government in 1950. In general, the internal organization of provincial and local health sections follows that of the Ministry, with adaptations according to the size of the jurisdiction and its particular health problems. As part of the National Councils and other local government organizations, they are subject to the control and direction not only of the Ministry of Health but also of other governmental agencies. Since budgeting, planning, employment of medical personnel, operation of hospitals, clinics, and other institutions are all governed by central directives and plans, the local health units have little administrative autonomy.

In addition to these regular agencies, permanent Committees of Sanitary Orderliness are attached to the presiding bodies of provincial and local administration. They mobilize the local population for health and sanitation activities and carry out "sanitary enlighten-ment" through press, radio, films, lectures and informal talks in workshops, schools, lecture rooms, and housing units.

MEDICAL CARE

During the interwar period a fairly extensive system of public hospitals was operated by central, provincial, and local governments; private hospitals were operated by individuals and organizations. Under the revised law of 1948 the Ministry of Health was given the power to expropriate the private institutions, and today few, if any, exist. Most hospitals are operated by the Ministry of Health or by provincial and local governments. Some are directed by the social insurance authorities. Such government agencies as the armed services, the political police, and the Ministry of Transportation operate hospitals for their own personnel and dependents. It is reported that military hospitals are now admitting civilian patients.

As in the Soviet Union, there are "open" hospitals, to which all people are admitted, and "closed" hospitals, which admit only the workers employed by the operating agency and their families. Within the "closed" system there are hospitals which cater only to the upper political and governmental groups and those individuals particularly favored by the Party. It is said that these institutions are far superior to those in the "open" system.

OUTPATIENT TREATMENT. Outpatient treatment is given for the most part in circuit health centers—the lowest units of the medical care system—and county health centers, which supplement the circuit centers with more specialized treatment. Both are under the administration of county units of local governments, but a mu-nicipality may be exempt from county jurisdiction and then become responsible for its own health centers. The health centers are also re-sponsible for disease prevention, medical supervision of preschool and school-age children, maternity care, and general matters of hygiene.

CLINICS AND CLINICAL HOSPITALS. Those hospitals and outpatient centers which are used for training of professional personnel are called clinical hospitals or clinics. Along with their training functions, they also serve the general public.

PRIVATE MEDICAL PRACTICE. With the exception of those who are unable to carry a full-time practice because of age or disability, all physicians and dentists are required to practice at least a minimum number of hours per day in some agency of the state medical service. They are permitted to carry on additional private practice from their homes. Since 1953 doctors and dentists have organized cooperative clinics in which they have combined their private practices at reduced fees. In the spring of 1957 the government began a limited encouragement of these cooperatives.

MOTHER AND CHILD CARE. Special emphasis is placed upon medical care for mothers and children. Shortly after the re-establishment of the Polish Government an educational program in this field was launched with the assistance of UNRRA and UNICEF. Special hospitals have been established for mothers and children. Most of the larger clinics and health centers have separate obstetrical and pediatric departments. Nurseries and kindergartens for infants and children of working mothers are operated under the supervision of the Ministry of Health.

HEALTH RESORTS. The government has made much of the development of health resorts at the sea, in the mountains, and at medicinal springs. They include special hospitals—such as tuberculosis sanitaria and rest homes for convalescents—under the jurisdiction of the health authorities, and vacation homes and hotels operated by trade unions (see chap. 12).

HEALTH EDUCATION AND FIRST AID. Health education and first-aid training are directed by the health authorities but largely carried on through various other agencies. The Polish Red Cross has a major part in organizing first-aid stations and in training Red Cross members and nonmembers in first-aid techniques. Youth groups, trade unions, and women's organizations also give instruction in personal hygiene, farm sanitation, child care, and the like.

PAYMENT FOR MEDICAL CARE. By law, all workers and employees in both the socialized and private sectors of the economy, and their dependents, are covered by compulsory social insurance paid entirely by the employer. There is no time limit upon the provision of free medical care and hospitalization for either the worker or his family. Drugs are also provided free or at very low cost—reported to be about 10 percent of the retail price.

Those eligible for the free medical care may, if they so desire, consult private physicians at their own expense. Persons not covered by social insurance must pay the going rates of private practitioners and standard charges for hospital care.

PERSONNEL. The training of all medical personnel is under the direction of the Ministry of Health. Nurses, technicians, and midwives are sent to secondary-level vocational schools; physicians, dentists, and some technicians attend institutions at the university level. The great need for medical personnel of all kinds in the years just after World War II led to the system of training *felczerzy,* modeled upon the *feldsher* system in the USSR. These physicians' assistants, for whom there were no counterparts in the interwar period, received training midway between that for a doctor and that for a nurse. They were expected to work as assistants to physicians, caring for simple conditions on their own but referring more complicated diagnosis and treatment to the physician. In May 1957 the Ministry of Health announced that the training of *felczerzy* would be discontinued. Those already trained are to be allowed to enter medical schools in the second year of the full course, and no entrance requirements will be required of outstanding students.

Practically all medical personnel are required by law to work at least part-time in state health institutions. The choice of a location for practice is regulated in part by the availability of positions in those institutions. The Ministry of Health has also established a system of norms designed to assure efficient distribution of medical personnel throughout the country. The norms were developed by consultation with the health authorities of both the National Councils and organizations of health service employees; they limit the number of physicians, dentists, *felczerzy,* nurses, technicians, and midwives who may practice in a given area. The practitioner must notify the Ministry of his intention to establish practice in a certain place; permission may be given or denied on the basis of the norms. If there are a number of applicants in excess of the norm for a particular area, competitions may be held to determine the selection.

Under a 1950 law, which was to have expired in January 1955, the Ministry of Health was empowered to draft physicians, dentists, and pharmacists away from their regular practice and place of residence for two years of service in communities or on circuits where the lack of personnel created a serious threat to the lives of the population. In such cases housing was to be provided, the costs of moving paid by the state, and the right to return to the former practice or position guaranteed. Whether this temporary measure expired on the date provided or was extended is not known.

Until early 1957 graduates of all types of medical training schools were required to work at an assigned position for three years following graduation. Penalties for refusal to accept either the assigned area of practice or the draft service have been severe.

Salaries of medical personnel, regulated by the government, are very low. In April 1957 the Minister of Health reported to the *Sejm* that the salary of a doctor working a 7-hour day was between 900 and 1,680 złotys a month; the higher sum was paid to a doctor in practice for 15 years. This was only slightly above the pay for nurses and other medical personnel. (The average pay of the Polish wage earner in 1955 was slightly over 1,000 złotys a month.)

EQUIPMENT AND SUPPLIES. Production of medical equipment and drugs is under the direction of the Ministry of Health. Considerable emphasis has been placed upon the establishment of factories, but the problems have been great. Practically all supplies and equipment had been destroyed or confiscated by the Germans by 1944. UNRRA assistance in medical supplies amounted to $28.7 million; UNICEf and other organizations also provided assistance. It is reported that in the mid 1950's only 20 percent of the requirements for pharmaceuticals were being met by domestic production, the remainder through imports. High duties were placed upon drugs sent from abroad to individuals. The duties have recently been lowered, and many sought-after medicines are now being sent in packages from friends and relatives abroad. Legal outlets for them have been established, but the sales policies do not ensure regular availability; consequently drugs find their way to the black market.

Operation of Health Services

The shortage of hospitals after the war was acute; despite the great improvement, facilities still are very inadequate.

According to official statistics, the number of hospital beds has increased markedly since 1938. The figures for 1955 seem highly inflated, however, in the light of a statement by the Minister of Health, in the spring of 1957, that there were 26,000 hospital beds available —45 per 10,000 population. (In 1955 there were approximately 64 beds per 10,000 population in the USSR; in 1954 there were 98 per 10,000 in the United States.)

During the last few years the Polish press has published much official and private criticism of hospital conditions. Although there have also been reports of hospitals that are very well-equipped, adequately staffed, and efficiently operated, it seems undoubtedly true that most are far below standard, especially in rural areas.

There had been a chronic shortage of physicians, dentists, and nurses in Poland for decades before World War II—just as there had been in general throughout the world. The shortage became especially acute in Poland during and after the war: practically all the Jewish doctors, of whom there were many before the war, were killed.

An increase in the number of medical schools, a shorter course of study, and the official effort to expand the system of health care have brought some improvement. But the number of qualified medical personnel still lags considerably behind that of the USSR, western Europe, or the United States. In 1955 there were about 6.7 physicians, 2.5 dentists, and 17.9 nurses per 10,000 population. The Minister of Health announced in the spring of 1957 that there were about 20,500 doctors in practice—about 1 physician to care for approximately 1,350 persons. (In the United States in 1954 the ratio of physicians to population was 1 to 735, and there were 359 dentists and 244 graduate nurses per 10,000 population.)

The distribution of medical personnel varies greatly among the various provinces, and even more widely between urban and rural areas. Compulsory assignments have not succeeded in correcting this unevenness of distribution. The lack of housing, particularly family housing, is one of the most important factors in the failure to improve rural and small town medical service; some young physicians who have reported to their assigned posts are said to have been forced to return home because they were unable to find living accommodations even after as much as a year. Another factor is the greater numbers of people in the rural areas that each doctor must serve, with facilities and equipment much less adequate than in the cities. Moreover, the lack of public transportation and the great difficulties (priorities and cost) in obtaining automobiles often make it impossible for the doctor to cover his required circuit of health centers.

The low pay, long hours of work, and bureaucratic control have had an extremely deleterious effect upon the quality of service and upon the morale and morals of the medical profession. Many a doctor is forced to hold more than one position in the socialized health institutions and to take private patients in order to support himself and his family. He is required to see a stated number of patients every day in the clinics and health centers and is unable, therefore, to give each proper attention. He must also fill out large numbers of forms and reports.

One of the most difficult tasks assigned to the physician is that of reducing absenteeism in the labor force. Doctors' certificates are required for most excused absences, and there is a quota on the number which a physician may issue in a given time. Thus the physician is caught between the regulations and the needs of his patients. Although house calls are not generally made unless the patient has a fever of 102 degrees, one of the purposes of the call is to determine whether or not the reported illness is real. A doctor can issue a certificate for ten days of absence from work, a specialist for fifteen days, and the head of a health center one for as long as thirty days.

Government regulations also impinge to a certain degree upon the type of treatment that a doctor may prescribe. For example, psychiatric treatment must be based upon the theories of Pavlov, as it has been in the Soviet Union. Officially, methods which have become standard in western Europe and the United States are forbidden, but it is reported that such limitations are simply ignored by many psychiatrists.

Officials and the public often complain that physicians and other medical personnel are inadequately trained. The shortening of the course of study of the medical vocational schools, in order to increase the number of graduates, has forced the partially trained to assume duties which should be performed by professionals with greater skill and knowledge.

The government has taken some steps to remove the difficulties under which medical personnel has been operating. Pay increases are recognized to be essential, but no definite action on them has been taken as yet. The decentralization of medical administration is to include some lessening of the paper work now required and of the administrative controls over performance of duties. Housing is to be provided for doctors taking up practice in rural areas. The training period for physicians has been extended to five years, and the new curriculum is to include, in addition to professional courses, humanistic, social, and philosophical studies. Time is to be provided for independent research and study. Medical authorities feel that medical schools should cease to be advanced vocational schools and should become "academic schools" in the fullest sense. To that purpose it has been suggested that they be transferred from the jurisdiction of the Ministry of Health to that of the Ministry of Higher Education. Standards for admission to schools of nursing are also to be raised, and the direction of the schools is to be placed in qualified professional hands. The number of applicants accepted by the medical schools is to be reduced so that greater stress may be placed upon the quality of training.

It has also been proposed that the disbanded doctor guilds be re-established as independent organizations, in the hope that they would improve medical ethics and provide for an exchange of professional information. The medical profession feels that such activities are not possible under the present trade union organization—which includes all levels of public health workers from hospital janitors to chief surgeons. The proposed guild organization would also emphasize professional competency rather than political qualifications.

The weekly official organ of the Public Health Service, *Służba Zdrowia,* made the following appraisal of the condition of Polish health services on January 13, 1957.

It would be senseless to close one's eyes to the ruins of the majority of the hospital buildings, to the crowding in old stone buildings in which various clinics are located, to the lack of apparatus, instruments, and equipment. All this, in connection with very low wages of doctors and nurses, has a fatal effect on the quality of the services, and sometimes even makes it impossible to render them.

All nonindustrial construction, including medical installations, has had a relatively low priority in postwar economic expansion. Often, additional hospital beds are created by overcrowding already crowded wards and utilizing other space in existing buildings. Although some equipment is now manufactured in Poland, much of it still must be imported. The local items are often reported to be imperfect and of inferior quality.

Locally produced drugs and pharmaceuticals, such as penicillin, are reported to be inferior and to contain impurities. The tuberculosis vaccines which were used in the 1955 inoculation campaign produced severe reactions and a number of deaths; the insufficiency of X-ray equipment has made it impossible to carry out the proposed tuberculosis-prevention plan for periodic examination of the whole population.

State pharmacies are often unable to fill prescriptions because of the unavailability of the necessary drugs. Medical authorities strictly limit doctors in the use of drugs that are in short supply. An official source stated that in 1957 only 75 percent of the demand for foreign medicines would be met.

Consumer Goods and Services

COMMODITIES

In 1945 the productive organization of Poland was in complete chaos—supplies of consumer goods were nonexistent, and the population was in dire need of basic articles of food, clothing, and shelter. Through the concentrated efforts of the government and the people, with considerable assistance from UNRRA and other outside organizations, the situation improved during the years until 1948, when the government's plan for accelerated expansion and development of industry gave the production of producers goods priority over the production of consumer goods.

As a result of this policy the Polish consumer has since been faced with high prices, low quality, and chronic shortages. The per capita consumption of basic items of food and clothing has shown very little change since 1949. The consumption of grains—a dietary staple—increased less than three kilograms (about six and a half pounds) between 1949 and 1954. Meat and fat consumption increased slightly more. Cigarette consumption has risen considerably, but average consumption is barely more than three cigarettes per day.

Shopping at state stores has always meant waiting in long lines. (It is reported that some individuals make a business of standing in line for others.) Although there have been several highly publicized cuts in state store prices since 1950, the cost of basic items has not been appreciably reduced. Prices on the free market have varied in accordance with supply and demand (see chap 16). With a monthly wage of little more than 1,000 złotys, it is clear that the average worker can barely manage to purchase absolute necessities.

In October 1956 the government announced the latest series of selective price cuts—15 to 40 percent reductions on some industrial articles, cotton textiles, footwear, "numerous" household items, and some foods. Prices on some other items, among them furniture, paper, newspapers, and periodicals, have been raised as part of the current attempt to establish a pricing policy which will enable all industries to operate at a profit instead of on partial subsidy (see chap. 15).

Although enough food has been available during the last few years to maintain an acceptable caloric level, the average diet is still predominantly starch and almost completely lacking in variety. Clothing has been expensive and of poor quality and workmanship. Official sources have criticized clothing producers for discontinuing production of better-quality merchandise and concentrating upon inferior materials and garments—in sharp contrast to the former textile production of the Lodz manufacturers, which, even before World War I, was known world wide for its excellent quality. Except in special stores restricted to the use of elite groups—and abolished after October 1956—nonessential items and luxury goods such as watches, radios, electrical appliances, certain foodstuffs, high-quality clothing, jewelry, and the like have been either prohibitive in price or nonexistent.

While warning the people again and again that improvements would be slow, the Gomułka government has revised the 1957 budget to include increased investment in facilities for the production of consumer goods. Decentralization of administration is designed to improve both production and distribution, and workers' councils are being urged to exercise ingenuity in putting unused productive capacity of their plants to the manufacture of consumer goods.

PUBLIC SERVICES

The production of electricity has more than doubled since 1938 but only a small proportion of it is used by domestic consumers. In 1955 per capita consumption in households was officially reported at 40.8 kilowatt hours, roughly the equivalent of one low-wattage light bulb burning for 2 hours daily. Only about 35 percent of the villages have been electrified. Although electricity is installed in most of the newer urban housing, it is probably insufficient for major electrical appliances. Such appliances in any case are difficult to purchase; it is reported that a refrigerator cost 3,000 złotys in 1956.

According to official figures (1955), of a total of 729 cities, 433 had a water network, 410 a sewer system, and only 236 a gas system. An entire city is rarely serviced, and few, if any villages have these facilities. Water is generally obtained in urban areas from communal wells or hydrants and in the countryside from lakes, streams, ponds, or individual or community wells. Little of the supply reaches the standard of potability required in the United States.

HOUSING

Housing constitutes one of the most critical problems in Poland today. It is not a new problem: during the interwar period industrialization and urbanization had already produced overcrowding in the cities; in the country it had been always rare for peasant dwellings to have more than two rooms and families were always large. Wartime destruction made the situation infinitely worse. The first postwar Minister of Reconstruction estimated that some 39 percent of all urban dwelling rooms, more than a sixth of all farmhouses, and many public buildings had been destroyed; 70 percent of Warsaw, 65 percent of Wroclaw, and 45 percent of Poznan lay in ruins. The reconstruction program of the new government at first gave priority to both essential industries and related living areas; after 1948, however, industry received by far the greater attention. Until 1949 most investment was concentrated upon the repair and reconstruction of the least damaged properties. After that time only enough new housing was actually constructed to assure uninterrupted production; efforts were made to provide in particular for such areas of new industrial development as Nowa Huta. New construction could not even meet normal replacement needs.

The last official comprehensive figures on housing are for 1950. There was an over-all average density of 1.54 persons per room, but 1-room dwellings housed, on the average, just under 3 persons. Any change in room density since 1950 has probably been slight. In June 1957 a Warsaw newspaper reported that thousands of inhabitants of the city were still living in squalor in ruined buildings, cellars, attics, sheds, and overcrowded barracks; that many inhabited structures were on the point of collapse; and that 2,500 married couples were compelled to live separately because they could not find accommodations. Congestion in rural areas is higher than in the cities—about 1.92 persons per room.

The Gomułka government has tried to step up the construction of housing. Planned investment in dwelling construction and allocation of credit funds for private construction have been increased. Allocation of housing and supervision of construction have been made the responsibility of local people's councils. Companies for production of building materials have been organized under the joint ownership of the state and groups of private engineers.

Improvement in the allocation and distribution of building materials to rural areas is receiving particular attention. The Ministry of Building has also been giving assistance and encouragement to the organization of firms for the production of building materials, "on the principle of state-private partnership." Many of the 25 to 40 such firms that have been organized are being directed by engineers and administrators formerly with the Central Boards. The firms will receive from the government raw materials and capital equipment for which they will pay in installments. The finished products will be sold en bloc to the Ministry of Building at state-set prices. The needs of other customers, including individual builders, may also be met, but in such cases the raw materials must be provided by the customer. Prefabricated, concrete units will be one of the most important items of production.

The administration and management of public housing, as well as control over cooperative housing, have been functions of the Ministry of Municipal Economy, which works through the people's councils on the local level. The Ministry sets generally low rental rates, varying somewhat according to the size of the city, neighborhood, type of structure, and the availability of utilities and services. Between 1951 and early 1957 it also established allocations and set norms for space allowances—formerly functions of the people's councils and now returned to them.

Norms for living space range from 5 to 12.5 square meters (6 to 15 square yards) per person. Extra space is allowed people who work at home, doctors, lawyers, writers, the chronically ill, and "those who have distinguished themselves by special services to People's Poland." The legally defined space allowances are not as small as those in the USSR. Although they are by no means met in present housing, they do tend to be observed in the occupancy plans for new apartment houses. Details of the actual administration and allocation of housing space are not known, but a Warsaw newspaper reported in October 1956 that persons who arbitrarily occupied premises would be legally evicted and that allocation of new housing would be made upon the basis of greatest need. Apparently, as in the USSR, people have been simply moving into new or partially constructed buildings without authority and have often been allowed to remain. The need for housing is so great that various extralegal practices have undoubtedly been indulged in to obtain living space.

The postwar government never completely prohibited either private or cooperative housing, though both were placed under the control of the public housing administration and a number of co-operative building organizations were dissolved and properties confiscated. Today the government is relying heavily upon individual builders and cooperatives in its efforts to relieve the tremendous housing shortage. It is proposed that cooperative apartments and one-family houses be excluded from the jurisdiction of the state administrative agencies. The Cooperative Social Building Enterprise is to be revived and will resume both the production of building materials and the organization of actual construction operations. Housing cooperatives will be its chief customers. According to the official plans, cooperatives will erect almost one third of the new dwelling space in the next few years.

Individuals are also being encouraged to build their own homes. The government has provided repayable loans and has given assistance in the acquisition of building plots and the preparation of building plans. The building-materials industry has been instructed to make special efforts to assist private builders. In the past it was quite usual for private building to be halted for lack of nails, window frames, and other needed materials.

In what is a real innovation the central government and municipalities are planning to build dwelling units, usually consisting of no more than four apartments, which will be offered for sale to individuals and to cooperatives either for cash or by installments. It has also been announced that buildings formerly earmarked for private businesses, small boarding homes in health resorts, and land within town boundaries which has been set aside for small truck-gardening establishments will be offered for sale to private home builders.

Standard of Living

On the basis of available indices, the standard of living in Poland is, and has been, considerably lower than that of the United States and the countries of western Europe. Before World War II it was much the same as that of Italy and the countries of eastern Europe. According to a United Nations study which referred to conditions in the summer of 1956, Poland ranked below the Soviet Union, Czechoslovakia, and East Germany, on a par with Hungary, and slightly above Bulgaria and Rumania.

REAL WAGES

Control of wages and prices has been one of the methods used by the Polish Government to restrict purchasing power of the people and to channel a high proportion of the national income into development of nonconsumer production (see chap. 13). Although there have been a number of selective price reductions and wage increases, the price of consumer goods and services has increased considerably faster than the purchasing power of the people. According to official figures, the index of average real wages of workers in the socialized economy showed an increase of 28 percent from 1949 to 1955. This index reflects a rise during the same period of 77 percent in the state prices of consumer goods and services and an increase in money wages of 126 percent. The real wages increase is questionable; even if accurately compiled, the real wages index makes no allowance for the prevailing shortage of goods which obliges people to buy basic commodities, when available, well above state-set prices.

Since October 1956 there have been a number of wage increases and some price adjustments. Coal miners received the first increases; successive increases affected engineering and technical workers in metallurgy and in the chemical and light industries. In August 1957 the government announced that streetcar workers, nurses, lumberjacks, and workers in the lime and cement industry would receive wage increases in the "immediate future." Official reports indicate that altogether the pay raises in 1956 and 1957 have given about 4.2 million persons average increases of more than 20 percent in most industries and 40 percent in mining. The government admits that the new rates are still too low and that the average family must continue to supplement its income from other sources. Concurrent with the pay raises there have been selective price cuts—and some increases—in industrial items and foodstuffs. There are no data by which the effects of these adjustments on real wages can be estimated. Prices of goods have increased on the free market, and the government has charged that there are many illegal increases of prices as well as price increases by cooperatives for their services. The official effort at present is to hold the price line against the inflationary pressures of increased wages by assuring adequate supplies. The limited adjustments far from satisfy the demands of the people, and the balance between wages, prices, and supplies is extremely precarious.

FAMILY BUDGETS

In the summer of 1956, *Życie Gospodarze,* a leading economic journal, estimated that the average cost of food and clothing for a male worker was 548 złotys per month. It calculated that a family of four—father, mother, teen-ager, and infant—would be required to spend a minimum of 1,728 złotys per month for food and clothing, provided that a daily intake of 2,800 calories was maintained; since the average wage earner makes only 1,077 złotys per month, such a family would not be able to afford even those necessities, let alone rent, utilities, and necessary incidentals. Although family allowances provide some additional income, they do not make up the deficit, and most wives or/and other family members must also work. The journal recognized this condition when it stated that over four fifths of the total labor force do not earn enough to maintain much more than a bare subsistence level. In spite of free medical care and sickness benefits, pensioners are in an even worse position.

According to preliminary reports of a government study of representative family budgets, there has been little change in the first quarter of 1957. The study dealt with the families of workers, engineers, and technical and administrative employees in coal mines, foundries, and machine and textile plants. Workers in the mines were the only group who reported average wages greatly in excess of the 1956 estimated average—they are among the best-paid workers in Poland. Wages in the foundries and machine industry were better than average, those in the textile industries about average; the engineers, technologists, administrative employees, and clerks received wages somewhat higher than those of the workers in the respective industries. Yet even among these workers, better paid than the average, income was insufficient to cover the amount spent on food and industrial goods, except in the case of the white-collar group in mining.

In none of the groups was the total family income made up of the wages of just one worker. Expenditures for food ranged from 49 percent of the total family income among the lowest paid to just over one third among the highest. According to the researchers, this may be an underestimation: the data covers only the first quarter of the year and omits the bulk of potato purchases, for example, which are made in the fall. Between 65 and 80 percent of family income was spent on food and industrial goods combined, leaving relatively small amounts for services, taxes and collections, savings, and the like.

Relatively little information is available regarding the budgets of peasant families. There are strong indications, however, that in the main the peasants are better off than the workers.

SOCIAL CONSEQUENCES OF THE STANDARD

As a direct result of the low wage level and high living costs, many wives have been forced to take jobs. The government has relied heavily upon the recruitment of women in enlarging the labor force to meet the plans for rapid industrial development; in part, wages and prices have been manipulated so as to achieve that end. The free nurseries and kindergartens provided for preschool children enable many women to work without extra expense for child care, but the double duty of a job and housekeeping—particularly when shopping for necessities consumes so much time—means considerable strain and pressure. In addition, both husband and wife are often forced to work considerably longer than the legal eight hours per day. (The apparent increase in average real wages during the past few years has probably been attained through increased hours of work rather than higher rates of pay.) The scattering of the family during working hours and the physical and mental fatigue that results from the day's work make it extremely difficult to maintain "normal" family relationships (see chap. 19).

Low salaries have resulted in widespread lowering of moral standards. Bribery and corruption—almost a necessity—in all phases of the country's life are reported by observers. Thievery and cheating are so usual that that they are often shrugged off by the authorities and condoned by the people—because "everyone is doing it."

An alarming increase in alcoholism among both adults and juveniles has been reported in the press. The poor housing conditions, long hours of extremely hard work, lack of recreational facilities, and the generally difficult and monotonous existence led by many of the people may well be causal factors. Certainly these factors have a detrimental effect upon the health of the people. It is probable that they are also related to the increase of prostitution and juvenile delinquency or "hooliganism" which is currently causing concern among officials and the general public.

Altogether the low standard of living is an important contributing factor to the social problems facing Poland today. Solution of the problems depends in large part upon the success of present official efforts to rehabilitate the total economy.

FORMAL EDUCATION

COMMUNIST THEORY AND PRACTICE ASSIGN TO THE EDUCATIONAL system a major role in the attainment of a socialist society. Control of that system is, therefore, one of the prime targets in the Communist take-over of any country. In 1948 when political control of Poland had been consolidated, the Party moved quickly to bring the educational system under its control and to reorganize the schools and the curricula to accomplish its goals. These were to produce as quickly as possible a labor force trained in the skills needed for the planned economic development of the country, and to develop loyal, enthusiastic, disciplined adherents to the Party and its policies.

Such goals were in total opposition to the humanistic and individualistic educational emphases of the interwar Polish school system; they clashed, moreover, with the traditional value pattern of the Polish people (see chap. 22). Learning and education have been held in high regard for centuries by Poles of all classes. Until the latter part of the eighteenth century almost all education was "classical"; the principal subjects of study were history, philosophy, languages, the arts, and the sciences. The development of individual critical ability, independence of thought, and freedom of expression and inquiry was jealously guarded in the universities and encouraged in the lower schools.

The educational program of the government of interwar Poland emphasized broad general studies but was only partially successful in extending the system to all children by enactment of a law for seven years of compulsory education. Although standard courses of study were given in all schools, teachers and administrators were allowed a great degree of freedom in applying them. The universities were self-governing and had almost complete control over appointments, admissions, certification of graduates, and the development of courses of study. Neither the government nor community organizations had the power to restrict freedom of expression and inquiry.

The Communist government greatly expanded the size of the school system but narrowed its range and scope of studies and brought it under tight centralized government control. All the curricula, from those of primary schools to universities, were drastically revised to implement a program of indoctrination and technical training. Almost all general education courses except for some study of languages and social science were eliminated and replaced primarily by vocational and technical courses and those directed toward supporting the current —and changing—communistic interpretation of history. The universities became advanced vocational schools rather than centers of intellectual activity. Teachers chafed under the strict control of the Party, the government, and the many semiofficial bodies established to regulate the content and administration of the school program.

Many educational leaders and students took advantage of the atmosphere of relative relaxation after the death of Stalin in 1953 to criticize the restrictions on the universities' freedom and independence and the excessive emphasis on technical and vocational training. By 1955 it became apparent that the system was producing neither dedicated Communists nor sufficiently qualified technical personnel. Consideration of various schemes of reorganization began in Party and governmental circles, and a few minor changes were made.

Since October 1956 the Gomułka government has granted some autonomy to the universities; religious education has been reinstated in the primary and secondary schools; and a promise has been made to eliminate ideological and factual distortions. The universities have been given the right to elect the members of the Commission on Higher Education as well as the membership of their own governing bodies. They have also been given authority to develop their own courses of study. A reorganization of the whole system, with a view to establishing a general education program, is now (1957) under consideration.

There is no doubt that the economic needs of Poland demand not only continuation but improvement of vocational and technical education. Qualified observers are convinced, however, that a compromise can be worked out between a general elementary and secondary curriculum and one exclusively devoted to technical training. A greater dilemma is posed by the pressure of the demands for academic freedom in the universities and for the removal of propaganda from the texts in all courses of study. Since political controls over education are part of the system under which Poland is governed it is unlikely that the government and Party will give them up.

The Interwar School System

The three partitioning powers had quite different policies on the education of Poles under their respective jurisdictions. There was this similarity, however, though elementary training was provided to varying extents and under varying conditions, education above the elementary level was largely restricted to the upper classes.

In the Prussian areas there was a system of compulsory eight-year education, conducted in German. Instruction in Polish and the public use of the Polish language were in general prohibited; the Poles in their homes, however, used their own language and preserved the traditions of Polish culture. There were no universities in the territory but qualified Polish students could attend universities in Germany or other countries.

In the Russian-occupied regions relatively little provision for education—and none in the Polish language—was made until 1905, when a Polish educational organization was permitted to establish private schools in all but the eastern areas. Qualified Polish students could be admitted to the University and the Institute of Technology in Warsaw, both Russian institutions, but these institutions were boycotted by the Poles after the abortive 1863 uprising. A considerable amount of advanced training was given by illegal nationalist organizations—"Flying Universities" which changed their places of meeting almost daily in order to escape the police. Their orientation was largely political and attendance was limited.

In Austrian-occupied Poland a system of compulsory four-year education for Polish children, with teaching in Polish, was maintained and university training was available. The Polish universities of Cracow and Lvov continued to be centers of Polish culture and intellectual activity, as they had been before the partitions, devoting special attention to Polish literature. By the outbreak of World War I the general school system had been extended to most of the rural areas of Galicia.

After 1918 the new Polish Government was faced with the task of creating a unified system for the areas within the new borders and filling the need for new schools, equipment, and trained teachers. The long pent-up desire for education among the people and the rapid increase in the birth rate swelled the number of children clamoring for admission to the schools. The government worked toward the development of a seven-year compulsory school system, which was finally provided by law in 1932. Although considerable progress had been made by the outbreak of World War II the majority of Polish children were still getting only four years of education.

GENERAL SCHOOLS

Following French and German models, the general school system of the interwar period was divided into a seven-year elementary school for children aged 7 to 14 and a secondary school with two stages—a four-year *gimnazjum* and a two-year *liceum*. Broad general education rather than early specialization was stressed and the curricula were uniform in all schools on each level.

The curriculum of the elementary schools included language (Polish or minority) and literature, history, geography, arithmetic and geometry, natural science, drawing, singing, and physical training. Two hours a week of religious instruction were compulsory in all grades through the *gimnazjum*. This instruction varied according to the pupil's religious affiliation and parents could request that their child be exempted from it. In the elementary grades almost one quarter of the classroom hours during the entire seven years were devoted to the study of literature and language, including one foreign language. Arithmetic and geometry were the next most important subjects. History and natural history were not taught as separate courses until the fifth grade, geography not until the third. In all seven grades a few hours a week were devoted to drawing, singing, and physical training.

The curriculum of the *gimnazjum* provided a continuation of the broad general training, with increased requirements for languages and sciences; drawing became an elective course, and singing was dropped entirely. Required courses included religion, Polish language, Latin (which in later years was often dropped in favor of a second modern language), a modern language, usually French or English (or in later years, German), history, geography, biology, physics, chemistry, mathematics, and physical training. Graduation from the *gymnazjum* was formally recognized by the "little matura" certificate which qualified the student for entrance into a *liceum* or a vocational school.

The *liceum* offered university preparatory courses and was divided into four departments—classics, humanism, physico-mathematics, and natural science. Rather than exhaustive treatment of any specific subject the departments provided a broad, general base for the specialization of the universities. The academic level of the *liceum* was as high as that of the first two years of college in the United States, if not higher. At graduation from the *liceum* the student was awarded a "certificate of maturity," which was a prerequisite for entrance into a university.

The emphasis of the curricula on all levels was upon the acquisition of knowledge and information; in the higher grades the development of critical ability was also emphasized. Discipline was strict, students had little or no choice of courses, and the work load, even in the lower grades, was heavy. Little attention was given to vocational training, and character training was left to the family and the Church. There was neither student participation in discipline through student government organizations nor provision for extra-curricular activities. The popular clubs—Scouts, Girl Guides, and various athletic clubs—were not directly sponsored by the schools.

Almost all elementary and secondary schools were day schools. The state supported most of the elementary schools, but about two thirds of the secondary schools were supported by private institutions. All were under the general supervision of the Ministry of Religious Denominations and Education. Despite the central administrative and supervisory control and the uniform curricula, individual schools had great independence in handling their own problems and administration.

VOCATIONAL SCHOOLS

Vocational schools were established to meet the growing demand for skilled labor and technicians. The school reform law of 1932 provided for four types: technical schools, which included industrial and artisan, agricultural and gardening training; commercial schools; schools for teaching women household skills and handicrafts; and continuation schools for young people already at work. Like the general schools, they were divided into *gimnazjum* and *liceum* levels, though some provided one or two years of training on the elementary school level. Most of them were organized and supported by local municipal authorities, by factories, or to a small extent by private associations and industries. Some were maintained by the government, but in most instances the state simply paid the teachers' salaries. All were under the general supervision of the Ministry of Religious Denomination and Education.

UNIVERSITIES

Before World War I there were in partitioned Poland only three institutions of higher education which gave their instruction in the Polish language—the University of Lvov, the University of Cracow, and the Institute of Technology of Lvov. The University and Institute of Technology in Warsaw were Russian institutions which were converted into Polish schools in 1918. Soon after 1918 new state universities were established at Poznan and Vilna. In addition, seven professional schools on the university level were organized by the government and six privately supported universities were founded.

Training in all the institutions of higher education was completely specialized. Students selected their courses from the prescribed curriculum of their chosen "faculty." They were treated as adults and pursued their studies without discipline from university authorities except that which was exerted by the very rigorous academic Standards. Successful completion of four years of study qualified students for the degree of *Magisterjum*. Doctorates were awarded for original and independent research.

Autonomy of the universities was established by the law of 1933. They elected their own rectors and appointed their own professors, a jealously guarded right; investiture was a solemn, formal occasion. The universities also established their own curricula, academic standards, and teaching methods. They controlled the admission of students, awarded degrees, and generally enjoyed a high degree of freedom in teaching and inquiry. Professors were held in high esteem by the people and the government. Close relationships were maintained with academic and scientific institutions and developments in western Europe.

The Present School System

ORGANIZATION

GENERAL SCHOOLS. Seven years of compulsory education are still required, and the elementary schools, renamed "basic schools," remain much the same in structure as they were before the war. The secondary schools, however, have been radically changed. Since 1948 the *gimnazjums* and the *liceums* have been merged into *liceums* providing four years of training, thus reducing secondary education by two years from the interwar standards. Recent proposals have suggested the addition of another year. Not all schools include the complete course, some providing grades 1 to 7, and others only grades 8 to 11. A uniform course of study is offered in all and children who have completed basic school are accepted by all *liceums*.

Changes in the curricula of both basic schools and *liceums* were radical. All semblance of general education was dropped; the course of study was completely oriented toward the acquisition of language skills and the sciences. The science courses put primary emphasis on practical applications and techniques. The language courses and the study of the Constitution are especially used for indoctrination in theory and ideology, although all other courses also include some ideological propaganda.

During the spring of 1957 various proposals were made for the reorganization of the elementary and secondary school system—such as extension of the system to twelve years, introduction of more general education courses, and separation of technical and vocational training from general education along the lines of the interwar system. A special commission is now working upon plans for a thorough revision of the school system but pending its decision definite steps have been taken to reduce the propaganda content. A commission of professional historians has been appointed to write textbooks which are "in accord with historical truth." History courses which deal with World War II, for example, will include material about the activities of the non-Communist Home Army.

While religious instruction was never formally prohibited in the schools (see chap. 5), the teaching of religion was gradually but steadily reduced until it was practically nonexistent. Parents were "encouraged" by various means to request that their children be exempted from religious instruction. Schools without religious instruction were established under the pretext of transforming them into schools of the Society of Children's Friends, an anti-religious organization. Apparently, much of the permitted religious instruction was given by pro-Communist priests and laymen.

In the fall of 1956, after agreement was reached between the new Polish Government and the Catholic Church, religious instruction was reinstated in the basic schools and *liceums*. Parents may request that their children be exempted from such instruction, but, according to all reports, considerable popular pressure has been brought to bear against children who do not take it. The government has made numerous appeals against such discrimination and asks for a similar spirit of tolerance toward nonbelievers. The wave of reaction against the nonbelievers seems to be subsiding.

VOCATIONAL SCHOOLS. In the years after the war the most rapid growth and the most thorough curriculum revision took place in the vocational schools as the government made plans to supply rapidly increasing demands for trained labor in developing industry. By the 1955–56 school year more than 500,000 adults and young people were enrolled in the various types of vocational schools. The new courses of study were based on the officially proclaimed premise that training of unspecialized, generally skillful workers was not only unnecessary but harmful in an era of steady progress in technical matters and increasing specialization of production. Instruction was narrowed by eliminating "the ballast of superfluous knowledge" and by "placing greater stress on teaching those subjects and exercises which are essential when practising a given trade." Vocational training increasingly became an adjunct to production, with students spending part- or full-time in actual work in factories.

Three kinds of vocational schools were established: preparatory trade schools, basic trade schools, and the *technikums* (a term adopted from the Soviet system). The preparatory trade schools are designed to produce semiskilled workers. They accept students 16 to 19 years of age who have had 4 years of elementary schooling but no vocational training. The course lasts from 5 to 11 months and, although there are some elements of general education, consists largely of practical work in a factory.

The basic trade schools, like the Soviet *rabfak,* are designed to train skilled workers in several hundred industrial trades. They provide a 2-year course of instruction for graduates of the 7-year elementary school. Some of them are organized for young people who have already begun work; practical training is given on the job and theoretical instruction in the classroom. Others admit young people who have not begun work and provide both theoretical and practical instruction. In all of them training is directed toward the mastery of techniques. Generally, 3 consecutive days a week are devoted to general and theoretical instruction and 3 to practical work. The factory work is supervised by designated skilled workers from the plant.

The *technikums* give 3 to 4 years of instruction to elementary school graduates and are designed to train technicians and administrative personnel. General courses from the *liceum* are taught along with theoretical and practical work in a specialty. Graduates receive both certification as technicians and the certificate of maturity which qualifies them for admission to institutions of higher education. The *technikums* also provide after-hours instruction and correspondence courses for working youth.

Vocational training for agriculture is organized on much the same basis as that for industry. There are also training schools for those wishing to enter the merchant marine, the fishing industry, and certain phases of medicine, law, and fine arts. Vocational training for adults is offered in night and special schools and by correspondence. All are designed to produce skilled but not professional personnel. Graduates of the vocational schools were until early 1957 required to spend a certain period, generally three years, on an assigned job. Compulsory assignment has now been abolished.

HIGHER EDUCATION. The remodeling of Polish higher education began in 1947. The number of schools increased rapidly but the training was more and more restricted to engineering and applied science. Such instruction in the humanities and the social sciences as remained became exposition of the theory and practice of Marxism-Leninism. Courses in Marxism-Leninism, dialectic, historical materialism, and history of the working-class movement (actually a history of the movement in the USSR), were required of all students, whatever their specialization. Many of the new institutions were devoted to training in a single specialty. Universities simply included several specialized institutions under the same administration. Courses of study in all schools of the same specialty became uniform, and the curriculum was set by government administrative authorities. Students were allowed practically no freedom in the selection of subjects. Institutions of higher education became extensions of the vocational schools instead of the centers of learning they had been during the interwar period. Work assignment for three years was until early 1957 compulsory for graduates, just as it was for vocational school graduates.

Of the more than 130,000 students enrolled in institutions of higher education during the 1955–56 session, about 44 percent were studying in schools of engineering (see Table 37). Some 14 percent were in universities and about 18 percent in medical schools. The fact that only some 3 percent of the students were enrolled in teacher training institutions throws light on the over-all poor quality of education; the fact that fewer than 10 percent were in agricultural training reflects the relatively minor emphasis given agricultural development under the Six-Year Plan.

A great effort was made by the government to increase the number of women at all levels of training. By 1956 they made up about a third of the student body in the institutions of higher education but they were not uniformly distributed in the various professional fields.

Plans for reorganizing higher education are being developed today by the Central Council on Higher Education and there has been considerable discussion of various proposals in the press and at educational conferences. But, except for an extension in 1956 of the length of the courses from four to five years, there have been no changes in the curricula. Discussion and criticism among both students and teachers concerning the inadequacies of university training have greatly increased. Their suggestions for reorganization center around reinstatement of the social sciences, division of higher education into academic and vocational sections, and "removal from the curricula of everything incompatible with scientific truth and bearing on dogmatism." There is no indication that the required courses in Marxism-Leninism will be dropped.

ADULT EDUCATION. Beginning in 1949 a vigorous and much publicized campaign was launched to wipe out illiteracy among adults and to give them the equivalent of the full seven years of the basic school. The courses include the last three years of the general school, as well as secondary school, basic trade school, and *technikum* training. Instruction is given in the evenings; sometimes special courses are arranged for day study during vacations. Correspondence schools, particularly in agriculture, are operated by various schools and by institutions of higher education.

SPECIAL SCHOOLS. World War II left Poland with an estimated 700,000 physically disabled persons, most of them children. A four-phase program of rehabilitation and training—which included vocational counseling, training and/or retraining, placement, and protection in employment—was initiated in November 1950. Training was given in special institutions for both children and adults, at industrial establishments, and in homes when the disabled person was unable to attend courses.

MINORITY-LANGUAGE SCHOOLS. The ethnic homogeneity achieved as the result of postwar boundary changes and population transfers greatly reduced the need to maintain schools conducted in non-Polish languages. However, the government has continued the prewar policy of supporting such schools, although the number of students has steadily decreased. In 1956, 13,000 students were attending primary minority-language schools and less than 1,000 were enrolled in *liceums*. About 70 percent of the total number attended German or Belorussian schools, with the former having a slightly higher enrollment. Some 2,000 young people were in Slovak schools, and about 1,000 in Yiddish and Hebrew institutions. Czech and Lithuanian schools had very small enrollments.

ADMINISTRATION

The administration of the Polish educational system, as in the Soviet Union, is highly centralized. Until late 1956 practically all school activities from the primary grades through the universities were subject to detailed direction from administrative agencies of the Polish Government and the Party. The autonomy of the school authorities had been practically eliminated and the number of official and semiofficial agencies concerned with school administration and operation had greatly increased. In recent months various steps toward decentralization have been taken and more are to be included when final plans for reorganization of the whole system are completed.

GENERAL AND VOCATIONAL SCHOOLS. The general schools are under the jurisdiction of the Ministry of Education and its provincial and local offices. Vocational schools until recently were under the general supervision of the Council for Vocational Education, but financed and operated by various ministries. Agricultural schools, for example, were operated by the Ministry of Agriculture; art and music schools by the Ministry of Art and Culture; teacher training institutions by the Ministry of Education; and law *technikums* by the Ministry of Justice. The Council appointed the directors of all the schools, drew up the courses of study, approved the appointment of teachers, and maintained its own inspectorate. In September 1956 the *Sejm* passed a bill abolishing the Central Council and transferring the vocational schools to the jurisdiction of the Ministry of Education. It appears that operation of the schools will remain in the hands of the various related ministries.

HIGHER EDUCATION. All institutions of higher learning are under the jurisdiction of the Ministry of Higher Education, which also directly operates the universities, higher economic schools, higher agricultural schools, polytechnical schools, and the higher engineering schools. Under its general supervision, the Education, Health, Culture and Arts, and Justice Ministries and the Committee for Physical Education direct the higher schools in their respective areas.

Before 1957 the Ministry of Higher Education also was responsible for the organization of scientific research, the establishment of curricula, the selection of teaching personnel, and the selection and preparation of candidates for admission to the higher schools. For most of his decisions and plans, the minister had to have the approval of the Central Council of Higher Education, which was part of the . Ministry. The Council was appointed by the President of the Republic upon recommendation of the Minister of Higher Education; two thirds of its members were active scientific workers. The Council had a part in the development of the state plans for education and in the examination of the qualifications of nominations for teaching and administrative posts. It was required to pass on all changes in existing organization and in curricula of higher schools. The Central Qualifications Commission examined all candidates and awarded all degrees.

In one of the two major changes effected in recent months, the universities have been given the right to elect the members of the Central Council for three-year terms. The government considers the increased control of policy by the universities to be a first step in the eventual reorientation of higher education toward the training of scientists and the encouragement of independent work and scholarship. The Council has been given the task of working out the new organization of the higher schools.

The universities now elect their own governing bodies—the senate, rector, departmental councils—which have considerable authority in the choice of personnel and the planning of scientific research and curricula. They also may make management decisions within the framework of the budget approved by the Ministry.

CONTROLS ON EDUCATION

Although in theory the educational administrative apparatus provided for considerable participation by teachers and educators in planning, policy-making, and operation, actual control was after 1948 in the hands of the Party; by 1950 the entire school system was subservient to the educational goals defined by the Party. Control was maintained both by organizations operating within the schools, such as the youth organizations, and by those operating throughout Poland, such as the Society of Children's Friends and the Schools Welfare Committees.

PLANNING. Detailed development of the educational system is an integral part of economic and political planning. Economic plans specify the number of semiskilled, skilled, technical, and professional personnel to be graduated annually; the establishment of schools and adaptation of curricula geared to those goals. Under the Six-Year Plan (1950–55) admission to schools, particularly those on the higher levels, was designed to meet the goal of "the creation of a new intelligentsia connected through unbreakable bonds with the working class and with the working peasants." It was specified that peasant and working-class youth should constitute 70 percent of all students in secondary and higher schools, and the social background and ideological "suitability" of candidates for admission were carefully examined.

The current Plan continues to specify the number of graduates that the schools are expected to produce but there is no longer much emphasis upon social class composition of the student body. Applicants for admission are still required, however, to submit a detailed life history. Levels of performance and work norms are also specified. A student who "disturbs the plan of education of cadres" by failing in his examinations, for example, is subject to punishment. The nature of the punishment is not explained.

PERSONNEL SELECTION. An important method of Party control is the appointment to key positions and many other lesser posts of "reliable" personnel who can be counted on to carry out Party directives and checks on the performance of their associates. It can be assumed that Party members hold the positions of authority in the various ministries and commissions, at least on the national level, but the functions of the various administrative agencies overlap so much that no single individual has the authority to make decisions.

At the beginning of Communist power the selection of teachers willing to carry out the directives of the administration was a major problem, particularly on the university level where the traditions of independence and academic freedom were strongest and where the war losses had been especially heavy.

It is highly probable that, as in the Soviet Union, the proportion of Party members among teachers varies according to subjects they teach and their positions in the school system. Party membership would be small among teachers in the lower schools and among those who teach such subjects as mathematics, in which the opportunity for indoctrination is slight.

YOUTH ORGANIZATION. Youth organizations had been strong before the war but not directly concerned with the schools. In 1948 they were remodeled to conform with the Soviet Komsomol and Pioneers. The Union of Polish Youth (Związek Młodzieży Polskiej—ZMP) was an adjunct of the Party and to a considerable extent amounted to a training ground for future members. It had specific functions in the secondary schools and institutions of higher education: to mobilize support for schools rules; to help fulfill scholastic requirements; and to spread the ideology of communism. In official phraseology, it was to aid in cooperation with the teaching staff in "combating the influences of an alien ideology." Other duties of members included various types of "social work," such as teaching illiterates; working on state farms during harvest times; and helping in the activities of the Boy Scouts and Girl Guides.

Designed to organize and promote the young people's enthusiasm for communism, the ZMP served indirectly as an agency of control of both the youth and the teachers. Membership was not compulsory, but members received better grades, found easy entrance into institutions of higher education, and received preferred job assignments. Apparently many students joined to obtain such privileges rather than out of political conviction.

The Polish Boy Scouts and Girl Guides prior to 1948 had not differed much from their counterparts in other lands. In the 1948 remodeling they retained their prewar names and such activities as camping and handicrafts but were assigned to indoctrinate children between the ages of 9 and 14 years.

Since October 1956 some reorientation of the activities of the various youth organizations has taken place. The Boy Scout and Girl Guide organizations have been detached from the Party and have reverted to the functions they had before the war; the ZMP was disbanded in December 1956. During the spring and summer of 1956 a number of independent youth organizations with political orientation were formed; at the beginning of 1957 most of them were amalgamated into two remaining groups—the Union of Rural Youth (Związek Młodzieży Wiejskiej—ZMW) and the Union of Socialist Youth (Związek Młodzieży Socjalistycznej—ZMS). For a while they tried to maintain a policy of political independence, but within a few months they were brought back under the control of the Party (see chap. 6).

"SERVICE FOR POLAND." "Service for Poland" (Słuzba Polsce—SP) was a paramilitary organization for youths between 16 and 21 years of age, directed by the Ministry of Defense and led by the ZMP in the schools. It was organized in troops and brigades in schools, factories, villages, and urban centers. Service in the SP was compulsory. For youths below conscription age, work was limited to six months; those of draft age, but not called up, worked until the term of military service began. The required time might be served in a series of short periods, but usually in a single term from May to October. Thirty-two hours a week were devoted to "social work" of various kinds—help on state farms, road construction and repair, teaching in the schools for illiterates, or other special jobs which the government was sponsoring. The remainder of the time was devoted to "political upbringing," military conditioning, sport, and recreation.

"Service for Poland" was greatly resented. It was disbanded in the fall of 1956, at the same time that compulsory job assignment for graduates was abolished. Its military functions have been taken over by the League of Soldiers' Friends. The need of the economy for trained rather than unskilled labor will be met now through direct arrangements between enterprises and schools.

SOCIETY OF CHILDREN'S FRIENDS. The Society of Children's Friends, which also has been disbanded, was officially described as a "mass social organization assembling all those who desire to cooperate with the People's State in the field of up-bringing the young generation." It operated a number of schools, paralleling the general schools, in which the children were given "strong bases for a scientific outlook on the world, free from all prejudices and superstitions." General schools were transferred to the jurisdiction of the Society as a pretext to eliminate the teaching of religion in the schools. The Society was disbanded after the reinstatement of religious education in the schools, but its place was taken by the Lay Schools Society, which has similar aims.

GENERAL PUBLIC AGENCIES. Under the aegis of the Party, supervision of the schools by so-called "social elements" was established by ministerial order in 1945. Three types of organizations were directed to carry out the order—Education Commissions, Parents' Committees, and Schools Welfare Committees. The Commissions were semiofficial bodies with supervisory power, while the two kinds of committees had the responsibility of stimulating community participation and support for educational policies and school activities.

The Education Commissions functioned in the educational administrations of the provincial and local governments and supervised schools, courses of study, students' boarding establishments, rest centers, and places of work. Especially concerned with maintaining the "democratic spirit of school education," they checked and reported on the "proper" expenditure of budgeted funds by the local educational and cultural authorities and helped in the enforcement of school attendance regulations.

Each Parents' Committee was composed of the principal of a school, ex officio, one teacher, a representative of the local Schools Welfare Committee, and representatives of the parents of the children attending the school. Each Schools Welfare Committee was composed of representatives of local works councils and of the factory committee, the principal of the school, a teacher and a representative of the Parents' Committee. Through public meetings and visits to parents both committees were expected to assist in the proper indoctrination of children and parents and at times to supervise classroom activities. In addition, the Parents' Committee was expected to provide needy children with food, clothing, and texts.

In the spring of 1957 the government announced that the Education Commissions and the Committees would restrict their activities to the maintenance and equipment of school plants and would have no influence on educational policies. Undoubtedly they will continue to function for rallying community interest in the schools and as agencies for indoctrination.

EVALUATION

Evaluation of the Polish educational system is complicated by a number of factors. No systematic, objective study of the schools is available. On the one hand, the system has been officially criticized for failing to indoctrinate youth in the theories and practices of communism, as well as for failing to develop a technically proficient labor force.

On the other hand, the volume of semiofficial and popular dissatisfaction with such goals has been growing, and the system is being in effect severely criticized for failing to fulfill the goal of the interwar school system—education that would prepare persons for making independent, individual judgments. While the school system has been materially expanded, it evidently has failed to fulfill either official or traditional goals. The present situation is still too fluid to show whether there will be any real change in the official goals or simply a change in the methods by which they are to be attained.

GROWTH OF THE SCHOOL SYSTEM. Since the interwar period enrollment in the elementary general schools has decreased along with the decrease in the total population. The ratio of pupils to the total population, however, has remained approximately the same—about one in eight. The slight enrollment increase in the urban elementary schools is a reflection of the urbanization of the population. In view of the almost complete destruction during World War II of the schools, equipment, and personnel of the interwar system, the present physical status of the school system represents a considerable accomplishment.

There has been in addition a marked increase in the number of schools which offer the complete seven years of elementary schooling. In the 1937–38 school year only 15 percent of the elementary schools offered seven years of instruction and only about 23 percent of the pupils were enrolled in them. During the 1955–56 session 60 percent of the elementary schools offered the full course and 90 percent of the school children were enrolled. Before the war only 9 percent of the rural schools included seven grades and only a quarter of the rural pupils were enrolled in them; in 1955–56 almost 60 percent of the rural schools offered the full course and enrolled 83 percent of the pupils in it.

The most marked postwar educational developments have been the growth of adult education and vocational schools and increased enrollment in the universities. Although there were before the war a number of primary schools for adults, there were none for secondary-level training. At present several thousand adult primary schools have a total enrollment of over 70,000, and just under 200 adult secondary schools have more than 50,000 enrolled. Such schools are part of the continuing effort of the government to reduce illiteracy and raise the educational level of the workers. Although vocational schools existed during the interwar period, they were not comparable to the present-day system of vocational secondary schools, in which just ten years after establishment of the system some 440,000 young people are being trained. The number of students attending institutions of higher education has more than tripled.

LITERACY. According to the 1930 Polish census, some 5.5 million people—about 23 percent of the population over 10 years of age—were illiterate. By 1945 the figure had dropped, owing both to educational progress and the loss of the eastern areas where the illiteracy rate was higher than in the other parts of the country; the number of illiterates was estimated at 2 million, or 10 to 11 percent of the population over 10 years of age. In 1949 a law was passed requiring registration of all persons unable to read or write. Some 1.2 million persons complied. Special schools and classes were set up to provide both basic and more advanced training for adults. A government representative stated that by 1952 "illiteracy had been eliminated as a mass phenomenon." While it is not possible to verify this claim, the concerted effort to reduce illiteracy seems to have met with much success.

QUALITY OF TRAINING. Both Communist officials and opponents of the government have been most severe since 1955 in their criticism of the universities, and to a lesser degree they have also criticized the other institutions of higher education as well as the elementary and secondary schools. The main targets have been the lack of general education courses and the early specialization required of students. In effect, the criticism has been of the goals established by the Six-Year Plan—the production in the shortest possible time of technicians and specialists. The basic schools have not given sufficient training to those who continue on to the universities, and specialization in the vocational schools has been so narrow that students are reportedly unable to work at any job but the specific one for which they were trained. The universities, which were to develop leaders in the sciences, have become little more than advanced technical schools.

There has also been indirect criticism of Party control over the content of textbooks and courses and its restrictions on materials from western Europe and the United States, and of the lack of regard for objectively determined fact. Instruction and learning have tended to become mere recitation of stereotyped dogma and formula; independence of thought and development of critical ability have been stifled. Although there are individual scientists of high caliber, the general level of scholarship is said to be low in comparison with that of the West and of the USSR (see chap. 21).

FAMILY

THE POLISH FAMILY IS CHARACTERIZED BY MARKED INTERNAL strain and attenuation of family ties which are the final product of a long process of disintegration. Before Poland's partition in the late eighteenth century the family was given cohesion by an ideal of family solidarity extending to a large number of relatives by blood and marriage. The ideal, which is still held by all strata of the population, stressed the feeling of belonging to the family group, the integration of activities of family members to obtain common objectives, the utilization of family resources for needy members, and the maintenance of continuity between the parental family and new family units. By the end of the nineteenth century, however, family ties had become so attenuated that the ideal was rarely attained except by upper-class and intelligentsia families. The nuclear family of husband, wife, and children, rather than the extended family (which includes many other relatives), became the norm among all social groups.

During the interwar period the pattern of values taught within the family contained certain contradictions which in practice seriously strained family relationships. The discipline exerted by the father was strict and harsh, especially among peasant and worker families. Unquestioning obedience was expected of a child; at the same time, the child was expected to become self-reliant, strong-willed, and independent of spirit. The goal of independence was stressed in the family not only as a virtue in the context of the basic Polish value system but as a practical attribute necessary for survival in the outside world. The dual emphasis on unquestioning obedience and independence subjected the child throughout the formative period of his life to two opposing pressures, creating strong tensions that often resulted in serious clashes between parents and children.

Among upper-class urban families the antagonism was often re-

ve to counteract somewhat the harshness of the parents' discipline—
y often indulge their godchildren and, if the real parents die, they
quently assume responsibility for the child.

Through example and precept the child is taught to discipline
himself. Ideally, restraint must be shown in all things. Eating, speaking, walking, and even dying are to be done with dignity. To show
one's hunger or eagerness for food is considered bad taste both in
the countryside and in the cities. Within the family, age and sex
must be respected. Sisters are expected to obey brothers, and seniority
among brothers must be observed. Drilled in good manners, the child
is sharply rebuked for falling short of the standards of dignity. The
dictates of etiquette, though varying in form by social class, often
carry moral force, and to be rude is to offend another person's honor.

A young person achieves honor by mastering himself. The child
must exercise self-control at all times and curb his tongue and temper,
but he must at the same time be ready to defend his honor at all
costs. He is expected to show courage and to overcome all fear of
pain. In both city and country, children's games often involve the
competitive performance of feats of bravery and the ability to sustain
pain. Many of the "hooligan" exploits reported in the Polish press
seem to have the character of these childhood and adolescent feats of
bravado.

The period of adolescence is seen as a time when a man "lives
himself out," "noises himself out," an important phase during which
he can be irrational, idealistic, passionate, stubborn, dreamy. He may
have many love affairs before marriage in order to prove his
masculinity. A Polish girl, on the other hand, is ideally supposed to
remain a virgin until marriage, although exceptions may be tolerated
as long as the girl does not become pregnant and as long as her sex
life does not attract public attention. The traditional standards of
sexual morality are gradually changing; especially in the cities unmarried girls are less expected to be virgins, and unmarried men are
less expected to brag about their numerous love affairs and great sexual
experience.

It is also during adolescence that children may take a stand
against the authoritarianism of their parents, particularly that of the
father. The quarrels are sometimes very intense. The son of a peasant
may assert his individuality and independence by beginning to struggle
for control of the family land. In intelligentsia families a youth's
rebellion against authority may take the form of imaginary heroism
and similar fantasies. Much of the idealism and dramatic behavior
characteristic of adolescence among the intelligentsia is carried over
into adult life.

MARRIAGE AND ESTABLISHMENT OF THE HOUSEHOLD

Marriage is a high point in the life of both sons and daughters. The son becomes master of his own household when he achieves economic independence and emancipates himself from family ties. In both city and country it is felt that only parents and unmarried children should live together. A newly married couple makes the greatest effort to set up a separate household but this is extremely difficult today given the acute housing shortage and the dearth of building materials.

In the city a young man may very quickly achieve material and social independence. He has adult status legally when he is eighteen and may soon establish a family of his own, preferably with the permission and help of his parents. Dependence upon parental permission, however, seems to be breaking down.

A peasant youth, on the other hand, may have to wait for independence until his late twenties or early thirties; as long as he lives and works on land belonging to his parents he possesses neither social nor economic independence. Each son is supposed to receive a portion of the family land when he marries, but there is no binding rule determining the size of the share. The paternal control is a source of great uncertainty and there is considerable conniving among sons to win the father's good graces. A daughter receives her share of the inheritance in the form of clothes, livestock, and occasionally a small piece of land as a dowry and is not usually involved in the competition for the estate of the father. The custom of providing a dowry is reportedly disappearing in the cities.

For a girl, marriage may mean both triumph and sorrow. She is happy in achieving the goal toward which all of her training and ambition has been shaped—finding a husband and household of her own. During the wedding she is the center of attention. As a wife, however, she must, in the country, face an endless round of daily toil; in the city, she must often take a job outside the family. Peasants and workers both appear to feel that greater hardships are faced by wives than by husbands; in the middle and upper classes, the men are apt to ruefully contrast their relatively free period of adolescence with the "gray life" of the family.

During the interwar period wedding ceremonies and the attendant festivities were lavish affairs in both city and country. Among the peasants they involved a whole village or neighborhood and sometimes extended for as long as a week. The lavish custom is no longer followed in the cities, where the cost would now be prohibitive, but persists in the countryside to some degree.

Eventually, a married couple has to accept responsibility for the care of parents or grandparents. This is especially true in the country;

after the marriage of the peasant's youngest son, the father is left landless or with only a small share of his former land, and he and his wife are then under strong compulsion to convert themselves into dependents of their children. The father retains authority in the peasant family only as long as he is in full possession of his property. After the marriage of all his children he is forced, by custom and by the threats of his adult sons if he does not comply, to withdraw from active work on the land and to live with one or more of his sons. This enforced retirement, stripping him of all property and authority, is dreaded by the peasant, but he can do little about it. Frequently a father draws up before a notary a formal inheritance agreement specifying the food and care to be given him by his son or sons and even the kind of coffin and suit of clothes in which he will be buried. It is not uncommon to include a clause in the agreement binding the children to honor their aged parents. The upkeep of parents, however, is often strongly resented, and the agreement may be ignored by the children, giving rise to many domestic battles and endless lawsuits. Peasant stories often refer to an aged parent or grandparent turned out of the house or even murdered.

In the cities parents or grandparents can support themselves to a later age without depending upon the children. There are indications that the help of grandparents in the working-class home today is much appreciated; they can care for the children in the absence of the parents, and their old-age pensions make a contribution to the family budget.

Family and State

During the interwar period the Polish Government enacted no uniform law on domestic relations. Such matters as marriage, family, guardianship, and inheritance were governed by several conflicting legal systems in different parts of the country. In the former Prussian provinces, the German civil code was in force, a civil marriage was mandatory and matrimonial cases were within the exclusive jurisdiction of civil courts. In central Poland, French law and some Russian statutes were applied. In the eastern areas, prerevolutionary Russian law was in force, a religious marriage was required, and matrimonial cases generally were decided by ecclesiastical courts. In southern Poland, Austrian law had authority and only a religious marriage was valid.

No divorce was legally possible for Catholics. In some provinces divorce was permitted for persons belonging to non-Catholic denominations and Catholics could obtain a divorce by renouncing Roman

Catholicism and embracing, at least formally, the Lutheran or Greek Orthodox faith. This device was increasingly used during the interwar period by members of the Polish upper classes.

Legislative efforts aimed at unifying the various legal systems in Poland began as early as 1919. A draft of a new law relating to marriage, published in 1931, provided for a uniform civil marriage ceremony and for the jurisdiction of civil courts in matrimonial cases. The Roman Catholic Church vigorously opposed the introduction of compulsory civil marriage and the draft never reached the *Sejm* for legislative action.

The need for a unified marriage law became urgent after World War II when millions of persons found themselves transplanted from the jurisdiction of one law to another. The demoralization of war, moreover, had seriously undermined the foundations of family relations. Faith in the permanence of many traditional values had been shaken. Standards of morality were losing much of their force. Children were often neglected, and discipline and authority in the home were weakened.

Poland's postwar government exhibited an early concern for the family as a social institution. It emphasized its solicitude for the durability of family life but sought to use the family for its own ends. Marital and family relations were gradually removed from the authority of the Church and brought under the jurisdiction of state courts. Parents were made responsible to the state for the preparation of disciplined, obedient citizens who would be conscious of their duties to society and the government.

The Communist government issued a series of decrees on marriage and divorce in 1945 and 1946. A Family Code was adopted on June 27, 1950, and went into effect on October 1. Openly patterned on Soviet laws, it outlines the basic juridical principles regulating family life in Poland today.

A marriage is considered valid only when both parties declare jointly before a civil registrar their intent to enter into marriage. The law does not prohibit a religious ceremony, but it emphasizes the exclusiveness of the civil forms: "Unless the declarations are made before the officer of vital statistics, the marriage is not concluded at all." Ecclesiastic jurisdiction in matrimonial matters is not recognized.

A marriage can be terminated by annulment or divorce. Annulment is considered an exceptional means for terminating a marriage concluded in defiance of legal prohibitions. Marriages are null and void, for example, if a person is of unsound mind and mentally defective or if a previous marriage has not been dissolved. The divorce provision reads:

> If for important reasons a complete and lasting discord has occurred in the marital relations, either spouse may ask the court to dissolve the marriage by divorce.

Specific grounds for divorce are not mentioned in the law, and it is up to the court to determine whether there is sufficient cause for divorce. The rights and duties of a divorced couple with regard to the custody and property of minor children are decided by the court.

In line with the Soviet program of "emancipating women," Poland's Family Code places great stress on the principle of equality between husband and wife and legally deprives the husband of his traditional authoritarian position as "head of the family." The code permits a Polish woman to hyphenate her name with her husband's. Each spouse may dispose of his or her personal possessions acquired before marriage, without the participation of the other; property held in common, however, must be jointly administered. The father and mother have identical rights and duties with regard to their children, and all family matters of importance must be decided jointly. Either spouse may ask for a court decision in case of dispute.

Both parents have the duty to rear their children in a manner compatible with the "interests of society." Children must be prepared to work for the good of the community and be brought up so that they will know how to fulfill their duties to the state, the nation, and "democracy." The execution of parental authority may be supervised by the state. Illegitimate children are granted equal rights with legitimate offspring; a child born out of wedlock has the right to bear his father's name.

The code was an attempt to make the family a government-protected social institution. The government stressed the principle that marriage is a durable and lifelong union. It indicated its desire to strengthen and stabilize the family and to give the marriage ceremony a solemn character. The registrar of civil status was expected to impress upon a couple the importance of matrimony to the state and the community. Divorce proceedings were made highly unattractive and difficult, involving high court and lawyers' fees. To encourage childbirth, monthly family allowances based on the number of children in the family were instituted.

Despite such concern for the permanence of family ties the government contributed in many ways to undermining the stability of family relations. In the Polish context, the secularization of marriage and admissibility of divorce for cause amounted to a revolutionary step designed, in part, to undermine the authority of the Catholic Church. The extension of divorce facilities, moreover, has done much to weaken the durability of marriage and family bonds, and state intervention in the rearing of the family has helped to reduce parental influence and discipline in the home.

The economic and social changes that followed World War II have tended to perpetuate and intensify the strains within the Polish family. Poverty and lack of housing, particularly in the cities, have led to the enforced separation of many couples and of many parents and children, and have contributed to a wave of broken marriages. In some cases children have become so great an economic burden that they are no longer wanted. As a result of their new economic independence, moreover, marriage is for many women, no longer the main fulfillment of life. Although the desire for personal attachments and for a home has not been destroyed, it has become increasingly difficult to establish strong family ties and a stable home life.

For the past several years official concern has been expressed in the Polish press over the increase of divorce, adultery, illegitimacy, abortion, juvenile delinquency, and prostitution. No official statistics on the number of persons seeking divorce have been released, but an article in the literary weekly *Nowa Kultura* reported that divorce cases in Poland had doubled in number between 1952 and 1954 and in 1955 the number was 250 percent over the 1952 figure.

Most of the divorce cases reportedly involve peasants who have migrated to the cities, members of the intelligentsia, and youths. The ratio between rural and urban divorces in one province is reported to be one to nine. Although the courts are obligated by law to do their utmost to reconcile estranged spouses, an article in *Nowe Prawo* (June 1956) disclosed that more than 80 percent of divorce requests were being granted. Fifty percent of the men and 70 percent of the women involved in divorce cases had been married before the age of twenty-five.

Increases in the number of illegitimate children and of illegal abortions forced the government to show a greater interest in birth control. A law was passed in April 1956 permitting doctors to carry out abortion for medical reasons and also in cases of "difficult material circumstances." In October 1956 the Ministry of Health reported that 60 percent of the women applying for permission to terminate pregnancy were of working-class origin, while 30 percent came from the intelligentsia and 10 percent from the peasantry. The report noted that the number of hospital admissions after illegal operations had decreased since the enactment of the abortion law, but that hospital facilities were inadequate to take care of all the women seeking abortion.

For a great number of women, abortion, being contrary to their religious beliefs and training, is a deeply shameful and embarrassing proceeding. Yet in many cases economic pressure appears great enough to overcome such scruples. Cardinal Wyszyński stated publicly in April 1957 that it came as a "painful discovery" to him that "it was women who led to the victory of the principles of death over the principles of life, those very women whom we thought to be the mainstay of the Church in Poland." With the shortage of contraceptives and an apparent reluctance of many people to make use of them, abortion is likely to remain the chief method of birth control in Poland for some time.

The Polish Government is now placing great emphasis upon the direct responsibility of parents in the upbringing of children but it can do little to enforce compliance and the institution of the family is likely to suffer from internal strains for a considerable time to come.

SOCIAL ORGANIZATION

THE STRUCTURE OF POLISH SOCIETY REFLECTS THE SOCIAL, economic, and political changes that have occurred in the country over the past four decades. The most important change, still in process, is the transition from a basically agricultural to an industrial economy. This has meant a disappearance of the traditional peasant-landlord class pattern, the emergence of a growing industrial labor force, and the rise of a newly trained technical and managerial bureaucracy.

Poland has not undergone, as has the Soviet Union, a social revolution in which an aroused populace led by an ideologically inflamed vanguard consciously overthrew the existing class system. Rather, the postwar government, through its economic and political policies, has attempted to shape the social structure in such a way as to further its program of rapid industrialization. It has replaced the prewar upper classes, most likely to offer resistance to Communist rule, with a political, intellectual, and managerial elite which has been offered privilege and power in return for support of the government and its policies.

While the present class groupings in the society—based primarily on education, occupation, political power, and economic status—meet the model for a socialist industrial society, the values held by each group are far from what is desired by the government.

The peasant is not a worker producing agricultural products on a piece-rate basis for the government to distribute to the other classes of the society. He clings to his own plot of land, works it as an individual owner, and begrudges any produce to the government; he will not work with other peasants for the "collective good" or for the achievement of a socialist society. The industrial worker dislikes the fact that he must work with his hands, does not take to labor discipline, and aspires to a nonmanual job. He does not feel loyalty to his factory or an obligation to produce for the state for the benefit of other classes in the society. While many of the white-collar bureaucracy and the intelligentsia today have worker and peasant backgrounds, they do not, as the government had hoped they would, feel a kinship to the workers and peasants. They hold to the traditional Polish value system which sees physical labor as demeaning. They expect and receive material preferment over the workers and peasants.

The population sees the increased educational opportunities offered by the government as a positive program facilitating social mobility; those who obtain the education look on the process as a change in class status which entitles them to a desk job. The government sees the program in terms of the needs of the economy for educated and trained agricultural, industrial, and managerial personnel.

In the past, the existence of class differences was an accepted, everyday fact of life for all Poles. The present possibilities for mobility, however, have produced dissatisfaction with the fact that everyone cannot rise to power and prestige and resentment of the excessive special benefits and privileges that are accumulated by one group, the political and managerial elite. There has been what the workers call an "overproduction of intelligentsia."

Polish Society before World War II

During the fifteenth and sixteenth centuries, which constituted one of the most prosperous periods in the history of Poland, Polish society was composed of three major social classes: the landed nobility (*szlachta*), which alone could take part in political life, the city and town bourgeois; and the peasantry.

The *szlachta,* about 10 percent of the total population, monopolized the wealth and political power of the country. All dignitaries of the Polish Church and administrators of the state belonged to the nobility. Most of the land was in the hands of the king, the Church, or the large landowners. The mass of the peasants, nearly 80 percent of the population, were attached to bishoprics or abbeys or the estates of noble families, working the land as serfs and without freedom to move except by permission of the landlord.

Unlike the gentry of other western countries, the *szlachta* retained a strong tradition of clan ties and organization and never developed the rigid hierarchy of social ranking observable in the feudal countries of western Europe. A dictator to his serfs, the Polish noble deemed himself the king's equal. He regarded himself as a joint ruler of the country, proud of his right to elect the king (see chap. 2). Yet, while nominally enjoying political equality, the members of the *szlachta* differed strikingly in their economic position. A small number of great nobles, known as the "magnates," possessed most of the wealth and exercised actual leadership in society. The economic preponderance of a dozen families virtually created as many petty kings competing for power and position through intrigues and factional struggles. Below the clans of magnates were the far more numerous lesser gentry, many of whom owned little or no land and were sometimes as destitute as the peasants. They possessed the right to vote but generally gave their allegiance to this or that magnate who granted them land or privileges in return. As a class, however, the *szlachta* considered itself the "nation" and guarded its political rights against both the peasantry and the townsmen.

The urban class, which had grown and flourished with the rise of towns and cities during the fourteenth and fifteenth centuries, was composed largely of immigrant elements—Jews, Germans, and other non-Poles. These merchants, shopkeepers, and craftsmen were kept outside of the main stream of Polish culture and society. Their outlook differed from that of both the gentry and the peasants, who had an aversion for trade and valued neither time nor industry (see chap. 22).

The process of urbanization was arrested late in the sixteenth century. The *szlachta* began to envy and fear the townsmen, many of whom became wealthy, and progressively curbed their activities by legislation. Viewing the towns as parasitic the rulers of the state maintained economic policies which led to the ruin of once prosperous urban communities and prevented the development of a middle class.

This situation changed only after the partitioning of Poland at the end of the eighteenth century (see chap. 2) when members of the nobility were deprived of their political power and much of their land. During the nineteenth century city life began to revive. With the growth of business and industry the sons of dispossessed land-owners, forsaking the countryside, became bankers, teachers, journalists, doctors, lawyers, and engineers. The peasants, increasing rapidly in numbers during most of the nineteenth century, were emancipated by their foreign rulers. Part of the surplus peasant population was absorbed into the rising urban proletariat, another part joined the flow of emigration overseas.

Hitherto almost exclusively agricultural, the Polish provinces acquired a new and varied urban look. Industrial workers grew in strength and began to take an interest in political affairs. Gradually there emerged a new urban social group, the intelligentsia, composed of former members of the gentry and of persons from worker and peasant families who had forced their way into higher education. Members of the intelligentsia varied greatly in background and training but all saw themselves as the cultural leaders of the Polish nation and looked forward to the day when they might lead their country to independence.

The principal change in the social structure during the interwar period was an accentuation of trends which had already emerged—a reduction in the size of the peasantry and the landed gentry groups, an increase of the working class, the intelligentsia, and the bourgeois. By 1939 the peasants represented 60 percent of the population, workers (including artisans, skilled and unskilled laborers) 15 percent, and the intelligentsia, 10 percent. The remaining 15 percent was made up of the landed gentry, the bourgeois, and such marginal groups as domestic servants and soldiers.

The peasants, workers, and intelligentsia had different degrees of social prestige and of access to social and economic opportunities, and their styles of life were distinctive. While the dividing lines between the groups were relatively clear, within each group there was a great deal of differentiation, the peasants being the most homogeneous.

THE INTELLIGENTSIA

The members of the intelligentsia were less a cohesive class than sharers in certain common standards of education, culture, and style of life. Ethnically, the intelligentsia included some assimilated Germans and Jews. Occupationally, it embraced professors, writers, artists, journalists, university students, doctors, army officers, lawyers, clergymen, and other professionals. The largest single group was comprised of the white-collar workers—bureaucrats and clerks—all of whom had at least a secondary education. The intelligentsia concentrated primarily in large urban centers, but white-collar workers, teachers, and priests in the towns and villages usually thought of themselves as members of the intelligentsia and were generally so regarded despite their low salaries and rural isolation.

The values of the *szlachta* persisted in the intelligentisa. Manual labor and trade were despised as crass and demeaning. During the latter part of the nineteenth century the dispossessed gentry had gone en masse into even the poorest white-collar jobs in preference to business, crafts, or manual labor, except for a few who were connected with such activities as the making or sale of objects of art, book publishing, and so forth.

Theoretically membership in the intelligentsia was open to any person who possessed the requisite education and culture. Higher education was the major determinant of social prestige; the diploma from an institution of higher learning, then as now, bestowed dignity and a title. The minimum educational requirement for intelligentsia membership was graduation from the *gimnazjum*—secondary school (see chap. 18). But only the wealthier familes could send their children to secondary schools or universities and, since advantageous social connections were also important for establishing oneself in a suitable profession, entrance into the intelligentsia was in fact limited to relatively few.

The values of the intelligentsia were colored by the long period of exaggerated, idealistic, exile patriotism from 1795 to 1918 when Poland was under foreign occupation (see chap. 22). Most members of the intelligentsia were political conservatives, but some supplied leadership for the peasant and workers' movements. Anticlericalism was less pronounced in Poland than in France or Italy but there was considerable conflict between the clergy and some intellectuals with respect to the actual exercise of ideological leadership and influence.

THE GENTRY

The landed gentry continued to be a distinctive social group and exerted considerable influence under the Piłsudski regime. Far more homogeneous than the intelligentisa, they constituted a closed aristocracy. They observed a pretentious code of manners and conformed meticulously to external symbols of their superior status and breeding. Politically they clung to conservative and clerical parties.

Although they were called *ziemianie* (landowners), the gentry as a class included those persons who prided themselves on their hereditary aristocracy, even if they no longer owned land and had lived in the city for generations. By the same token, the *ziemianie* group excluded many actual owners of country estates, because they were of peasant, bourgeois, or foreign origin and not born into the gentry class; such a person might be referred to as *"nouveau riche,"* or "a city man owning land."

Typically, the Polish country squire lived in a mansion on the outskirts of the village. Even in a family inferior to the richer peasants in land or wealth, the "landowner's" house was unmistakable. It was built in a distinctive style, often with several columns around the porch. A large, stone-fenced park often surrounded the house, and, starting from an impressive gate, a road lined with old trees led to the house entrance.

THE BOURGEOIS

Immediately after the end of World War I, when the devastated country needed industrial development, economic policies favoring the commercial bourgeois were adopted. This group, long a relatively unimportant part of the Polish society, gained in numbers and strength during the interwar period. The bourgeois could be described as a social class, however, only in the sense that its members shared a common economic role and lived in the cities.

A major division among the bourgeois was that between the Jews—a culturally unassimilated ethnic group—and the Polish and German businessmen, merchants, and shopkeepers. The Jews constituted in reality a *petit bourgeois,* managing one-man enterprises. Most of them were engaged in commerce but approximately 20 percent owned and ran small industries. In western Poland there were many assimilated German businessmen.

Some of the Polish merchants in small towns and cities were of peasant birth and maintained their social contacts with the home village rather than with the city. At the other extreme, a number of the prospering and successful bourgeois of interwar Poland came from upper-class families and tended to share the values and way of life of the intelligentsia or the gentry.

The political role of the Jews was distinctly marginal (see chap. 6). The Polish bourgeois were not very active politically, but as a group they supported the clerical and conservative parties. While businessmen and shopkeepers prospered and became to an unprecedented degree socially respectable after World War I, they continued to be accused of stinginess, love of comfort, softness, and lack of patriotism by their Polish compatriots of other classes.

THE WORKERS

The working class gained most of its members from the surplus rural population. During the whole interwar period many Polish workers had to make the transition from agricultural to industrial work. This meant a gradual breakdown of peasant insularity and an accelerated acquisition of patriotic ideals. A small number of worker groups—miners, carpenters, masons, printers, and tilemakers—had traditions extending back to the craft guilds of the Middle Ages. Although many of the artisans now worked in factories, some of them had preserved the guild-nurtured tradition of craftsmanship.

Workers gradually became conscious of their common interests in regard to better wages and working conditions; they were often split, however, on how to attain these goals. The majority supported the Polish Socialist Party, whose leaders were also union heads, but concerted action by the workers was rare.

Certain distinctions existed between workers employed on government and municipal enterprises, laborers in private enterprises, unskilled workers, and small artisans. The government or municipal enterprise workers had the highest status; they received higher salaries, were paid on a monthly rather than a weekly basis, enjoyed numerous fringe benefits, and had a measure of job security. The more skilled and well-organized laborers in private enterprises also earned wages much above the national average—in some cases above that earned by the white-collar intelligentsia. These and the government workers were often able to save enough money to buy their own homes—a mark of prestige.

There was considerable social distance between skilled and unskilled laborers. The unskilled were largely peasants who supplemented their farm income during the winter in the towns and cities while their wives and children remained in the village. The skilled mechanic or other urban worker sometimes called his assistant simply "the peasant." Frequently the peasant migrant remained marginal in the urban setting, and he was often condemned for his role in depressing wage levels.

The small artisans were bakers, cobblers, milliners, tailors, cartwrights, blacksmiths, and potters. In terms of self-identification, style of life, and social status, they had far less in common with the merchants or the intelligentsia than with the other urban workers. Even those employing several helpers or apprentices were typically inferior in wealth, position, and influence to the unionized industrial workers. The *chałupniks*—home-workers—were perhaps the most exploited class in Poland. They and their families produced handmade goods at home under contract with an outside employer and were not covered by the labor laws of the interwar period. Many of the artisans, especially the cobblers and tailors, were Jews.

THE PEASANTS

The peasants, constituting over 60 percent of the population, continued to be the real base of the society. Their numbers were not reflected, however, in proportionate influence, for actual social and economic liberation of the serfs lagged far behind the legal emancipation. Despite the emigration of over two million Poles in the interwar period, overpopulation remained the central, unalleviated rural problem.

Depending upon the region and the local situation the peasants varied greatly in economic and social standing. Generally speaking, they were much better off in western Poland than in the eastern region, where the land was poor and the landlords were largely Russians.

Ownership of land was the principal source of prestige among peasants, and the principal social division was between those who worked their own land, the *gospodarze*, and the landless. A few of the *gospodarze* were fairly wealthy, with large landholdings. Small flower and vegetable gardens often surrounded their houses, and the houses were usually part of the village cluster. The poorer peasants lived in small houses or huts close to each other; their fields might be at some distance from the village.

There were two types of landless peasants—the *fornals* or *dworaks* (from *dwor,* the term for the squire's mansion), who worked as laborers for the landed gentry, and the *parobeks,* who worked as itinerant day laborers. The *fornals* were employed on a yearly basis; the contract usually extended throughout the worker's lifetime and sometimes through that of his son and grandson. Conditions varied, but generally they lived in barracks on the estate and received a small part of their wages in cash and the rest in kind. They were also given the use of land for a garden.

The *parobeks* took whatever agricultural work was available, whether from a landlord or a peasant. In some cases they were supplementing income from very small plots of land they might own. There were attempts to unionize the *parobeks,* and several strikes occurred during the early years of independence, but the organizing movement soon lost strength.

Regional and economic differences among the peasants, large and important as they were, were reflected to only a minor degree in peasant culture. With regard to their values, customs, aspirations, and style of life, the peasants were the most homogeneous of all the Polish classes. From the point of view of the landed gentry there was not much difference between the landowning *gospodarze* and other peasants. And a *gospodarz* was not wanting in deference and respect to the village squire, even though no longer his serf or even his employee; there was always the possibility that a peasant might at some time be forced to seek employment or favors which only this member of the gentry class could dispense.

The Polish peasants as a whole had little political consciousness. The various peasant political parties which came into existence in the 1920's had very small followings. The parties sought agricultural reforms and measures which would immediately benefit the peasants, but beyond that they allied themselves with other groups at all points of the political spectrum (see chap. 6).

Contemporary Society

In their treatment of the Polish population the Germans made little distinction between social classes. They did, however, attempt specifically to eliminate all known leaders of the intelligentsia. The landed gentry lost their land, fled, or were killed or imprisoned. Most of the intelligentsia were forced to engage in manual labor for the Germans, although some escaped into the countryside or sought a precarious existence through black-market activities. The Germans closed all high schools and universities and required the youth to register and attend "vocational schools" which were little more than factories; many of the youth from intelligentsia families were forced into manual labor. In the large urban centers such as Warsaw, Poznan, and Lodz there were underground schools, many of them run by priests, which perpetuated the Polish tradition of classical, liberal arts education (see chap. 18).

Many factory workers were shipped off to Germany to work. Those in Poland were paid starvation wages in the German-controlled factories and forced to maintain high production under the most brutal conditions. Despite severe penalties, there were persistent slowdowns, sabotage, and widespread stealing; the work produced was purposefully inferior.

At the beginning of the German occupation the peasants generally maintained an insularity from the events surrounding them. Many were able to take advantage of food shortages by selling produce in the black market; throughout the period the peasants maintained themselves better than did the other classes. But the German forced labor program, the system of produce quotas enforced by the death penalty, mass evictions, and enforced transfers of population finally produced a change in their attitudes. The peasants finally joined the mainstream of the Polish patriotic tradition, with the formation of the Peasant Battalions, part of the underground resistance.

The German occupation thus wiped out some classes and produced a degree of attitudinal homogeneity among all of them. The landed gentry, as a class, disappeared. The virtual extermination of the Jews left a gaping void in Polish economic and commercial life. For all classes, including the peasant, loyalty to the Polish nation was brought into sharp focus. But patriotism also was identified with slacking on the German-controlled job, shoddy workmanship, and evasion of authority, reinforcing the Polish distaste for manual labor. The universal reaction to the German educational policy made education—and the nonmanual job it leads to—a value for all groups of the population.

There are today four major social groupings or classes—an upper class or intelligentsia, a nonmanual white-collar bureaucracy, a working class, and a peasantry. There is in addition a very small but growing group of private shopkeepers and artisan entrepreneurs, recruited from all classes, which has recently been encouraged to fill the void in private trade (see chap. 16). Within each of these groupings there are subdivisions; economically each group tends to shade into the other. In terms of social prestige and attitudes, however, two lines—one between workers and nonmanual employees and the other between the urban population and the peasantry—are clear cut.

THE INTELLIGENTSIA

The intelligentsia includes the political elite of the Polish United Workers' Party and the other "allied parties" (see chap. 6), many of whom are also *Sejm* deputies; officers in the armed forces; producing intellectuals; some professional people; and the higher clergy. While the grouping is thus extremely diverse, members of the intelligentsia all have a university education or are self-educated and receive the largest share of the material and social rewards the society has to offer. The highest proportion of Party membership comes from this class. Contrary to the situation in the USSR, however, Party membership has not been essential for inclusion in the intelligentsia. The Polish Government has tended to recognize the ability of the individual—whether of peasant or worker origin—regardless of his willingness to belong to the Party.

The inclusion of plant managers and other highly placed technical personnel in the intelligentsia marks a transition from the older Polish pattern to one more in keeping with socialized industrialization. In the past these people either owned the factories or formed a group of technicians who, because of their training and interests, were counted as upper bourgeois but, because of their close tie-in with commerce and industry, were not considered intelligentsia. A gradual shift seems to be taking place, so that highly qualified technical personnel, even though lacking broad educational background, are through their power and position counted as part of the intelligentsia.

Primary and secondary school teachers, doctors, and other professionals are members of this class grouping, more on the basis of educational background and social prestige than of actual material endowments or power. They are the lowest-paid group of the intelligentsia.

THE WHITE-COLLAR BUREAUCRACY

With the development of an industrial society within the framework of an enormous and complex bureaucratic structure, there has been a considerable increase in the number of clerks and petty bureaucrats. In the prewar period such nonmanual workers, on the basis of occupation and education, were part of the intelligentsia; they are no longer counted as such, since most do not have the necessary educational qualifications. An official survey (May 1957) showed that 60 percent of the white-collar workers have not completed a secondary education. They aspire to be in the intelligentsia, but those in the lowest ranks fare no better economically than the skilled workers, and some fare much worse.

A large number of white-collar workers are former peasants or industrial workers who, upon completing primary school, received a year or so of highly technical but practical training and have been given positions of power in industrial enterprises. They are relatively well-paid, though not as well as they wish, and many of them are extremely young. In some factories, for example, the average age of managerial personnel reportedly is between twenty-five and twenty-seven.

THE WORKERS

This group has increased more than any other since the end of the war. In terms of what its members can contribute to the economy—based largely on their skill—they are subdivided into skilled workers, semiskilled, and unskilled. Both the skilled and semiskilled have received more on-the-job training than formal educational background, and they generally are at least second generation workers. The unskilled workers are largely first generation workers from peasant families and have gone through a short vocational training course or have simply started work without completing primary school (see chap. 18).

Coal miners, no matter what their skill, have been granted better wages than any other working group. This is a reflection of the dependence of the economy, both internally and for foreign exchange, on coal. There persists, however, a chronic shortage of coal miners.

Most workers receive such a low wage that both members of the family must work. Most Poles feel that women belong in the home, and this feeling has lately been reflected in the government's approach to unemployment, which is one of taking women out of the work force. Economic pressure, however, continues to force many women into the labor group and about one third of the working force in the socialized sector of the economy, outside of agriculture, consists of women (see chap. 12).

THE PEASANTS

The postwar land reform (see chap. 14) resulted in a multiplication of small, uneconomic peasant holdings and, coupled with the government's program of rapid industrialization, led to a large migration out of the countryside. Peasants constitute about 45 percent of the population today, in contrast to 60 percent in 1939. Most of the peasants who remained on the land have suffered less economic hardship since the war than the workers. The poorest peasants, and those with lowest status, are the agricultural workers on state farms, who are regarded as being little better than the landless laborers (*fornals*) of the interwar period.

The Communist government has had great difficulty in winning the loyalty of the peasants. They have held on to their individual plots of land, fiercely resisted attempted collectivization, and remained deeply hostile toward governmental authority. The Party tried to create a following among peasant youths by offering them increased educational opportunities, technical and vocational training, and an opportunity to enter managerial positions. This policy, however, had unanticipated consequences. A great many young peasants streamed into the cities in search of education, glamor, and excitement. Many were trained as agricultural technicians and agronomists, then refused to go back to the farms. Instead, they took jobs in factories or found other employment in the cities; many of them engaged in the black market and in "hooligan" activities. It is difficult in many rural communities today to find young men below the age of twenty-five.

Social Dynamics

The Communist government has attempted to manipulate the social structure to serve its political and economic programs. Remnants of the prewar gentry and intelligentsia who could be expected to oppose Communist rule were deprived of power, influence, and livelihood. In Party propaganda, the working class—"in alliance with the working peasants"—was accorded a "leading role in the country." Many young workers and peasants were given education and training for technical and managerial positions in the society and hailed as the future leaders of "People's Poland." For example, only 18 percent of the students in the universities in 1946 were of worker or peasant origin; in 1952 the figure jumped to 59 percent. In return, the working class was expected to serve as the active core of support for the state, while the peasantry was asked to supply the foods and products necessary for industrial expansion.

The present social structure, however, does not in fact serve the purposes of the kind of industrial society envisioned by the Communist rulers. Many former workers and peasants, once having acquired a little education, have eagerly adopted the views and ways of life of the intelligentsia. As members of the new managerial bureaucracy, many find little satisfaction in their technical responsi-

372

bilities and have little motivation or drive to build an efficient industrial system. The majority of graduates from academic institutions refuse to accept jobs directly related to production.

Most workers and peasants continue to work only enough to take care of their immediate needs. Although many workers are ready to demand a larger share in the planning, management, and profits of their enterprises, they have not strongly developed factory habits and are unwilling to submit to managerial discipline. The peasants show little interest in making their small landholdings more efficient, and they seem to see little relationship between their farming and the needs of the economy as a whole.

Through propaganda and exhortation, the Gomułka government is appealing to all classes for a greater sense of community responsibility for national economic problems. Gomułka has repeatedly emphasized that continued industrialization will benefit all classes by providing employment for a rapidly growing population, and he has asked that each class accept its share of sacrifice, work, and responsibility.

Among and within the various social classes, however, the sense of cooperation is weakly developed. While all groups are united in their support of national independence and patriotic ideals, they are divided in their day-to-day life by strong prejudices, enmities, and jealousies. The educated regard the peasants and their way of life with contempt. The workers resent the privileges and powers of the "intellectuals"; their relations with the managerial personnel of factories are frequently marked with tension and hostility. Both workers and peasants feel strongly that they are exploited and unjustly taxed and that there is great inequity in the present social system. Members of the intelligentsia still reap the highest material and social rewards.

Although the workers and peasants more or less accept the superior position of the intelligentsia in the social scale, they bitterly resent the fact that those already well off in terms of salary and social standing should be given additional privileges. Some of these privileges—the special stores, for example—have been abolished by the Gomułka government, but strong resentments still remain. A group of Poznan workers recently asked Gomułka why manual workers still do not get the same welfare benefits as "intellectual workers," and Gomułka replied that the "rights" of the intellectual workers were established long ago and could not easily be abolished.

One of the major means whereby the Communist government has attempted to achieve control over the social structure—and thereby integrate the functioning parts of the society—has been the creation of mass organizations on the basis of class lines. None of the prewar mass organizations, such as trade unions and political parties, had ever represented all the members of a single social class. Each social class reflected a diversity of political orientations, and a variety of political parties competed for the support of the members of any one social group. The organizations that did at least speak on behalf of the membership of a social class—such as the Polish Socialist Party—were internally divided into numerous factions, each with its own goals and interests, and their members rarely acted in concert.

The postwar government took over the existing trade unions and political parties, abolishing some and consolidating others, and tried to shape them into instruments of mass control (see chap. 6). Each major social class was to have its own political organization through which the Party hoped to channel its directives and appeals. But this attempt to impose unity from above created much bitterness among Poles of all classes, who jealously guarded their sense of individuality and uniqueness (see chap. 22). They resented being submerged in a "mass movement," preferring to participate in the activities of small, independent groups where they could express themselves as individuals. The government, failing to eliminate factionalism and separatist tendencies within its mass organizations, has been able to accomplish little in its effort to create a regimented society, responsive to the political and economic needs of the state.

ART AND INTELLECTUAL EXPRESSION

POLAND'S ARTISTIC AND INTELLECTUAL HERITAGE, WHILE SHAR-
ing much with the general western tradition, is strongly imbued with
national feeling and patriotism and possesses at times a marked religious character. Historically, Polish formal artistic and intellectual
activity was an undertaking by and for the landed gentry; it might on
occasion have been directed at the upper classes of other countries,
such as France and Italy, but seldom if ever at the masses of the
Polish people. By the turn of this century, however, the spirit and
message of upper-class Polish accomplishment, especially that of the
nineteenth century, began to filter down to a rising middle class; during the interwar period it reached all other groups in the population
and continues to do so today.

When in the tenth century Poland adopted the Christianity of
the Latin or Roman rite rather than that of the Greek or Byzantine,
it became culturally a part of the West. Latin was the prevailing
language in Polish literary production until the sixteenth century.
The Renaissance—in the sixteenth century—came to Poland from
remote but friendly Italy and helped to produce the first great age of
Polish art, literature, and learning. In the latter part of the sixteenth
century the Reformation contributed to the development of a vernacu-
lar literature, although many Polish writers, anxious to reach the
wider public of the outside world, continued to use Latin up to the
end of the seventeenth century. In the second half of the eighteenth
century Poland enjoyed an artistic and intellectual revival under the
stimulus of French cultural and political influences.

During the nineteenth century, when Poland languished under
foreign rule, the leading intellectuals, writers, and artists lived abroad
as exiles and Paris became the radiating center of Polish literary
and artistic expression. Stimulated by the spirit of European Romanticism and nationalism the exiles dedicated themselves to the task of

serving as the spiritual leaders of their nation in bondage. Their works, charged with intense patriotic feelings, espoused political programs and visions which could find no other outlet. Poetry, in particular, was permeated with religious and patriotic mysticism and became for Polish intellectuals the supreme manifestation of the nation's continued existence. The mass of Polish peasants, however, were not reached by this literary expression of a nationalistic mystique. They preserved their sense of "Polishness" by clinging to their native speech, their Catholic faith, and their traditional folkways, songs, dances, and arts.

Today, the nineteenth-century literary heritage is the common property of almost the entire nation. It is especially remembered and loved as Poland's greatest cultural achievement, and has taken on in the eyes of most Poles the glory and dignity of a great national institution. Polish accomplishments in other arts such as music and painting, as well as in scholarship and science, share some of the same honor and glory. The literary and artistic achievements of Poland's intellectual elite since World War I are less known and valued by the mass of the population.

After Poland regained its independence in 1918 broader outlets for political energy and interest were created and much of Polish intellectual life was freed from an almost exclusive concern with politics although some writers of course continued to be preoccupied with political and social problems.

Polish writers and artists, as well as scholars and scientists, enjoyed until World War II considerable autonomy in thir work. But following World War II, and particularly after 1949, all artistic and intellectual endeavor was called upon to reflect and propagate the Marxist-Leninist ideology as interpreted in the USSR. In practice this meant that Polish intellectuals and artists had to disown western influences, accept Soviet-Russian models of artistic, literary, and scientific production, and become propagandists of the current Party line. To the extent that they accepted, at least publicly, the Party as "the leader of life in every domain" they received considerable material support from the state. The literacy drives, educational improvements, and intensive development of mass-communication media made the intellectuals most important in the life of the country; as a consequence they were subjected to intense pressure from the Party.

The attempt to transform Poland's artistic and intellectual environment into the Soviet image proved a difficult process, and it failed to affect much more than surfaces. Although some writers, artists, and scholars were genuinely converted to faith in communism, many skillfully resisted the Party's political demands. Scholars frequently concealed original research behind the formal garb of ideological pronouncements and quotations from the classics of communism. Many older writers chose silence or turned to translating foreign classics. Others attempted to communicate "forbidden" thoughts to the public by the subtle use of metaphor, allegory, and play on words. The reading public, in turn, developed a strong sensitivity to hidden meanings: messages of resentment, revolt, and hope were read into novels, plays, and sometimes even into the text of the official Party press.

A strong spirit of cultural and national independence survived to find vigorous and open expression after Stalin's death in 1953. Writers, artists, and intellectuals vented their dissatisfaction with bureaucratic Party controls of cultural activity. The cultural rebellion gathered momentum throughout 1955 and in time gave voice to general disillusionment and frustration with existing conditions of life. Polish literature and art once more became vehicles for expressing national aspirations.

A wave of popular dissatisfaction and intellectual ferment helped bring Władysław Gomułka back to power as leader of the Party in October 1956 (see chap. 2). The Gomułka government quickly acknowledged the demands of intellectuals and artists for greater freedom of expression and for closer contacts with western artistic and intellectual movements. Thereupon, Poland's artistic and intellectual life became extremely animated, colorful, and expressive. Debates questioning many fundamentals of communist ideology mounted in the press. The vigor and spirit of the intellectual ferment began to disturb the government, and in March 1957 censorship was tightened and the publication of criticism of the USSR or of communist doctrines was forbidden. Gomułka apparently felt that the further questioning of ideological tenets menaced the stability of his regime or relations with the Soviet Union.

Whether or not the regime will find it necessary to take stronger action to curb the intellectual freedom won thus far cannot be determined. It appears unlikely, however, that a full-scale counteraction against the "liberalization" in Polish cultural life can succeed without harsh repression and without alienating those groups whose support is of crucial importance to the regime today.

Literature

ROMANTIC HERITAGE

Poland's Romantic period, encompassing roughly the years between the national insurrections of 1830 and 1863, is remembered by Poles as the greatest period in the history of their literature. To this epoch belongs the profusion of lyrical and epic poems written by exiles and abounding with patriotic symbolism and allegory.

Drawing upon Polish folklore and legend for inspiration, the Romantic writers protrayed a world of premonitions, riddles, and mysteries. Ancient beliefs and superstitions, the magic of witches, ghosts, and spirits, the spell of secluded cemeteries and chapels—all became symbols of some hidden truth. Much of the literature was penetrated with tragedy, pessimism, and bitterness and filled with accusations, invectives, didactic opinions, and long personal confessions. At the same time it conveyed a sense of spiritual ecstasy and revelation, and the mystical faith that the suffering of the Polish people would lead to a regeneration of the universe gave the poetry a distinctive beauty.

The three most widely remembered poets of the Romantic period are Adam Mickiewicz (1798–1855), Juliusz Słowacki (1809–49), and Zygmunt Krasiński (1812–59). Mickiewicz is considered by Poles to be their greatest poet, and passages from his works still are recited from memory. His semi-Biblical *Books of the Polish Nation* presents a synthesis of Polish history and is marked with a sense of reverence for Poland's past. In this and other works he saw Poland crucified, as Christ was crucified, for being the standard-bearer of mankind's spiritual values and ideals, but eventually rising from the dead to bring the world a more righteous order. Mickiewicz is also thought of as the nation's teacher—a man who soothed its sufferings and who united the Polish cause with that of humanity's struggle for a better future. He gave whole generations an armor, a "religion of the fatherland," which helped them survive and fight oppression. The following prose translation from the opening lines of his last great poetic work, *Pan Tadeusz,* known to every Polish schoolboy, illustrates the blend of religious and national feeling that permeates much of his writing:

> Holy Virgin, who protectest bright Czestochowa and shinest above the Ostra Gate in Wilno! Thou who dost shelter the castle of Nowogrodek with its faithful folk! As by miracle thou didst restore me to health in my childhood—when offered by my weeping mother to thy protection, I raised my dead eyelids, and could straightway walk to the threshold of thy shrine to thank God for the life returned me—so by miracle thou wilt return us to the bosom of our country. Meanwhile bear my grief-stricken soul to those wooded hills, to those green meadows stretched far and wide along the blue Niemen; to those fields painted with various grain, gilded with wheat, silvered with rye; where grows the amber mustard, the buckwheat white as snow, where the clover glows with a maiden's blush, where all is girdled as with a ribbon by a strip of green turf on which here and there rest quiet pear-trees.

Mickiewicz is regarded not only as a great patriot, but also as a supreme artist and master of the Polish word. Poles consider many of his descriptive passages—telling of foggy mornings and starry nights, rain and thunderstorms, the world of plants and animals, ponds, meadows, and woods at various times of the day or night, in different lights and innumerable colors—flawless and unsurpassed in the whole of Polish poetry.

Słowacki is seen as the second greatest Polish Romantic poet. He combined fairy lore with serious drama, weaving fancies round tragedy of ambition and crime to create the first great dramas in the Polish language. Many of his writings bear the influence of foreign works, particularly those of Shakespeare and Byron. Like Mickiewicz, Słowacki was deeply concerned with the fate of his nation. His *Agamemnon's Grave,* a poem which compares the struggle of ancient Greece with the Polish insurrection of 1830, is an outburst of bitterness and indignation. In this work he lamented that Poland's "angel's soul" was imprisoned within the nobleman's "coarse skull," insisting that this skull must be broken so that Poland might rise once more in a completely new form—"new, naked, bathed in the slime of the Styx, sculptured in one piece of clay."

Słowacki's tragic drama *Lilla Weneda* (inspired in part by Byron's *Childe Harold*) is imbued with dark foreboding about the future of Poland. An inevitable doom hangs over the heroes, sounding a note of warning and despair. His *Anhelli,* written with great simplicity and in a Biblical tone, contains the grim prophecy that his generation would not live to see a free fatherland. Elaborating on the messianic theme Słowacki insisted that the existing generation had to die and be utterly forgotten before Poland could rise again, and he called upon Poles to prepare themselves for martyrdom. These ideas provided a powerful stimulus for the hopeless uprising inside Poland in 1863.

The concept of Poland's messianic role in history found its final poetic crystallization in the works of Krasiński; he, Mickiewicz, and Słowacki were called the "trinity of seers." Although Krasiński was the least gifted poet of the three, he was perhaps the greatest exponent of Poland's spiritual nationalism. In *Dawn,* a song in praise of the beauty of woman and of nature, he kept alive the faith that Poland, sacrificed for the sins of the world, would rise again as the herald of God's Kingdom on earth.

The Romantic period produced a galaxy of lesser poets and writers, and though a time of national tragedy, it also gave Poland its best comic writer. Almost totally unaffected by contemporary conditions, Aleksander Fredro (1793–1876) wrote witty and sparkling plays (*Maidens' Vows, Ladies and Hussars, Vengeance*), which continue to provide light and diverting entertainment today. These plays were influenced in part by Molière but are bright with national coloring.

Although the period was distinguished for its poetry, prose also played a part in keeping the national spirit alive. Józef Kraszewski (1812–87) is regarded as the father of the Polish novel. He was the author of some 500 works of fiction, which encompassed the history of Poland from its dawn up to his own day. His numerous historical novels won him the title of "the Walter Scott of Poland."

POST-ROMANTIC PERIOD

The Romantic literature of Poland reached its zenith by the 1850's and then declined. Polish literature found a new orientation after the insurrection of 1863—the last outburst of political Romanticism in nineteenth-century Poland. Stimulated by the system of positivism elaborated by Auguste Comte, new writers advocated adaptation to day-to-day reality in place of religious exaltation and romantic dreams. In Poland, as elsewhere in Europe, the new realism found expression in the novel, which at this time began its rise to predominance of literary forms.

The novels of Kraszewski were still linked with the romantic past; the characteristic tendencies of the new age of realism were more definitely represented in the works of B. Prus (the pen name of Aleksander Głowacki, 1847–1912). His large-scale novels—*The Emancipated Women, The Doll*—give an excellent picture of Polish middle-class and professional life. His descriptions of life in Warsaw have been compared to Dickens' treatment of London; like Dickens, Prus is pre-eminent as a humorist. Somewhat similar to Prus in outlook, a woman novelist, E. Orzeszkowa (1841–1910), gained note as an advocate of social reform.

The works of another master of realism, Henryk Sienkiewicz (1846–1916), remained imbued with strong patriotic feeling. He chose Poland's heroic wars of the stormy seventeenth century as the subject matter of three huge epic novels, *With Fire and Sword, The Deluge,* and *The Little Knight,* jointly known as *The Trilogy,* which became enormously popular in Poland. His later novel on early Christianity under Nero, *Quo Vadis?,*was his most popular work abroad. Another novel, *The Knights of the Cross,* depicted the conflict between the Polish-Lithuanian Commonwealth and the Knights of the Teutonic Order in the early fifteenth century. Sienkiewicz was awarded the Nobel prize in 1905.

The works of Władysław Reymont (1867–1925), presenting a

vast panorama of Polish peasant life and imbued with tragic pathos, also tower high above those of many other novelists in the latter part of the nineteenth century. His prose epic, *The Peasants*, translated into all European languages, was hailed by foreign critics as the perfect picture of peasant life in world literature. It depicts the whole of life in the Polish countryside—with its customs, traditions, rituals, parties, personal passions, and social conflicts—against the background of the unending annual pageantry of the seasons. For it Reymont received the Nobel prize in 1924.

Other Polish novelists who gained prominence before World War I include G. Zapolska (1860–1921), a pioneer of the naturalistic trend, who laid bare in clinical fashion the hypocrisy and egotism of contemporary life; Z. Niedzwiecki (1865–1916), who wrote under the distinct influence of Maupassant; S. Żeromski (1864–1925), who pictures the hopelessly gray and oppressive daily reality of Polish provincial life.

Under the pen name Joseph Conrad, Józef Konrad Korzeniowski (1857–1924) became one of the great English novelists. Some of his countrymen in Poland, however, have never quite forgiven him for abandoning his native tongue.

In comparison with the number of outstanding novelists during this period, the roll of eminent poets is short. The works of Poland's first great woman poet, Maria Konopnicka (1842–1910), express great sympathy for the poor and oppressed. An appreciation for the growing social importance of the peasant and the factory worker is a keynote of her many lyrics. Some of her poems have become popular songs. The poems of Poland's most outstanding philosophical lyrist, Jan Kasprowicz (1860–1926), possess an elemental strength and have as their theme the struggle of a heroic human spirit against an apparently unconquerable and permanent power of evil.

The greatest playwright at the turn of the century, Stanisław Wyspiański (1869–1907), was also a gifted poet and painter. Reacting against the spirit of political resignation that permeated much of Polish life after the 1863 insurrection, he denounced the lethargy of his contemporaries and did much to revive the sense of national patriotism in Poland. His works with their criticism of social inertia and call to national action possess in the eyes of Poles today a dignity equal to that of the great Romantics.

Toward the end of the nineteenth century the rising literary generation, reacting against Positivism, turned toward antirealism. Christened "Young Poland," the new literary trend found support in the similar reaction in other European literatures at the time.

INTERWAR PERIOD

Lyric poetry dominated the literature of the first decade of interwar Poland. The tone of poetry at this time was set by the young "Skamander" poets, a group which derived its appellation from the title of a literary monthly. Their attitude toward the aims of poetry was expressed by J. Lechoń: "And in springtime let me look at the spring and not at Poland." They did not avoid the immediate problems of contemporary life but did insist that these should be presented in a way appropriate to the art of poetry rather than to moral or political instruction. The most important representatives of the "Skamander" group included J. Tuwim (1894–1954), A. Słonimski (b. 1895), J. Lechoń (pen name of L. Serafinowicz, 1899–1956), K. Wierzyński (b. 1894), M. Pawlikowskà (1895–1945), and W. Broniewski (b. 1898).

A variety of trends were represented in the literature of the period. A so-called "avant-garde" group of poets, influenced by such movements as futurism, expressionism, and surrealism, sought to bring about a radical reform in lyric poetry by discarding traditional rhythms and creating a language so new and different that it sometimes became unintelligible. Its representatives included T. Peiper (b. 1891), C. Miłosz (b. 1911), J. Przyboś (b. 1901), J. Kurek (b. 1904), M. Czuchnowski (b. 1909), and J. Czechowicz (1903–39).

The novel gradually moved again to the foreground with the beginning of the second decade of the interwar period and owes much for its development to a number of women authors, among them Z. Nałkowska (1885–1954), M. Kuncewicz (b. 1897), and Z. Kossak-Szczucka (b. 1890). The works of Maria Dąbrowska (b. 1892) particularly achieved popularity and possess some of the epic breadth found in the works of Tolstoy. Well-known men novelists included F. Goetel (b. 1890) and J. Kaden-Bandrowski (1885–1944).

Many of the novelists of this period were engrossed with a hunger for "authenticity" and "truth." With exact and dispassionate descriptions they captured the contemporary urban middle-class atmosphere of convention, sham, petty lies, and hypocrisy. Searching for new means of expression, they employed new and refreshing techniques in the composition of plots: abandonment of the chronological sequence of events; parallel simultaneous development of several actions; flashbacks of all kinds; mingling of various points of view in presenting characters and events; dramatization of dialogue. But while given to innovation in the structure of the novel, most writers of the period remained within the framework of realistic verisimilitude.

POSTWAR PERIOD

The Communist regime installed in Poland after World War II went to great pains to harness for its own purposes the creative energies of writers, poets, artists, scholars, and intellectuals in general. The policy of the Party in the domain of cultural life may be roughly divided into two stages: (1) a period of caution, and (2) a period of extensive subordination of intellectuals and their works to the demands of the Party. The year 1949 was the dividing line between the policy stages—the year in which Communist control spread to all aspects of Polish life.

During the immediate postwar years the regime had engaged in little direct interference in the cultural field. Literary clubs and circles appeared all over the country. Eminent prewar writers were welcomed as participators in the cultural life of the country and were given substantial material benefits and privileges. The more prominent or more trustworthy obtained good apartments and were provided with impressive summer quarters in nationalized country estates. Royalties for books and articles were much higher than before the war, and larger printings of books were made.

The regime encouraged grandiose speeches about the role of the intellectuals, who were endowed not only with prestige and considerable financial means but also with the appearance of great power. Contact with the "masses" was regulated through the agencies of the Ministry of Culture and Art. Extensive trips by writers and poets were organized for the purpose of giving lectures, reading original works, and conducting discussions with groups of factory workers, peasants, office clerks, and students. Certain words, themes, and ideas were politically taboo, but in general the writers were not yet issued specific instructions and in the lectures to factory workers were free to popularize such varied subjects as Copernicus or modern French poetry.

Many Polish writers and poets who had happened to be in Soviet Russia during the war were given high status as cultural officials. Some had been Communists since before the war but most were simply intellectuals with progressive leanings who had been very eager to defeat the Germans and liberate Poland. It was mainly this group which helped the new regime to install a bureaucratic apparatus for Communist control of Polish cultural life.

The Party's offensive to subordinate literary expression to its own aims was touched off in January 1949 at a Writers' Congress held in Szczecin and attended by Soviet as well as Polish writers. Communist spokesmen condemned writers for failing to inject enough "socialist content" in their works and for neglecting Marxist principles. Writers were told to accept the Party as judge of their works, and their organizations and professional associations were then brought under strict Party supervision and control. The other arts underwent the same process of regimentation.

Party supervision of the content of new works was achieved through censorship and control over the physical means of literary production. Polish literature was required to submit to the principles of Soviet aesthetic theory—"socialist realism"—and was transformed into a propaganda instrument. Some of the most outstanding authors —among them, J. Lechón, K. Wierzyński, C. Miłosz, M. Kuncewicz —escaped to the West. The better authors who continued to write in Poland—J. Tuwim, A. Słonimski, K. Brandys, K. I. Gałczynski, J. Iwaszkiewicz, T. Breza, and others—managed to show occasional flashes of talent in their work. The bulk of literary output, however, was devoted to political themes, and, in the main, outstanding works were rare. Polish and foreign classics enjoyed considerably more popularity than the new literature produced under Party dictation.

Polish writers and intellectuals strongly resented ideological regimentation, even though many paid lip service to Party doctrines, and in 1950 the regime complained of "a paralysis of creative will amidst our writers."

Interpretive Arts

THEATER

The drama ranks second only to literature in popular esteem in Poland. For Poles, who tend to see their own life and history as filled with drama and romance, the spell of the stage possesses a special potency. Their love of the theater borders on adoration, and actors are almost worshiped for possessing a "divine" gift. The fact that the wife of Poland's present Prime Minister (Cyrankiewicz) is a noted actress may, indeed, be an asset to his public career. Theatergoing is one of the most important social activities of the urban population, particularly the intelligentsia who consider it a serious and edifying experience, not entertainment.

In the nineteenth century Poland produced the three great dramatic writers already mentioned: Fredro, Słowacki, and Wyspiański. In addition, almost all of the Polish poets of that period wrote poetry in dramatic form. During the interwar period the best Polish plays were written by novelists rather than playwrights and there was no major dramatic development during those twenty years. Of contemporary playwrights, Z. Skowroński and J. Lutosławski are perhaps the best known today. Productions of foreign plays—French, English, German—have always been and continue to be very popular; tickets for their performances are invariably difficult to obtain.

The Party attempted after 1949 to harness the theater in the service of propaganda, but did not succeed in bringing about any radical changes. Plays considered "ideologically worthless"—for the most part French and German farces and comedies—were eliminated from the repertoire. The number of Polish and foreign classics performed was increased, but theater directors were taxed with the necessity of interpreting a play in accordance with the canons of the ideology as adapted by the current Party line. *Hamlet,* for example, was to be presented in such a way as to "bare the emptiness of the feudal world" with its "hypocrisy, corruption, sloth, and debauchery." The works of G. B. Shaw were given official approval on the basis that they unmasked the "mortal sins" of capitalism.

Such interference did little to change the tastes of the theatergoing public, which seized every opportunity to register disapproval of Communist policies. Pro-Communist actors, especially when imported from abroad, were given an icy reception, while those known to have no Communist connections received overwhelming ovations. The Party's attempt to regiment the theater has diminished considerably in recent months.

BALLET

Although Polish ballet was built on a well-developed folk dance tradition, it was and is primarily an urban enjoyment. Ballet stars are popular but they do not enjoy the wide and intensive adoration accorded them in the Soviet Union and some western countries. During the interwar period the ballet suffered from low standards of production, a shortage of choreographers and scenarios, and a neglect of the classical repertoire.

The ballet was given considerable state support after World War II. A system of state ballet schools was organized on the Russian pattern and a great deal was done to raise the level of training of dancers. The education of dancers today emphasizes classical and folk dancing but also admits some elements—such as "expressive" dancing—which are not fully recognized in the Soviet system.

FILMS

During the interwar period Polish film productions were generally of poor quality, and the best and most popular pictures were imported from abroad. Since the end of World War II Polish films have benefited greatly from Soviet cinema techniques. Acting, camera work, and musical themes are today of very good quality. Some of the films dealing with the war, the German occupation, and contemporary social problems were sufficiently impressive to win prizes at Venice. Many others produced in the postwar period have, however, suffered from mediocre scripts designed to fulfill some propaganda assignment.

Much of such propaganda is probably effective in rural communities now served by mobile cinema units. In the cities foreign films, particularly from France and Italy, continue to have the greatest popular appeal, and tickets for them are often sold on the black market. The best-liked Polish films are those which deal with historical themes—a life of Chopin was very popular—and which contain a lavish display of costumes and music.

OTHER INTERPRETIVE ARTS

A great number of outstanding performing musicians have been Poles. The pianists Józef Hofmann, Ignacy Paderewski, Artur Rubinstein, Wanda Landowska, the violinist Bronisław Hubermann, and the orchestra conductor Artur Rodziński are among those who have won world fame. Many Poles have been noted as particularly talented pianists and often win high honors at international piano competitions and musical festivals. Polish contributions to piano pedagogy and the development of piano technique have been outstanding.

Orchestral and singing groups are popular, and operettas and foreign musical shows are also greatly enjoyed. Jazz concerts are in considerable vogue at present—in fact, a veritable mania for western popular music and other such forms of entertainment has developed in Poland over the past year.

Numerous folk dance and singing groups such as the Mazowsze are particularly liked throughout the country. Many are supported by the state for their excellent propaganda value and are enthusiastically received at home as well as abroad.

Cabaret theater, based on Parisian examples, was very popular during the interwar period, providing an outlet of burlesque and criticism of the current scene. Humorous and extremely sharp political satire, often written by well-known poets and writers, was presented in the cabarets of the larger Polish cities in the form of short dramatic sketches, songs, and poems. This form of entertainment disappeared from Polish life after World War II but has lately been revived and is now enjoying enormous success.

Music

Though limited to the works of a few outstanding composers, Polish achievements in music are the source of great national pride. Frédéric Chopin (1810–49), unlike his peers in literature, stands alone in his time as Poland's greatest musician. He is, for Poles, the musical embodiment of the nation's spirit.

The violinist Henri Wieniawski (1835–80) won considerable recognition as a composer later in the century. The more popular and successful composers during the interwar period included J. Maklakiewicz, Roman Palestar, and Karol Szymanowski, the last being considered Poland's greatest since Chopin. These composers were influenced by German and French trends in music but also attempted to create a style of their own based on native folk music.

Immediately after World War II music in Poland enjoyed a lively revival. Musical societies were formed in all principal cities, and numerous academies and schools of music were built. Gradually, however, the state assumed control of the publication of music scores and presented Soviet achievements as the only ones worthy of emulation. Composers also were told to purge their works of western influences and to make greater use of folk motifs in their compositions. Recent events have led to a relaxation of such restrictions, and Polish musicians today are showing an avid interest in the development of modern music abroad.

Fine Arts

The fine arts in Poland have been strongly influenced by the general European tradition; almost from the moment of its conversion to Christianity, Poland absorbed and assimilated influences from abroad.

Poland's immediate neighbor, Germany, exerted a strong influence as late as the fifteenth century. Traces of Gothic are preserved in a number of churches and buildings in Cracow, which in the fifteenth century became a center of arts and crafts, as well as of science and learning, and gave Poland one of the greatest sculptors of the time in Europe—Wit Stwosz—whose works in the late Gothic style influenced Polish artists up to the middle of the sixteenth century and are today highly valued.

The artistic forms of the Renaissance were brought to Poland by Italian artists at the beginning of the sixteenth century. Zygmunt I (r. 1506–48), married to a Sforza of Milan, surrounded his court with Italian architects and sculptors. Native artisans imitated Italian models in building palaces and castles for temporal and spiritual lords throughout Poland. Many structures contained mixed Gothic and Renaissance elements. Intricate geometrical and floral ornamentations preserved late Gothic styles, while profiles of arcades and capitals were of a purely Renaissance character. Subordinated to architecture, painting and sculpture were employed primarily as ornament and decoration.

The baroque style was introduced into Poland in the seventeenth century. Throughout central and eastern Poland new churches and buildings were erected which equaled those of Prague and Vienna. The Church of the Sisters of the Holy Sacrament in Warsaw and the Church of St. Anne in Cracow are among the best examples of this period. The royal castle in Warsaw was reconstructed in baroque. Some of the buildings of Warsaw University also bear the imprint of this style. Baroque evolved into rococo during the eighteenth century.

During the nineteenth century neoclassical or Empire styles were used throughout Poland for city mansions, country houses, churches, and public buildings. The typical design of Polish country houses, which persists even today, was established at this time: one-story, with front columns and a porch. The buildings erected in Prussian Poland reveal the influence of a German or "Berlin" classicism. Neo-Gothic was not used extensively, though there are such outstanding examples of it as the Cathedral of St. John in Warsaw and the courtyard of the Jagiellonian Library in Cracow.

The nineteenth century produced no masterpieces of Polish sculpture. Polish painting, however, began to acquire prominence. The huge and crowded canvases of Jan Matejko (1838–93), recognized as Poland's greatest painter, depict numerous scenes out of Polish history.

In close contact with European trends in art during the interwar period, Polish painters absorbed such movements as cubism and formism, but also found new inspiration in the color and design of traditional peasant decorative arts. Interwar Poland also produced a number of able artists in the fields of sculpture, wood engraving, drawing, and illustration. The development of both sculpture and wood engraving was greatly influenced by the traditions of peasant art, particularly the woodcut. In the field of wood engraving the expressive works of Władysław Skoczylas (1883–1934) are held in especially high esteem.

Polish architects also found many new opportunities for creative work in the wake of World War I. Some patterned their work on the classical styles of the late eighteenth and nineteenth centuries. Others, rejecting conservative forms, favored rationalism and simplicity. Many incorporated in their work the decorative elements peculiar to Polish peasant art. The general trend during the interwar period was toward a monumental style in architecture which on the whole possessed little inspiration or originality.

The ideological regimentation of the fine arts after World War II paralleled developments in other fields. Polish painters, architects, and sculptors protested vigorously that artists should be free to seek their own means of expression, but open protest became increasingly difficult after 1949, and the fear of losing job, prestige, and privileges induced many to submit to the Party's demands. Some gave up their professions or continued to work privately, refusing to allow exhibition of their works. Others fled the country and established themselves abroad, among them F. Topolski, whose sensitive drawings and illustrations have attracted particular attention in the West.

The works exhibited after 1949 were chiefly of a propagandistic nature. A great deal of money was spent by the state to organize exhibitions and to popularize art in general; permanent and traveling exhibitions of Soviet and Polish painting and sculpture attracted great crowds. Well-organized museums in Cracow, Warsaw, Poznan, and other cities became important centers of propaganda activities. The effort to popularize the fine arts apparently had some success. At the same time, the rebuilding of Warsaw according to Soviet styles, which Poles considered pretentious and ugly, deeply wounded Polish pride.

Events over the past year have restored to Polish artists much of the freedom of expression that previously had been lost. An increasing number of paintings, drawings, and illustrations exhibited today display considerable imagination and originality.

Folk Art

Folk song, dance, legend, poetry, sculptural wood carving, pottery, weaving, embroidery, and other arts and crafts hold an important place in the life of the Polish peasantry. Marked regional and local variations are found, and in all of the peasant arts there is also great scope for individual variation. Perhaps the most outstanding characteristic of Polish folk art is the peasant's love for an immense diversity of color and ornamentation and for intricacy of design.

Each region has its own distinctive costumes, songs, dances, and traditions. Costumes and dances serve, perhaps, as the most important symbols of regional and national identification for the peasants. The mazurka, a dashing dance originating in the Mazovian plains, is among the most popular of national dances. The stately polonaise, originating as a drawing-room dance of the upper classes, has been adapted for ceremonial occasions. The polka is primarily a dance of the suburbs. The krakowiak presents a striking contrast in lively and melancholy spirits. The dances of the mountain regions of southern Poland are especially vigorous, exciting, and colorful.

Polish folk songs deal with such universal themes as love, laughter, sorrow, and bondage. Old ceremonial songs are sung at weddings, funerals, christenings, at the end of harvest, and at other familial or social festivals. New songs are composed spontaneously for special occasions.

Tales and legends contain a mixture of religious and secular motifs: the lives of saints, the battles of ancient kings, the contest between knights and dragons, the heroism of ancient bandits and robbers. The folk epic or saga is absent from Polish folklore. Although the religious and magical significance of many of the tales has been forgotten, the stories themselves still provide considerable aesthetic enjoyment.

Wood carving, pottery, embroidery, weaving, and other decorative arts are well developed throughout Poland. In all of these arts, individual virtuosity and originality are highly prized by the peasants. Weaving and embroidery display a great variety of techniques and color combination. The most noted carving—abstract designs, figures of saints, scenes from everyday life or from the Bible—is found in the southern mountain regions. Wooden dolls, dressed in traditional peasant costumes, are popular in all parts of the country.

The practice of coloring Easter eggs is a tradition reaching back to the eleventh century and has developed into an elaborate and complex art. The designs used may include motifs from plant and animal life, stylized representations of household objects, and geometric patterns. Paper decoration is a more recent but extremely popular form of Polish folk art. Mazes of intricate designs are cut out freehand from glossy paper and used to decorate walls, windows, and cupboards. The designs may include dots, squares, hexagons, circles, conical shapes, wreathes of wheat, stylized trees, animals, and birds. Lacelike curtains for windows and baskets for flowers are also cut out of paper. Paper cutouts are often used to add color to festive occasions.

The Communist regime has taken a great interest in the development of folk art. Many folk artists have been organized into cooperatives through which they are provided with work and guaranteed the sale of their products. Numerous art festivals are devoted to exhibits of peasant weaving, embroidery, paper decoration, pottery, and wood carving. The Ministry of Culture and Art organizes competitions for folk artists and craftsmen, who are given a chance to win prizes, diplomas, and honorable mentions. Much of this is done for propaganda purposes, and folk artists are rewarded for producing works which reflect such new themes and motifs as "The Fight for Peace," "The Tractor," but although some peasant art may be thus artificially sustained, a great deal of it remains rooted in tradition.

Scholarship and Science

Poland was an important center of humanistic learning during the fifteenth and sixteenth centuries. The process of Latinization fostered by the Roman Catholic Church facilitated the rapid reception of the Renaissance. The University of Cracow, founded in 1364, was reorganized in 1400 after the pattern of the Sorbonne and became an intellectual center for eastern Europe. By the end of the fifteenth century it was one of the most important seats of scholarship and humanistic activity in the western world. The greatest scholar produced by Renaissance Poland and one of the greatest figures of the western world, Nicolaus Copernicus (Mikołaj Kopernik, 1473–1543), was educated in Cracow, later going to Italy to study further in mathematics, astronomy, canon law, medicine, and economics.

Cracow attracted scores of teachers and students from abroad until well on in the sixteenth century, but during the troubled seventeenth century the tradition of scholarship and science declined and after the partitions was carried on by only fitful and fragmentary efforts. In the late nineteenth century a number of Poles once more achieved eminence in the world of learning. Distinguished scholars appeared in such fields as linguistics, literary criticism, and historiography, and also made important contributions to scientific research. Two Polish scientists at Cracow (Wróblewski and Olszewski) succeeded in liquefying air in the 1880's. Natanson (1864–1937) won international fame as a mathematical physicist and is also considered one of the masters of Polish scientific prose. Raciborski (1863–1917) contributed to the development of all branches of botanical research. Cybulski (1854–1922) developed a method of registering the action of the heart, which found world-wide medical acceptance.

A great deal of Polish learning and talent at this period was scattered over the globe. The University of Chile at Santiago de Chile was organized by the mineralogist Domeyko (1802–89). Highly original work on the evolution of law was done by Professor L. Petrażycki (1867–1931) at St. Petersburg. Important exploring in North Africa was done by the geographer and botanist J. Dybowski (1855–1930). Malinowski (1884–1942) won great renown as a pioneer in the field of anthropology and occupied a chair at the University of London and was later a visiting professor at Yale University. Maria Skłodowska-Curie (1867–1934), daughter of a Polish scientist and educator, completed her scientific education in Paris and there with her French husband Pierre did the research that led to the discovery of radium. She shared in two Nobel prizes. The international recognition given to these outstanding Polish scholars and scientists is a source of great pride in Poland today.

INTERWAR PERIOD

During the interwar period distinguished research in the physical and social sciences was conducted in the academic centers of the new Poland. Those engaged in scholarly pursuits enjoyed high social prestige, and a number of notable Polish scholars played important roles in the political life of the country. Professor W. Swiętosławski (b. 1881), a distinguished chemical physicist, for a time occupied the post of Minister of Education. Professor Ignacy Mościcki (1867–1946), a pioneer in industrial chemistry, was elected President of the Republic in 1926. Infeld, (b. 1898), a nuclear physicist, collaborated with Einstein and is today head of the Institute of Theoretical Physics at Warsaw University.

The men of learning who achieved particular distinction during the interwar period, at home and abroad, included Professor E. Romer (1871–1954), director of the school of geography and mapmaking at Lvov; Krzyżanowski (b. 1873), Poland's foremost economist, who presided over the school of political economy at Cracow; Professor F. Znaniecki (b. 1882), head of the Poznan school of sociology, who became well known in English-speaking countries through his books on the Polish peasant in America; Professor W. Sierpiński (b. 1882), head of a famous school of pure mathematics in Warsaw; Professor J. Łukasiewicz (b. 1878), in charge of the school of mathematical logic in Warsaw. During this period in scientific research emphasis was generally placed upon the theoretical rather than the applied sciences.

The humanities continued to be represented by outstanding scholars. Work in the fields of history, literary criticism, linguistics, and logic was especially noteworthy.

POSTWAR PERIOD

Following World War II Polish scholarly and scientific activities were brought under total state control and direction. The policies of the Communist regime had both beneficial and detrimental effects upon Polish learning. Organizational changes in the work of scientific institutions led to improvements in team work and in the planning of research, and the physical sciences were able to benefit from Soviet advances in their respective fields. At the same time, the doctrinal demands of the ideology hampered independent research, particularly in the biological and social sciences, and became a source of frustration for many engaged in scholarship.

Despite such restraints, many Polish scholars remained devoted to the ideals of scholarly integrity. By giving lip service in their works with exclamations against prewar and western scholarship and by quoting numerous Russian authors, some were able to publish their own findings. Since Gomułka's recent return to power Polish scholarship and science appear to have won considerable freedom from the ideological fetters of the Stalinist past.

Recent Trends

Communist efforts to regiment Polish thought and culture proved far from successful. The regime failed to transform the thinking habits and tastes of Polish writers, artists, scholars, and their public. To survive, many paid lip service to Party doctrines, but even convinced Communists retained private reservations about the Sovietization of Poland's artistic and intellectual life.

Direct criticism of the regime and its official philosophy became difficult and dangerous after 1949. Literary and artistic debates, however, provided intellectuals with an outlet for disguised political writing. Artists and intellectuals reacted to the new atmosphere of relaxation that followed Stalin's death in 1953 with a sense of relief and a determination to profit from the easing of restraints. In April 1954 the Party found it necessary to discuss shortcomings in cultural propaganda, and writers and artists were criticized for failing to "educate" the masses effectively. This set off a vigorous controversy in various literary and cultural publications, in which Polish writers assailed the discouragement of experimentation, dictation from above, and restrictions on the artist's freedom of expression.

This ferment continued unabated for a year. In July 1955 the Party reminded writers, in a mild reproof of their criticism of the Party line, that the principles of "socialist realism" remained valid, but it was conceded that they had been interpreted too rigidly.

Simultaneously, the cultural "thaw" spread to other fields. Young painters were authorized in July 1955 to stage an exhibit of new works in which they could be as "western" as they liked. A storm of controversy developed when a prominent Communist sociologist, Józef Chałasiński, sharply criticized the application of Leninist philosophy to the social sciences.

The questioning of Soviet aesthetic criteria and Marxist ideology led to an open expression of disillusionment with the regime's political and economic policies. In August 1955 a Warsaw weekly literary review published "Poem for Adults" by Adam Ważyk, which created a sensation in Poland as well as in the West. Ważyk was a leading Communist poet whose works, including an ode to Stalin, had previously contained little of worth. Suggesting in the title of his new poem that the poetry of the Stalinist period was for children, he now painted a grim picture of actual life in Poland. He spoke of people "who wait for justice" and of the prevalence of alcoholism, hooliganism, bandits, and social decay. He attacked Party doctrine, demanding that people should not be forced to believe in "chimeras," but he did not confess a loss of basic political faith. The poem concluded with an appeal for a change in policy, though not in leadership:

> *for a clear truth,*
> *for the bread of freedom,*
> *for burning reason,*
> *for burning reason.*
>
> *We demand these every day.*
> *We demand these through the party.*

Other published articles and poems, full of bitterness and irony, were equally sensational.

The official denunciation of Stalin in February 1956 at the Twentieth Congress of the Communist Party of the Soviet Union gave impetus to fresh demands for greater creative freedom in Poland. Poles continued to speak out, and their right to do so was hailed by Władysław Gomułka when he returned to power as head of the Party in October 1956.

Since then Poland's artistic and intellectual life has been one of remarkable ferment and excitement. Wrtiers, artists, and scholars who previously had refused to bow to Party dictation were now acclaimed as heroes, whereas those who had followed the Party line were in many cases accused of servility. The revival of satirical, political revues in the theater was greeted enthusiastically.

The literary scene has been enriched by the appearance of young and new writers who have been extremely bold and outspoken in their display of intellectual independence. A particularly talented newcomer is Marek Hłasko, hailed by some Poles as the "voice of the generation." A Polish critic singled out Hłasko in February 1957 as a writer who "explodes with moral indignation," who "touches upon the naked truth of our life," and whose works are "imbued with wrath over human dignity which has been trodden upon."

In practically all fields of intellectual and artistic endeavor there has been a great reaction against the enforced cultural isolation of the "Stalinist" era. Almost anything coming from the West is seized upon enthusiastically, sometimes only for the sake of novelty, sometimes as a demonstration against communism. Polish newspapers are now offering young readers "mass instruction" in "Rock 'n Roll."

Editions of western light fiction, particularly detective stories, are quickly sold out. American newspapers and magazines are now available and have been received with considerable interest. Polish publications look increasingly more like those of the western countries. Children's comic books are being edited on the lines of American comic strips. Magazines devoted to Wild West adventures, science-fiction, and other light entertainment are extremely popular.

Poland's more serious writers, musicians, architects, painters, scholars, and scientists, are showing an immense and almost fervid interest in western arts and sciences today. Soviet models of literary, artistic, and scientific productions are being discarded with elation, except where they possess some practical value, as in the physical sciences. In April 1957 Poland accepted a grant of $500,000 from the Ford Foundation (long an object of Soviet propaganda abuse) to stimulate cultural, scientific, and technical exchanges with western Europe and America. Dr. Henry T. Heald, president of the Foundation, noted in his announcement of the grant that:

> . . . the universities and scholars and students of Poland have given us strong evidence, which we have investigated very carefully, of their desire to renew relations with the free institutions of Europe and the United States.

A delegation from the Rockefeller Foundation visited Poland in February 1957 to study the possibility of establishing a similar program of cultural exchange.

By permitting a more critical attitude and a greater freedom for the expression of opinion, the present regime has undoubtedly gained much. It can maneuver with greater elasticity, and, under the guise of greater reasonableness, has been able to persuade many people of its sincerity and patriotism. By permitting at least a portion of the truth to be spoken, it may hope that Poland's artists and intellectuals will be animated with a more persuasive communist spirit.

At the same time the current intellectual unrest and spirit of independence is being viewed with growing unease. The regime apparently fears that its ideological position may be threatened and has recently attempted to exclude doctrinal matters from intellectual debate. In time, reversion to tightening of controls in the intellectual sphere may be thought necessary. But since the regime has through propaganda, improved schooling, and improved communications built up a broad following for Polish intellectuals, a future official stifling of the hopes for complete intellectual and artistic liberation would probably be difficult and arouse much resentment.

VALUES AND ATTITUDES

POLAND IS A WESTERN NATION. THE CREATION OF THE POLISH state and its adoption of Christianity were simultaneous and the Poles have viewed themselves for centuries as an outpost of the Latin Christian world. The significant attitudes and forms of behavior of the Polish people revolve around the value placed on individual dignity, initiative, originality, and self-expression. The uniqueness of the Polish people in part lies in the intensity with which they hold these and other values of the Catholic West. In terms of Poland's present alignment with the Soviet Union, it is significant that Poles always have identified Russia, tsarist or Soviet, as an alien culture hallowing conformity and the submersion of the individual in the state.

Poles are trained from early childhood to exercise self-command and are brought up with the conviction that the individual can rule himself. Discipline is to be found in the individual, rather than enforced by the institutions of society. The ideal person is independent, strong, and self-reliant. The feeling that each person is unique and should be allowed considerable freedom for self-expression is sustained by the Roman Catholic belief in the sacredness of the human person. This sense of personal dignity and difference is fundamental to a Pole's behavior as a member of society and the nation.

Socially, individualism is expressed through the Pole's unwillingness to submerge himself in any group or submit to authority, except when it becomes clearly necessary for national or individual survival. In the absence of a perceived threat the society is fragmented, governmental authority evaded, and there is extreme political factionalism, great conflict within the family, village, and nation, and a general unwillingness to work together.

The individual will first look to his own interests and only secondarily to those of others. Self-interest, however, is not simply a question of material aggrandizement. The individual is concerned with protecting his identity. His actions and those of others are considered as they affect his honor. To back down from a position, to compromise, to admit error is to lose honor.

Honor also is related to something outside the individual—the nation. Polish individualism has been shaped by the Polish historical milieu. The Polish approach to life bears the deep imprint of more than a century of subjugation during which Poles were unable to shape their own destiny. For over a hundred years Poles lived on the defensive and glorified their ability to withstand overwhelming pressure. A proud intelligentsia tradition of self-sacrifice in the name of Poland produced an ideal of heroism as an end in itself which eventually was adopted by the mass of the population.

In contrast to the ideal of heroic action, the toil of everyday life takes on a dull, gray, uninteresting cast. Work, seldom an end in itself, is an often despised necessity—unconnected with honor or the welfare of the nation. For both peasants and intelligentsia, work is a means of supplying immediate gratification. Practical concerns tend to be given only enough time and effort to insure one's present wellbeing. Frugality and concentration on laborious accumulation of material things to be enjoyed sometime in the future are for the most part not valued.

But everyday life must go on. The nation does not exist in a perpetual state of crisis. National and individual honor cannot be defended at every turn. Despite the obsession with individualism, a minimum of social order, cooperation, and organization is necessary. The Polish social order is preserved through an emphasis on social forms—through which an essential minimum of predictability and cooperation is established. But order as such is not a part of the basic Polish value system.

In daily face-to-face relationships Poles expect of each other a show of mutual respect. Great stress is placed upon the proper forms of behavior. The dignity of an individual should never be offended. Courtesy, etiquette, and a certain formality are the basis of everyday human relations. A Pole is willing to work with others in an organization so long as the forms are such as to allow him to express his individual opinion. A person must be open in his dealings with others and should express himself freely, sincerely, and with feeling.

Since the end of World War II the Communist government has attempted to establish and enforce unity and conformity in social, political, and economic life. In so doing, it deeply violated the individualism that Poles hold dear. It insisted that the individual submerge himself in the Party and its auxiliaries; it created numerous mass organizations for indoctrination. But the Poles refused to conform. The peasants refused to be pressured into collectives. The workers demonstrated that they would not be bound by labor-discipline laws or by production quotas which they had no part in establishing.

For ten years the government has exhorted the people to work hard, "to build socialism" for a better tomorrow; except during the initial task of reconstruction they have elicited little response. Recently the Church has also appealed to the nation to shoulder the burden of wearisome, long toil that is necessary if all are to benefit economically and if Poland is to maintain itself as an independent nation. The Poles, however, seem to see little connection between dull toil and their survival as a nation.

The needs of industrialization have also conflicted with the value system. Not only is there a lack of discipline in the labor force but in many cases Poles refuse to enter occupations which would put them on the production line. The economy needs efficient farm workers, mechanics, practicing engineers, yet the positions most sought after, even with respect to the poorest white-collar job, are those which carry the aura of "intellectual activity."

The fundamental source of conflict between the state and the people has been the government's insistence on Soviet forms and its obvious subservience to the USSR. The October 1956 events marked a shift in the relationship between the two countries; for the Poles, Gomułka is the symbol of their new, if limited, independence. While Gomułka has been made by the situation, his appeal is a personal one and he stands on what he is able to accomplish. His government has attempted to return to forms of organization which preserve and encourage individuality. Workers' councils, greater freedom for intellectual expression, debates in the *Sejm,* peasant discussion and freedom to reject collectivization, and various other government programs, all are part of this effort to demonstrate a return to Polish values and forms.

The Individual and Society

Good manners and dignified behavior are highly valued by all classes. In the Polish village personal relationships are very formal and marked with great reserve. Rural discourse, studded with rhymed proverbs, is measured and deliberate. The peasant takes great pains to preserve his own dignity while respecting that of others. To be lacking in formality, politeness, and dignity is to be crude and to offend another person's honor.

In the cities personal behavior is freer and more spontaneous, but etiquette and courtesy are as important as in the countryside. A person is expected to be cordial with others but not boisterous and lacking in tact. Self-respect demands a display of good manners; little courtesies dot all of life. It is believed that each person one deals with should be made to feel that he is respected as an individual and that greetings, though correctly formal, should express a certain warmth of feeling. The emphasis on courtesy is sometimes overtly made light of in the cities today, but the practice of good manners in daily life continues to be regarded as essential for any person of integrity, refinement, and "culture."

Hospitality to others, including strangers, is stressed. No matter how poor the peasant family, a stranger or a guest must be made to feel welcome. It is a custom among peasants on Christmas Eve to serve an extra plate for "the guest beyond the mountain or for a passing wanderer or beggar." According to a peasant saying, "God enters the home when a guest enters in." Among the upper classes also visitors are traditionally welcome and looked upon as an honor.

Deference, politeness, and respect are reflected in the very language used by a Pole in his relations with others. There is a variety of forms of politeness for a variety of occasions. The great concern with individual dignity, however, makes a Pole very sensitive to any personal slight, insult, or injury. He is easily offended if not shown the proper forms of respect. An ill-mannered guest is deeply resented and viewed with contempt. Rudeness is considered an assault on one's honor and an insult is seldom overlooked—even if the opportunity for retaliation comes only long afterward. Poles, thus, are quick to quarrel; honor must be protected at any cost, and no compromise is permitted.

In relations with others each mature person is expected to hold some kind of individual viewpoint—as an extension of his personality —and defend it against other individuals or even the rest of the community. A Pole will apologize readily for losing his temper or displaying bad manners but admits to faulty judgment only with the greatest difficulty. To confess that one was wrong is a matter of great shame and Poles find it hard to understand a person who has honestly changed his mind.

GROUP SOLIDARITY

The strong need to preserve one's personal autonomy is a particularly important aspect of a Pole's behavior as a member of a group. If he identifies himself with a group he feels he must defend it from outside criticism and attack. Just as a Pole believes in the uniqueness of every man, he feels that his own particular village, community, or political party is unique. The forced merger of the rival Socialist and peasant political associations after World War II, for example, and their incorporation into a Communist-dominated popular front produced great bitterness and resentment among the rank and file of these organizations. The achievement of unity and cooperation between separate organizations is ordinarily very difficult unless all are equally threatened from outside.

The Party's struggle against factionalism, particularly in the political field, has been especially noteworthy since the return of Gomułka. In the atmosphere of relative political freedom that followed the October crisis the government found it hard to contain the pressures of diverse and conflicting interests within and outside the Party. Although Party propaganda has insisted that unity does not mean "absorption" or "liquidation," fear of losing independence by uniting with a rival group seems very strong. The official press has admitted that it will take time, effort, and considerable tact before the "unification concept" can be given "meaning and life."

Stressing his own self-reliance the individual is not particularly inclined toward cooperation with others unless all share a common danger. Despite the proliferation of governmental controls, for example, public officials frequently make their own decisions and often abuse their position or power for personal advantage. Collusion, graft, and corruption, typical of the interwar administration, continue to plague the Communist government. Marian Rybicki, former Minister of Justice, complained before a session of the *Sejm* in July 1957:

> . . . immense material and moral damage is being inflicted upon the nation . . . by the activities of diverse cliques which succeeded in occupying frequently key positions in enterprises and in industrial and commercial institutions and in monopolizing in their hands all kinds of privileges, for instance, the allocation of imported goods in great demand, flats, credits, and building materials for private construction.

The individual, in the last analysis, refuses to submerge himself within a group. He reserves the right to act on his own. Among the peasants there is strong reluctance to share work and land with neighbors and little borrowing or lending of implements or household goods is done. In the cities even the forms of courtesy and etiquette are bypassed when it is necessary to line up at a bus stop or to obtain goods in a store.

Although the individual rarely turns to his family for understanding and seldom loses himself in any cause but that of the nation, he finds great emotional support and intellectual satisfaction in friendship, which, as the one relationship which is developed by choice of the individual, is lasting and highly valued. True friendship must be a relationship of equals and is tested by sacrifice and loyalty. Friendships are highly selective, few, and intense. They transcend political lines; it is not uncommon for a Polish Communist to shelter a non-Communist friend. Loyalty to a friend, however, does not necessarily demand a complete frankness about one's entire inner life. A fundamental part of an individual's life is never exposed even to the closest intimates.

The Pole's obsession with personal autonomy and integrity so fragment loyalties and interests that few existing institutions or values contribute to working out the problems of a modern state. There is unity in language, religion, national consciousness, patriotism, but in little else. Within the society there is little concerted and effective action on the part of groups or individuals for anything not directly related to the defense or welfare of Poland.

The unity that can be created on the basis of commonly held national ideals, however, is dramatically illustrated by the argreement reached between the Church and the government following Gomułka's return to power. Spokesmen for the Church as well as Catholic laymen and writers have consistently stressed that they have no intention of minimizing the differences between Marxists and Catholics but that loyalty to Poland was more important than all the differences— and under present circumstances no other form of government for Poland was possible.

Although the national ideal is frequently vague, amorphous, and subject to individual interpretation, competing political groups have always subscribed to the same national symbols. In general, most Poles support the Church in its insistence that national ideals must include independence, a "respect for human dignity and freedom," and the maintenance of close ties with western civilization. In his sermons Cardinal Wyszyński has made a special point of describing Latin and Roman culture as one of the most beautiful and greatest achievements of mankind and has emphasized several times the importance of renewing and stregthening Poland's bonds with the West. Communist efforts to wean Poland from the West was one of the major sources of popular resentment prior to October 1956.

The Gomułka government is now identifying itself with the national ideal as understood by the people. By stressing the "Polish road" to socialism it has indicated it will no longer be totally subservient to Russia. Party leaders speak in favor of a greater freedom for individual self-expression, initiative, and responsibility. The government is encouraging the resumption of cultural contacts with the

West. The rights of the Church in matters of faith have been recognized. In attempting to pursue an independent course without provoking Russian intervention, the government leaders found that they possessed, for the first time, the support of a united nation—as was demonstrated during the elections of January 1957.

Popular approval of the national goals incorporated into Gomułka's program, however, does not mean that the people willingly accept or respect the authority of the Party or of the government as such. The government's efforts to diminish the appearance of command by emphasizing persuasion rather than coercion, without relinquishing political power, have served to intensify resistance to governmental controls. In the atmosphere of new-found freedom, many Poles have availed themselves of the opportunity to riot, strike, and to criticize and attack the institutions of authority.

AUTHORITY AND LEADERSHIP

The attitude of a Pole toward authority and leadership is colored by his feeling that every person should have the strength and ability to exercise initiative and responsibility, and by his conviction that each individual possesses equal dignity and equal rights. Direction from outside authority or the preeminence of one man over his fellows is resented by almost all Poles. The right to criticize officials freely is cherished.

While there is a basic unwillingness to submit to leadership, Poles do, however, recognize the need for some authority—as a necessary evil—in society. A person who represents a specific authority will usually be given at least a minimum of cooperation and obedience. The individual occupying a position of authority is expected to show respect to those who come under his jurisdiction, and he will inspire great hostility if he is dictatorial, brusque, and insensitive in his dealings with others. The degree to which a leader is respected, then, depends largely on his personal qualities; if he is honest, frank, and shows a sensitive concern for the feelings and dignity of others he is likely to win popular support.

The importance of these qualities in a public official was illustrated in a meeting between Prime Minister Cyrankiewicz and Poznan factory workers in July 1957. During the Poznan riots of June 1956, Cyrankiewicz had threatened the workers with severe reprisals. This had produced great indignation among the workers. After Gomułka's return to power a delegation of Poznan workers demanded that Cyrankiewicz make a personal apology for his conduct at the time of the uprising. The Prime Minister went to Poznan in July 1957 to talk with the workers and to explain his position. By a display of frankness and sincerity he was able to appease much of the hostility he had previously provoked.

There is one type of leader whom Poles will freely admire and readily follow—a selfless champion of national ideals and a courageous defender of the nation's honor. He must be devoid of all personal ambition and pretensions. He is honored less as a person than for the ideals which he represents. One does not support such a leader; one puts faith in him. Poland's historical military heroes and the poets of the Romantic period are seen in this light. After World War I many Poles regarded Piłsudski as such a leader, and it is possible that Gomułka is viewed in this light by some of his followers today.

If entrusted with authority and responsibility a Pole feels strongly that he must have the freedom to make his own decision. The ability to make quick decisions without requiring previous instructions is greatly valued; to be bound by detailed instructions is highly resented. The centralization of power under the Communists and the intrusion of rigid Party dictates into almost all spheres of life produced widespread discontent within and outside the Party.

Discipline within the Party has been difficult to enforce. The imposition of uniform decisions from above and the Russian pattern of providing everybody with the same instructions and the same things to say created strong resentments at all levels of the hierarchy. Whenever possible, local Party officials and activists interpreted their instructions in their own way and attempted to meet specific problems on their own initiative.

The population, in turn, found the dictatorial attitude of government and Party officials intolerable. The laws, regulations, and demands of the state were met with passive resistance and evasion. Violence against local officials was not uncommon. The Party leadership attempted, particularly after 1948, to enforce its rule by terror and coercion but never achieved total control over the society. To have made control really effective the government would have had to resort to force on a scale which probably would have risked civil war.

Gomułka's present search for more viable methods of government includes an experimentation with more acceptable forms of leadership. And for some time before Gomułka's return to power local Party officials had already been trying to find new ways of eliciting the cooperation and support of the people for specific programs and activities. An incident reported in the Warsaw press, January 1956, is significant in this regard.

A local Party committee at Nowa Huta was attempting to get the peasants of a certain village to start a cooperative brickkiln. Most of the peasants were curtly informed that a meeting of the village would be held at a certain time to discuss "official matters" and that attendance was obligatory. About twenty villagers, however, received another announcement simply stating that at a specified time the project of organizing a cooperative brickkiln would be discussed in the village. Only those peasants who received the nonobligatory announcement attended the meeting and decided to join the cooperative. The local Party secretary was quoted as commenting: "I think that those new forms are better adapted to human nature. For that reason, it is not necessary to 'urge' the people too much."

Such "new forms" of leadership and direction have been given much stress in Party propaganda since the return of Gomułka. Party activists have been exhorted not to "stand on a podium" if they want to gain authority with the masses. Officials have been told to listen to individual complaints and grievances. Recent press articles indicate that local Party committees and government organs have been swamped with complaints as a result of the campaign to make officials more responsive to popular sentiment.

Gomułka wants to preserve the Party's control over the formulation and direction of broad national policies. At the same time he appears eager to stimulate personal initiative in the solution of day-to-day economic and social problems. This attempt to reconcile authority with personal freedom presents the Party with numerous difficulties. Since October 1956 the government has had to fight not only manifestations of greater resistance to its authority but also a tendency on the part of many Poles to concern themselves primarily with vague, abstract national programs rather than concrete and immediate tasks —a tendency that reflects an important aspect of the Pole's attitude toward everyday life and work.

The Temper of Life

Color and style are sought in individual speech and mannerism. Decorative arts occupy an important place within and outside the home. The art of enjoying life and giving it beauty is highly prized by Poles and practiced even under the most difficult circumstances. During the Warsaw uprising in 1944, for example, young insurgents sometimes risked their lives behind the German lines in order to find flowers for their girls.

Among all classes great stress is placed on finding enjoyment in the present. Weddings, baptisms, harvest festivals, religious celebrations, and holidays are high spots in the peasant's routine and always involve a great deal of dancing, singing, drinking, visiting, and telling of tales. With the city dweller theaters, movies, night clubs, and sporting events are immensely popular. Among the upper classes, although the open-air life of riding, hunting, and giving lavish parties on one's estate is now only a memory, a good time is still found in small informal parties and countryside excursions. For the intelligentsia, private salons and cafes where one can gossip, discuss politics or literature, or play cards are highly valued aspects of life. Long hours in conversation and long walks are very common. A person need only to lie down on the grass and look at the sky to spend his time profitably.

A Pole finds great difficulty in relating long-range social or economic problems to his immediate, plodding day-to-day labor. Instead, such problems are embellished as abstractions and rarely considered in terms of effective, practical action. Writers and intellectuals, for example, are repeatedly criticized for limiting their concern with important issues to "those bold projections of thought, scintillating in the originality of generalizations." A typical complaint appeared in *Trybuna Ludu* in May 1957: "There is a great deal of this tendency to save Poland and the world with a single article."

Polish workers, similarly, are frequently criticized by Party authorities for engaging in endless debates and quarrels about general class and national interests instead of settling down to solve immediate and specific problems in their own factories. The tendency to avoid concrete issues was also satirized (May 1957) in the Warsaw weekly *Szpilki:*

Query: Our workers' council is extremely active. We get together every week, and sometimes even more frequently. We discuss the national economic plan, we plan the further consolidation of individual ministries, we establish their spheres of competence, etc. Recently we worked out detailed projects regarding the liquidation of central administrative bodies. We're hurt by the fact that there are comrades who don't appreciate our contribution and bluntly imply that we should occupy ourselves with plant matters.

Reply: Don't pay any attention to that. It is their envy which speaks. The devil with plant matters! There'll be time for that, once you've settled the national economic policy.

Trybuna Ludu has repeatedly stressed the theme that mere discussion cannot be expected "to yield in some miraculous way larger quantities of coal, steel, motorcycles, cars, radio sets, footwear," and that talks, debates, analyses, and generalizations must be accompanied by "effective work." The Gomułka government has had great difficulty in trying to persuade the people that only their own willingness to work harder and to produce more can eventually raise Poland's living standards.

But work is not idealized, or even valued. The peasant must work very hard in order to maintain his family, but he is not greatly concerned with more efficient ways of doing his job. Feeling that his best efforts can be frustrated by unforseen circumstances, he tries to provide for the uncertainties of the future by fulfilling religious and magical ceremonies and leaving the rest "up to God." Except for a small number of skilled workers and artisans most Polish industrial laborers (many of recent peasant origin) find factory work distasteful and do not value workmanship, efficiency, or the quality of products. Slackness and absenteeism are major problems in Polish industry today.

Among the intelligentsia there is a tendency to look down on any kind of physical labor. The type of work which is most valued is that which involves intellectual activity. A sharp distinction is made between the "life of the spirit" and the "gray life" of everyday existence. Having absorbed many of the traits and attitudes of the old Polish nobility, the *szlachta,* the intelligentsia tend to view themselves as the "aristocrats of thought and spirit." Learning and education are viewed as ends in themselves. To have broad intellectual interests is a mark of "culture" and sophistication, but little emphasis is placed on the practical use of one's knowledge, despite the government's effort to popularize vocational training.

Public leaders today, both lay and clerical, are seeking to create a more positive attitude toward work and everyday problems by appealing to the people's sense of patriotism. Alarmed at the extent of idleness and absenteeism in many enterprises and mines, one government paper called for a "national campaign to awaken the awareness of work being a duty."

The Gomułka government has expended great effort in the attempt to revive the spirit of "organic labor"—a slogan which had been popular during the latter part of the nineteenth century when many Poles temporarily abandoned efforts at direct political resistance to support day-to-day educational and economic reforms (see chap. 2). The present government is trying to exploit this aspect of the patriotic tradition; with a sense of great urgency, Gomułka has insisted that the people manifest their concern for the fate of their nation by practical and constructive labor. The Church has supported this attempt to persuade Poles that sweat, rather than blood, is needed in Poland today. Shortly after his release from confinement in October 1956, Cardinal Wyszyński appealed to the nation:

> Poles know how to die magnificently, but, my brothers, Poles must learn to work magnificently. Death may bring quick glory, but to live in toil, suffering, pain, and sacrifice for years is greater heroism. And this heroism is needed today.

In subsequent sermons and speeches, the Primate stressed the theme that the concern of the people should be to work for a future when the hungry are fed, the naked clothed, and the poor assured a roof over their heads. Despite such exhortations, a rapid change in popular attitudes toward work as such appears unlikely.

Poles are apt to daydream about the future. The habits of economy and living on a budget are not well developed in the home, frugality, industry, and the amassing of wealth are not particularly valued, and the future is rarely viewed in concrete terms.

The Fatherland

The people of Poland have a strong sense of national identity and a deep love for their land. They have clung tenaciously to their native speech, their religion and culture, through generations of foreign oppression. Their attachment to the land—its rivers, field, and woods —is matched by pride in their history and tradition of struggle for national independence. Their devotion to Poland as a national entity is intense and almost religious.

ITS SYMBOLS

The traditional Polish national symbol is a white eagle. According to legend, the first King of the Poles while hunting came upon a huge white eagle hovering over a nest of young and making a strange cry. These pure white birds were absolutely unknown in the land and the King looked upon them as a prophetic sign. He is said to have built his home at the site and named it Gniezno ("Nest-town")—one of the oldest cities in Central Europe—and chose the white eagle as his emblem. The old tales often refer to Poland as the Land of the White Eagle.

The white eagle, crowned, on a red field became the traditional Polish coat of arms and except for the crown has been retained as the official coat of arms of the present Polish state. The traditional colors, white and red, also have been retained in the national flag.

The present national anthem originated among Dąbrowski's Polish Legion fighting under Napoleon in the hope of obtaining the support of France for the cause of their fatherland (see chap. 2):

Poland is not Yet Lost

While we live she is existing,
Poland is not fallen;
We will win with swords resisting,
What the foe has stolen.

We'll cross where Warta's surging
Gloomily its waters,
With each blade from sheath emerging
Poland's foes to slaughter!

Hence unto the field of glory,
Where the life blood's streaming;
Where with talons red and gory,
Poland's eagle's screaming.

Poland! shall the foe enslave thee
Sadly and forever;
And we hesitate to save thee?
Never, Poland, Never!

(Chorus)
March, March, Dąbrowski,
From Italy's Plain;
Our Brethren shall meet us
In Poland again!

Communist efforts to popularize "The International" have been unsuccessful. It is played by bands on official occasions, but Poles do not like to sing it.

ITS PERSONIFICATION AND ROLE

During the nineteenth century Polish poets and writers expressed the sufferings and hopes of their nation in religious imagery which continues to inspire many Poles today. Poland has been frequently identified with the figure of Christ—crucified, buried, and risen. As Christ's martyrdom was necessary to fulfill God's design for man, so Poland's subjugation, the poets felt, would some day be followed by freedom and a better world. Polish independence, attained in 1918 and again anticipated after World War II, was often described as the "Resurrection."

Poland has also been represented as a beautiful, ethereal young woman, usually in the act of breaking her chains of bondage. To some extent this feminine saintly Poland is identified with the Holy Virgin, "the Queen of the Polish Crown." Love for her must be sublime and without thought of reciprocation. The ideal Pole is always ready to sacrifice his life for her and expects no reward.

Polish tradition has stressed the role of Poland as a guardian of Christianity and of western culture against eastern barbarians. Polish writers have often spoken of their country as the bastion of European civilization. The most popular heroic episodes of Polish history involve the defense of western Europe. Polish troops stopped the Tatar advance in 1241. The seventeenth-century Polish King, Jan Sobieski, is remembered for saving Europe from the Turks at Vienna. In 1920 the Polish Army, under the command of Piłsudski, stopped the Russian Bolsheviks at the gates of Warsaw in what Poles have called "the miracle on the Vistula."

ITS REGIONS AND ROLE

Poland traditionally is said to have four corner cities—Poznan, Cracow, Lvov, and Vilna (the last two are now part of the USSR). Warsaw, in the center, is often referred to as "the heart of Poland," and "Poland's broken heart," or as "the Paris of the North." It is the site of many heroic episodes in recent Polish history. During the 1944 uprising many Poles came from a distance to "die in Warsaw."

Cracow, capital of Poland until 1609, is viewed as the cradle of national culture and science, steeped in tradition and learning. The whole city is one great museum. On Wawel Hill, overlooking the Vistula, the historic Palace of Polish kings and the Cathedral enshrine a thousand years of Polish hopes, ambitions, achievements, and memories.

Poznan, founded before the advent of Christianity to Poland, became the first Polish see (tenth century) and has been the seat of the Primate ever since. It was a nucleus of the Polish state. The annual trade fair in Poznan is a custom which harks back to the Middle Ages. One of Poland's oldest cities it is becoming increasingly industrialized and is noted for the somewhat radical political temper of its students and workers.

Czestochowa, in south central Poland, is the country's most revered religious center. On Jasna Gora—Mountain of Light—which dominates the city, is a Pauline monastery with the highest spire in Poland. It contains the shrine of Our Lady of the Black Madonna, which hundreds of thousands of pilgrims visit annually. The Holy Virgin of Czestochowa is regarded by Poles as the protectress of the Polish nation.

Few Poles have been satisifed with their modern territorial boundaries. When Poland regained its independence in 1918 some political leaders wanted to establish a state which would embrace the areas belonging to Poland before the eighteenth-century partitions. Since then practically all Poles have recognized that a return to the frontier of 1772 is impossible, although many now strongly feel that the western territories taken from Germany after World War II and the eastern areas incorporated into the USSR both rightfully belong to the Polish nation. Most Poles, however, appear very sensitive to their geographic and military weakness and have all but abandoned dreams of territorial aggrandizement.

Citizenship and Patriotism

Poles tend to believe that a man born a Pole cannot stop being one. The children and grandchildren of Polish emigrants are often said to have a "Polish nature" which will come to the fore in the important moments of life. It is felt that the adoption of foreign citizenship does not in any way affect one's "Polishness" (*Polskość*), so often exalted in the national poetry and literature.

All Poles are expected to be patriots. Oppression during the nineteenth century created a proud intelligentsia tradition of heroic self-sacrifice in the name of national ideals, a tradition that has since then been absorbed by all classes of society. It glorifies courageous behavior, bravado, and fearless persistence in the face of all attacks and the refusal to admit "moral" defeat.

Since World War II, however, a growing number of Poles have felt that this type of idealism can only lead to national suicide. The writer A. Janta remarked in 1949:

> We are taught from the time that we are little that there are ideals for which it is worth while to die. . . . There is a price which a man can pay, but which a nation cannot afford if it wants to survive.

Immediately after Gomułka's return in October 1956 the government insisted that the people's patriotism be manifested in practical, constructive daily work. This was coupled with a plea to remain calm and disciplined and to avoid emotional excesses. As one government spokesman put it:

> Ordinary national common sense today dictates that we should distinguish between emotional and rational thinking. Throughout the course of history this has been on the whole an art alien to Poles. For this we had to pay in blood, ruins, and poverty. For the first time we have amazed the world by a revolution without barricades. The man in the street says: "We behaved like Englishmen, and we made a handsome profit!" This is not just the best way—it is the only possible way. Let us always remember the actual situation, the possi-

bilities and dangers. Let us always ask ourselves the question: "What can our action lead to, whom is it going to help and whom could it harm?"

In the immediate wake of Gomułka's bloodless "revolution," however, public sentiment ran high. The Hungarian revolt helped to inflame anti-Soviet feelings throughout Poland. On October 24, 1956, thousands of youths marched through the streets of Warsaw, shouting anti-Soviet slogans and setting up rhythmic chants of "Katyn! Katyn! Katyn!"—a reference to the alleged massacre of 10,000 Polish officers in the Katyn forest by the Russians in 1940. Anti-Soviet riots took place in Poznan and Szczecin (Stettin) early in December. In other cities Soviet soldiers were manhandled and military vehicles were set on fire.

At the same time the government and various public leaders, both lay and clerical, appealed for "a sense of greater realism." Gomułka bitterly criticized "citizens and comrades hotheaded enough not to be guided by reason but only by feelings and reflexes." University students were urged by their elders to "remember" the Warsaw uprising. An article in the literary weekly *Nowa Kultura* recalling the great acts of revolt in Polish history, deplored that Poles "never had more to sell than their blood," and that they always "lost their shirt in the end."

The effect of all these exhortations was to temper the radical and idealistic moods of the population. With the help of the great influence of the Church, the people were persuaded to "listen to the voice of reason" during the parliamentary elections held on January 20, 1957. For the first time the Communist elections were held without pressure at the polls. The people were not intimidated during the elections, as had previously been the case, and were given the opportunity to freely cross out the names of the candidates selected by the government (see chap. 6). The majority of the population indicated that it would accept the only government Poland could have at that time.

Despite this display of caution and realism, however, the old ideals of romantic and heroic behavior continue to possess great potency. Cardinal Wysziński, for example, has stressed sweat, rather than blood, as the means of insuring the nation's survival and renewal, but he has also stated that the Church will not turn its back on the ideals of sacrifice and martyrdom, if they become necessary in order to defend "the Nation, the Church, the Fatherland, and God." Addressing a group of Polish-American women at Jasna Góra in May 1957, the Primate declared:

But you should know: we remain on the Polish land full of confidence, we shall not give in, even if we have to fertilize it once again with our own blood, just as our fathers did. . . . Perhaps they may say about us: "You are going too far—maybe too far!" And we will reply: Yes! we are going very far, we are going very far, even to prison if need be. And this is not heroism, this is a duty which we do with confidence that God will ultimately win.

Statements of this kind continue to arouse great pride and admiration among the people. The conflict between patriotic ideals and the demands of political reality is likely to find sharp expression in Polish life for a considerable time to come.

Table 1. Population of Poland

(in thousands)

Province[a]	1931	1946	1950	1955	Percent Change 1931 to 1946	1946 to 1950	1950 to 1955
Warsaw (including Warsaw City)	3,552	2,662	2,809	3,245	-25.1	5.5	15.5
Bydgoszcz	1,566	1,457	1,470	1,597	- 7.0	0.9	8.6
Poznan	2,311	2,086	2,109	2,304	- 9.7	1.1	9.2
Lodz (including Lodz City)	2,385	2,015	2,047	2,210	-15.5	1.6	8.0
Kielce	1,858	1,702	1,659	1,763	- 8.4	- 2.6	6.3
Lublin	2,069	1,753	1,640	1,719	-15.3	- 6.5	4.8
Bialystok	1,194	944	952	1,040	-20.9	0.8	9.2
Olsztyn	1,030	442	675	811	-57.1	52.8	20.1
Gdansk	1,065	732	891	1,082	-31.3	21.6	21.4
Koszalin	789	585	514	632	-25.8	-12.1	23.0
Szczecin	941	308	508	661	-67.3	65.1	30.1
Zielona Gora	884	347	560	678	-60.7	61.4	21.1
Wroclaw	2,604	1,769	1,735	1,986	-32.1	- 1.9	14.5
Opole	1,040	792	811	887	-23.8	2.3	9.4
Katowice	2,608	2,363	2,635	3,040	- 9.4	11.5	15.4
Cracow	2,195	2,133	2,147	2,359	- 2.8	0.7	9.9
Rzeszow	1,801	1,535	1,371	1,530	-14.7	-10.7	11.6
Total Population	29,892	23,625	24,533	27,544	-21.0	3.8	12.3

(a) Prewar boundaries adjusted to 1950; postwar provincial boundaries as of year cited.

Sources: Adapted from Mauldin, W. Parker, and Akers, Donald S., The Population of Poland, p. 122, and from Polska Rzeczypospolita Ludowa: Główny Urząd Statystyczny, Rocznik Statystyczny 1956 (Polish People's Republic: Main Statistical Administration, Statistical Yearbook 1956), p. 44.

Table 2. Growth of Polish Cities[a]
(cities with population of 50,000 or more in 1955)

City	Population (in thousands)				Percent Change			Economic Activity
	1921	1939	1946	1955	1921 to 1939	1939 to 1946	1946 to 1955	
Warsaw	937	1,289	479	1,000.6	37.6	-62.8	109.0	Capital; chemicals; riverport; textiles; eng.; steel.
Lodz	452	672	497	674.2	48.7	-26.0	35.6	Eng.; textiles; paper.
Cracow	184	259	299	428.2	40.8	15.4	43.2	Riverport; paper; chemicals; eng.; metallurgical center.
Wroclaw	528	621	171	378.6	17.6	-72.5	121.4	Riverport; textiles; chemicals; eng.
Poznan	169	272	268	374.9	60.9	-1.5	39.9	Riverport; eng.; iron founding; chemicals.
Gdansk	195	250	118	242.9	28.2	-52.8	105.8	Baltic port; eng.
Szczecin	233(b)	268	73	229.5	15.0	-72.8	214.4	Baltic port; elec. power; eng.; iron; textiles; paper.
Katowice	50	134	128	199.9	168.0	- 4.5	56.2	Coal; lead; zinc; mining; foundries; chemicals.

(continued)

Tables

Table 2 (continued)

Bydgoszcz	88	141	135	202.0	60.2	- 4.3	49.6	Riverport; eng.; textiles; chemicals; lignite.
Zabrze	67	126	104	182.8	88.1	-17.5	75.8	Coal; steel; eng.; chemicals.
Bytom	53[b]	101	93	180.7	90.6	- 8.0	99.4	Coal; lead; zinc; eng.
Czestochowa	80	138	101	149.7	72.5	-26.8	48.2	Iron; steel; textiles.
Chorzow	73	110	111	141.4	50.7	0.9	27.4	Coal; iron; steel; chemicals; eng.
Gliwice	69[b]	114	96	134.8	65.2	-15.8	40.4	Chemicals; iron; steel.
Lublin	94	122	99	132.2	29.8	-18.9	33.5	Eng.
Gdynia	1.3	120	78	129.6	913.1	-35.0	66.1	Baltic port.
Sosnowiec	86	130	78	124.4	51.2	-40.0	59.5	Elec. power; eng.
Radom	62	--	69	118.1	---	---	71.1	
Walbrzych	37[b]	64	73	110.3	73.0	14.1	51.1	Coal; chemicals.
Bialystok	77	107	57	97.2	39.0	-46.7	70.5	Eng.; chemicals; textiles; sawmilling.
Torun	---	---	80[c]	92.5	---	---	15.6	Eng.
Nowy Bytom	---	---	---	79.3	---	---	---	Coal; lead; zinc; eng.
Kielce	---	---	50[d]	73.9	---	---	47.8	Eng.; sawmilling.
Bielsko-Biala	---	---	27[d]	67.1	---	---	148.5	----------
Kalisz	---	---	48	66.1	---	---	37.7	----------
Elblag	---	---	21	65.9	---	---	213.8	Baltic port; eng.; elec. power.

(continued)

Table 2 (continued)

Wloclawek	---	---	48	59.5	---	---	24.0	Sulphur; sawmilling.
Siemianowice	---	---	---	59.4	---	---	---	----------
Tarnau	---	---	33(d)	58.8	---	---	78.2	----------
Grudziadz	---	---	37	57.2	---	---	54.6	Sawmilling.
Swietochlowice	---	---	---	56.3	---	---	---	----------
Opole	53	---	28	55.6	-47.2	98.6	---	Eng.
Olsztyn	---	---	29	55.5	---	83.8	---	Sawmilling; elec. power.
Szopienice	---	---	---(d)	52.7	---	---	---	Iron.
Rzeszow	---	---	29(d)	52.1	---	79.7	---	Eng.; manganese.
Legnica	---	84	24	51.8	-71.4	115.8	---	Textiles.
Pabianice	---	---	37	51.7	---	39.7	---	Textiles.

(a) Within administrative boundaries effective in the year given unless otherwise noted.
(b) 1919, including the military in barracks.
(c) 1950.
(d) 1947.

Sources: Adapted from Polska Rzeczypospolita Ludowa: Główny Urząd Statystyczny, Rocznik Statystyczny 1956, pp. 57-59, and from Oxford Regional Economic Atlas: The USSR and Eastern Europe, pp. 110-133.

Table 3. Vital Rates in Poland, 1955
(number per 1,000 population)

Province	Natural Increase	Births	Deaths
Poland	19.4	29.0	9.6
Warsaw City	16.1	23.7	7.6
Warsaw	17.9	28.0	10.1
Bydgoszcz	20.5	30.6	10.1
Poznan	17.1	27.1	10.0
Lodz City	12.9	22.1	9.2
Lodz	15.3	25.7	10.4
Kielce	18.1	28.3	10.2
Lublin	16.7	25.8	9.1
Bialystok	17.6	27.8	10.2
Olsztyn	28.9	39.1	10.2
Gdansk	26.4	35.0	8.6
Koszalin	31.8	41.0	9.2
Szczecin	31.7	40.7	9.0
Zielona Gora	30.3	39.4	9.1
Wroclaw	28.0	36.7	8.7
Opole	18.8	28.8	10.0
Katowice	14.8	24.2	9.4
Cracow	17.2	26.8	9.6
Rzeszow	16.6	26.6	10.0

Source: Adapted from Polska Rzeczypospolita Ludowa: Główny
Urząd Statystyczny, Rocznik Statystyczny 1956, pp. 61-62.

Table 4. Population of Poland by Sex and Age in 1955[a]
(percent of totals)

Age	Total	Men	Women
Total Population	27,544,000	13,229,000	14,315,000
2 Years and Under	7.8	8.3	7.4
3 to 6 Years	9.7	10.4	9.1
7 to 13 Years	12.1	12.7	11.5
14 to 17 Years	6.3	6.7	6.1
18 to 24 Years	12.0	12.5	11.5
25 to 29 Years	8.5	8.7	8.4
30 to 39 Years	12.7	12.4	13.0
40 to 49 Years	12.5	12.0	12.9
50 to 59 Years	9.8	9.2	10.3
60 to 69 Years	5.4	4.6	6.0
70 and Older	3.2	2.5	3.8
Median Age	25.2	23.66	26.6

[a] Population estimates.

Source: Adapted from Polska Rzeczypospolita Ludowa: Główny Urząd Statystyczny, Rocznik Statystyczny 1956, p. 45.

Table 5. Social Composition of the Polish United Workers' Party
(percentage)

Year	Workers	Intelligentsia	Peasants and Others
1948	53.6	17.6	28.8
1949	57.1	22.8	20.1
1950	50.6	28.9	20.5
1954	48.3	36.4	15.3
1957	44.5	39.5	16.0

Source: Adapted from Free Europe Press: Research and Analysis Department, Communist Party Congresses in the Soviet Bloc: Part II, Poland, p. 4.

Table 6. Polish Newspapers and Periodicals

(figures are for 1956, except when marked by *, indicating Spring 1957 announced circulation.)

A. Chief Polish Party Newspapers and Periodicals

Central Committee of the PZPR	Province	Frequency	Copies Published	
Chłopska Droga (Peasant's Way)		Weekly	302,000	Chief Party journal for peasants.
Nowe Drogi (New Ways)		Monthly	---	Chief theoretical journal of the Party; national and international politics, economics, news of Party.
Polityka (Politics)		Weekly	---	Founded March 1957 by Gomulka faction of the PZPR; political and social problems and international economic problems.
Sztandar Młodych (Youth's Banner)		D ex Sun	381,000	Organ of Union of Socialist Youth.
Trybuna Ludu (People's Tribune)		Daily	500,000 230,000*	Authoritative organ of the Party.
Trybuna Wolności (The Tribune of Freedom)		Weekly	165,000	General; 3 editions--1 for East Poland, 1 for West Poland, 1 for capital.

(continued)

Table 6 (continued)

Życie Partii (Party Life)	Province	Frequency Monthly	Copies Published ---	Directed to Party activists.
Provincial Parties				
Gazeta Białostocka (Bialystok Gazette)	Białystok	D ex Sun	57,000	
Gazeta Krakówska (Cracow Gazette)	Cracow	D ex Sun	100,000	
Gazeta Pomorska (Pomeranian Gazette)	Bydgoszcz	D ex Sun	87,000	
Gazeta Poznańska (Poznan Gazette)	Poznan		100,000	
Gazeta Robotnicza (Worker's Gazette)	Wroclaw	D ex Sun	143,000	
Gazeta Zielonogórska (Zielona Gora Gazette)	Zielona Gora		37,000	
Głos Koszaliński (Voice of Koszalin)	Koszalin		29,000	
Głos Olsztyński (Voice of Olsztyn)	Olsztyn		37,000	

(continued)

Table 6 (continued)

Provincial Parties

	Province	Frequency	Copies Published
Głos Robotniczy (Labor's Voice)	Lodz	D ex Sun	136,000
Głos Szczeciński (Voice of Szczecin)	Szczecin	D ex Sun	36,000
Głos Wybrzeża (Voice of the Seashore)	Gdansk	D ex Sun	79,000
Nowiny Rzeszówskie (News of Rzeszow)	Rzeszow	D ex Sun	48,000
Słowo Ludu (The People's Word)	Kielce		60,000
Sztandar Ludu (People's Banner)	Lublin	D ex Sun	48,000
Trybuna Mazowiecka (Tribune of Mazowsze)	Warsaw		43,000
Trybuna Opolska (Opole Tribune)	Opole		73,000
Trybuna Robotnicza (Worker's Tribune)	Katowice	D ex Sun	401,000

(continued)

Table 6 (continued)

B. Important Polish Non-Party Newspapers and Periodicals

Title	Place of Publication	Frequency	Copies Published	Type and Sponsorship
Dookoła Świata (Around the World)	Warsaw	Weekly	180,000	General.
Dziennik Bałtycki (Baltic Daily)	Gdansk	Daily	60,000	
Dziennik Łódzki (Lodz Daily)	Lodz	Daily	---	
Dziennik Polski (Polish Daily)	Cracow	D ex Sun	55,000	Czytelnik Press Institute.
Dziennik Zachodni (Western Daily)	Katowice	Daily	126,000	
Express Wieczórny (Evening Express)	Warsaw	D ex Sun	250,000	Prasa.
Głos Pracy (Voice of Labor)	Warsaw		180,000 81,000*	Central Council of Trade Unions.
Głos Wielkopolski (Voice of North Western Poland)	Poznan		84,000	

(continued)

Table 6 (continued)

	Place of Publication	Frequency	Copies Published	Type and Sponsorship
Gospodarka Planowa (Planned Economy)	Warsaw	Monthly	---	Polish Economic Press; formerly State Economic Planning Commission.
Gromada Rolnik Polski (Community Polish Farmer)	Warsaw	3 times weekly	1,150,000 ---*(a)	For peasants.
Ilustrawany Kurier Polski (Illustrated Polish Express)	Bydgoszcz	Daily	72,000	
Kierunki (Directions)	Warsaw	Weekly	30,000	PAX.
Kobieta i Życie (Woman and Life)	Warsaw	Weekly	450,000	Illustrated; for women.
Kurier Szczeciński (Szczecin Express)	Szczecin	Daily	35,000	
Łódzki Express Ilustrawany (Lodz Illustrated Express)	Lodz	Daily	97,000	Illustrated; general.
Nowa Kultura (New Culture)	Warsaw	Weekly	--- 70,000*	Independent; formerly Polish Writers' Union organ.
Panorama (Panorama)	Edited Katowice Printed Warsaw	Weekly	150,000	General illustrated; emphasis on Silesian problems.
Państwo i Prawo (State and Law)	Warsaw	Monthly	11,175	Polish Academy of Science and Institute of Legal Sciences.

(continued)

Table 6. (continued)

	Place of Publication	Frequency	Copies Published	Type and Sponsorship
Po Prostu (Simply Speaking)	Warsaw	Weekly	--- 150,000*	Young intelligentsia; political-cultural.
Przegląd Kulturalny (The Cultural Review)		Weekly	70,300 70,000*	Social; cultural review.
Przekrój (Cross-Section)	Cracow	Weekly	385,000	Illustrated; general.
Przyjaciółka (Women's Friend)	Warsaw	Weekly	2,000,000 1,790,000*	Illustrated; for women.
Przyjaźń (Friendship)	Warsaw		289,000	Polish-Soviet Friendship Society.
Samopomoc Chłopska (Peasant Mutual Aid)	Warsaw	Weekly	48,000	Peasant Self-Help Association.
Słowo Polskie (Polish Word)	Wroclaw	Daily	64,000	
Słowo Powszechne (The Universal Word)	Warsaw	Daily	100,000	PAX.
Świat (The World)		Weekly	165,000	Illustrated; current events, arts, literary matter.
Świat i Polska (The World and Poland)		Weekly	---	

(continued)

Table 6 (continued)

	Place of Publication	Frequency	Copies Published	Type and Sponsorship
Świat Młodych (World of Youth)	Warsaw	Weekly	220,000 185,000*	For youth 11-17 years.
Szpilki (The Pins)	Warsaw	Weekly	105,000	Satirical.
Twórczość (Creation)	Cracow	Monthly	---	Literary.
Tygodnik Demokratyczny (Democratic Weekly)	Warsaw	Weekly	20,000	Democratic Party.
Tygodnik Powszechny (Universal Weekly)	Cracow	Weekly	30,000	Catholic.
Zielony Sztandar (Green Banner)		3 times weekly	150,000	United Peasant Party.
Żołnierz Wolności (Soldier of Freedom)		D ex Sun	---	Polish Army; formerly Ministry of National Defense.
Życie Literackie (Literary Life)	Cracow-Katowice	Weekly	40,000*	Political, literary.
Życie Warszawy (Warsaw's Life)	Warsaw	D ex Sun	200,000	Czytelnik.

(a) Always very popular but has had a sizable reduction.

426

Table 7. Selected Polish Periodicals for Foreign Readers

Title	Frequency	Description	Language
Information Bulletin	Monthly	Journal of International Affairs Department of the PZPR.	English, French, German, Russian
Poland	Monthly	Prestige pictorial.	English, French, German, Polish, Russian, Spanish.
Polish Foreign Trade	Bimonthly	Foreign trade journal.	English, French, German, Russian, Spanish.
Polish Trade Union Review	Quarterly	Prestige labor pictorial.	English, French, German, Russian, Spanish.

Source: Adapted from Kirkpatrick, Evron M. (ed.), Target: The World, p. 83.

Table 8. Distribution of Radio Receivers, 1955
(number of owners and subscribers in thousands)

Province	Total				Urban Areas			
	Number	Number per 1,000 Population	Tube Sets (%)(a)	Loud-speakers (%)(a)	Number	Number per 1,000 Population	Tube Sets (%)(a)	Loud-speakers (%)(a)
Poland	3,000	108.9	56	44	1,985	164.5	66	34
Warsaw City	207	206.6	76	24	207	206.6	76	24
Warsaw	198	88.5	34	66	108	187.0	44	56
Bydgoszcz	180	112.6	57	43	126	173.9	63	37
Poznan	259	112.2	54	46	174	170.5	66	34
Lodz City	117	173.0	84	16	117	173.0	83	17
Lodz	138	90.1	31	69	77	173.0	42	58
Kielce	111	63.0	36	64	56	135.3	59	41
Lublin	137	79.8	31	69	56	163.4	54	46
Bialystok	85	82.0	26	74	45	165.7	40	60
Olsztyn	77	95.2	49	51	47	181.7	47	53
Gdansk	156	143.8	67	33	121	176.1	73	27
Koszalin	68	108.4	57	43	38	151.8	55	45
Szczecin	90	136.0	61	39	59	150.9	71	29
Zielona Gora	84	123.2	52	48	43	151.0	58	42
Wroclaw	249	125.3	69	31	156	139.3	77	23
Opole	103	116.3	52	48	45	173.7	51	49
Katowice	431	141.8	69	31	336	156.4	74	26
Cracow	202	85.7	51	49	124	145.3	66	34
Rzeszow	108	70.5	31	69	50	156.5	46	54

(continued)

Table 8 (continued)

| | Total | | | | Rural Areas | | | |
Province	Number	Number per 1,000 Population	Tube Sets (%) (a)	Loud-speakers (%) (a)	Number	Number per 1,000 Population	Tube Sets (%) (a)	Loud-speakers (%) (a)
Poland	3,000	108.9	56	44	1,015	65.6	34	66
Warsaw City	207	206.6	76	24	---	---	---	---
Warsaw	198	88.5	34	66	90	54.2	19	81
Bydgoszcz	180	112.6	57	43	54	61.4	41	59
Poznan	259	112.2	54	46	85	66.1	31	69
Lodz City	117	173.0	84	16	---	---	---	---
Lodz	138	90.1	31	69	61	56.3	16	84
Kielce	111	63.0	36	64	55	41.0	13	87
Lublin	137	79.8	31	69	81	58.3	14	86
Bialystok	85	82.0	26	74	40	52.5	10	90
Olsztyn	77	95.2	49	51	30	53.9	53	47
Gdansk	156	143.8	67	33	35	88.2	49	51
Koszalin	68	108.4	57	43	30	79.4	60	40
Szczecin	90	136.0	61	39	31	114.7	42	58
Zielona Gora	84	123.2	52	48	41	102.8	46	54
Wroclaw	249	125.3	69	31	93	107.2	57	43
Opole	103	116.3	52	48	58	95.4	53	47
Katowice	431	141.8	69	31	95	106.9	54	46
Cracow	202	85.7	51	49	78	51.8	28	72
Rzeszow	108	70.5	31	69	58	48.0	17	83

(a) Based upon number of sets, which deviates slightly from number of subscribers.

Source: Adapted from Polska Rzeczypospolita Ludowa: Główny Urząd Statystyczny, Rocznik Statystyczny 1956, p. 354.

428

Table 9. Poland's Mineral Products Potential After Frontier Revision[a]

(thousands of metric tons)

Product	Prewar Boundaries	Postwar Boundaries	Percentage Increase (+) or Decrease (-)
Pit Coal	36, 200	64, 650[b]	+ 78.6
Coke	2, 124	5, 353	+ 152.0
Brown Coal	18	7, 611	+ 41, 200.0
Iron Ore	792	865	+ 7.9
Crude Oil	501	141	- 71.9
Salt	603	537	- 10.9
Potash	522	nil	- 100.0
Lead and Zinc Ore	492	1, 214	+ 146.8

[a] Based on 1937 output figures.
[b] Output of coal in postwar boundaries reached a peak of over 90 million tons in 1943.

Source: Adapted from United Nations Relief and Rehabilitation Administration, Industrial Rehabilitation in Poland (Operation Analysis Papers, No. 35), p. 6.

Table 10. Principal Employment of
Occupationally Active Population, Poland

(in percent)[a]

Principal Source of Income	1931 [b]	1950 [c]
Agriculture	63.8	53.3
Industry and Manual Trades	11.0	17.7
Construction	1.0	3.9
Transport and Communications	1.9	3.6
Trade Turnover[d]	4.2	4.9
Science, Education and Culture	1.1	2.3
Health Protection and Social Welfare	0.7	1.3
Total	100.0	100.0

[a] Base of percentages not given.
[b] For the sake of comparability with 1950, the necessary regroupings were performed and the jobless, together with their dependents, are eliminated--6 percent of total population.
[c] Proportion of the jobless in total population for 1950 is not given.
[d] Including restaurants.

Source: Adapted from Polska Rzeczypospolita Ludowa: Główny Urząd Statystyczny, Rocznik Statystyczny 1956, p. 47.

Table 11. Employment in Polish Socialized Industry, 1955

Type of Industry by Ministries	Number of Workers	Percent
Heavy Industry		
Ministry of Metallurgy	236,806	8.8
Mining (coal)	345,560	12.8
Central Petroleum Office	9,837	0.4
Electric Power	53,106	2.0
Ministry of Machine Industry	183,178	6.8
Ministry of Motor Industry	180,090	6.7
Ministry of Chemical Industry	123,234	4.6
Total	1,131,811	42.1
Light Industry and Consumer Products		
Light Industry	422,192	15.7
Agriculture and Food Industry	120,476	4.5
Meat and Dairy Industry	87,020	3.2
Small Industry and Crafts	155,987	5.8
Central Union of Labor Cooperatives	259,179	9.6
Internal Trade	46,789	1.7
Ministry of Purchasing	23,475	0.9
Central Office of Peasant Self-Help Cooperatives	26,363	1.0
Total	1,141,481	42.4
Construction and Forest Products		
Construction Materials Industry	92,230	3.4
Wood and Paper Industry	78,503	2.9
Forestry	52,170	1.9
Total	222,903	8.2
Transportation		
Railways	52,697	2.0
Highway and Air Transportation	25,979	1.0
Navigation	23,371	0.9
Total	102,047	3.9
Not Specified	92,341	3.4
Grand Total	2,690,583	100.0

Source: Adapted from Polska Rzeczypospolita Ludowa: Główny Urząd Statystyczny, Rocznik Statystyczny 1956, p. 106.

Table 12. Labor Productivity in Poland, 1946-54

Year	Index (1937 = 100)	Increase (percent)
1946	55	--
1947	64	16
1948	81	27
1949	87	7
1950	95	9
1951	108	14
1952	122	13
1953	135	11
1954	144	7

Source: Adapted from Free Europe Press (Research and Analysis Department), Relationships Between Labor Productivity and Wages in the Satellites: Part II, Poland, p. 20.

Table 13. Operations of the General Savings Bank of Poland, 1953-55

Savings Activities	1953	1954	1955
Savings Account Books (in thousands)	3,682	4,029	4,480
Savings Deposits[a] (mil. złotys)	436	751	1,274
Turnover (mil. złotys)	2,412	2,937	4,667
Checking Activities			
Number of Accounts[a] (in thousands)	78	95	84
Demand Deposits (mil. złotys)	324	380	399
Turnover (mil. złotys)	22,516	22,199	22,480
Other Services in the Competence of Financial Settlements[a]			
(in thousands)	5,774	9,117	7,817
Amounts Involved (mil. złotys)	1,213	1,903	1,977

[a]At the beginning of the year.

Source: Adapted from Polska Rzeczypospolita Ludowa: Główny Urząd Statystyczny, Rocznik Statystyczny 1956, p. 300.

Table 14. Polish Planned Budgets, 1955-57

(in billions of złotys)

	1955	Percent of Total Budget	1956	Percent of Total Budget	1957	Percent of Total Budget
Revenue						
Socialized Sector	105.3	86.3	116.8[a]	82.7	119.9[a]	85.4
Taxes from Nonsocialized Sector	6.2	5.1	5.9	4.2	4.7	3.3
Direct Taxes	6.6	5.4	7.2	5.1	5.9	4.2
Loans	1.1	0.9	1.2	0.8	2.9	2.1
Other and Unidentified	2.8	2.3	10.2[b]	7.2	6.9[b]	5.0
Total	122.0	100.0	141.3	100.0	140.3	100.0
Expenditures						
National Economy	60.8	52.9	73.5	53.7	75.0	54.0
Social and Cultural	28.9	25.1	32.4	23.7	40.1	28.9
National Defense	11.9	10.4	12.0	8.8	10.2	7.3
Administration	10.3	9.0	10.1	7.4	10.2	7.3
Other and Unidentified	3.0	2.6	8.9[c]	6.4	3.3	2.5
Total	114.9	100.0	136.9	100.0	138.8	100.0
Surplus	7.1		4.4		1.5	

[a] Including receipts from social insurance; shown as a separate item after 1955.
[b] Since 1956 also including "surplus from past years."
[c] Including clearing accounts from past years.

Sources: Adapted from Polska Rzeczypospolita Ludowa: Główny Urząd Statystyczny, Rocznik Statystyczny 1956, p. 295, and from Dziennik Ustaw Rzeczypospolitej Polskiej (Gazette of Laws of the Republic of Poland), No. 12, 1956, and from Trybuna Ludu, March 10, 1957.

Table 15.   Changes in Selected Budgetary Expenditures,
Poland, 1953-57
(in percentages)

	1953	1955	1956	1957
Total Expenditures	100.0	118.3	140.9	142.9
National Economy	100.0	121.8	147.3	150.3
Social and Cultural	100.0	123.0	137.9	170.6
National Defense	100.0	113.3	114.3	97.1
Administration	100.0	104.0	120.0	103.0

Source: Adapted from available Polish budgetary information of respective years.

Table 16.   Polish Budgetary Revenues, 1954-55
(in millions of złotys)

	1954	Percent of Total	1955	Percent of Total
TOTAL REVENUES	116,817.0	100.0	124,281.8	100.0
Socialized Sector	86,348.3	73.9	92,712.2	74.6
Taxes				
Turnover	57,256.9		56,460.3	
Income	1,481.1		1,649.0	
Remittance of Profits	7,980.7		10,784.6	
Errors and Omissions	14,423.3		19,259.2	
Overplan Turnover	2,413.7		832.6	
Other	2,792.6		3,726.5	
Nonsocialized Sector	5,639.5	4.8	5,786.4	4.7
Taxes				
Turnover	671.5		814.7	
Income	810.8		764.7	
Land	4,001.7		4,021.9	
Other	155.5		185.1	
Taxes and Payments from Individuals	6,335.7	5.4	7,123.0	5.7
Taxes				
On Earnings	4,987.8		5,757.3	
On Realty Transactions	46.7		55.2	
Treasury Fees	251.1		250.2	
Local Budgetary Revenues	1,050.1		1,070.3	

(continued)

Table 16 (continued)

Loans and Investments	968.5	.9	1,188.9	1.0
Foreign Loans	521.8		590.4	
Interest Earned by Financial Institutions	446.7		598.5	
Other Revenues	4,107.9	3.5	3,274.4	2.6
Social and Cultural Services	304.5		330.7	
Property	100.7		53.5	
Licenses	1,155.0		249.3	
Customs Duties and Excise Taxes	362.5		419.8	
Other (including fines, confiscations interest on overdue loans, etc.)	2,185.2		2,221.1	
Social Insurance	12,567.6	10.8	13,556.4	10.9
Transfers and Carry-overs	849.5	.7	640.5	.5

Source: Adapted from Polska Rzeczypospolita Ludowa: Główny Urząd
Statystyczny, Rocznik Statystyczny 1956, p. 296.

Table 17. Polish Landholding and Farm Output, 1955.

	Type of Farm Ownership		
	Private	Collective	State
Share in Farm Land	78.8	8.6	12.6
Share in Total Output	83.9	7.7	8.4
Share in Livestock Production	91.0	4.0	5.0
Value of Output per Hectare of Arable Land, in Złotys	621.1	517.3	393.7

Source: Adapted from Koenig, Ernest, "A New Farm
Policy for Poland," Foreign Agriculture, Vol.
XXI, No. 5 (May 1957).

Table 18   Livestock in Poland, 1938-55

(thousand heads, midyear)

Year	Horses	Cattle	Pigs	Sheep
1938[a]	3,916	10,554	7,525	3,411
1938[b]	3,148	9,924	9,684	1,940
1946	1,730	3,910	2,674	727
1947	2,016	4,746	4,274	983
1948	2,297	5,748	4,626	1,410
1949	2,538	6,365	6,122	1,621
1950	2,800	7,203	8,134	2,198
1951	2,884	7,203	7,320	2,572
1952	--[c]	7,240	7,539	2,906
1953	2,720	7,385	9,730	3,330
1955[d]	3,000	9,500	10,500	3,800
1955[e]	2,560	7,912	10,888	4,243

[a] Prewar boundaries.
[b] Postwar boundaries.
[c] Not available.
[d] Plan.
[e] Actual.

Sources: Adapted from Alton, Thad Paul, Polish Postwar Economy,
1955, p. 216, and from Polska Rzeczypospolita Ludowa:
Główny Urząd Statystyczny, Rocznik Statystyczny 1956,
p. 136.

Table 19.   Share of Polish State-Owned, Cooperative, and Private
Industry in Total Production, 1955
(in percentages of total production)

Industry	Socialized Sector			Private Sector
	Total	State	Cooperative	
Ferrous Metallurgy	100.0	97.9	2.1	---
Nonferrous Metallurgy	100.0	100.0	---	---
Fuel Industry	100.0	99.9	0.1	---
Electric Power	100.0	100.0	---	---
Machine and Equipment Building	99.9	94.1	5.8	0.1
Consumer Metal and Electrical Appliances	98.6	71.1	27.5	1.4
Chemical	99.1	94.0	5.1	0.9
Rubber	99.9	85.3	14.6	0.1
Pharmaceutical	100.0	90.4	9.6	---
Construction Materials	99.4	89.8	9.6	0.6

(continued)

Table 19 (continued)

Glassmaking	99.6	77.7	21.9	0.
Porcelain and Ceramics	99.9	92.7	7.2	0.
Lumber and Lumber Processing	98.4	73.5	24.9	1.
Cellulose and Paper	100.0	100.0	---	--
Paper Processing and Office Materials	99.9	64.8	35.1	0.
Typographical	100.0	77.6	22.4	—
Textile	100.0	84.9	15.1	--
Leather and Footwear	99.9	71.2	28.7	0.
Musical Instruments	100.0	89.3	10.7	--
Consumer Foods	98.7	84.8	13.9	1.
Salt	100.0	100.0	---	--
Refrigeration	100.0	100.0	---	--
Fats	98.7	87.5	11.2	1.
Other Branches (including buttons and haberdashery, toys, brush-making, and fodder)	96.8	73.5	23.3	3.
Total	99.5	88.6	10.9	0.

Source: Adapted from Polska Rzeczypospolita Ludowa: Główny Urzą Statystyczny, Rocznik Statystyczny 1956, pp. 85-86.

Table 20. Polish Production of Pig Iron, Steel, and Zinc, Selected Years, 1938-60

Year	Pig Iron (million tons)	Crude Steel (million tons)	Crude Zinc (thousand tons)
1938	0.9	1.4	108.0
1947	0.9	1.6	74.0
1950	1.4	2.5	112.8
1955[a]	3.5	4.6	197.6
1955[b]	3.1	4.4	156.2
1960[a]	5.1	7.2	190.0

[a] Plan.
[b] Actual.

Sources: Adapted from Alton, Thad Paul, The Polish Postwar Econom 1955, p. 177, and Trybuna Ludu, August 3, 1956.

Table 21. Production of the Polish Chemical Industry
Selected Years, 1938-55

		1938	1948	1950	1955
Gross Output Index		100	---(a)	---(a)	602(b)
Sulphuric Acid (in 1,000 tons)		189	218	283	449
Caustic Soda	"	30	48	65	162(b)
Calcium Carbide	"	64	162	173	---(a)
Fertilizers:					
Superphosphate	"	36	45	---(a))	
Nitrogen	"	51	54	---(a))	285
Potassium	"	108	0	---(a))	
Dyes	"	2,000	3,100	4,300	7,900(b)
Automobile Tires	"	1,260	2,505	4,394	---(c)

(a) Not available.
(b) Plan.
(c) 1955 production figures not available but in 1956, 3.5 million rubber tires were produced. For 1957, production in excess of 4 million tires is scheduled.

Source: Adapted from Alton, Thad Paul, The Polish Postwar Economy, 1955, p. 179.

Table 22. Output of Tractors, Machine Tools, and Agricultural
Implements in Poland, Selected Years, 1937-60

Year	Agricultural Tractors (thousands)	Metalworking and Woodworking Machine Tools (thousand metric tons)	Agricultural Machines and Implements (thousand metric tons)
1937(a)	---(b)	2.04	21.2
1947	0.3(c)	4.61	36.4
1950	3.7	12.54	39.6
1955(d)	11.0	70.80	---(b)
1955(e)	8.0	27.20	---(b)
1960(d)	10.6	58.30	---(f)

(a) Production within prewar boundaries.
(b) Not available.
(c) Planned production.
(d) Plan.
(e) Actual.
(f) 1960 Plan figures not available but Five-Year Plan goal is given as a 369 percent increase over 1955, in comparable prices.

Sources: Adapted from Alton, Thad Paul, The Polish Postwar Economy, 1955, p. 183, and from Trybuna Ludu, August 3, 1956.

Table 23. Production of Selected Industrial Consumer Goods in Polan
Selected Years, 1937-60

Year	Bicycles (thousands)	Leather Shoes (million pairs)	Cotton Fabrics (million meters)	Wool Fabrics (million meters
1937	39	1.5	399	40
1947	79	2.7	257	32
1950	99	7.9	431	54
1955(a)	---(b)	22.2	608	75
1955(c)	167	---(b)	558	74
1960(a)	600	---(b)	681	87

(a) Plan.   (b) Not available.   (c) Actual.

Sources: Adapted from Alton, Thad Paul, The Polish Postwar Econom
1955, p. 185, and Trybuna Ludu, August 3, 1956.

Table 24. Polish Retail Trade Outlets as of December 31, 1955.

	Total	Stores	Kiosks, Booths, Mobile Vendors
All Sectors	132,588	94,322	38,266
Socialized Trade	118,529	87,515	31,014
State	39,238	26,988	12,250
Cooperative	79,291	60,527	18,764
Rural Coops	48,652	41,936	6,716
Urban Coops	30,639	18,591	12,048
Private Trade	14,059	6,807	7,252

Source: Adapted from Polska Rzeczypospolita Ludowa: Główny
Urząd Statystyczny, Rocznik Statystyczny 1956, pp. 224-25.

Table 25. Polish Socialized Retail Trade Turnover, 1955
(in millions of złotys)

	Amount	Percen of Total
Total Turnover	128,945	100.0
Retail Trade	112,681	87.4
Trading Organizations	110,173	85.4
Workers' Supplies Departments	1,919	1.5
Commission Sales	589	0.5

(continued)

Table 25 (continued)

Food Serving Establishments	9,542	7.4
Public Establishments	7,188	5.6
Workers' Canteens	1,439	1.1
Others[a]	915	0.7
Sales to Population from Marketing and Wholesale Enterprises	988	0.8
Sales to Population Directly from Production and Allotments in Kind	5,734	4.4

[a] Including canteens of the Union of Consumer Cooperatives, maintained by labor establishments and other establishments.

Source: Adapted from Polska Rzeczypospolita Ludowa: Główny Urząd Statystyczny, Rocznik Statystyczny 1956, p. 222.

Table 26. Structure of Polish Imports and Exports,
Percentage Distribution by Commodity Groups, 1951–55

	1951	1952	1953	1954	1955
	Imports				
Machinery, Equipment and Transport Facilities:	39.1	40.0	41.4	32.6	30.9
Industrial Plants	2.4	7.0	9.4	10.4	9.8
Power and Electrical Industry	6.9	6.0	6.3	4.7	4.2
Surface Transportation Equipment	8.4	6.9	6.4	5.0	5.9
Raw and Other Materials:	47.9	45.5	49.8	51.1	51.7
Fuels	2.9	3.4	3.6	4.1	4.7
Materials for Heavy Industry	14.5	16.9	19.7	20.8	20.4
Materials for Light Industry	26.4	21.9	22.5	22.7	23.7
Agricultural Supplies	4.1	3.3	4.0	3.5	2.9
Food Products	7.6	10.5	6.2	13.0	13.0
Manufactured Consumer Goods	5.4	4.0	2.6	3.3	4.4
Total Imports	100.0	100.0	100.0	100.0	100.0

(continued)

Table 26 (continued)

Exports

Machinery, Equipment and Transport					
Facilities:	7.5	10.9	12.9	10.9	13.1
Metal Cutting Machine Tools	0.6	0.6	0.8	0.6	0.5
Vehicles and Rolling Stock	6.6	8.2	7.7	6.2	6.7
Ships	0.1	1.9	3.3	2.9	4.0
Raw and Other Materials:	68.8	65.3	60.8	63.3	64.2
Coal and Coke	49.4	47.4	41.9	47.1	46.6
Iron and Zinc	8.5	8.4	8.6	7.3	8.0
Cement	0.7	0.7	0.9	0.7	0.9
Lumber and Paper	4.4	3.8	4.4	4.2	3.7
Food Products	16.7	15.9	18.2	17.3	15.5
Manufactured Consumer Goods	7.0	7.9	8.1	8.5	7.2
Total Exports	100.0	100.0	100.0	100.0	100.0

Source: Adapted from Polska Rzeczypospolita Ludowa: Główny Urząd Statystyczny, Rocznik Statystyczny 1956, p. 248.

Table 27. Foreign Trade of Poland by Major Areas in 1955[a]

(in million dollars)

Country	Polish Imports		Polish Exports	
	Value	Percent	Value	Percent
Soviet Bloc	600.0	64.4	563.5	61.7
USSR	314.0	33.7	280.4	30.7
Germany, Democratic Republic	122.1	13.1	125.1	13.7
Czechoslovakia	79.2	8.5	74.9	8.2
China, People's Republic	35.4	3.8	34.7	3.8
Hungary	30.7	3.3	26.5	2.9
Rumania	12.1	1.3	12.8	1.4
Bulgaria	6.5	0.7	9.1	1.0
Non-Soviet Areas	331.8	35.6	350.0	38.3
United Kingdom	41.9	4.5	77.6	8.5
France	34.5	3.7	12.8	1.4
Argentina	28.9	3.1	21.9	2.4
Australia	28.9	3.1	---	---
Germany, Federal Republic	23.3	2.5	29.2	3.2
Austria	17.7	1.9	28.3	3.1
Finland	15.8	1.7	32.9	3.6
Sweden	14.9	1.6	21.0	2.3
Belgium	12.1	1.3	3.7	0.4
Turkey	12.1	1.3	15.5	1.7

Table 27 (continued)

Italy	8.3	0.9	6.4	0.7
All Other	93.4	10.0	100.7	11.0
Grand Total	931.8	100.0	913.5	100.0

(a) Converted at official rate of exchange of 4 złotys to $1.

Note: Polish imports to the United States in 1955 amounted to $25.8
million, $19 million of which consisted of canned cooked hams
and other prepared pork. Exports were valued at $3.2 million,
half of which were in wool rags and used clothing.

Source: Adapted from Polska Rzeczypospolita Ludowa: Główny
Urząd Statystyczny, Rocznik Statystyczny 1956, p. 249.

Table 28. Polish Imports and Exports of Selected Commodities

to and from the USSR in 1955

Exports

	Unit	Total	To USSR	Exports to USSR in Percentage of Total
Coal	thousand tons	24,300.0	8,200.0	33.7
Coke	"	2,200.0	434.0	19.7
Rolled Products	"	247.0	52.0	21.1
Zinc and Zinc Sheets	"	92.0	55.0	59.8
Caustic and Calcium Soda	"	51.8	36.8	71.0
Cement	"	674.0	69.0	10.2
Sugar	"	372.3	215.0	57.7
Cotton Cloth	million meters	57.5	5.0	8.7
Woolen Cloth	"	5.8	4.2	72.4
Railway Rolling Stock	million rubles	182.0	174.0	95.6
Ships	"	148.0	125.0	84.5
Machinery and Equipment	"	480.0	304.0	63.3

Imports

	Unit	Total	From USSR	Imports from USSR in Percentage of Total
Grain	thousand tons	1,154.0	400.0	34.7
Hardened Fats	"	4.6	4.6	100.0
Cotton	"	95.2	70.3	73.8
Crude Oil	"	545.0	408.0	74.9
Oil Products	"	465.7	145.4	31.2
Gasoline	"	420.0	94.0	22.4

(continued)

Table 28 (continued)

Iron Ore	thousand tons	4,407.0	3,000.0	68.1
Zinc Concentrates	"	80.1	35.8	44.7
Machinery and Equipment	million rubles	1,152.0	486.0	42.2
Means of Transport (without tractors)	"	217.0	75.0	34.6
Tires	"	47.0	19.0	40.4

Note:

Besides the commodities given above, Poland imports from the USSR considerable amounts of manganese and chromium ores, copper and nickel.
Source:

Adapted from Trybuna Ludu, April 21, 1956.

Table 29. Proportion of Intra-Bloc Trade in the Trade of Satellites
(in percent)

Country	1937	1948	1949	1950	1951	1952	1953	1954	1955
Poland	7	41	43	59	58	67	70	70	64
Czechoslovakia	11	32	45	55	60	71	78	72	69
Hungary	13	34	46	61	67	71	77	70	61
Rumania	18	71	82	83	80	85	84	72	79
Albania	5	38	100	100	100	100	100	--(a)	97
East Germany	--(a)	--(a)	--(a)	65	75	74	76	75	72

(a)Not available.
Source:

Adapted from U.S. Department of Commerce: Bureau of Foreign Commerce, citing from Planovoye Khozyaistvo, (Planned Economy), Moscow April 1957, p. 9.

Table 30. Rates of Disability Pensions in Poland
(percentage of the calculated wage base)

	Cause of Disability		
	Industrial Accident or Disease	Other	
Disability Category	Employment Categories 1 and 2	Employment Category 1	Employment Category 2
I	100	70	60
II	75	50	40
III	50	40	30

Source: International Labor Office, Poland: Old-Age, Invalidity and Survivors' Insurance (Legislative Series, 1954 - Pol. 2), p. 12

RECOMMENDED FURTHER READING

The following are recommended as additional reading on the basis of quality and general availability.

Alton, Thad Paul. *The Polish Postwar Economy.* New York: Columbia University Press, 1955.

Benet, Sula. *Song, Dance, and Customs of Peasant Poland.* London: Dobson, 1951.

Biliński, J. M. *Trade Unions. (The Pattern of Life in Poland,* Vol. XIII.) Paris: Mid-European Research and Planning Centre, 1952.

Buell, Raymond L. *Poland: The Key to Europe.* (3rd. ed.) New York: Knopf, 1939.

Carlton, Richard K. (ed.). *Forced Labor in the "People's Democracies."* New York: Praeger, 1955.

Constitution of the Polish People's Republic. Warsaw: Książka i Wiedza, 1953.

Craig, Gordon A., and Gilbert, Felix (eds.). *The Diplomats, 1919–1939.* Princeton, N. J.: Princeton University Press, 1953.

Danilewicz, M. L. *Periodical and Non-Periodical Publications. (The Pattern of Life in Poland,* Vol. VIII.) Paris: Mid-European Research and Planning Centre, 1952.

Dolan, E. "Post-War Poland and the Church," *American Slavic Review,* XIV (February 1955), 84–92.

Douglas, Dorothy W. *Transitional Economic Systems: The Polish Czech Example.* London: Routledge & Kegan Paul, 1953.

Dziewanowski, Marian K. "Communist Poland and the Catholic Church," *Problems of Communism,* III, No. 5 (September–October 1954), 1–8.

Gorove, Stephen. "The New Polish Constitution," *Washington University Law Quarterly,* V, No. 3 (June 1954), 261–282.

Gottman, Jean. *A Geography of Europe.* (2d ed.) New York: Holt, 1954.

Graham, Malbone W. *New Gvernments of Eastern Europe.* New York: Holt, 1927.

Greene, Graham. "Catholic Temper in Poland," *Atlantic Monthly,* CXCVII (March 1956), 39–41.

444

Gross, Feliks. *The Polish Worker*. New York: Roy, 1945.

Gryziewicz, Stanisław. *Labour Legislation*. (*The Pattern of Life in Poland*. Vol. XI.) Paris: Mid-European Research and Planning Centre, 1952.

Grzybowski, Kazimierz. "Evolution of the Polish Labor Law," *Studies of the Association of Polish Lawyers in Exile in the United States*, n. d., pp. 80–96.

———. "Trade Unions in Communist Poland," *Problems of Communism*, V, No. 5 (September–October 1956), 16–21.

———. "Workers Councils in Poland," *Problems of Communism*, VI, No. 4 (July–August 1957), 16–19.

Institut National de la Statistique et des Etudes Economiques. *Mémento Economique la Pologne*. (Mémentos Economiques Série M. 8.) Paris: Presses Universitaires de France, 1954.

Jarecka, Louise. *Made in Poland: Living Tradition of the Land*. New York: Knopf, 1949.

Jones, Ralph A. "Polish Local Government Reorganized on Soviet Model," *American Slavic and East European Review*, X (February 1951), 56–68.

Korab, A. "Poland: The Search for Independence," *Problems of Communism*, V, No. 6 (November–December 1956), 10–16.

Kridl, Manfred. *A Survey of Polish Literature and Culture*. New York: Columbia University Press, 1956.

Kulischer, Eugene M. *Europe on the Move: War and Population Changes, 1917–47*. New York: Columbia University Press, 1948.

Lednicki, Wacław. *Life and Culture of Poland: As Reflected in Polish Literature*. New York: Roy, 1944.

Lowenthal, R. "Revolution Over Eastern Europe," *Problems of Communism*, V, No. 6 (November–December 1956), 4–9.

"Marriage and Family Under Communism," *East Europe*, VI, No. 3 (March 1957), 22–31.

Mauldin, W. Parker and Akers, Donald S. *The Population of Poland*. Washington, D. C.: Government Printing Office, 1954.

Miłosz, Czesław. *The Captive Mind*. New York: Knopf, 1955.

———. "Poland: Voices of Disillusion," *Problems of Communism*, V, No. 3 (May–June 1956), 24–30.

———. The Seizure of Power. New York: Criterion, 1955.

Montias, John. "Unbinding the Polish Economy," *Foreign Affairs*, XXXV, No. 3 (April 1957), 470–484.

Moore, Wilbert E. *Economic Demography of Eastern and Southern Europe*. Geneva: League of Nations, 1945.

Reddaway, W. F., *et al.* (eds.). *Cambridge History of Poland, to 1935*. 2 vols. Cambridge: Cambridge University Press, 1950 and 1951.

Rose, William John. *Poland: Old and New*. London: Bell, 1948.

———. *The Rise of Polish Democracy*. London: Bell, 1944.

Rudzinski, Aleksander Witold. "Sovietization of Civil Law in Poland," *The American Slavic and East European Review*, XV, No. 2 (April 1956), 216–243.

Schmitt, Bernadotte, E. (ed.). *Poland*. Berkeley: University of California Press, 1947.

Seton-Watson, Hugh. *Eastern Europe Between the Wars, 1918–1941.* Cambridge: Cambridge University Press, 1945.

Sharp, Samuel L. *New Constitutions in the Soviet Sphere.* Washington, D. C.: Foundation for Foreign Affairs, 1950.

————. *Poland: White Eagle on a Red Field.* Cambridge: Harvard University Press, 1953.

Shotwell, James T., and Laserson, Max M. *Poland and Russia, 1919–1945.* New York: King's Crown Press for the Carnegie Endowment for International Peace, 1945.

Shuster, George N. *Religion Behind the Iron Curtain.* New York: Macmillan, 1954.

Simon, Brian. *Education in the New Poland.* London: Lawrence & Wishart, 1954.

Stankiewicz, Wladislaw J., and Montias, J. M. *Institutional Changes in the Postwar Economy of Poland.* (Mimeograph Series No. 21.) New York: Mid-European Studies Center, 1955.

Sulimirski, Tadeusz. *Primary, Secondary and Adult Education.* (The Pattern of Life in Poland, Vol. III.) Paris: Mid-European Research and Planning Centre, 1952.

————. *The Universities, Professional Education and Science.* (Ibid., Vol. IV.) Paris: Mid-European Research and Planning Centre, 1952.

Super, Paul. *The Polish Tradition.* London: Allen & Unwin, 1939.

Szułdrzyński, Jan. *The Situation of the Catholic Church.* (The Pattern of Life in Poland, Vol. XVI.) Paris: Mid-European Research and Planning Centre, 1953.

Taylor, Jack. *Economic Development of Poland, 1919–1950.* Ithaca, N. Y.: Cornell University Press, 1952.

Thomas, William I., and Znaniecki, Florian. *The Polish Peasant in Europe and America.* 2 vols. New York: Knopf, 1927.

Ulam, Adam B. *Titoism and the Cominform.* Cambridge: Harvard University Press, 1952.

University of Chicago. *Contemporary Poland: Society, Politics, Economy.* HRAF Subcontractor's Monograph, 1955.

Valkenier, E. "Catholic Church in Communist Poland, 1945–1955," *Review of Politics.* XVIII (July 1956), 305–326.

Zinner, Paul E. (ed.). *National Communism and Popular Revolt in Eastern Europe: Events in Poland and Hungary.* New York: Columbia University Press, 1956.

Zweig, Ferdynand. *Poland Between Two Wars: A Critical Study of Social and Economic Changes.* London: Secker & Warburg, 1944.

OTHER USEFUL SOURCES

Appleby, J. "Poland Today," *Contemporary Review,* CLXXXVI (September 1954), 138–142.

Bain, Leslie B. "Can Gomulka Reconcile the Irreconcilable?" *The Reporter,* May 30, 1957, 23–25.

Baldwin, Roger N. (ed.). *A New Slavery: Forced Labor: The Communist Betrayal of Human Rights.* New York: Oceana, 1953.

446

Beazley, R. "Poland and Russia Yesterday and Today," *Quarterly Review,* CCLXXXV, No. 574 (October 1947), 541–553.

Beck, Col. Joseph. *Dernier Rapport, Politique Polonaise 1926–1939* (Last Report, Polish Policy). Paris: Editions de la Bacconiere, 1951.

Benet, Sula. "Patterns of Thought and Behavior in the Culture of Poland." New York: Columbia University Press, 1952. (Unpublished manuscript.)

Betts, R. R.(ed.). *Central and South East Europe.* London and New York: Royal Institute of International Affairs, 1950.

Black, Cyril E.(ed.). *Challenge in Eastern Europe.* Twelve Essays. New Brunswick, N. J.: Rutgers University Press, 1954.

————.(ed.). *Readings on Contemporary Eastern Europe.* New York: Mid-European Studies Center, 1953.

Blackett, P. M. S. *Atomic Weapons and East-West Relations.* Cambridge: Cambridge University Press, 1956.

Bolanowski, J. E. *A New Polish Grammar.* Milwaukee: Polonia, 1941.

Boswell, A. Bruce. *Poland and the Poles.* New York: Dodd, Mead, 1919.

Bourdet, C. "It's a Workers' Poland," *Nation,* CLXXXIII (December 1, 1956), 471–473.

Boyd, Louise A. *Polish Countrysides.* New York: American Geographical Society, 1937.

Brandes, George. *Poland.* New York: Macmillan, 1903.

British Broadcasting System: Monitoring Service. *Summary of World Broadcasts. Part IIA. Poland, Czechoslovakia, Eastern Germany, Finland.* September 1956, *passim.*

Brock, Peter. "Early Years of the Polish Peasant Party, 1895–1907," *Journal of Central European Affairs,* XIV (October 1954), 219–235.

Buell, Raymond L. "Foreign Policy of Poland," *Foreign Policy Reports,* XIV, No. 18 (December 1938), 210–220.

Caesar, A. A. L. "On the Economic Organization of Eastern Europe; Poland," *Geographical Journal,* CXXI (December 1955), 454–455.

"Cardinal and the Commissar," *Time,* LXIX, No. 20 (May 20, 1957), 96–104.

Cardwell, A. S. "Communist Attack on Polish Church," *Christian Century,* LXXIII (February 22, 1956), 232–233.

————. "Poland's Red Elite Live the Life of Riley," *Saturday Evening Post,* CCXXVII (February 5, 1955), 10.

Carlton, Richard. *The Economic Role of Forced Labor in Eastern Europe.* (Mimeograph Series No. 35.) New York: Mid-European Studies Center, 1954.

Ciechanowski, Jan. *Defeat in Victory.* New York: Doubleday, 1947.

"Communist 'Red Cross,'" *America,* XC (September 1, 1956), 494.

Constitution de la République de Pologne du 17 Mars 1921. Warsaw, n. d.

Constitution (Fundamental Law) of the Union of Soviet Socialist Republics. New York: The National Council of American-Soviet Friendship, n. d.

Corbridge-Patkaniowska, M. *Teach Yourself Polish.* London: English Universities Press, 1948.

Council on Foreign Relations: John C. Campbell(ed.). *The United States in World Affairs, 1947–1948*. With an introduction by Dean Acheson. New York: Harper, 1948.

————. *The United States in World Affairs, 1948–1949*. With an introduction by General George C. Marshall. New York: Harper, 1949.

Crossman, R. H. S. "New Revolution in Poland," *New Statesman and Nation*, May 5, 1956, 476; "Discussion," May 19, 1956, and June 2, 1956, 628.

"Current Economic Developments in Europe," *Economic Bulletin for Europe*, VIII, No. 2 (August 1956), 1–40.

Czapski, Jan. *The Inhuman Land*. (Trans., Gerard Hopkins.) New York: Sheed & Ward, 1952.

Czerwinski, Marcin. "The Transit," *East Europe*, VI, No. 6 (June 1957), 6–9.

Degras, Jane T.(ed.). *The Communist International, 1919–1943 Documents*. (Vol. I, *1919–1922*.) New York: Oxford University Press, 1956.

Dembowski, J. *Science in New Poland*. London: Lawrence & Wishart, 1952.

Deutscher, I. "October Revolutions, New Style," *Reporter*, XV (November 15, 1956), 14–17.

Dewar, Margaret. *Soviet Trade with Eastern Europe, 1945–1949*. London: Royal Institute of International Affairs, 1951.

"Dilemma of the Polish Economy," *World Today*, X (March–May, 1954), 122–135, 172–182.

Djilas, Milovan. "The Storm in Eastern Europe," *New Leader*, XXXIX, No. 47 (November 19, 1956), 3–6.

Douglas, Dorothy W. *Transitional Economic Systems: The Polish Czech Example*. London: Routledge & Kegan Paul, 1953.

Dunin-Borkowski, Władysław, and Stypulkowska, Alexandra. *The Administration of Justice*. (*The Pattern of Life in Poland*, Vol. V.) Paris: Mid-European Research and Planning Centre, 1952.

Dyboski, Roman. "Economic and Social Problems of Poland," *International Affairs*, XVI, No. 4 (July–August 1937), 579–600.

————. *Poland*. New York: Scribner, 1933.

Dziennik Ustaw Rzeczypospolitej Polskiej (Gazette of Laws of the Republic of Poland). 1928, No. 38, Law No. 382. Decree of the President of the Republic of March 22, 1928, concerning medicinal establishments.

————. 1939, No. 54, Law No. 342. Law of June 15, 1939, concerning public health service.

————. 1948, No. 55, Law No. 434. Law of October 28, 1948, concerning social institutions of the health service and planned administration in the service of health.

————. 1950, No. 3, Law No. 21. Decree of the Minister of Health of December 16, 1949, concerning the acquisition by the nation of the medicinal establishments of local governments.

————. 1950, No. 36, Law No. 327. Law of July 18, 1950, changing the law concerning social institutions of health service and planned administration in the service of health.

448

————. 1950, No. 36, Law No. 334. Law of July 20, 1950, concerning the establishment of Work Healing.

————. 1954, No. 37, Law No. 160. Concerning the National Sanitary Inspection.

Dziewanowski, Marian K. "Foundation of the Communist Party of Poland," *American Slavic Review,* XI (April 1952), 106–122.

————. "Genealogy of a Party: Origins and Beginnings of the Communist Party of Poland." Unpublished Ph.D. thesis, Harvard University.

————. "Poland, 1950–1954," *Journal of Central European Affairs,* XV (January 1956), 379–394.

————. "Revolution of 1904–1905 and the Marxist Movement of Poland," *Journal of Central European Affairs,* XII (October 1952), 259–275.

The Economist (London), 1955, *passim.*

1957 Editor & Publisher International Year Book, Vol. XC, No. 9 (February 28, 1957).

"Electric Power," *News from Behind the Iron Curtain,* V, No. 9 (September 1956), 17–18.

"Eyewitness Reports," News from Behind the Iron Curtain, V, No. 5 (May 1956), 16–17.

"Dentistry in Poland," *News from Behind the Iron Curtain,* V. No. 9 (September 1956), 726.

Fabre, Michel-Henry. *Théorie des Démocraties Populaires: Contribution à l'Etude de l'Etat Socialiste* (Theory of the People's Democracies: Contribution to the Study of the Socialist State). (*Bibliothèque de la Faculté de Droit d'Ager,* Vol. V.) Paris: A. Pedone, 1950.

Farman, Carl H. *Health and Maternity Insurance Throughout the World, 1954.* Washington, D. C.: Department of Health, Education, and Welfare, 1954.

"Ferment in the Polish Economy," *News from Behind the Iron Curtain,* V, No. 4 (April 1956), 3–10.

"The First Day of the Month," *News from Behind the Iron Curtain,* V, No. 4 (April 1956), 28–29.

Fisher, Harold Henry. *America and the New Poland.* New York: Macmillan, 1928.

Folejewski, Zbigniew. "Polish Poetry During the Last War," *American Slavic and East European Review,* X, No. 3 (October 1951), 216–225.

Foreign Broadcast Information Service. *Broadcasting Stations of the World. Part I: According to Country and City.* Washington, D. C.: Government Printing Office, 1955.

————. *Broadcasting Stations of the World. Part II: According to Frequency.* Washington, D. C.: Gvernment Printing Office, 1955.

————. *Broadcasting Stations of the World. Part III: According to Station Name or Slogan.* Washington, D. C.: Government Printing Office, 1955.

————. *Broadcasting Stations of the World. Part IV: FM and TV Stations.* Washington, D. C.: Government Printing Office, 1955.

Free Europe Press: Polish Section. *Alphabetical List of Deputies to the New Polish Parliament (SEJM).* New York, March 21, 1957.

————. *First Attack in Poland upon the Principle of Collectivization.* (Edward Lipinski, "Revisions," *Nowa Kultura,* September 9, 1956; Edward Ochab [speech], *Trybuna Ludu,* September 10, 1956; Roman Zambrowski [speech], *Trybuna Ludu,* September 26, 1956.) New York, October 4, 1956.

————. *Poland's Citizens Militia (MO).* New York, September 24, 1954.

————. *A Polish Agnostic on the Issue of Tolerance Between Believers and Non-Believers in Polish Schools.* (Translation of an article by E. SZ., "The Confession of an Agnostic," *Kierunki* [Catholic Weekly], February 3, 1957.) New York, February 28, 1957.

————. *Warsaw Denies West German Report on "Kontrasty" and Its Alleged Pro-German Attitude.* (Translation of article by Eugeniusz Guz, "Wrong Direction," *Po Prostu,* February 3, 1957.) New York, February 27, 1957.

————. *Yugoslavia Recommended as Model for Poland.* (Translated statements from *Trybuna Ludu,* September 21, 1956.) New York, October 5, 1956.

Free Europe Press: Research and Analysis Department. *Brief Biographies of the Nine Top Leaders of the Polish United Workers' [Communist] Party (PZPR).* (Research Report No. 48.) New York, February 7, 1957.

————. *Communist Party Congresses in the Soviet Bloc: Part II, Poland.* New York, 1954.

————. *Electoral Procedures for Forthcoming Local National Elections in Poland (December 5, 1954).* (Research Project No. 22.) New York, November 5, 1954.

————. *Health Services in Poland: The Statistics, the Reality, the Prospects.* (Research Report No. 5.) New York, July 6, 1954.

————. *The Household Plot: A Study of Private Farming Within the Collective Farm.* (Research Report No. 36.) New York, May 24, 1955.

————. *New Sovkhozes: Polish Regime's Attempt to Escape Kolkhoz Impasse.* (Research Report No. 23.) New York, November 16, 1954.

————. *Polish Collectivization Drive Bogs Down.* (Research Report No. 17.) New York, September 27, 1954.

————. *The Principles of the Budget System in Poland.* (Research Report No. 12.) New York, September 1, 1954.

————. *Relationships Between Labor Productivity and Wages in the Satellites: Part II, Poland.* (Research Report No. 40.) New York, August 4, 1955.

Frumkin, Gregory. *Population Changes in Europe Since 1939.* London: Allen & Unwin, 1951.

Fryde, Matthew M. *Selected Works on Polish Agrarian History and Agriculture.* (Mimeograph Series No. 6.) New York: Mid-European Studies Center, 1952.

Gardner, Monica M. *Poland.* London: Black, 1917.

Gasiorowski, Zygmunt J. "The German-Polish Nonaggression Pact of 1934," *Journal of Central European Affairs,* Vol. XV, No. 1 (April 1955).

Gawalewicz, Maryan. *The Queen of Heaven.* New York: Dial, 1929.

Goetel, Ferdynand. *From Day to Day*. (Trans., Winifred Cooper.) New York: The Literary Guild, 1931.

Górka, Olgierd. *Outline of Polish History*. (2d ed.) London: Alliance Press, 1945.

Gorski, Zdzisaw. "Polish Imports and Its Problems," *Handel Zagraniczny* (Foreign Trade), Vol. II, No. 5 (May 1956).

Gross, Feliks. *The Polish Worker*. New York: Roy, 1945.

Gryziewicz, Stanisław. *Agriculture*. (*The Pattern of Life in Poland*, Vol. XII). Paris: Mid-European Research and Planning Centre, 1952.

————. *Polish Fuel and Power in the Soviet Economic Sphere*. (Mimeographed Series No. 23.) New York: Mid-European Studies Center, 1954.

Grzybowski, Kazimierz. "La Continuité Légal dans les Démocraties Populaires" (Legal Continuity in the People's Democracies), *Revue Politique et Parlementaire*, July 1952, 55–63.

————. "Poland—Workers' Councils," *Highlights of Current Legislation and Activities in Mid-Europe*, V, No. 6 (June 1957), 245–262.

————. "Private Rights and Administration of Justice in Communist Poland," *Federal Bar News*, II, No. 4 (January 1955), 99–102.

————. "Vocational Rehabilitation in Communist Poland," *Highlights of Current Legislation and Activities in Mid-Europe*, III, No. 4 (April 1955), 119–123.

Gsovski, Vladimir,(ed.). *Church and State Behind the Iron Curtain*. New York: Praeger, 1955.

Gsovski, Vladimir, and Grzybowski, Kazimierz(eds.). *Land and Peasant*. (*Government, Law, and Courts Behind the Iron Curtain*, Part VIII.) International Commission of Jurists, 1955.

————. *New Substantive Criminal Law*. (*Ibid.*, Part III.) International Commission of Jurists, 1955.

————. *Worker and Factory*. (Preliminary ed.) (*Ibid.*, Part VII.) International Commission of Jurists, 1955.

Gsovski, Vladimir, and Jann, Edmund C.(eds.). *Forced Labor and Confinement Without Trial in Poland*. Washington, D. C.: National Committee for a Free Europe, 1952.

Halecki, Oscar. *Borderlands of Western Civilization*. New York: Ronald Press, 1952.

————. *Contemporary Poland*. In Leonid I. Strakhovsky(ed.), *A Handbook of Slavic Studies*, Cambridge: Harvard University Press, 1949.

Hallett, George H., Jr. *Proportional Representation: The Key to Democracy*. (2d ed., revised.) New York: National Municipal League, 1940.

Hansen, Harry(ed.). *World Almanac and Book of Facts for 1955*. New York: New York World-Telegram, 1955.

Hazlitt, H. "They've Had It," *Newsweek*, XLVIII (November 19, 1956), 106.

Hedlam-Morley, Agnes. *The New Democratic Constitutions of Europe*. New York: Oxford University Press, 1928.

Henderson, H. W. *An Outline of Polish-Soviet Relations*. Glasgow, n.d.

Hertz, Aleksander, "The Case of an Eastern European Intelligentsia," *Journal of Central European Affairs,* XI, No. 4 (January 1951), 10–26.

Heyn, Gerhard. *Ostdeutschlands Landwirtschaft und ihre Ueberschusse* (East Germany's Agriculture and Its Surpluses). Bonn, Germany: Deutscher Agrar-Verlag, n.d.

Hoag, Clarence G., and Hallett, George H., Jr. *Proportional Representation.* New York: Macmillan, 1926.

Hooker, Nancy (ed.). *The Moffat Papers.* Cambridge: Harvard University Press, 1956.

Hottelet, Richard C. "Inside Defiant Poland," *The Saturday Evening Post,* CCXXIX, No. 36 (March 9, 1957), 19, 99–102.

"Housing," *East Europe,* VI, No. 6 (June 1957), 26–30.

"Housing," *Polish Facts and Figures,* February 9, 1957.

"How Poland Has Gone Downhill Under Communism," *U. S. News and World Report,* XLI (November 2, 1956), 29.

Hulek, A. "Vocational Rehabilitation of the Disabled in Poland," *International Labour Review,* LXXIV (July 1956), 46–55.

Humphrey, Grace. *Piłsudski, Builder of Poland.* New York: Scott & More, 1936.

Humphrey, Grace. *Poland the Unexplored.* Indianapolis: Bobbs-Merrill, 1931.

International Cooperation Administration. *Survey of East-West Trade in 1955.* Washington, D. C.: Government Printing Office, 1956.

International Labor Office. *Polish Social Insurance and Pension Laws.* (Legislative Series, 1948, Pol. 2; 1949, Pol. 1; 1954, Pol. 2; 1955, Pol. 2.)

International Monetary Fund. *International Financial News Survey* (Washington, D. C., weekly publication), 1956, *passim.*

International Public Opinion Research, Inc. "Media of Communications and the Free World as Seen by Polish Refugees." New York: International Public Opinion Research, 1952. (Unpublished manuscript.)

International Year Book and Statesmen's Who's Who 1957. London: Burke's, 1957.

Jordan, Peter. *Poland's Frontiers.* London: Maxlove, 1945.

Kabes, Vladimir, and Sergot, Alfons. *Blueprint of Deception.* The Hague: Mouton, 1957.

Karski, Jan. *Story of a Secret State.* Boston: Houghton Mifflin, 1944.

Kelly, Eric P. *The Land of the Polish People.* Philadelphia: Lippincott, 1952.

Kerstein, Edward S. *Red Star over Poland.* Appleton, Wisconsin; Nelson, 1947.

Kertesz, Stephen (ed.). *The Fate of East Central Europe.* South Bend, Indiana: Notre Dame University Press, 1956.

Kirpatrick, Evron M. (ed.). *Target: The World.* New York: Macmillan, 1956.

Kister, Hannah. "A Recent Visit to Poland," *Publishers Weekly,* CLXXI, No. 5 (February 1957), 32–35.

Koehl, R. L. "Deutsche Volksliste in Poland, 1939–1945" (German People's List in Poland), *Journal of Central European Affairs,* XV (January 1956), 354–366.

452

Koenig, Ernest. "Land Reform in Poland," *Foreign Agriculture*, XVII, Nos. 7–8 (July–August 1953), 139–144.

———. "A New Farm Policy for Poland," *Foreign Agriculture*, Vol. XXI, No. 5 (May 1957).

Korbonski, Stefan. *Fighting Warsaw*. London: Allen & Unwin, 1956.

Kostanick, H. L. "Population Changes in Poland," *Geographical Review*, XLV (October 1955), 578–579.

Kotiuzynski, Antoni, *Agricultural Insurance in Poland 1927–1950*. (Mimeograph Series No. 16.) New York: Mid-European Studies Center, 1954.

Kowalczyk, Leon S. *Poland's Chemical Industry*. (Mimeograph Series No. 9.) New York: Mid-European Studies Center, 1953.

Kowalczyk, W. *State-conducted Commerce*. (*The Pattern of Life in Poland*, Vol. XV.) Paris: Mid-European Research and Planning Centre, 1952.

Kracauer, Siegfried, and Berkman, Paul L. *Satellite Mentality*. New York: Praeger, 1956.

Kulischer, Eugene M. *The Displacement of Population in Europe*. Montreal: International Labour Office, 1943.

"Labor Productivity in the Captive Nations," *News from Behind the Iron Curtain*, V, No. 5 (May 1956), 19–28.

Landau, L. "Seasonal Emigration from Poland to Germany and Latvia," *International Labour Review*, XL (August 1939), 195–208.

Lane, Arthur Bliss. *I Saw Poland Betrayed*. New York: Bobbs-Merrill, 1948.

Lane, Marie Dresden. "Social Worker's Glimpse Behind the Iron Curtain," *Public Welfare*, IX, No. 8 (October 1951), 178–183.

Lerski, Jerzy J. *Economy of Poland* (Report A-23.) Washington, D. C.: Council for Economic and Industry Research, 1954.

Leslie, R. F. "Education in Poland," *New Statesman and Nation*, LI (June 2, 1956), 628–629.

Leszczycki, Stanisław. "The Geographical Bases of Contemporary Poland," *Journal of Central European Affairs*, VII, No. 4 (January 1948), 357–373.

Lewinski-Corwin, Edward H. *Political History of Poland*. New York: Polish Book Importing Company, 1917.

"Liberal Editors Dismissed," *East Europe*, VI, No. 6 (June 1957), 41.

Ligocki, Edward E. *Legends and History of Poland*. New York: Nelson, 1943.

Machray, Robert. *Poland 1914–1931*. New York: Dutton, 1932.

MacKiewicz, Stanislas. *Col. Beck and His Policy*. London: Eyre & Spottiswood, 1944.

Malara, Jean, and Rey, Lucienne. *La Pologne d'Une Occupation à l'Autre (1944–1952)* (Poland from One Occupation to Another). Paris: Editions du Fuseau, 1952.

Mallory, Walter (ed.). *Political Handbook of the World*. New York: Harper (for the Council on Foreign Relations), 1957.

Mead, Margaret, and Métraux, Rhoda (eds.). *The Study of Culture at a Distance*. Chicago: University of Chicago Press, 1953.

Meyer, Peter, *et al. The Jews in the Soviet Satellites*. Syracuse, N. Y.: Syracuse University Press, 1953.

Mikołajczyk, Stanisław. *The Rape of Poland.* New York: McGraw-Hill, 1948.

Modlinski, Eugeniusz. "Social Insurance in Poland," *The New Central European Observer,* II, Nos. 23, 24 (November 12 and November 26, 1949), 272 and 288.

Monitor Polski: Dziennik Urzędowy Polskiej Rzeczypospolitej Ludowej (Polish Monitor: Official Gazette of the Polish People's Republic). No. A-3 (January 16, 1951), Item No. 40. Resolution of the Presiding Body of the Government of December 30, 1950, in the matter of appointing a Scientific Council attached to the Ministry of Health.

————. No. A-17 (1951), Item No. 228. Resolution No. 82 of the Presiding Body of the Government of February 3, 1951, concerning granting of medical benefits.

————. No. A-8 (January 25, 1952), Item No. 76. Instruction No. 8 on the matter of the internal organization and placements in the divisions of the bodies of provincial national councils.

————. No. A-5 (January 24, 1953), Item No. 46. Resolution No. 22 of the Council of Ministers of January 10, 1953, concerning the temporary organizational statute of the Ministry of Health.

————. No. A-28 (March 28, 1953), Item No. 329. Resolution No. 193 of the Council of Ministers of March 14, 1953, on the matter of changing the temporary organizational statute of the Ministry of Health.

————. No. A-22 (February 26, 1954), Item No. 365. Instruction of the Minister of Health of February 18, 1954, concerning the specific sphere of action of the committees of sanitary orderliness attached to presiding bodies of national councils.

————. No. 1 (January 10, 1955), Item No. 2. Resolution No. 888 of the Council of Ministers of December 18, 1954, concerning the change of Instruction No. 8 in the matter of internal organization and placements in the divisions of presiding bodies of national councils.

Moor, Paul. "Revolt of the Polish Musicians," *Harper's,* CCXIV, No. 1282 (March 1957), 78–81.

"Moscow's Uncle Tom," *Newsweek,* XLV (May 2, 1955), 40.

Murphy, Charles J. V. "The Polish Salient," *Fortune,* LV, No. 5 (May 1957), 124–127.

Namier, L. B. *Diplomatic Prelude, 1938–1939.* London: Macmillan, 1948.

————. *Europe in Decay.* London: Macmillan, 1950.

Nash, Edmund. "Labor Conditions in Poland," *Monthly Labor Review,* July 1944.

"New Poland Achieves Some Liberties," *Life,* LXII (January 14, 1957), 22–29.

"New Road for Poland's Parliament?" *The Economist,* CLXXX (September 29, 1956), 1031.

New York Times, September 1956, *passim.*

Newman, Bernard. *The People of Poland.* London: Polish Publications Committee, 1943.

————. *Russia's Neighbor: The New Poland.* London: Victor Gollancz, 1946.

454

News from Behind the Iron Curtain (now *East Europe*) 1955, *passim.*

Nöel, Léon. *L'agression Allemande contre la Pologne* (The German Aggression Against Poland). Paris: Flammarion, 1946.

Nowak, Antoni. *Preliminary Notes on Political Institutions in Poland. (The Pattern of Life in Poland,* Vol. I.) Paris: Mid-European Research and Planning Centre, 1952.

—————. *The Supreme Organs of Authority. (The Pattern of Life in Poland,* Vol. II.) Paris: Mid-European Research and Planning Centre, 1952.

"Nuclear Notes," *Science,* CXXIV (July 6, 1956), 21.

"October's Aftermath," *East Europe,* VI, No. 4 (April 1957), 3–10.

Office Belge du Commerce Extérieur. *Pologne. (Série Etudes de Marché.)* Brussels: June 1956.

Oxenfeldt, Alfred R. *Economic Systems in Action.* New York: Rinehart, 1952.

Oxford Regional Economic Atlas: The USSR and Eastern Europe. New York: Oxford University Press, 1956.

Paprocki, Stanisław (ed.). *Minority Affairs and Poland: An Informatory Outline.* Warsaw: Nationality Research Institute, 1935.

Pares, Richard, and Taylor, A. J. P.(eds.). *Essays Presented to Sir Lewis Namier.* London: Macmillan, 1956.

Parkes, James. *The Emergence of the Jewish Problem, 1878–1939.* New York: Oxford University Press, 1946.

Patkaniowska, K. *Essentials of Polish Grammar.* Glasgow: Polish Library, 1944.

Pawlowicz, Tadeusz. *Interview with a Polish Youth.* New York: Radio Free Europe, Information Department, February 1955.

Peaslee, Amos J. *Constitutions of Nations.* (2d ed.) 3 vols. The Hague: Matrinus Nijhoff, 1956.

Petrusewicz, K. "Science News," *Science,* CXXI (January 14, 1955), 52.

Piłsudska, Aleksandra. *Piłsudski.* New York: Dodd, Mead, 1941.

"Poland and Trade," *Newsweek,* November 5, 1956, 102.

"Poland," *Europa: The Encyclopaedia of Europe.* London: Europa, n. d.

"Poland, Her Neighbors and the West," *Round Table,* XXVIII (*September* 1938), 753–767.

"Poland: Labor Discipline," *Highlights of Current Legislation and Activities in Mid-Europe,* IV, No. 3 (March 1956), 73–76.

Poland: Ministry of Foreign Affairs. *The Polish White Book: Official Documents Concerning Polish-German and Polish-Soviet Relations 1933–1939.* London: Hutchinson, n. d.

"Poland, Nuzzling up to Canada, Talks of Buying Much More Wheat," *Business Week,* July 7, 1956, 101.

"Poland Revisited," *News From Behind the Iron Curtain,* V, No. 2 (February 1956), 21–27.

"Poland's Democratic Election," *America,* XCVI (January 19, 1957), 440.

"Poland's Revolution," *East Europe,* VI, No. 2 (February 1957), 3–15.

"Poland's Youth Debates," *New York Times,* January 20, 1957, 12–13.

"Polish Airline Details Post-War Growth," *Aviation Week,* September 3, 1956, 45.

"The Polish Election," *East Europe,* VI, No. 3 (March 1957), 3–12.

"Polish League for Mental Hygiene," *Mental Hygiene,* XXII (July 1938), 507–508.

Polish Press Summary. Prepared by the American and British Embassies in Warsaw. May 1957, *passim.* (Mimeographed.)

Polish Research and Information Service. *Public Health in Poland.* New York, 1949.

————. *Social Legislation in Poland.* New York, 1948.

————. *Social Welfare in Poland.* New York, 1949.

Political Handbook of the World: Parliaments, Parties, and Press. New York: Harper, 1957.

"La Politique Sociale en Pologne" (The Social Policy in Poland), *Revue Française du Travail,* No. 1–2 (January–February 1949), 49–58.

Polska Rzeczypospolita Ludowa: Główny Urząd Statystyczny, *Rocznik Statystyczny 1956* (Polish People's Republic: Main Statistical Administration, *Statistical Yearbook 1956*). Warsaw: Nakładem Głównego Urzędu Statystycznego, 1956.

Poray, J. B. and Żeromska, O. S. *Art and Literature. (The Pattern of Life in Poland,* Vol. VII) Paris: Mid-European Research and Planning Centre, 1952.

Prigrada, Anthony. *International Agreements Concerning the Danube.* (Mimeographed Series No. 6.) New York: Mid-European Studies Center, 1953.

Radio Free Europe: Information and Reference Department. *Elements in the Conduct and Control of Polish Communist Propaganda.* (Special Report No. 49.) New York: October 17, 1952.

Reddaway, W. F., *et al.* (eds.). *Cambridge History of Poland, to 1935.* 2 vols. Cambridge: Cambridge University Press, 1950 and 1951.

Reitlinger, Gerald. *The Final Solution.* New York: Beechhurst, 1953.

"Relations Between Poland and Eastern Germany," *World Today,* VII (September 1951), 370–376.

"Religious Faith and Love of Liberty That Led to Change," *Life,* XLI (November 5, 1956), 42–43.

Research in Contemporary Cultures Project Files, Institute for Intercultural Studies. Margaret Mead, Director. (Unpublished documents.)

Retinger, J. H. (ed.). *All About Poland.* London: Minerva, 1940.

"Retreat from Stalinism in Poland," *The Economist,* CLXXIX (April 28, 1956), 384.

Reymont, Ladislas. *The Peasants.* 4 vols. New York: Knopf, 1924.

————. *The Promised Land.* New York: Knopf, 1927.

Rochlin, R. P. *Die Wirtschaft Polens von 1945 bis 1952* (The Economy of Poland from 1945 to 1952). Berlin: Duncker & Humblot, 1954.

Rosada, Stefan, and Gwozdz, Jozef. *Forced Labor and Confinement Without Trial in Poland.* Washington: Mid-European Law Project, 1952.

————. "Sources of Legal Information in Poland," Reprint from *Law Library Journal,* Vol. XLVI, No. 2 (May 1953).

456

Rose, William John. "Czechs and Poles as Neighbors," *Journal of Central European Affairs,* XI (July 1951), 153–171.

———. *Poland: Old and New.* London: Bell, 1948.

Rosenthal, Celia S. "Deviation and Social Change in the Jewish Community in a Small Polish Town," *American Journal of Sociology,* LX, No. 2 (September 1954), 177–181.

———. "Functions of Polish Trade Unions: Their Progression Toward the Soviet Pattern," *British Journal of Sociology,* VI (September 1955), 264–276.

———. "Social Stratification of the Jewish Community in a Small Polish Town," *American Journal of Sociology,* LIX (July 1953), 1–10.

Rudzinski, Aleksander Witold. *Polish Public Administration Before World War II.* (Mimeograph Series No. 30.) New York: Mid-European Studies Center, 1954.

———. "Sovietization of Civil Law in Poland," *The American Slavic and East European Review,* XV, No. 2 (April 1956), 216–243.

Rudzki, Adam. *Organization of Transportation in Captive Europe.* (Mimeograph Series No. 10.) New York: Mid-European Studies Center, 1954.

———. *Railroad Systems in Captive Europe.* (Mimeograph Series No. 13.) New York: Mid-European Studies Center, 1954.

———. *Roads, Waterways, and Seaports of Captive Europe.* (Mimeograph Series No. 15.) New York: Mid-European Studies Center, 1954.

Russification of Poland. New York: Polish Research and Information Service, 1950.

Sapieha, Virginia. *Polish Profile.* New York: Carrick & Evans, 1940.

Scaevola (pseud.) *A Study in Forgery.* London: J. Rolls, 1945.

Schechtman, J. B. *European Population Transfers, 1939–1945.* New York: Oxford University Press, 1946.

Schlesinger, Rudolf. *Central European Democracy and Its Background.* London: Routledge & Kegan Paul, 1953.

Schmitt, Bernadotte E. (ed.). *Poland.* Berkeley: University of California Press, 1947.

"Science in Poland," *Nature,* CLX (August 16, 1947), 219.

Scottish League for European Freedom. *Who's Who of the Regime in Poland.* Edinburgh: 1947.

Seton-Watson, Hugh. *The East European Revolution.* London: Methuen, 1950.

Shackleton, Margaret Reid. *Europe: A Regional Geography.* New York: Longmans, Green, 1954.

Sharp, Samuel L. "Red and Black in Poland," *New Republic,* CXXIX (October 12, 1953), 11–13.

Shneiderman, S. L. "Before the Earthquake in Poland," *Reporter,* XV (November 15, 1956), 18–19.

Siekanowicz, Peter. *Legislation on Sovietization of Industry and Commerce in Poland.* Washington, D. C.: Mid-European Law Project, 1954.

Skrzyński, Aleksander J. *Poland and Peace.* London: Allen & Unwin, 1923.

Skrzypek, Stanislaw. "Agricultural Policies in Poland," *Journal of Central European Affairs*, XVI (April 1956), 45–70.

————. "Real Wages in Poland," *Slavic and East-European Studies*, I, Part 3 (August 1956), 179–187.

Slomka, Jan. *From Serfdom to Self-Government*. (Trans., William J. Rose.) London: Minerva, 1941.

Soviet Security Agencies in Postwar Poland. (Mimeograph Series No. 17.) New York: East European Fund, 1952.

Sovietization of Culture in Poland. Paris: Mid-European Research and Planning Centre, 1953.

"Standard of Living," *News from Behind the Iron Curtain*, V, No. 9 (September 1956), 26–27.

"Standard of Living in Poland," *Polish Affairs*, August 1956, 5.

Stanisławski, J. *Dictionary: English-Polish and Polish-English*. New York: Roy, n. d.

Stankiewicz, Wladislaw J. and Montias, J. M. *Institutional Changes in the Postwar Economy of Poland*. (Mimeograph Series No. 21.) New York: Mid-European Studies Center, 1955.

Starr, Richard F. "The Central Committee of the United Polish Workers' Party (PZPR)," *Journal of Central European Affairs*, XVI, No. 4 (January 1957), 371–383.

————. "Military Potential of Communist Poland," *Military Review*, July 1956, 41–47.

————. "Political Bureau of the United Polish Workers' Party," *American Slavic Review*, XV (April 1956), 206–215.

————. "Political Framework of Communist Poland." Unpublished Ph.D. dissertation (Microfilm AC-1,7735), University of Michigan, 1954.

————. "Secretariat of the United Polish Workers' Party (PZPR)," *Journal of Central European Affairs*, XV (October 1955), 272–285.

————. "Ten Years of the Polish People's Republic," *American Mercury*, LXXXI (November 1955), 133–137.

Stern, Harold P. *Struggle for Poland*. Washington: Public Affairs Press, 1953.

Stevens, E. "Poland Today," *Look*, XX (July 24, 1956), 17.

Stolz, George. *Forced Labor in the Soviet Orbit*. New York: Mid-European Studies Center, 1954.

Strakhovsky, Leonid I. (ed.). *A Handbook of Slavic Studies*. Cambridge: Harvard University Press, 1949.

Stroński, Stanisław. *The Two Polish Constitutions of 1921 and 1935*. Glasgow: The Polish Library, 1944.

Stypulkowski, Z. F. *Invitation to Moscow*. London: Thames & Hudson, 1951.

"A Survey of Poland," *The Statist*, November 24, 1956, special supplement.

Szembek, Comte Jean. *Journal, 1933–1939*. Paris: Librarie Plons, 1952.

Szober, Stanisław. *Gramatyka Języka Polskiego* (Polish Grammar). Warsaw, 1931.

Szułdrzyński, Jan. *The Family*. (*The Pattern of Life in Poland*, Vol. VI.) Paris: Mid-European Research and Planning Centre, 1952.

458

"Tale of Polish Socialism," *Foreign Affairs*, XXVIII, No. 1 (October 1949), 125–142.

Tepicht, J.(ed.). *The Polish Countryside in Figures.* (3d ed., abridged.) (Institute of Agricultural Economics) Warsaw: Foreign Languages Publishing House, 1954.

Thomas, William I, and Znaniecki, Florian. *The Polish Peasant in Europe and America.* 2 vols. New York: Knopf, 1927.

"Trade Union Plenum," *News from Behind the Iron Curtain*, V, No. 3 (March 1956), 42.

Turosienski, Severink. *Poland's Institutions of Higher Education.* (U. S. Office of Education Bulletin, 1936, No. 14.) Washington, D. C.: Government Printing Office, 1936.

Ulam, Adam B. *Titoism and the Cominform.* Cambridge: Harvard University Press, 1952.

Umiastowski, R. *Poland, Russia and Great Britain.* London: Hollis & Carter, 1946.

United Nations. *Report of the Special Committee on the Problem of Hungary.* (A/3592.) 2 vols. 1957.

United Nations: Department of Economic and Social Affairs. *Economic Survey of Europe in 1956.* Geneva, 1957.

———. *Statistical Yearbook 1955.* New York, 1956.

———. *World Economic Survey 1955.* New York, 1956.

United Nations: Department of Social Affairs. *Methods of Social Welfare Administration.* New York, 1950.

United Nations: Economic and Social Council. *Forced Labor* (A report by the Secretary-General of the UN and the Director-General of the ILO). Report E/2815, December 15, 1955. New York, 1955.

United Nations: Economic Commission for Europe. *The European Housing Situation.* Geneva, 1956.

United Nations: Food and Agricultural Organization. *Report of the FAO Mission to Poland.* Washington, 1948.

———. *State of Food and Agriculture, 1948.* Washington, 1948.

United Nations: International Labour Organization. *Report of the Ad Hoc Committee on Forced Labour.* Geneva, 1953.

UNESCO. *World Communications: Press, Radio, Film, Television.* (3d ed.) New York, 1956.

UNRRA: Division of Operation Analysis. *Agriculture and Food in Poland.* (Operation Analysis Papers, No. 3.) London: UNRRA European Regional Office, July 1946. Revised edition.

———. *Finance in Poland.* (*Ibid.,* No. 44.) London: UNRRA European Regional Office, April 1947.

———. *Foreign Trade in Poland.* (*Ibid.,* No. 7.) London: UNRRA European Regional Office, September 1946. Revised edition. (*Ibid.,* No. 40.) London, April 1947.

———. *Health Conditions in Poland.* (*Ibid.,* No. 31.) London: UNRRA European Regional Office, June 1946.

————. *Impact of UNRRA on the Polish Economy.* (*Ibid.,* No. 45.) London: UNRRA European Regional Office, April 1947.

————. *Industrial Rehabilitation in Poland.* (*Ibid.,* No. 2.) London: UNRRA European Regional Office, July 1946. Revised edition. (*Ibid.,* No. 35.) London, April 1947.

————. *Poland's Need for Assistance in 1947.* (*Ibid.,* No. 9.) London: UNRRA European Regional Office, October 1946.

————. *Transport Rehabilitation in Poland.* (*Ibid.,* No. 1.) London: UNRRA European Regional Office, June 1946. Revised edition. (*Ibid.,* No. 36.) London, April 1947.

U. S. Congress, 82d, 2d Session, House. *Polish Documents Report of the Select Committee on Communist Aggression.* (Appendix to Committee Report on Communist Takeover and Occupation of Poland.) House Report 2684, Part 4. Washington, D. C.: Government Printing Office, 1955.

U. S. Congress, 83d, 2d Session, House. *Communist Takeover and Occupation of Poland. Special Report No. 1 of the Select Committee on Communist Aggression.* House Report 2684, Part 3. Washington, D. C.: Government Printing Office, 1955.

————. *Summary Report of the Select Committee on Communist Aggression. Ibid.,* Part 16. Washington, D. C.: Government Printing Office, 1955.

————. *Tenth Interim Report of Hearings before the Select Committee on Communist Aggression: Poland, Rumania, and Slovakia.* Washington, D. C.: Government Printing Office, 1954.

————. *Trends in Economic Growth: A Comparison of the Western Powers and the Soviet Bloc.* Washington, D. C.: Government Printing Office, 1955.

U. S. Congress, 85th, 1st Session, Senate. Committee on Foreign Relations. *Report on the Soviet Union, Poland, and Czechoslovakia, August 1956.* (Report of Senator Russell B. Long.) Washington, D. C.: Government Printing Office, 1957.

U. S. Department of State. *Foreign Relations of the United States: The Conference at Malta and Yalta, 1945.* (Department of State Publication 6199.) Washington, D. C.: Government Printing Office, 1955.

————. *Moscow's European Satellites.* (Department of State Publication 5914, European and British Commonwealth Series 48.) Washington, D. C.: Government Printing Office, 1955.

U. S. Library of Congress: Legislative Reference Service. *Trends in Economic Growth: A Comparison of the Western Powers and the Soviet Bloc.* (A Study prepared for the Joint Committee on the Economic Report, 83d Congress, 2d Session.) Washington, D. C.: Government Printing Office, 1955.

U. S. Library of Congress: Mid-European Law Project. *Digest-Index of East European Law: Poland.* Washington, D. C., n. d.

————. *Highlights of Current Legislation and Activities in Mid-Europe, passim,* Washington, D. C., 1956.

U. S. Library of Congress: Reference Department. *Postwar Foreign Newspapers* (A Union List). Washington, D. C., 1953.

U. S. Office of Strategic Services: Research and Analysis Branch. *The Polish Provisional Government of International Unity.* (Research and Analysis No. 3180.) Washington, D. C., 1945.

U. S. Social Security Administration: Division of Research and Statistics. *Major Changes in Social Security Legislation, 1940–50.* (Supplement to *Social Security Legislation Throughout the World,* Report No. 16, Division of Research and Statistics.) Washington, D. C.: Federal Security Agency, 1951.

————. *Major Changes in Social Security Legislation, 1951.* (*Ibid.*) Washington, D. C.: Federal Security Agency, 1952.

————. *Major Changes in Social Security Legislation, 1952.* (*Ibid.*) Washington, D. C.: Department of Health, Education and Welfare, 1953.

————. *Social Security Legislation Throughout the World.* (Report No. 16.) Washington, D. C.: Government Printing Office, 1949.

University of Chicago. *Contemporary Poland: Society, Politics, Economy.* HRAF Subcontractor's Monograph, 1955.

Voigt, F. A. "Poland, Russia and Great Britain," *The Nineteenth Century and After.* Reprinted by Polish and American Congress, 1943.

"Wage Increases for Administrative Workers," *News From Behind the Iron Curtain,* V, No. 8 (August 1956), 46–47.

Wajnryb, M. "Economic and Social Importance of the Central Industrial District of Poland," *International Labour Review,* XXXVIII (November 1938), 660–666.

Wandycz, Piotr S. "The Soviet System of Alliances in East Central Europe," *Journal of Central European Affairs,* XVI, No. 2 (July 1956), 177–184.

Warriner, Doreen. *Revolution in Eastern Europe.* London: Turnstile Press, 1950.

Wepsiec, Jan (comp.). *Polish Newspapers in 1953: A Union List.* New York: Mid-European Studies Center, Free Europe Committee, 1955.

Werth, Alexander. *Poland Today.* New York: Polish Research and Information Service, 1948.

Wiktorowicz, S. *State-Owned Industries.* (*The Pattern of Life in Poland,* Vol. XIV.) Paris: Mid-European Research and Planning Centre, 1952.

Winston, Victor H. "The Polish Coal Mining Industry," *The American Slavic and East European Review,* XV, No. 1 (February 1956), 38–70.

Wojcicka, Janina. *Higher Education in Poland.* (Mimeograph Series No. 12.) New York: Mid-European Studies Center, 1954.

————. *Libraries in Communist Poland.* (Mimeograph Series No. 31.) New York: Mid-European Studies Center, 1954.

————. *Polish Abbreviations: A Selective List.* Washington, D. C.: Library of Congress, 1955.

"Workers Demand Self-Management," *News From Behind the Iron Curtain,* V, No. 11 (November 1956), 46.

World Health Organization. *Annual Report of the Director-General, 1949.* (Official Records of the World Health Organization No. 24.) Geneva, 1950.

Date Due